alan
rogers

C000184628

the best campsites
in Spain & Portugal

alan rogers publishing
experts in camping for over 40 years

Compiled by: Alan Rogers Guides Ltd

Designed by: Vine Design Ltd

Additional photography: T Lambelin, www.lambelin.com
Maps created by Customised Mapping (01769 540044)
contain background data provided by GisDATA Ltd

Maps are © Alan Rogers Guides and GisDATA Ltd 2011

© Alan Rogers Guides Ltd 2011

Published by: Alan Rogers Guides Ltd,
Spelmonden Old Oast, Goudhurst, Kent TN17 1HE
www.alanrogers.com Tel: 01580 214000

British Library Cataloguing-in-Publication Data:
A catalogue record for this book is available
from the British Library.

ISBN 978-1-906215-49-1

Printed in Great Britain by Stephens & George Print Group

Contents

Alan Rogers - in search of 'the best'

Alan Rogers Guides were first published over 40 years ago. Since Alan Rogers published the first campsite guide that bore his name, the range has expanded and now covers 27 countries in six separate guides. No fewer than 20 of the campsites selected by Alan for the first guide are still featured in our 2011 editions.

There are many thousands of campsites in Spain and Portugal of varying quality: this guide contains impartially written reports on almost 300, including many of the very finest, each being individually inspected and selected. We aim to provide you with a selection of the best, rather than information on all – in short, a more selective, qualitative approach. New, improved maps and indexes are also included, designed to help you find the choice of campsite that's right for you.

We hope you enjoy some happy and safe travels – and some pleasurable 'armchair touring' in the meantime!

" ...the campsites included in this book have been chosen entirely on merit, and no payment of any sort is made by them for their inclusion."

Alan Rogers, 1968

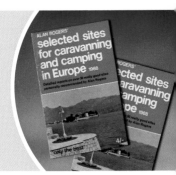

How do we find the best?

The criteria we use when inspecting and selecting campsites are numerous, but the most important by far is the question of good quality. People want different things from their choice of site so we try to include a range of campsite 'styles' to cater for a wide variety of preferences: from those seeking a small peaceful campsite in the heart of the countryside, to visitors looking for an 'all singing, all dancing' site in a popular seaside resort. Those with more specific interests, such as sporting facilities, cultural events or historical attractions, are also catered for.

The size of the site, whether it's part of a chain or privately owned, makes no difference in terms of it being required to meet our exacting standards in respect of its quality and it being 'fit for purpose'. In other words, irrespective of the size of the site, or the number of facilities it offers, we consider and evaluate the welcome, the pitches, the sanitary facilities, the cleanliness, the general maintenance and even the location.

Expert opinions

We rely on our dedicated team of Site Assessors, all of whom are experienced campers, caravanners or motorcaravanners, to visit and recommend campsites. Each year they travel some 100,000 miles around Europe inspecting new campsites for the guide and re-inspecting the existing ones. Our thanks are due to them for their enthusiastic efforts, their diligence and integrity.

We also appreciate the feedback we receive from many of our readers and we always make a point of following up complaints, suggestions or recommendations for possible new campsites. Of course we get a few grumbles too – but it really is a few, and those we do receive usually relate to overcrowding or to poor maintenance during the peak school holiday period. Please bear in mind that, although we are interested to hear about any complaints, we have no contractual relationship with the campsites featured in our guides and are therefore not in a position to intervene in any dispute between a reader and a campsite.

Independent and honest

Whilst the content and scope of the Alan Rogers guides have expanded considerably since the early editions, our selection of campsites still employs exactly the same philosophy and criteria as defined by Alan Rogers in 1968.

'telling it how it is'

Firstly, and most importantly, our selection is based entirely on our own rigorous and independent inspection and selection process. Campsites cannot buy their way into our guides – indeed the extensive Site Report which is written by us, not by the site owner, is provided free of charge so we are free to say what we think and to provide an honest, 'warts and all' description. This is written in plain English and without the use of confusing icons or symbols.

Looking for the best

Highly respected by site owners and readers alike, there is no better guide when it comes to forming an independent view of a campsite's quality. When you need to be confident in your choice of campsite, you need the Alan Rogers Guide.

- Sites only included on merit

- Sites cannot pay to be included

- Independently inspected, rigorously assessed

- Impartial reviews

- Over 40 years of expertise

Written in plain English, our guides are exceptionally easy to use, but a few words of explanation regarding the layout and content may be helpful. In Spain we have used the 16 official administrative regions, whilst in Portugal we use the five regions defined by the Portugal Tourist Board. A full page introduction to each region highlights its main areas of interest, places to visit and the local cuisine.

Region

Index town
Site name
Postal address (including area) T: telephone number. E: email address
alanrogers.com web address (including Alan Rogers reference number)

A description of the site in which we try to give an idea of its general features – its size, its situation, its strengths and its weaknesses. This section should provide a picture of the site itself with reference to the facilities that are provided and if they impact on its appearance or character. We include details on pitch numbers, electricity (with amperage), hardstandings etc. in this section as pitch design, planning and terracing affects the site's overall appearance. Similarly we include reference to pitches used for caravan holiday homes, chalets, and the like. Importantly at the end of this column we indicate if there are any restrictions, e.g. no tents, no children, naturist sites.

Facilities
Lists more specific information on the site's facilities and amenities and, where available, the dates when these facilities are open (if not for the whole season). Off site: here we give distances to various local amenities, for example, local shops, the nearest beach, plus our featured activities (bicycle hire, fishing, horse riding, boat launching). Where we have space we list suggestions for activities and local tourist attractions.

Open: Site opening dates.

Directions
Separated from the main text in order that they may be read and assimilated more easily by a navigator en-route. Bear in mind that road improvement schemes can result in road numbers being altered.

GPS: references are provided in decimal format. All latitudes are North. Longitudes are East unless preceeded by a minus sign e.g. 48.71695 is North, 0.31254 is East and -0.31254 is West.

Charges 2011 (or a general guide)

Maps, campsite listings and indexes

For this 2011 guide we have changed the way in which we list our campsites and also the way in which we help you locate the sites within each region.

We now include a map immediately after our Introduction to that region. These maps show the towns near which one (or more) of our featured campsites is located.

Within each regional section of the guide, we list these towns and the site(s) in that vicinity in alphabetical order.

You will certainly need more detailed maps for navigation, for example the Michelin atlas. We provide GPS coordinates for each site to assist you. Our three indexes will also help you to find a site by region and site name, by reference number or by the town where the site is situated.

Understanding the entries

Facilities

Toilet blocks

We assume that toilet blocks will be equipped with WCs, washbasins with hot and cold water and hot showers with dividers or curtains, and will have all necessary shelves, hooks, plugs and mirrors. We also assume that there will be an identified chemical toilet disposal point, and that the campsite will provide water and waste water drainage points and bin areas. If not the case, we comment. We do mention certain features that some readers find important: washbasins in cubicles, facilities for babies, facilities for those with disabilities and motorcaravan service points. Readers with disabilities are advised to contact the site of their choice to ensure that facilities are appropriate to their needs.

Shop

Basic or fully supplied, and opening dates.

Bars, restaurants, takeaway facilities and entertainment

We try hard to supply opening and closing dates (if other than the campsite opening dates) and to identify if there are discos or other entertainment.

Children's play areas

Fenced and with safety surface (e.g. sand, bark or pea-gravel).

Swimming pools

If particularly special, we cover in detail in our main campsite description but reference is always included under our Facilities listings. We will also indicate the existence of water slides, sunbathing areas and other features. Opening dates, charges and levels of supervision are provided where we have been notified. There is a regulation whereby Bermuda shorts may not be worn in swimming pools (for health and hygiene reasons). It is worth ensuring that you do take 'proper' swimming trunks with you.

Leisure facilities

For example, playing fields, bicycle hire, organised activities and entertainment.

Dogs

If dogs are not accepted or restrictions apply, we state it here. Check the quick reference list at the back of the guide.

Off site

This briefly covers leisure facilities, tourist attractions, restaurants etc. nearby.

Charges

These are the latest provided to us by the sites. In those cases where 2011 prices have not been provided to us by the sites, we try to give a general guide.

Reservations

Necessary for high season (roughly mid-July to mid-August) in popular holiday areas (i.e. beach resorts). You can reserve many sites via our own Alan Rogers Travel Service or through other tour operators. Or be wholly independent and contact the campsite(s) of your choice direct, using the phone or e-mail numbers shown in the site reports, but please bear in mind that many sites are closed all winter.

Telephone Numbers

All numbers assume that you are phoning from within Spain or Portugal. To phone Spain from outside that country, prefix the number shown with the relevant International Code '00 34' and then the number indicated. To phone Portugal prefix the number shown with the International Code '00 351'.

Opening dates

These are advised to us during the early autumn of the previous year – sites can, and sometimes do, alter these dates before the start of the following season, often for good reasons. If you intend to visit shortly after a published opening date, or shortly before the closing date, it is wise to check that it will actually be open at the time required. Similarly some sites operate a restricted service during the low season, only opening some of their facilities (e.g. swimming pools) during the main season; where we know about this, and have the relevant dates, we indicate it – again if you are at all doubtful it is wise to check.

Sometimes, campsite amenities may be dependent on there being enough customers on site to justify their opening and, for this reason, actual opening dates may vary from those indicated.

Some campsite owners are very relaxed when it comes to opening and closing dates. They may not be fully ready by their stated opening dates – grass and hedges may not all be cut or perhaps only limited sanitary facilities open. At the end of the season they also tend to close down some facilities and generally wind down prior to the closing date. Bear this in mind if you are travelling early or late in the season – it is worth phoning ahead.

The Camping Cheque low season touring system goes some way to addressing this in that many participating campsites will have all key facilities open and running by the opening date and these will remain fully operational until the closing date.

You're on your way!

Whether you're an 'old hand' in terms of camping and caravanning or are contemplating your first trip, a regular reader of our Guides or a new 'convert', we wish you well in your travels and hope we have been able to help in some way.

We are, of course, also out and about ourselves, visiting sites, talking to owners and readers, and generally checking on standards and new developments.

Our Accommodation section

Over recent years, more and more campsites have added high quality mobile home and chalet accommodation. In response to feedback from many of our readers, and to reflect this evolution in campsites, we have now decided to include a separate section on mobile homes and chalets.

If a site offers this accommodation, it is indicated above the site report with a page reference where full details are given. We have chosen a number of sites offering some of the best accommodation available and have included full details of one or two accommodation types at these sites. Please note however that many other campsites listed in this guide may also have a selection of accommodation for rent.

We wish all our readers thoroughly enjoyable Camping and Caravanning in 2011 – favoured by good weather of course!

The Alan Rogers Team

Cantabria
page 127

Pais Vasco-Euskadi
page 133

La Rioja
page 137

Asturias
page 121

Galicia
page 117

Navarra
page 141

Porto & North
page 175

Castilla y Léon
page 111

isbon &
e do Tejo
age 164

Aragón
page 145

Catalunya
page 16

Beiras & Centre
page 170

Madrid
page 107

Extremadura
page 99

Balears
page 152

Alentejo
page 159

Castilla-La Mancha
page 103

Comunidad
Valenciana
page 62

Andalucia
page 82

Murcia
page 78

Algarve
page 154

The Alan Rogers Awards

The Alan Rogers Campsite Awards were launched in 2004 and have proved a great success.

Our awards have a broad scope and before committing to our winners, we carefully consider more than 2,000 campsites featured in our guides, taking into account comments from our site assessors, our head office team and, of course, our readers.

Our award winners come from the four corners of Europe, from southern Portugal to Slovenia, and this year we are making awards to campsites in 13 different countries.

Needless to say, it's an extremely difficult task to choose our eventual winners, but we believe that we have identified a number of campsites with truly outstanding characteristics.

In each case, we have selected an outright winner, along with two highly commended runners-up. Listed below are full details of each of our award categories and our winners for 2010.

Alan Rogers Progress Award 2010

This award reflects the hard work and commitment undertaken by particular site owners to improve and upgrade their site.

Winner	
FR40100	Camping du Domaine de la Rive *France*

Runners-up	
AU0060	Ferienparadies Natterer See *Austria*
IT60360	Camping Ca'Pasquali *Italy*

Alan Rogers Welcome Award 2010

This award takes account of sites offering a particularly friendly welcome and maintaining a friendly ambience throughout reader's holidays.

Winner	
FR38010	Kawan Village le Coin Tranquille *France*

Runners-up	
NL6630	Camping Ter Spegelt *Netherlands*
IT62485	Camping Conca d'Oro *Italy*

Our warmest congratulations to all our award winners and our commiserations to all those not having won an award on this occasion.

The Alan Rogers Team

Alan Rogers Active Holiday Award 2010

This award reflects sites in outstanding locations which are ideally suited for active holidays, notably walking or cycling, but which could extend to include such activities as winter sports or water sports.

Winner

DE3820	Camping Havelberge *Germany*

Runners-up

SV4415	Camping Terme Catez *Slovenia*
FR65090	Camping du Soleil de Pibeste *France*

Alan Rogers Motorhome Award 2010

Motorhome sales are increasing and this award acknowledges sites which, in our opinion, have made outstanding efforts to welcome motorhome clients.

Winner

NL6200	Camping Erkemederstrand *Netherlands*

Runners-up

UK1340	Cornish Farm Touring Park *England*
FR30120	Campéole Ile des Papes *France*

Alan Rogers 4 Seasons Award 2010

This award is made to outstanding sites with extended opening dates and which welcome clients to a uniformly high standard throughout the year.

Winner

ES81300	Camping Int. de Calonge *Spain*

Runners-up

UK0970	Cofton Country Holidays *England*
DE3455	Gugel's Dreiländer Camping *Germany*

Alan Rogers Seaside Award 2010

This award is made for sites which we feel are outstandingly suitable for a really excellent seaside holiday.

Winner

FR83120	Camp du Domaine *France*

Runners-up

CR6716	Camping Lanterna *Croatia*
ES82000	Camping Cala Llevadó *Spain*

Alan Rogers Country Award 2010

This award contrasts with our former award and acknowledges sites which are attractively located in delightful, rural locations.

Winner

NL6425	Camping De Twee Bruggen *Netherlands*

Runners-up

FR24010	Kawan Château le Verdoyer *France*
UK7830	Glen Nevis Caravan Park *Scotland*

Alan Rogers Rented Accommodation Award 2010

Given the increasing importance of rented accommodation on many campsites, we feel that it is important to acknowledge sites which have made a particular effort in creating a high quality 'rented accommodation' park.

Winner

SV4270	Kamp Koren Kobarid *Slovenia*

Runners-up

FR66070	Yelloh! Village le Brasilia *France*
ES84830	Camping Tamarit Park Resort *Spain*

Alan Rogers Unique Site Award 2010

This award acknowledges sites with unique, outstanding features – something which simply cannot be found elsewhere and which is an important attraction of the site.

Winner

PO8175	Zmar-Eco Camping Resort *Portugal*

Runners-up

DK2170	Klim Strand Camping *Denmark*
ES80330	Camping Las Palmeras *Spain*

Alan Rogers Family Site Award 2010

Many sites claim to be child friendly but this award acknowledges the sites we feel to be the very best in this respect.

Winner

ES80400	Camping Las Dunas *Spain*

Runners-up

IT60030	Centro Vacanze Pra' Delle Torri *Italy*
LU7620	Europacamping Nommerlayen *Luxembourg*

Alan Rogers Readers' Award 2010

We believe our Readers' Award to be the most important. We simply invite our readers (by means of an on-line poll at www.alanrogers.com) to nominate the site they enjoyed most.

The outright winner for 2010 is:

Winner

IT60200	Camping Union Lido Vacanze *Italy*

Alan Rogers Special Award 2010

A special award is made to acknowledge sites which we feel have overcome a very significant setback, and have not only returned to their former condition, but can fairly be considered to be even better than before. In 2010 we acknowledge one campsite which suffered storm damage and we feel qualifies for this award, but also wish to acknowledge the campsites of the Argens valley, Var, France, which suffered serious flood damage in June 2010 and have made highly impressive recoveries.

FR17340	Camping Au Port-Punay *France*
The campsites of the Argens valley	*Var, France*

Crossing the Channel

One of the great advantages of booking your ferry-inclusive holiday with the Alan Rogers Travel Service is the tremendous value we offer. Our money-saving Ferry Deals have become legendary. As agents for all major cross-Channel operators we can book all your travel arrangements with the minimum of fuss and at the best possible rates.

(Please note we can only book ferry crossings in conjunction with a campsite holiday reservation)

Just call us for an instant quote
01580 214000

The aims of the Travel Service are simple

- To provide convenience - a one-stop shop to make life easier.

- To provide peace of mind - when you need it most.

- To provide a friendly, knowledgeable, efficient service
  – when this can be hard to find.

- To provide a low cost means of organising your holiday
  – when prices can be so complicated.

When you book with us, you will be allocated an experienced Personal Travel Consultant to provide you with personal advice and manage every stage of your booking. Our Personal Travel Consultants have first-hand experience of many of our campsites and access to a wealth of information. They can check availability, provide a competitive price and tailor your holiday arrangements to your specific needs.

- Discuss your holiday plans with a friendly person with first-hand experience

- Let us reassure you that your holiday arrangements really are taken care of

- Tell us about your special requests and allow us to pass these on

- Benefit from advice which will save you money – the latest ferry deals and more

- Remember, our offices are in Kent not overseas and we do NOT operate a queuing system!

Call us for advice or an instant quote
01580 214000
or visit **www.alanrogers.com/travel**

Look for a campsite entry like this to indicate which campsites we can book for you.

The list is growing so please call for up to the minute information.

alan rogers travel

It's all on-line

www.alanrogers.com/travel is a website designed to give you everything you need to know when planning your Alan Rogers inspected and selected campsite holiday. You'll find it useful for images and background information – allowing you to make a fully-informed decision. Then 'click' to book or just call us to discuss.

Our friendly, expert team of travel consultants is always happy to help on

01580 214000 – but they do go home sometimes!

www.alanrogers.com/travel

- Find latest special offers on campsites - instantly

- Check campsite availability - instantly

- Check ferry availability - instantly

- Find latest ferry deals - instantly

- Book your ferry online - instantly

[handwritten notes:]
08705 360360.
90254 7979
Paradone.es.
30063289.

Want our latest deals and offers?
Sign up for our regular email bulletin
www.alanrogers.com/subscribe

alan rogers travel

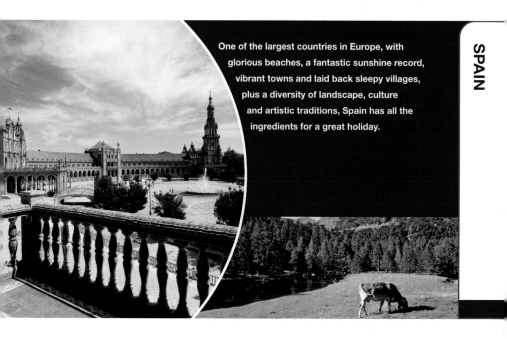

One of the largest countries in Europe, with glorious beaches, a fantastic sunshine record, vibrant towns and laid back sleepy villages, plus a diversity of landscape, culture and artistic traditions, Spain has all the ingredients for a great holiday.

Tourist Office

Spanish National Tourist Office
22/23 Manchester Square
London W1U 3PX

Tel: 020 7486 8077
E-mail: info.londres@tourspain.es
Fax: 020 7486 8034
Internet: http://www.tourspain.es

Spain has a huge choice of beach resorts to choose from. With charming villages and attractive towns, the Costa Brava boasts spectacular scenery with towering cliffs and sheltered coves. There are plenty of lively resorts, including Lloret, Tossa and Calella, plus several quieter ones. Further along the east coast, the Costa del Azahar stretches from Vinaros to Almanzora, with the great port of Valencia in the middle. Orange groves abound. The central section of the coastline, the Costa Blanca, has 170 miles or so of silvery-white beaches. Benidorm is the most popular resort. The Costa del Sol lies in the south, home to more beaches and brilliant sunshine, whilst in the north the Costa Verde is largely unspoiled, with clean water, sandy beaches and rocky coves against a backdrop of mountains.

Beaches and sunshine aside, Spain also has plenty of great cities and towns to explore, including Barcelona, Valencia, Seville, Madrid, Toledo and Bilbao, all offering an array of sights, galleries and museums.

Population

46 million

Capital

Madrid

Climate

Spain has a very varied climate. The north is temperate with most of the rainfall; dry and very hot in the centre; subtropical along the Mediterranean.

Language

Castilian Spanish is spoken by most people with Catalan (northeast), Basque (north) and Galician (northwest) used in their respective areas.

Telephone

The country code is 00 34.

Currency

The Euro (€).

Banks

Mon-Fri 09.00-14.00. Sat 09.00-13.00.

Shops

Mon-Sat 09.00-13.00/14.00 and 15.00/16.00-19.30/20.00.
Many close later.

Public Holidays

New Year; Epiphany; Saint's Day 19 March; Maundy Thurs; Good Fri; Easter Mon; Labour Day; Saint's Day 25 July; Assumption 15 Aug; National Day 12 Oct; All Saints Day 1 Nov; Constitution Day 6 Dec; Immaculate Conception 8 Dec; Christmas Day.

Flanked by the Pyrenees mountains and bathed by the Mediterranean Sea, Catalunya occupies the northeastern part of the Iberian peninsula. It has a strong identity, with a unique culture and language all of its own.

CATALUNYA IS COMPOSED OF FOUR PROVINCES: BARCELONA, TARRAGONA, LLEIDA AND GIRONA

THE REGIONAL CAPITAL IS BARCELONA

Barcelona is the historical capital of Catalunya and Spain's second leading city in both size and importance, after Madrid. The beautiful city has an impressive architectural heritage that includes the Gothic Quarter, with its cathedral, the old City Hall Building, the Episcopal Palace and the splendid Palace of the Generalitat. The city also boasts the work of the incomparable modernist architect Antonio Gaudí. In the centre of the fertile plain of the river Segre sits Lleida, capital of the province of the same name. Prominent atop a hill in the historic quarter of the city is the old cathedral or Seu Vella. The Costa Brava is the coastal zone that begins about 40 km. north of Barcelona and includes the entire shoreline of the province of Girona. It is an area of great natural beauty, formed by a succession of steep cliffs and small coves with finely grained sand. Some of its towns have been massively exploited for tourism but others, such as Tossa de Mar, still maintain their original size and fishing-village charm. The principal tourist centres on the coast include Roses, Sant Pere Pescador, L'Escala, L'Estartit, Palamós, Palafrugell, Platja d'Aro, S'Agaro, Sant Feliu de Guíxols, Lloret de Mar and Blanes. There are daily boat services which operate along the coast for most of the year.

Places of interest

Empúries: Greco-Roman city.

Figueres: birthplace of Salvador Dalí, museum displaying his finest work.

Girona: one of the oldest and most beautiful Catalan cities, 14th-century cathedral.

La Costa Dorada: stretches south from the Costa Brava to Tarragona, with beautiful, open, well maintained beaches.

Parque Natural de Aigüamolls de L'Empordà: park made up of three reserves, with wildlife and over 320 bird species.

Sitges: attractive beach town, museum of Cau-Ferrat featuring paintings by El Greco.

Tarragona: Roman remains of Tarraco, the original Roman city.

Cuisine of the region

Mediterranean influence with lots of tomatoes, garlic, fresh herbs, olive oil, onions, fish. Wild mushrooms in the autumn. Locally produced wines from Penedés, Conca de Barberá, Pla de Bages and Alella.

Calçots: green onions grilled on a barbecue.

Cod esqueixada: cod soaked in cold water then mixed with tomatoes, olives and onion.

Escalivada: vegetable stew with roasted aubergine and peppers.

Fuet, llonganisa, butifarra: local sausages.

Suquet: seafood casserole.

Recao de binefar: rice cooked with white beans, potatoes and chorizo.

For a map of northeast Catalunya, see the next page.

For latest campsite news, availability and prices visit
alanrogers.com

Albanya
Camping Bassegoda Park

Camí Camp de l'illa, E-17733 Albanya (Girona) T: 972 542 020. E: info@bassegodapark.com
alanrogers.com/ES80640

Surrounded by mountains alongside the Muga river, Bassegoda Park is a place to experience Spain in a natural environment but with a touch of luxury. This totally rebuilt site is in Albanya, on the edge of the Alta Garrotxa National Park, in an area of great beauty. In their own area, the 80 touring pitches are level and well shaded, all with electricity, water and drainage. Tents are dotted informally in the terraced forest areas. Particular care has been taken in the landscaping, layout and design of the whole site, but especially the most attractive pool, bar and restaurant, the hub of the site. These, with al fresco dining and night entertainment complement the natural setting. Regional wines and dishes are available in the reasonably priced restaurant. The enthusiastic young director, Estere Guerra (Steve) who speaks excellent English, and Laura have been working hard to make a stay at here a unique experience.

Facilities

A new main toilet building includes facilities for babies and disabled visitors. It is supplemented by three refurbished, clean blocks which are well positioned. Facilities for disabled visitors. Washing machine. Gas supplies. Supermarket. Pleasant bar and restaurant. Swimming pool. Playground. New leisure area with outdoor relaxation area and minigolf. Entertainment programme including children's entertainment. Walking, trekking and bicycle hire. Barbecue areas. Torches useful. Air conditioned bungalows to rent. Off site: Sailing 5 km. Riding 15 km. Golf 20 km. Beach 35 km. Limited public transport.

Open: 1 March - 11 December.

Directions

Site is north of Girona, west of Figueres. From Barcelona on the AP7/E15, take exit 4 and the N11 towards France. Then the GI 510 to Llers and GI 511 to St Llorenc de la Muga and Albanya. Site is well signed where the road ends. From France take exit 3 then the GI 510 to Llers. There is NO exit 3 northbound on the AP7/E15.
GPS: 42.30654, 2.70933

Charges guide

Per unit incl. 2 persons and electricity	€ 21,65 - € 35,30
extra person	€ 5,00 - € 6,85
child (3-10 yrs)	€ 4,95 - € 5,10
dog	€ 4,75

For latest campsite news, availability and prices visit
alanrogers.com

Ametlla de Mar

Camping Caravanning Ametlla Village Platja

Apdo 240, Paraje Santes Creus, E-43860 Ametlla de Mar (Tarragona) T: 977 267 784
E: info@campingametlla.com **alanrogers.com/ES85360**

This site within a protected area has been well thought out and is startling in the quality of service provided, the finish and the materials used in construction. The 373 pitches are on a terraced hillside above colourful coves with shingle beaches and two small associated lagoons (with a protected fish species). The many bungalows here have been tastefully incorporated. There are great views, particularly from the friendly restaurant. There is some train noise. The site is used by tour operators (30 pitches). It is a very good site for families or for just relaxing. The site is environmentally correct and local planning regulations are extremely tight including the types of trees that may be planted. No transit traffic is allowed within the site in high season.

Facilities

Three really good toilet blocks. Some private cabins. Motorcaravan services. Gas supplies. Supermarket (2/4-30/9; small shop incl. bread at other times). Good restaurant with snack menu. Bar with TV (2/4-30/9). Swimming pool. Sub-aqua diving. Kayaking. Fishing. Children's club and play area. Fitness room. Bicycle hire. Entertainment (July/Aug). Barbecue area. Fishing. Off site: Boat launching 3 km. Golf 15 km. Riding 20 km.

Open: All year.

Directions

From A7/E15 (Barcelona - Valencia) take exit 39 for l'Ametlla de Mar. Follow numerous large white signs on reaching village and site is 2.5 km. south of the village. GPS: 40.8645, 0.7788

Charges 2011

Per unit incl. 2 persons and electricity	€ 16,50 - € 36,50

Less for longer stays, especially in low season.

Amposta

Camping Eucaliptus

Platja Eucaliptus s/n, E-43870 Amposta (Tarragona) T: 977 479 046. E: eucaliptus@campingeucaliptus.com
alanrogers.com/ES85550

Ideally situated in the Delta del Ebro national park, a unique area of wetland (320 square kilometres) and close to the golden sands of Platja Eucaliptus. Arriving at Camping Eucaliptus is like finding an oasis after the extraordinary drive through flat marshland and rice fields. There are 264 small, level, shady grass pitches, 156 for touring, all with electricity (6A). The site is very well maintained and three modern buildings near the entrance house the reception, toilet block, shop, bar and restaurant. The terrace overlooks the pleasant pool area with lawned gardens for sunbathing and the campsite's own lagoon.

Facilities

The single toilet block is kept very clean and includes open style washbasins and good sized shower cubicles. Baby bath. Good facilities for disabled visitors. Laundry facilities. Dog shower. Well stocked shop. Gas supplies. Bar with satellite TV. Good restaurant and snack bar with takeaway. Play area. Swimming pool with paddling pool (1/6-15/9). Bicycle hire. Attractive barbecue area with covered seating. Large units may require two pitches (no extra charge in low season). Off site: Fishing 300 m. Boat launching 8 km. Sant Jaume with shops.

Open: 19 March - 26 September.

Directions

From the A7 take exit 41, signed Amposta, N340. Immediately after crossing river Ebro leave N340 signed Els Muntells and Sant Jaume. On entering Sant Jaume turn right over canal, signed Els Muntells. At T-junction turn left. Site on right in 6 km. just before beach. GPS: 40.65658, 0.77978

Charges guide

Per unit incl. 2 persons and electricity	€ 22,25 - € 31,30
extra person	€ 4,65 - € 6,55

Begur

Camping El Maset

Playa de Sa Riera, E-17255 Begur (Girona) T: 972 623 023. E: info@campingelmaset.com
alanrogers.com/ES81030

A delightful little gem of a site in lovely surroundings, El Maset has 107 pitches, of which just 20 are slightly larger for caravans or motorcaravans, the remainder suitable only for tents. The owner of some 40 years, Sr Juan Perez is delightful and his staff are very helpful. The site entrance is steep and access to the caravan pitches can be quite tricky. However, the owner's son will tow your caravan to your pitch. Some of the pitches are shaded and all have electricity, 20 also with water and drainage.

Facilities

Good sanitary facilities in three small blocks are kept very clean. Baby facilities. Washing machines and dryers. Unit for disabled campers (steep ground). Bar/restaurant, takeaway and shop. Swimming pool (all season). Solarium. Play area. Area for football and basketball. Excellent games room. Satellite TV. Internet access and free WiFi. Dogs are not accepted. Off site: Fishing and beach 300 m. Golf and bicycle hire 1 km. Riding 8 km.

Open: 1 April - 25 September.

Directions

From the C31 Figueres - Palamos road south of Pals, north of Palafrugell, take GI653 to Begur. Site is 2 km. north of the town; follow signs for Playa de Sa Riera and site (steep entrance). GPS: 41.96860, 3.21002

Charges guide

Per person	€ 5,56 - € 7,81
pitch incl. car	€ 7,70 - € 16,05
electricity	€ 4,28 - € 6,42

For latest campsite news, availability and prices visit
alanrogers.com

Begur

Camping Begur

Ctra d'Esclanya km 2, E-17255 Begur (Girona) T: 972 623 201. E: info@campingbegur.com
alanrogers.com/ES81040

The owners here have made a massive investment in making the site a pleasant place to spend time. There are some good supporting facilities including a pleasant swimming pool at its centre. The bar and snack bar are part of this new pool complex and it has been well designed with terraces and sunbathing area. The touring areas are protected from the sun by mature trees which are all numbered and protected. The 317 pitches are informally arranged on sloping sandy ground (chocks useful). Most pitches have electricity (10A), water and drainage.

Facilities

Two modern toilet blocks are fully equipped and include large showers. Excellent facilities for disabled campers. Baby bath. Washing machines and dryers. Motorcaravan services. Bar and snacks. Swimming pools (all season). Boules. Weight training room. Play area. Some children's entertainment in high season. Little farm with ponies, goats and chickens. Internet access. Off site: Restaurant and supermarket just outside gate. Village and beaches 1.5 km. Fishing 3 km. Golf 10 km. Riding 15 km.

Open: 1 April - 26 September.

Directions

From Girona take road east to La Bisbal and Palafrugell then Begur. Turn south towards Fornells, the site is well signed 3 km. south of Begur. GPS: 41.940216, 3.200079

Charges guide

Per unit incl. 2 persons	€ 22,00 - € 41,00
extra person	€ 3,50 - € 6,40
child (3-10 yrs)	€ 1,50 - € 3,50

No credit cards.

Bellver de Cerdanya

Camping Solana del Segre

Ctra N260 km 198, E-25720 Bellver de Cerdanya (Lleida) T: 973 510 310. E: sds@solanadelsegre.com
alanrogers.com/ES91420

The Sierra del Cadi offers some spectacular scenery and the Reserva Cerdanya is very popular with Spanish skiers. This site is situated in an open, sunny lower valley beside the River Segre where the far bank is a National Park (unfenced so children will need supervision). The immediate area is ideal for walkers and offers many opportunities for outdoor sports enthusiasts. The site is in two sections, the lower one nearer the river being for tourists, mainly flat and grassy with 200 pitches of 100 sq.m. or more, shaded by trees with 15A electricity. The upper area is taken by permanent units.

Facilities

Modern sanitary facilities are in a central building on the lower level, with extra Portacabin style units (unisex toilets/showers). Facilities for disabled campers are on the upper level (wheelchair users will experience problems). Laundry facilities. Motorcaravan services. Shop, bar and restaurant (1/7-15/9). Swimming and paddling pools (1/7-5/9). Indoor pool. Two play areas. Games room. River fishing. Dance area. Barbecue areas. Internet. Torches are required. Off site: Village with shops bars and restaurants. Riding 2 km. Bicycle hire and golf 10 km. Skiing.

Open: 1 July - 15 September.

Directions

Site is on left at the 198 km. marker on the N260 from Puigcerda to La Seu d'Urgell, well signed just beyond Bellver le Cerdanya. GPS: 42.372697, 1.760484

Charges guide

Per unit incl. 1 person and electricity	€ 28,50
extra person	€ 6,00
child (2-9 yrs)	€ 5,50
dog	€ 4,75

Blanes

Camping La Masia

Ctra Colon 44, E-17300 Blanes (Girona) T: 972 331 013. E: info@campinglamasia.com
alanrogers.com/ES82250

A large resort site, La Masia has 757 pitches with 300 for touring units. These pitches are flat, shaded by trees and in rows with some mobile homes inserted here and there. There is something for everyone in La Masia and the resort town is just outside the gate, as is the fine beach. A large, central building houses the main bar and restaurant. The jewel in the crown of the site is below this complex where you can enjoy an indoor heated pool, spas, massage, plunge pools and exercise pools, and pamper yourself in luxury in a Roman bath-style setting (extra charge).

Facilities

Six well maintained but basic toilet blocks provide facilities for disabled campers and a well equipped baby room. Motorcaravan services. Laundry facilities. Supermarket. Bakery. Restaurants. Snack bars. Swimming pools. Spa centre. Play areas. Boules. Bicycle hire. Barbecue area. Entertainment programme. Internet access and WiFi. ATM. Security boxes. Torches useful. Off site: Resort town and beach outside the gate. Fishing. Boat launching 200 m. Bicycle hire 500 m. Riding 3 km. Golf 5 km.

Open: 9 January - 9 December.

Directions

From exit 9 on the AP7 Girona - Barcelona road follow the N11 to the B600 towards Blanes. Before entering Blanes turn southwest following site signs at the roundabouts which will direct you to La Masia avoiding Blanes town (narrow roads and best avoided by large units). GPS: 41.66291, 2.78075

Charges guide

Per unit incl. 2 persons	€ 24,60 - € 45,50
extra person	€ 5,00 - € 6,00

Camping Cheques accepted.

For latest campsite news, availability and prices visit
alanrogers.com

Blanes
Camping Blanes

Avenida Villa de Madrid 33, Apdo 72, E-17300 Blanes (Girona) T: 972 331 591. E: info@campingblanes.com
alanrogers.com/ES82280

Camping Blanes is the first of the sites which edge the pedestrian promenade here and probably the smallest. Open all year, it is family owned and run and has been in the hands of the Boix family for 40 years. Antonio the son runs the site now with pride and care, speaking good English. With only 206 pitches, no bungalows or mobile homes and only five seasonal vans, it has a comfortable family atmosphere. Shade is provided by tall pines and because of this, some of the pitches are a bit irregular in shape and average between 60-80 sq.m.

Facilities	Directions
Smart, well equipped sanitary block with provision for disabled visitors (by key). Baby changing unit. Washing machines and dryers. Shop (15/6-15/9). Bar (1/4-12/10). Restaurant (7/7-25/8). Takeaway (7/7-25/8). Swimming pool. Play area. Beach alongside site. Car wash. Internet access and WiFi. Off site: All amenities of the town are within walking distance (500 m). Golf and riding 5 km. **Open:** All year.	Site is south of the town beside the beach before Camping Bella Terra and El Pinar. Follow signs for 'campings' until individual site signs appear. GPS: 41.65918, 2.77959

Charges 2011

Per unit incl. 2 persons and electricity	€ 25,20 - € 35,90

No credit cards in winter season.

Blanes
Beach Camp El Pinar

Avenida Vila de Madrid 39, E-17300 Blanes (Girona) T: 972 331 083. E: camping@elpinarbeach.com
alanrogers.com/ES82300

A long established campsite, El Pinar enjoys an excellent location on the southern edge of Blanes with direct access to the superb beach. The site is in two halves, arranged on either side of a large road that terminates just past the site entrance gates where it meets the very clean, sandy beach. One side of the site is more modern than the other. All the 450 touring pitches are on level sandy grass and all have 6A electricity. There is a degree of shade with younger trees on the newer side while the very old pine trees on the original, older side are impressive and provide a good deal of shade. The site roads are of fine gravel/coarse sand. The touring pitches are in the centre of the site whilst pitches for 115 bungalows and chalets to rent are placed round the perimeter. The buildings on the older side tend to look their age but are kept clean and whilst we were visiting a lot of work was being done in preparation for the new season. This site offers good value in a friendly, relaxed way with the wonderful beach close at hand.

Facilities	Directions
Sanitary facilities in two large blocks (one older but refurbished) include some private washbasins. Facilities for disabled visitors. Baby room. Cleaning is continual through the day. Full laundry facilities including ironing boards. Shop (all season). Bar/restaurant and takeaway (all season). Games room. Large swimming pool with adjacent paddling pool on the newer side (from 1/5). Multisport area. Bicycle hire. Simple play area. Miniclub (late June-early Sept). Beach. Off site: Bicycle hire 500 m. Boat launching 2 km. Riding 8 km. Golf 6 km. Tourist train into town (10 mins). Water theme park. Marina and harbour. Large town of Blanes with full tourist attractions. Boat excursions to other towns on the coast. **Open:** 16 April - 2 October.	From AP7 or C-32 motorways follow signs for Blanes. Site is the last travelling south from Blanes town centre. Follow camping signs in Blanes until you see the El Pinar sign. GPS: 41.6555, 2.77862

Charges guide

Per unit incl. 2 persons and electricity	€ 27,70 - € 35,30
extra person	€ 5,40 - € 6,60
child (2-10 yrs)	€ 4,30 - € 5,70
dog	€ 2,00

Discounts for pensioners and low season longer stays.

HOLIDAY ON THE BEACH... AND IN THE POOL

EL PINAR BEACH CAMPING

Waiting for you at EL PINAR BEACH CAMP: 300 metres of fine soft sand beach, pine woods, easy motorway access and organised events for everybody, every day. And that is not all! There is also a superb freshwater swimming pool in a carefully landscaped garden, a snack bar, a supermarket, organised activities, etc...Now at EL PINAR BEACH CAMP-more of everything! Discover us.

c. Villa de Madrid | E-17300 Blanes (Girona) | Tel.: (34) 972 33 10 83 | www.elpinarbeach.com

For latest campsite news, availability and prices visit
alanrogers.com

Blanes

Camping Bella Terra

Avenida Vila de Madrid 35-40, E-17300 Blanes (Girona) T: 972 348 017. E: info@campingbellaterra.com

alanrogers.com/ES82320

Camping Bella Terra is set in a shady pine grove facing a white sandy beach on the Mediterranean coast. There are 797 pitches with 600 for touring units, the rest taken by bungalows to rent (97) and by Spanish 'residents' (200). All pitches have 5/6A electricity and 134 are fully serviced. The site is in two sections, each with its own reception. The main reception is on the right of the road as you approach, with the swimming and paddling pools and delightful new pool bar and restaurant. The other half, which fills up first, has direct access to the beach and a supermarket with its own bakery.

Facilities

The newer side of the site has excellent new sanitary blocks with superb facilities for children and a baby room. The older side has older blocks which are clean, but dated. Provision for disabled visitors and laundry on both sides. Shop, restaurant, bar and takeaway. Outdoor swimming and paddling pools (from May). Playground. Fishing. Bicycle hire. Internet café and WiFi. Miniclub. For dogs, contact site first. Off site: Blanes town within walking distance. Road train to the resort (high season). Sailing 3 km. Golf 8 km. Riding 12 km.

Open: 27 March - 26 September.

Directions

Site is on the southwest side of Blanes. From exit 9 on the AP7 Girona - Barcelona road follow N11 to the B600 towards Blanes. Before entering Blanes turn southwest following site signs at the roundabouts which will direct you avoiding Blanes town which has narrow roads and is best avoided by large units. GPS: 41.6616, 2.77612

Charges guide

Per person	€ 4,50 - € 6,00
pitch	€ 16,40 - € 39,40

Borredá

Camping Campalans

Ctra Sant Jaume de Frontanyá km 1,5, E-08619 Borredá (Barcelona) T: 938 239 163
E: campalans@campalans.net alanrogers.com/ES91380

With its wonderful location in a quiet river valley with views of the surrounding mountains, Camping Campalans is an excellent site for enjoying this beautiful area. Combining camping with chalets and a hostel, the site has 40 small, grass touring pitches. The terraced pitches are below an old stone building housing reception, a comfortable bar, a restaurant and a small shop. The approach is by a steep, narrow, gravel mountain track and the site is 5 km. from the nearest village. However, for all but the largest units, the trip is well worth making. The site offers assistance with a 4x4 vehicle.

Facilities

One new toilet block, heated and with well equipped showers, washbasins and ensuite cabins. Laundry room and drying room. Motorcaravan services. Shop (1/6-31/8). Bar. Swimming pool (1/6-15/9). Play area. Large adventure trail for three age groups next to site. Lodges and bungalows to rent. Off site: Borredá with cafés and small shops 5 km. Big supermarket, banking and cheap petrol in Berga 22 km.

Open: 1 July - 31 August, weekends 1 Feb - 31 Dec.

Directions

From France via Puigcerda on the C-16, just before Berga turn left towards Ripoll. After Borredá turn left to Sant Jaume de Frontanyá. Site is east of the village, 1.5 km. on the left. GPS: 42.14583, 1.99954

Charges guide

Per person	€ 5,35
pitch incl. car	€ 12,84
electricity (5A)	€ 4,07

Calella de la Costa

Camping Botánic Bona Vista Kim

Ctra NII km 665,8, E-08370 Calella de la Costa (Barcelona) T: 937 692 488. E: info@botanic-bonavista.net

alanrogers.com/ES82400

While Calella itself may conjure up visions of mass tourism, this site is set on a very steep hillside some 3 km. out of the town. Any noise from the nearby coast road and railway gets lost as you gain height and it is a quite delightful setting with an abundance of flowers, shrubs and roses (1,700, all planted by the knowledgeable owner Kim, who has won prizes for his roses). The design of the site successfully marries the beautiful botanic surrounds with the wonderful views over the bay. Of the 160 pitches, 130 are for tourers, all with electricity and on flat terraces on the slopes, with some shade.

Facilities

The standard of design in the three sanitary blocks is quite outstanding for a small site. Some washbasins in cabins in the newest block. Baby room. Washing machines. Motorcaravan services. Bar/restaurant, takeaway and shop (all year). Outdoor pool (1/5-30/9). Large play area. Recreation park. Satellite TV. Internet point. Barbecue and picnic area. Entertainment (11/7-26/8). No cycling on site. Off site: Fishing 100 m. Bicycle hire 1 km. Riding and golf 3 km.

Open: All year.

Directions

From N11 coast road, site is signed south of Calella (km. 665), and is on the coastal side of road. The road is busy but site signs give ample warning of the entrance (shared ES82420). Entrance is very steep. From the Barcelona direction you must pass the entrance and turn at the roundabout in some 800 m. GPS: 41.606667, 2.639167

Charges 2011

Per unit incl. 2 persons	€ 38,75 - € 40,65
extra person	€ 7,73 - € 8,10

For latest campsite news, availability and prices visit

alanrogers.com

Calella de la Costa

Camping Roca Grossa

Ctra NII km 665, E-08370 Calella de la Costa (Barcelona) T: 937 691 297. E: rocagrossa@rocagrossa.com
alanrogers.com/ES82420

Roca Grossa's owners, the Bachs family, are very friendly and there is a very happy atmosphere in the campsite. Very steep slopes predominate at this site and there is a challenging 1 in 3, 100 m. climb from reception to the swimming pool at the top of the site. In high season a road train runs all day to ferry you up to the amenities, but the site is unsuitable for disabled campers. The bonus is some great views over the sea from most of the terraced, but flat and reasonably sized pitches. A 4x4 can site your unit.

Facilities

An amazing array of clean sanitary blocks means there is not far to walk from any area of the site. Large and small, all blocks are well kept with hot water throughout. Washing machines. Gas supplies. Shop. Pleasant bar (with internet access) and restaurant. Swimming pools (1/5-30/9). Playground. Road train. Tennis. Entertainment programme including children's entertainment. Excursions. WiFi. ATM. Torches useful. Off site: Beach, boat launching and fishing 50 m. Town 100 m. Indoor pool 1 km. Riding 1 km. Golf 2 km. Watersports nearby.

Open: 1 April - 15 October.

Directions

From A7 (Girona - Barcelona) take exit 9 or 10 for Malgrat del Mar on the N11. Turn south towards Calella and site is at 665 km. marker sharing an entrance with another campsite. Caravans are placed on pitches with site Landrover.
GPS: 41.60632, 2.63892

Charges guide

Per unit incl. 2 persons and electricity	€ 34,40
extra person	€ 7,10
child (under 10 yrs)	€ 6,25

No credit cards.

Calonge

Camping Internacional de Calonge

Ctra San Feliu/Guixols - Palamós km 7.6, E-17251 Calonge (Girona) T: 972 651 233
E: info@intercalonge.com alanrogers.com/ES81300

This spacious, well laid out site has access to a fine beach by a footbridge over the coast road, or you can take the little road train as the site is on very sloping ground. Calonge is a family site with two good sized pools on different levels, a paddling pool and large sunbathing areas. A great restaurant, bar and snack bar are by the pool. The site's 793 pitches are on terraces and all have electricity (5A), with 84 being fully serviced. The pitches are set on attractively landscaped terraces (access to some may be challenging). There is good shade from the tall pine trees and some views of the sea through the foliage. The views from the upper levels are taken by a tour operator and mobile home pitches. The pools are overlooked by the restaurant terraces which have great views over the mountains. A nature area within the site is used for walks or picnics. A separate area within the site is set aside for visitors with dogs. The beach is accessed over the main road by 100 steps and is shared with another campsite (ES81400).

Facilities

Generous sanitary provision includes some washbasins in cabins. No toilet seats. One block is heated in winter. Laundry facilities. Motorcaravan services. Gas supplies. Shop (26/3-30/10), Restaurant (1/2-31/12). Bar, patio bar (pizza and takeaway 27/3-24/10, weekends otherwise). Swimming pools (26/3-16/10). Playground. Electronic games. Rather noisy disco two nights a week (but not late). Bicycle hire. Tennis. Hairdresser. ATM. Internet access and WiFi. Torches necessary in some areas. Road train from the bottom of the site to the top in high season. Off site: Bus at the gate. Fishing 300 m. Supermarket 500 m. Golf 3 km. Riding 10 km.

Open: All year.

Directions

Site is on the inland side of the coast road between Palamós and Platja d'Aro. Take the C31 south to the 661 at Calonge. At Calonge follow signs to the C253 towards Platja d'Aro and on to site which is well signed. GPS: 41.83333, 3.08417

Charges guide

Per unit incl. 2 persons and electricity	€ 19,65 - € 44,65
extra person	€ 3,65 - € 7,85
child (3-10 yrs)	€ 1,85 - € 4,40
dog	€ 3,20 - € 4,05

No credit cards.

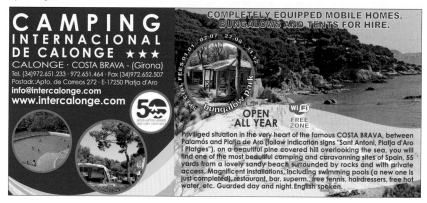

For latest campsite news, availability and prices visit
alanrogers.com

Calonge

Camping Treumal

Ctra 253 km 47.5, E-17250 Calonge (Girona) T: 972 651 095. E: info@campingtreumal.com

alanrogers.com/ES81400

This very attractive terraced site has been developed on a hillside around the attractive gardens of a large, spectacular estate house which is close to the sea. The house is the focus of the site's excellent facilities, including a superb restaurant with terraces overlooking two tranquil beaches, protected in pretty coves. The site has 551 pitches on well shaded terraces. Of these 409 are accessible to tourers and there are some 50 pitches on flat ground alongside the sea – the views are stunning and you wake to the sound of the waves. Electrical connections (6/10/16A) are available in all parts.

Facilities

Four well maintained sanitary blocks have free hot water in the washbasins (with some private cabins), controllable showers, and a tap to draw from for the sinks. New beach block. Washing machines. Motorcaravan services. Gas supplies. Supermarket, bar and takeaway. Restaurant (1/6-15/9). Beach bar. Fishing. Play area. Sports area. Games room. Satellite TV. Internet access and WiFi. ATM. Dogs are not accepted. Off site: Public transport 300 m. Bicycle hire 2 km. (delivered to site). Riding, golf 5 km.

Open: 1 April - 30 September.

Directions

Site is southeast of Girona on the coast 3 km. south of Palamós. It is best to avoid the town centre by using C31 (Girona - Palamós) road, leave at km. 320, and take road south to Sant Anthoni de Calonge. Take C253 south towards Platja d'Aro. Site is well signed. GPS: 41.83642, 3.08725

Charges 2011

Per unit incl. 2 persons	€ 23,70 - € 47,40
extra person	€ 4,30 - € 8,20

Discounts in low seasons. No credit cards.

Calonge

Camping Cala Gogo

Av. Andorra 13, E-17251 Calonge (Girona) T: 972 651 564. E: calagogo@calagogo.es

alanrogers.com/ES81600

Cala Gogo is a large traditional campsite with a pleasant situation on a wooded hillside with mature trees giving shade to most pitches. The 578 shaded touring pitches varying in size are in terraced rows, some with artificial shade, all have 10A electricity and water, and most have drainage. There may be road noise in eastern parts of the site. Some pitches are now right by the beach, the remainder are up to 800 m. uphill, but the 'Gua gua' tractor train, operating almost all season, takes people between the centre of site and beach and adds to the general sense of fun.

Facilities

Seven clean toilet blocks are of a high standard. Some washbasins in private cabins. New baby rooms. Facilities for disabled visitors. Laundry room. Motorcaravan services. Gas supplies. New supermarket. General shop. Restaurants and bars. Two heated swimming pools and paddling pool (lifeguards). Playground, crèche and babysitting service (extra charge). Sports centre. Bicycle hire. Kayaks (free). Internet access and WiFi (free). Medical service. Dogs are not accepted in high season. Off site: Golf 5 km. Riding 10 km. Aqua Park nearby.

Open: End April - end September.

Directions

Sant Antoni de Calonge is southeast of Girona. Leave the AP7/E15 at exit 6. Take C66 towards Palamós which becomes the C31. Use the C31 (Girona - Palamós) road to avoid Palamós town. Take the C253 coast road. Site is at km. 46.5, which is 4 km. south of Palamós. GPS: 41.83083, 3.08247

Charges guide

Per unit incl. 2 persons	
and electricity	€ 21,50 - € 48,25
extra person	€ 3,65 - € 7,60

Cambrils

Camping La Llosa

Camí de les Lloses, Ctra. N-340, km. 1143, E-43850 Cambrils (Tarragona) T: 977 362 615
E: info@camping-lallosa.com alanrogers.com/ES84770

La Llosa is situated close to the attractive seafront town of Cambrils. You will meet three generations of this family busy about the site, the younger members speak good English. The site is hidden in a residential area 100 m. from the excellent beach and promenade of Cambrils and has a pleasant pool with separate paddling area. The 300 touring pitches with 6A electricity, are level, shaded by trees (watch the overheads) and are traditional as are most of the facilities here. This site will appeal to campers who do not wish for the glitz and brashness of modern sites.

Facilities

Four clean, traditional sanitary blocks. Separate facilities for disabled campers, and a baby bath. Restaurant and bar (open all year; most other facilities open Easter-Oct). Washing machines. Well stocked supermarket. Outdoor pool with separate paddling pool. Bicycle hire. Multisports pitch. Limited entertainment programme in high season. WiFi. Internet access. Pets accepted. Train and bus 500 m. Accommodation for hire. Torches useful. Off site: Beach 100 m. Cambrils town 1 km.

Open: All year.

Directions

From A7 Valencia/Barcelona autoroute take exit 37 for Cambrils and the N340 to Cambrils. Site is near the 1143 km. marker on the N340 – well signed. GPS: 41.065339, 1.044585

Charges guide

Per unit incl. 2 persons	
and electricity	€ 24,00 - € 46,00
extra person	€ 4,70 - € 7,00
child (1-10 yrs)	€ 4,50 - € 5,75

For latest campsite news, availability and prices visit
alanrogers.com

Cambrils

Camping Playa Cambrils Don Camilo

Ctra Cambrils - Salou km 1,5, Avenida Oleastrum, E-43850 Cambrils (Tarragona) T: 977 361 490
E: info@playacambrils.com alanrogers.com/ES84790

A smart, well kept site with a canopy of mature shading trees. The site is 300 m. from the beach across a busy road. The small (60 sq.m) pitches are on flat ground, divided by hedges. There are many permanent pitches and a quarter of the site is given up to chalet style accommodation, which is generally separate from the touring pitches. Large units are placed in a dedicated area where the trees are higher. The very pleasant pool complex includes a smart glassed restaurant and bar with a distinct Spanish flavour reflected in the menu and tapas available throughout the day. As this is a popular site with Spanish families it is a good place to practise your language. The pool is long and narrow with separate children's pool and a large grassed and paved area for soaking up the sun. Entertainment for children is provided in high season. A big building at one end of the site near the railway (some passing train noise). consists of the supermarket, an attended electronic games room and a large play room.

Facilities

Three smart, attractively tiled modern sanitary buildings, offer sound, clean facilities with British style WCs and showers in separate buildings. Excellent facilities for disabled campers. Laundry facilities. Supermarket (April -Sept). Bar/snacks and separate restaurant (April-Sept). Swimming pools. Playground. Entertainment in high season. Miniclub. Huge electronic games room. Bicycle hire. Torches useful. Off site: Resort town has a wide range of shops, bars and restaurants. Boat launching 400 m. Fishing and golf 1 km. Riding 1.5 km.

Open: 15 March - 12 October.

Directions

Leave AP7 autopista at exit 37 and head for Cambrils and then to the beach. Turn left along beach road. Site is 1 km. east of Cambrils Playa and is well signed as you leave Cambrils marina. GPS: 41.06487, 1.08368

Charges guide

Per unit incl. 2 persons and electricity	€ 18,30 - € 41,81
extra person	€ 2,75 - € 5,25
child (under 9 yrs)	€ 1,95 - € 3,99

Camping Cheques accepted.

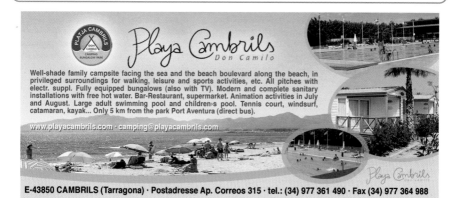
Cambrils

Camping Joan

182

Passeig Maritim 88, E-43850 Cambrils (Tarragona) T: 977 364 604. E: info@campingjoan.com
alanrogers.com/ES84780

Camping Joan is a family site to the south of the popular resort of Cambrils and with direct access to the sandy beach. There are 200 touring pitches of two different types, some being suitable for larger units. Most are between 60-90 sq.m. in size with 5A electrical connections and there is good shade. The 160 remaining pitches are used for mobile homes and chalets to rent. The site has a swimming pool, but obviously the main attraction here will be the beach. This is a lively site in high season with a varied and comprehensive programme of entertainment and activities for adults and children.

Facilities

Six sanitary blocks of which only four are available for the touring pitches. Bar, restaurant and takeaway meals. Supermarket. Swimming and paddling pools. Playground. Entertainment programme in high season, children's club. WiFi. Direct access to beach. Off site: Cambrils 2 km. Golf 8 km. Port Aventura 8 km.

Open: 27 February - 5 November.

Directions

Heading south on the AP7 motorway, leave at exit 37 (Costa Daurada) and join the southbound N340. Leave this road at the service station in La Dorada. GPS: 41.058899, 1.027774

Charges guide

Per unit incl. 2 persons and electricity	€ 17,90 - € 34,35
extra person	€ 2,90 - € 5,95
child (3-10 yrs)	€ 1,90 - € 4,95
dog	€ 1,50 - € 3,10

For latest campsite news, availability and prices visit
alanrogers.com

Camprodon
Camping Vall de Camprodon
Ctra C38 Ripoll a Camprodon, E-17867 Camprodon (Girona) T: 972 740 507. E: info@valldecamprodon.net
alanrogers.com/ES91225

This large holiday village is attractively situated in a wooded valley with cows grazing to one side, their pleasant bells often to be heard. A stream runs between the site and the road and the site lies a few yards above. There are 200 grass and gravel pitches many with shade, with just 40 for touring units, all with 4-10A electricity. There are some fully serviced pitches near the entrance. The Gomes family, who also own the nearby 'Els Roures' site, took over this complex a few years ago and since then have done all they can to turn it into a pleasant holiday destination.

Facilities

One centrally placed, fully equipped and well maintained toilet block. Very large en-suite bathroom for disabled visitors. Washing machines, dryers and ironing board (iron from reception). Shop. Bar/restaurant with simple menu (July/Aug). Swimming and paddling pools (July/Aug). Fishing. Tennis. Multisport court. Boules. Miniclub (July/Aug). WiFi. Off site: Golf and bicycle hire 2 km. Riding 6 km. Valley station of the railway to Nuria 40 km. Skiing 20 km. at Vallter 2000.

Open: All year.

Directions

From the N260 Figueres - Ripoll road after Olot continue towards Ripoll. Take C26 north via Valley of Bianya. After the tunnels turn right on C-38 to Camprodon. Site is halfway between St Pau de Seguries and Camprodon. GPS: 42.29033, 2.36242

Charges guide

Per person	€ 7,95
pitch	€ 10,50 - € 14,95
electricity (4-10A)	€ 3,60 - € 7,90

Camping Cheques accepted.

Cambrils
Camping Cambrils Park
182
Avenida Mas Clariana s/n, E-43850 Cambrils (Tarragona) T: 977 351 031. E: mail@cambrilspark.es
alanrogers.com/ES84810

This is a superb site for a camping holiday providing for all family members, whatever their ages. A drive lined with palm trees and flowers leads from a large, very smart, round reception building at this impressive modern site. Sister site to no. ES8480, it is set 500 metres back from the excellent beach in a generally quiet setting with outstanding facilities. The 504 slightly sloping, grassy pitches of around 90 sq.m. are numbered and separated by trees. All have 10A electricity, 55 have water and waste water connections, some have more shade than others and there are 325 chalets close by.

Facilities

Four excellent sanitary buildings are constantly cleaned and provide some washbasins in cabins, superb units for disabled visitors and immaculate baby sections. Huge serviced laundry. Motorcaravan services. Car wash. Quality restaurant. Takeaway. Supermarket, souvenir shop and bakery. Swimming pools. Tennis. Entertainment. Miniclub. Internet access. ATM. Gas supplies. Pets are not accepted. Off site: Beach 500 m. Fishing, bicycle hire 400 m. Riding 3 km. Port Aventura 4 km. Golf 7 km.

Open: 26 March - 12 October.

Directions

On west side of Salou about 1.5 km. from the centre, site is well signed from the coast road to Cambrils and from the other town approaches. Caution as there are many campsites with similar names off this road. GPS: 41.076463, 1.109238

Charges guide

Per person	€ 6,00
pitch incl. electricity	€ 15,00 - € 55,00

Camping Cheques accepted.

Canet de Mar
Camping Globo Rojo
Ctra N-II km 660.9, E-08360 Canet de Mar (Barcelona) T: 937 941 143. E: camping@globo-robo.com
alanrogers.com/ES82430

Camping Globo Roja is cleverly laid out in a semi-circular fashion. Within the various sectors, permanent campers and touring units stay alongside each other. The restaurant which serves authentic food and tapas, is within a sensitively restored farmhouse and is superb. The site is located on the beach road (N11) so is subject to some traffic noise, but the full shading of mature trees also absorbs the noise. The 170 flat pitches include 100 touring pitches, all with 10A electricity and with an average size of 70 sq.m. An excellent elevated pool and paddling pool are waiting for you to enjoy and the beach is close by.

Facilities

Two sanitary blocks have clean, modern equipment. Baby room. Facilities for disabled campers. Hot water throughout. Washing machines. Motorcaravan service areas. Shop. Bar. Restaurant. Takeaway. Swimming and paddling pools (with lifeguards). Miniclub. WIFI (free) in restaurant area. Playground. Pétanque. Electronic games. Dog bath. Car wash. Safes. Off site: Fishing 100 m. Golf and bicycle hire 5 km. Riding 7 km. Watersports 2 km.

Open: 1 April - 30 September.

Directions

Site is at the 660.9 km. marker on the N11. Leave the C-32 autoroute at exit 20 (AP7 exit 120) and follow signs to Canet de Mar. Site is well signed on both carriageways of the N11. GPS: 41.590903, 2.591951

Charges guide

Per unit incl. 2 persons and electricity	€ 22,50 - € 45,75
extra person	€ 4,50 - € 6,50

For latest campsite news, availability and prices visit
alanrogers.com

Castelló d'Empúries
Camping Caravaning La Laguna
Apdo 55, E-17486 Castelló d'Empúries (Girona) T: 972 450 553. E: info@campinglaguna.com
alanrogers.com/ES80150

La Laguna is a relaxed, spacious site on an isthmus within a Catalan national maritime park, on the migratory path of many different birds. It has direct access to an excellent sandy beach and the estuary of the river Muga (also a beach). The owners continue to spend much time and effort on improvements. The double lagoons are a most attractive feature. The 762 pitches (with just 41 mobile homes) are shaded and clearly marked on grass and sand, all with 6/10A electricity. There are also 47 fully serviced pitches. A very attractive bar/restaurant and sitting room overlook the lagoons and there are two swimming pools (one is heated in low season). A disco operates across the road from reception, keeping the noise away from the main site. A large riding school operates (May-September) and there are many other activities. The beach frontage is large and has a sailing school. It is said to be possible to cross over to Empuriabrava when the tide is out. There are many pleasant walks in this area and this a good site for family holidays.

Facilities

Five superb toilet blocks, placed to avoid long walks, have solar heated water. Laundry room. Bar, restaurant and takeaway. Comprehensive supermarket. Swimming pools (15/5-31/10). Football. Tennis (free in low season). ATM. Minigolf. Windsurfing and sailing schools (July/Aug). Fishing. Miniclub. Play areas. Bicycle hire. Riding. Entertainment programme and competitions. Satellite TV. Internet access and WiFi. Off site: Boat launching. Golf 15 km. Birdwatching (Ramsar area).

Open: 5 April - 31 October.

Directions

Castelló d'Empúries is east of Figueras on the coast. From AP7/E15 take exit 3 south or exit 4 north (note there is no exit 3 north) and then N11 to the C260 towards Roses. At Castelló d'Empúries roundabout (there is only one) follow signs to Depuradora (2 km) and 'camping' for 4 km. on a hard track road to the site. GPS: 42.2374, 3.121

Charges 2011

Per unit incl. 2 persons
and electricity   € 25,50 - € 49,70
No credit cards.

Castelló d'Empúries
Kawan Village Mas Nou
Mas Nou no. 7, E-17486 Castelló d'Empúries (Girona) T: 972 454 175. E: info@campingmasnou.com
alanrogers.com/ES80120

Some two kilometres from the sea on the Costa Brava, this is a pristine and surprisingly tranquil site in two parts split by the access road. One part contains the pitches and toilet blocks, the other houses the impressive leisure complex. There are 450 neat, level and marked pitches on grass and sand, a minimum of 70 sq.m. but most 80-100 sq.m, and 300 with electricity (10A). The leisure complex is across the road from reception and features a huge L-shaped swimming pool with a paddling area. A formal restaurant has an adjoining bar/café, pleasant terrace and rotisseria under palms.

Facilities

Three absolutely excellent, fully equipped sanitary blocks include baby baths, good facilities for disabled visitors. Washing machines. Motorcaravan services. Supermarket and other shops. Baker in season. Bar/restaurant, rotisserie and takeaway. Swimming pool with lifeguard (1/5-25/9). Tennis. Minigolf. Miniclub (July/Aug). Play areas. Electronic games. Internet access and free WiFi. Car wash. Off site: Riding 1.5 km. Fishing or bicycle hire 2 km. Beach 2.5 km. Public transport 1 km. Aquatic Park.

Open: 16 April - 25 September.

Directions

From A7 use exit 3. Mas Nou is 2 km. east of Castelló d'Empúries, on the Roses road, 10 km. from Figueras. Do not turn left across the main road but continue to the roundabout and return. Site is clearly marked. GPS: 42.26558, 3.1025

Charges 2011

Per unit incl. 2 persons
and electricity   € 23,50 - € 43,40
extra person   € 2,55 - € 4,95
Camping Cheques accepted.

For latest campsite news, availability and prices visit
alanrogers.com

Castelló d'Empúries
Camping Nautic Almata

Ctra. GIV- 6216 km 11,6, E-17486 Castelló d'Empúries (Girona) T: 972 454 477. E: info@almata.com
alanrogers.com/ES80300

In the Bay of Roses, south of Empúriabrava and beside the Parc Natural dels Aiguamolls de l'Empordá, this is a high quality site of particular interest to nature lovers (especially bird watchers). Beautifully laid out, it is arranged around the river and waterways, so will suit those who like to be close to water or who enjoy watersports and boating. It is worth visiting because of its unusual aspects and the feeling of being on the canals, as well as being a superb beachside site. A large site, there are 1,109 well kept, large, numbered pitches, all with electricity and on flat, sandy ground. There are some pitches right on the beach and on the banks of the canal. As you drive through the natural park to the site watch for the warning signs for frogs on the road and enjoy the wild flamingos. The name no doubt derives from the fact that boats can be tied up at the small marina within the site and a slipway also gives access to a river and thence to the sea. Throughout the season there is a varied entertainment programme for children and adults. The facilities on this site are impressive. Some tour operators use the site.

Facilities

Toilet blocks of a high standard include some en-suite showers with basins. Good facilities for disabled visitors. Washing machines. Gas supplies. Excellent supermarket. Restaurants and bar. Two separate bars and snack bar by beach where discos held in main season. Water-ski, diving and windsurfing schools. 300 sq.m. swimming pool. New tennis court. Squash. Fronton. Minigolf. Games room. Extensive riding tuition with own stables and stud. New children's play park. Fishing (licence required). Car, motorcycle and bicycle hire. Hairdresser. Internet access and WiFi. ATM. Torches are useful near beach. Off site: Canal trips 18 km. Aquatic Park 20 km.

Open: 14 May - 18 September (with all services).

Directions

Site is signed at 26 km. marker on C252 between Castello d'Empúries and Vildemat, then 7 km. to site. Alternatively, on San Pescador - Castello d'Empuries road head north and site is well signed. GPS: 42.1245, 3.0510

Charges 2011

Per unit incl. 2 persons	
and electricity	€ 28,30 - € 56,60
extra person (over 3 yrs)	€ 2,65 - € 5,30
dog	€ 5,00 - € 6,60
boat or jet ski	€ 9,75 - € 13,00

No credit cards.

Castelló d'Empúries
Camping Castell Mar

182

Platja de la Rubina, E-17486 Castelló d'Empúries (Girona) T: 972 450 822. E: cmar@campingparks.com
alanrogers.com/ES80100

This traditional-style and pricey site is a 450-metre walk from one of the very pleasant Gulf of Roses beaches (one of the closest beach gates is not used), and within the large Aiguamolls de l'Empordá nature reserve. It is also convenient for (but quite separate from) the latest tourist development and facilities at Empuria Brava. With some 310 pitches (160 for touring), it is smaller than many sites in this part of Spain and may be suitable for some families. The pitches, most with electricity, are of average size for the Costa Brava and are on level ground with some artificial shade added to the natural shade from the trees. There is a rather small outdoor pool (heated in low season), a restaurant and bar and an large open-air auditorium where a varied entertainment programme is provided in high season. A rooftop, terraced area is used for special occasions and enjoys pleasant views of the surrounding area. There are opportunities for most watersports nearby and reception can arrange excursions by canoe through the nature reserve. Security is very good – if you want to leave before 8 am. you must make prior arrangements. There are several tour operators (100 pitches) and a further 50 pitches have mobile homes to rent. English, French and Dutch spoken.

Facilities

The large, well maintained, modern toilet block is kept clean but there are no toilet seats. Some washbasins in cabins. Facilities for disabled visitors. Laundry facilities. Bar, restaurant/pizzeria and takeaway. Supermarket. Play area. Swimming pools. Many activities and limited entertainment over a long season. ATM. Security boxes. Torches required in some areas. Off site: Boat launching 500 m. Riding 1 km. Bicycle hire 3 km. Golf 10 km. Discounts at local attractions.

Open: 21 May - 18 September.

Directions

Castello d'Empuries is north of Girona and east of Figueres on the coast. From motorway AP7 take exit 3 south or exit 4 north (note there is no exit 3 north). Do not go into Castello d'Empuries or Empuriabrava, but continue on N11 to the C260 towards Roses. At km 40 La Rubina, turn and pass by La Llar restaurant, site is 1.5 km further. GPS: 42.25517, 3.1366

Charges 2011

Per unit incl. 2 persons	
and electricity	€ 18,00 - € 64,00
extra person	€ 5,00
child (3-10 yrs)	€ 3,50
dog	free

No credit cards.

For latest campsite news, availability and prices visit
alanrogers.com

www.almata.com

1ª Cat

N 42°.12.45
E 3° 05.10

amping Nautic Almata
Ctra. Giv-6216
17486 Castelló d'Empuries
Costa Brava-Girona-España
Tel:(34)972 454477
Fax:(34)972 454686
info@almata.com
www.almata.com

Offers on our
Website

Cubelles

Camping La Rueda

Ctra C31 km 146,2, E-08880 Cubelles (Barcelona) T: 938 950 207. E: larueda@la-rueda.com
alanrogers.com/ES83930

On arrival at La Rueda, you are met with an impressive security barrier opposite the reception building. The staff here speak good English and are very welcoming. Just inside the gate is a small pine forest where a more casual camping area is to be found offering plenty of shade. The remainder of the 300 flat, grassy pitches are set amongst young trees where some artificial awnings provide shade. At the far end of the site is a railway underpass (some noise) which leads to a long sandy beach. At the centre of the site and up a few steps, are a bar and snack bar.

Facilities

Two identical sanitary blocks, one on each side of the site. Although dated, they offer adequate facilities and are kept very clean. Some washbasins in cabins. Baby cubicle. Separate laundry room. Shop (weekends only in low season). Bar and snack bar with takeaway pizzas. Formal restaurant. Swimming pool (28/5-11/9). Games room. Play area. Entertainment (July/Aug). Off site: Fishing 200 m. Riding and bicycle hire 1 km. Golf 7 km.

Open: 16 April - 11 September.

Directions

La Rueda is very easy to find. It is on the C31 at 146.2 km. west of Cubelles.
GPS: 41.19987, 1.64335

Charges 2011

Per unit incl. 2 persons	
and electricity	€ 24,84 - € 45,13
extra person	€ 4,14 - € 6,90
child (1-9 yrs)	€ 2,90 - € 4,83
dog	€ 2,22 - € 3,70

El Vendrell

Camping Vendrell Platja

Avenida del Sanatori s/n, E-43880 Coma-ruga - El Vendrell (Tarragona) T: 977 694 009
E: vendrell@camping-vendrellplatja.com   alanrogers.com/ES84020

In the popular Calafell area, this site is set back from the sea across a beach road. Popular with tourists for many years, the area has apartment buildings, bars and restaurants, and is popular with families. The pitches (70 sq.m) are fairly close together, partially shaded by trees, and all have 6A electricity. Access to all the pitches is through one narrow central avenue of palms which is busy with foot and vehicle traffic. The pleasant pool area with more tall palms and grassy areas, has very wide slides that delight children and adults alike. There is a railway line at the western end of the site.

Facilities

Two well located and modern toilet blocks provide clean facilities with a unit for disabled campers and well equipped baby rooms. Washing machines. Car wash. Supermarket. Restaurant. Snack bar. Swimming pools and pool bar. Play areas. Boules. Bicycle hire. Entertainment and activity programmes. ATM. Security boxes. Torches useful. Internet access and WiFi. Off site: Resort town and beach nearby. Fishing. Bicycle hire 200 m. Riding 2 km. Golf 3 km.

Open: 1 April - 12 October.

Directions

From A7 or A16 take exit 31 for El Vendrell. Then go east to Sant Salvador, and north on coast road towards Platja Calafell. Site is well signed on this road west of the town centre. GPS: 41.1856, 1.5554

Charges guide

Per person	€ 4,50 - € 9,00
child (3-11 yrs)	€ 2,50 - € 8,50
pitch incl. electricity	€ 12,00 - € 23,50

Empúriabrava

Camping Internacional Amberes

Playa de la Rubina, E-17487 Empúriabrava (Girona) T: 972 450 507. E: info@campingamberes.com
alanrogers.com/ES80200

Situated in the 'Venice of Spain', Empúriabrava is interlaced with inland waterways and canals, where many residents and holidaymakers moor their boats directly outside their expensive homes on the canal banks. Internacional de Amberes is a large friendly site 200 m. from the wide, sandy beach, which is bordered on the east and west by the waterway canals. Amberes is a surprisingly pretty and hospitable site where people seem to make friends easily and get to know other campers and the staff. The site has 620 touring pitches, most enjoying some shade from strategically placed trees. All have electricity and water connections.

Facilities

Toilet facilities are in five fully equipped blocks. Washing machines. Motorcaravan services. Modern supermarket, bakery and shop. Restaurant/bar. Disco bar. Large takeaway/pizzeria. Watersports with windsurfing school. Organised sports activities, children's programmes and entertainment. Swimming pool. Bicycle hire. Playground. Pétanque. Tennis. Very smart internet café. WiFi. Dog shower. Apartments. Off site: Beach 200 m. Fishing 300 m. Boat launching 500 m. Riding 1 km. Golf 3 km. Public transport from site gate all season.

Open: 26 March - 17 October.

Directions

Empúriabrava is north of Girona and east of Figueras on the coast. From AP7/E15 take exit 3 south or exit 4 north (note there is no exit 3 north) and then N11 to the C260 towards Roses. At Empúriabrava follow 'camping area' signs to site. GPS: 42.25267, 3.1317

Charges guide

Per person	€ 3,60 - € 4,00
pitch incl. electricity and water	€ 14,50 - € 37,50
dog	€ 3,00 - € 3,30

No credit cards.

For latest campsite news, availability and prices visit
alanrogers.com

Esponellá
Camping Caravaning Esponellá

Ctra de Banyoles a Figueres km 8, E-17832 Esponellá (Girona) T: 972 597 074
E: informa@campingesponella.com alanrogers.com/ES80360

This large campsite has a lovely setting alongside a slow flowing river. The last 10 km. of the route here is well worth the trip, but careful driving is necessary with large motorhomes. There are 240 medium sized pitches, 140 for touring, many fully serviced, all with 5A electricity and shaded by trees. The better pitches are behind the reception office which is in a newer building. The site is very popular with Spanish campers who keep their caravans with large awnings here.

Facilities

Two old toilet blocks, a smaller one with only toilets and washbasins near the rental accommodations, and a newer one at the front part of the site. Some washbasins with only cold water. Small shop (Easter -Sept). Traditional restaurant, snacks and bar (all year). Three swimming pools. Play area. Boules. Minigolf. Small disco. Internet access. Barbecues are not permitted in summer. Off site: Hydrotherapy and massage centre next to site gate (April-Aug). Bus stop in the village.

Open: All year.

Directions

From Figueres towards Olot via the N260. Continue for 4 km. past Navata. Turn left in 12 km. over a smaller road to entrance of the site. Site is southeast of the village and well signed. GPS: 42.18166, 2.79499

Charges guide

Per unit incl. 2 persons and electricity	€ 24,70 - € 32,85
extra person	€ 5,20 - € 6,95
child (4-10 yrs)	€ 3,95 - € 5,30

Farga de Moles
Frontera Park

Ctra Seo d'Urgell - Andorra N145 km 8, E-25799 Farga de Moles (Lleida) T: 973 355 830
E: info@fronterapark.com alanrogers.com/ES91190

Frontera Park lives up to its name, as it is situated on the border with Andorra and makes an ideal base for visiting this small Principality. The site is strung out along the bank of a small river with no reported problems with flooding. There are 230 fairly small grass pitches, 50 for touring, with mountain views, trees giving some shade and 10A electricity. Spacious chalets are situated in the northern part of the site, away from the camping area. During the winter this is a good area for skiing in the Pyrenees. In summer there are hiking trails plus lakes and rivers, with many possibilities for wild water canoeing and swimming in this picturesque region.

Facilities

Two very clean toilet blocks have separate areas for ladies and men. Baby washroom but no facilities for campers with disabilities. Small bar with terrace. Cosy restaurant. The catering facilities, open all year, close on Wednesdays. Swimming pool and paddling pool (July/Aug) with grassy sunbathing area. Multisport field. Play area. Off site: Fishing. Riding. Golf. Lake with beach and sailing 8 km. Hiking trails. During the ski season many pistes 13 km.

Open: All year.

Directions

Site lies about 8 km. north of Seu d'Urgell and south of Andorra. From Seu d'Urgell take N145 towards Andorra. After 8 km. sign look out for site sign on the left mountain wall. Turn right to make a sharp left turn across the main road into the access road of the site. GPS: 42.42809, 1.4633

Charges guide

Per unit incl. 2 persons and electricity (	€ 20,00
extra person	€ 4,10
Camping Cheques accepted.	

Guardiola de Berguedá
Camping El Berguedá

Ctra B400 a Saldes km 3,5, E-08694 Guardiola de Berguedá (Barcelona) T: 938 227 432
E: info@campingbergueda.com alanrogers.com/ES91390

The short scenic drive through the mountains to reach the site is breathtakingly beautiful. Situated under trees this terraced campsite, in the area of the Cadi-Moixer Natural Park, is not far from the majestic Pedraforca mountain. A favourite for Catalan climbers and walkers, its amazing rugged peak in the shape of a massive stone fork gives it its name. Access to the site is quite easy for large units. Of the 73 small grass gravel pitches there are 20 for touring with 6A electricity. The campsite owners will do all in their power to make your stay here enjoyable. There are excellent facilities including, a large and a smaller outdoor pool, upstairs restaurant and bar. There is a Picassso museum at nearby Goso.

Facilities

Two clean, well equipped, heated modern toilet blocks. Facilities for campers with disabilities. Three private cabins with washbasin, toilet and bidet. Washing machines and dryer. Small shop, restaurant, bar and takeaway (w/ends only then 10/7-1/9). Outdoor pools (24/6-31/8). Play areas. Barbecues are not permitted except in communal area. Off site: Mountain biking. Artigas gardens by Gaudi. Picasso Museum. Museum of mines. Adventure park 5 km.

Open: Easter - 30 October.

Directions

From France via Puigcerda take the C-16, towards Berga. After Guardiola de Berguedá turn right towards Saldes. Site is on right after 3.5 km. GPS: 42.21642, 1.83692

Charges 2011

Per unit incl. 2 persons and electricity	€ 27,60
extra person	€ 5,60
child (1-10 yrs)	€ 4,45

For latest campsite news, availability and prices visit
alanrogers.com

Guils de Cerdanya
Camping Pirineus

Ctra Guils de Cerdanya km 2, E-17528 Guils de Cerdanya (Girona) T: 972 881 062. E: guils@stel.es

alanrogers.com/ES91430

This is a sister site to ES84200 and ES91440, with a well organized entrance and an immediate impression of space, green trees and grass – there is always someone watering and clearing up to maintain the high standards here. The pitches are neat, marked, of average size and organized in rows. Generally flat with some on a gentle incline, a proportion have water at their own sink on the pitch. Many trees offer shade but watch overhanging branches if you have a high unit. From the restaurant terrace you have fine views of the mountains in the background and the pool in the foreground.

Facilities

Two fully equipped sanitary blocks are kept spotlessly clean and can be heated. Good laundry facilities. Motorcaravan service point. Shop, bar and restaurant. TV/games room. Snooker. Heated swimming pool and circular paddling pool. Boules. Tennis. Outdoor sports. Play area and supervised clubhouse for youngsters. Excursions. Entertainment (high season). Dogs are not accepted. Off site: River fishing. Bicycle hire 2 km. Riding 4 km. Golf 6 km.

Open: 17 June - 11 September.

Directions

From Perpignan take N116 to Prades and Andorra. Exit at Piugcerda taking N250 signed Le Seu d'Urgell and almost immediately take second right for Guils de Cerdanya. Follow for 2 km. to site on right. GPS: 42.44312, 1.90583

Charges 2011

Per unit incl. 2 persons and electricity	€ 41,80
extra person	€ 6,60
child (3-10 yrs)	€ 5,50

Hospitalet del Infante
Camping-Pension Cala d'Oques

Via Augusta s/n, E-43890 Hospitalet del Infante (Tarragona) T: 977 823 254. E: info@caladoques.com

alanrogers.com/ES85350

This peaceful and delightful site has been developed with care and dedication by Elisa Roller over 40 years or so and she now runs it with the help of her daughter Kim and son-in-law Joost. Part of its appeal lies in its situation beside the sea with a wide beach of sand and pebbles, its amazing mountain backdrop and the views across the bay to the town and part by the atmosphere created by Elisa, her family and her staff – friendly, relaxed and comfortable. There are 152 pitches, mostly level and laid out beside the beach, with more behind on wide, informal terracing. Electricity is available although long leads may be needed in places.

Facilities

Clean and neat toilet facilities with hot water to showers (by token but free to campers). New heated unit with toilets and washbasins for winter use. Additional small block with toilets and washbasins at the far end of the site. Motorcaravan service point. Restaurant/bar and shop (1/4-30/10). Play area. Kim's kids' club. Fishing. Internet access and WiFi. Gas supplies. Torches required in some areas. Off site: Village facilities, incl. shop and restaurant 1.5 km. Bicycle hire and riding 2 km.

Open: All year.

Directions

Hospitalet del Infante is south of Tarragona, accessed from the A7 (exit 38) or from the N340. From the north take first exit to Hospitalet del Infante at 1128 km. marker. Follow signs in village, site is 2 km. south, by the sea. GPS: 40.97777, 0.90338

Charges 2011

Per unit incl. 2 persons	€ 15,00 - € 41,85
extra person	€ 4,95 - € 9,40
No credit cards.	

Hospitalet del Infante
Camping Naturista El Templo del Sol

E-43890 Hospitalet del Infante (Tarragona) T: 977 823 434. E: info@eltemplodelsol.com

alanrogers.com/ES85370

El Templo del Sol is a large, luxurious terraced naturist site with a distinctly Arabesque style and superb buildings in Moorish style. The owner has designed the magnificent main turreted building at the entrance with fountains and elaborate Moorish arches. The site has over 400 pitches of two different sizes, some with car parking alongside and 85 with full services. There is shade and the pitches are on terraces giving rewarding views over the sea. Attractive steps give ready access to the sandy beach. There is some daytime rail noise especially in the lower areas of the site where larger pitches are located.

Facilities

Excellent sanitary blocks and facilities for disabled campers. Washing machines. Supermarket. Health shop. Souvenir shop. Bars. Restaurant and snack bar (1/4-10/10). Swimming pools (20/3-15/10). Jacuzzi. Cinema. Games area. Boules. Separate children's pool and play area. Miniclub. Library. Safety deposit boxes. Hairdresser Entertainment. Bicycle hire. ATM. Dogs are not accepted. No jet skis. Off site: Fishing 100 m. Golf 2 km. (night time only). Bicycle hire 3 km. Riding 7 km.

Open: 22 March - 22 October.

Directions

From N340 south of Tarragona, exit at km. 1126 towards L'Hopitalet Plaja and follow signs. Heading north, near km. 1124, turn right immediately after a modern railway bridge and site is just 400 m. on the right. GPS: 40.97723, 0.90093

Charges guide

Per unit incl. 2 persons and electricity	€ 18,70 - € 47,65
extra person	€ 3,30 - € 9,00
child (under 10 yrs)	free - € 6,45

For latest campsite news, availability and prices visit

alanrogers.com

L'Escala

Camping L'Escala

Cami Ample, E-17130 L'Escala (Girona) T: 972 770 084. E: info@campinglescala.com
alanrogers.com/ES80700

Under the same ownership as Las Dunas (no. ES80400), but a complete contrast in terms of size and location. It is a small site with all the amenities of the town within easy reach and the beach within 100 m. and fabulous new sanitary facilities for 2010. The site has a canopy of fir trees giving excellent shade. There are 140 pitches of which 90 are for touring units, so reservation is essential. Unusually for a small site, all pitches have electricity, water and drainage. In season there is a bar and pizza oven. There is some road noise despite the very high wall between the site and the busy road alongside.

Facilities

New central toilet block of the highest quality with underfloor heating for cooler seasons and sliding glass doors. Wonderful facilities for children featuring tiled pirate ships. Laundry sinks with hot water. Shop, bar and pizza oven (all high season). Simple play area. Satellite TV. WiFi. No pets allowed. Modern bungalow apartments to rent. Off site: Public transport 500 m. Beach 100 m. Bicycle hire 500 m. Riding 3 km. Golf 15 km.

Open: Easter - last Sunday in September.

Directions

L'Escala is northeast of Girona on the coast. From A7/E15 autostrada take exit 5 towards L'Escala on GI 623. Turn north 2 km. before reaching L'Escala towards Sant Marti d'Ampurias. Site well signed on north side of town and beach. Watch for site name high on wall. GPS: 42.121, 3.13478

Charges guide

Per person	€ 3,00 - € 5,00
pitch incl. electricity	€ 18,00 - € 31,00

No credit cards. Discounts for longer stays.

L'Escala

Camping Illa Mateua

Avenida de Montgó 260, E-17130 L'Escala (Girona) T: 972 770 200. E: info@campingillamateua.com
alanrogers.com/ES80740

If you prefer a quieter site out of the very busy resort of L'Escala then this site is an excellent option. This large, family run site has a dynamic owner Marti, who speaks excellent English. The site is divided by the beach access road and has its own private access to the very safe and unspoilt beach. There are 358 pitches in the two parts of the site, all with 10A electricity, some on sloping ground although the pitches in the second part are flat. Established pine trees provide shade for most pitches.

Facilities

Very modern, fully equipped sanitary blocks are kept spotlessly clean by omnipresent cleaners. Brilliant facilities for children, and baby baths. Washing machines and dryers. Shop, restaurants, bars and takeaways. Swimming pools (20/4-12/10). Pool bar. Play areas. Kayak hire. Organised activities for children in high season. Diving school. Sports centre. Internet access and WiFi. ATM. Off site: Cala Montgó beach 100 m. Road train to town centre. Riding 2 km. Golf 10 km. Fishing 150 m.

Open: 21 March - 12 October.

Directions

Leave autopista A7 at exit 5 heading for Viladimat, then L'Escala. Site is well signed from town centre. Follow signs for Montgó and site is south of town beside the coast. Site has changed name so some signs may show the old name of Paradis. GPS: 42.11051, 3.16542

Charges guide

Per unit incl. 2 persons	€ 22,80 - € 44,00
extra person	€ 3,25 - € 6,00

No credit cards.

L'Escala

Camping Neus

Cala Montgó, E-17130 L'Escala (Girona) T: 972 770 403. E: info@campingneus.cat
alanrogers.com/ES80690

Camping Neus is set on the edges of a forest under mature pines with 190 pitches arranged on sets of terraces, all with 6A electricity. This mature site is being thoughtfully renovated. It is fenced from the road and facilities are mainly close to the reception building. A small pool with a circular paddling pool is welcome after a hot day's sightseeing; other site amenities include a tennis court and bar/restaurant. A new play area and a volleyball court have been added (2010) and gardens planted. The nearest beach at Cala Montgó is 850 m. away and easily accessible on foot. The usual range of resort entertainment is available there including sea kayaking and most watersports.

Facilities

Renovated sanitary blocks offer sound and clean facilities along with baby rooms and facilities for disabled campers. Bar. Restaurant. Takeaway. Shop. Play area. Swimming pool. Paddling pool. Tennis. Volleyball. Entertainment and activities in peak season. Club for children. WiFi. Motorcaravan service point. Off site: Resort of Cala Montgó with beach 850 m. Fishing. Kayaking. Diving. Tours and sightseeing.

Open: 28 May - 19 September.

Directions

Take exit 5 from the AP7 and the GI 623 to L'Escala. Continue to Riells and Montgó. Site is on the right shortly before reaching Cala Montgó. GPS: 42.1049, 3.15816

Charges guide

Per unit incl. 2 persons and electricity	€ 21,00 - € 43,00
extra person	€ 3,00 - € 5,00

For latest campsite news, availability and prices visit
alanrogers.com

L'Estartit

Camping Castell Montgri

183

Ctra Toroella - l'Estartit km 4,7, E-17258 L'Estartit (Girona) T: 972 751 630. E: cmontgri@campingparks.com
alanrogers.com/ES80070

This is a large, noisy, bustling, expensive site with all the modern paraphernalia of holiday-making. Over 50 per cent of this site is dedicated to catering for tour operators, and obviously so, but there are three designated areas for independent campers. These provide 590 terraced and flat pitches, some shaded but all with electricity. On arrival you are processed by rather impersonal staff. The site could be of interest to families with teenagers, offering the possibility for parents to rest whilst the youngsters enjoy their own type of holiday within the confines of the site.

Facilities

Toilet facilities are adequate, if not that luxurious, each area having its own block. Cleaning is continual (06.00-22.00) but with the numbers on site, queueing and litter can be a problem. Bars and restaurants. Pizzeria. Takeaway. Swimming pools. Supermarket and souvenirs. Tennis. Minigolf. Playground. Large screen TV. Disco. Entertainment programme and excursions. Free bus to L'Estartit. Internet access (expensive)and WiFi (charged). Torches required in some areas. Off site: Beach 1 km. Riding 500 m. Fishing 1 km. Bicycle hire 1 km. Golf 5 km.

Open: 15 May - 26 September.

Directions

Estartit is on the coast northeast of Girona. Leave the AP7/E15 and take the C66 towards Palamós. Then take the GI642 towards Parlava and the GI643 towards Torroella de Montgri. Site is well signed on the GI 641 Torroella de Montgri - L'Estartit road just north of the town on the left. GPS: 42.0511, 3.1827

Charges guide

Per person	€ 5,00
child (3-10 yrs)	€ 3,50
pitch incl. car and electricity	€ 9,00 - € 56,00

L'Estartit

Camping Les Medes

Paratge Camp de L'Arbre, E-17258 L'Estartit (Girona) T: 972 751 805. E: info@campinglesmedes.com
alanrogers.com/ES80720

Les Medes is different from some of the 'all singing, all dancing' sites so popular along this coast and the friendly family of Pla-Coll are rightly proud of their award winning site and provide a very warm welcome. With just 182 pitches, the site is small enough for the owners to know their visitors and, being campers themselves, they have been careful in planning their top class facilities and are aware of environmental issues. The 170 level, grassy touring pitches range in size from 70-80 sq.m. depending on your unit. All have electricity (5/10A) and the larger ones (around half) also have water and drainage.

Facilities

Two modern sanitary blocks can be heated and are extremely well maintained. Top class facilities for disabled visitors. Baby baths. Washing machines and dryer. Motorcaravan services. Bar with snacks and pizza. Restaurant (1/4-31/10). Shop. Swimming and paddling pools (1/5-15/9). Indoor pool with sauna, solarium and massage (15/9-15/6). TV room. Entertainment, activities and excursions (July/Aug). Bicycle hire. Internet access and WiFi. Dogs are not accepted July/Aug. Off site: Riding 400 m. Fishing 800 m. Beach 800 m.

Open: All year excl. November.

Directions

Site is signed from the main Torroella de Montgri - L'Estartit road GE641. Turn right after Camping Castel Montgri, at Joc's hamburger/pizzeria and follow signs. GPS: 42.048, 3.1881

Charges 2011

Per unit incl. 2 persons and electricity	€ 22,30 - € 40,50

Discounts outside high season and special offers for low season longer stays. No credit cards.

La Bordeta

Camping Caravaning Bedurá Park

Era Bordeta - Val d'Aran CN230 km 174,4, la Bordeta, E-25551 Lleida (Lleida) T: 973 648 293
E: info@bedurapark.com alanrogers.com/ES91240

Bedurá Park lies in the Val d'Aran at a height of 900 metres, surrounded by wonderful panoramic views. The surrounding woods are alive with a wide variety of wildlife, including deer, wild boar, capercaillies and pine martens. This is a perfect place for a quiet, yet active holiday. On site you can unwind around the swimming pool or take a leisurely drink in the bar. There are 173 small, well shaded, stony/grass pitches set out on terraces with 150 for touring, all with 5A electricity. Access for large units may be difficult due to the low trees. This is a haven for nature lovers and photographers.

Facilities

One large and one small toilet block with some washbasins in cabins plus facilities for campers with disabilities. Shop (1/6-30/9). Bar, restaurant and takeaway (24/6-30/9). Heated swimming and paddling pools (15/6-15/9). Miniclub (July/Aug). Games/TV room. Play area. Barbecues are not permitted except on a communal area. Animals are not accepted. Off site: Riding 12 km. Skiing 20 km. Vielha ice palace with ice rink, indoor pool 10 km.

Open: All year.

Directions

Site is on the N230, 12 km. from the French border and 10 km. north of Vielha. Leave A60 (French) autoroute at exit 17 and take N125 south to the border. Continue on N230 through Bossost then 4 km. to site at la Bordeta. GPS: 42.74969, 0.69804

Charges 2011

Per person	€ 5,50
pitch incl. electricity	€ 18,50 - € 23,55

No credit cards.

For latest campsite news, availability and prices visit
alanrogers.com

La Pineda
Camping La Pineda de Salou
Ctra Costa Tarragona - Salou km 5, E-43481 La Pineda (Tarragona) T: 977 373 080
E: info@campinglapineda.com **alanrogers.com/ES84820**

La Pineda is a clean, neat site north of Salou, just 300 m. from the Aquapark and 2.5 km. from Port Aventura, to which there is an hourly bus service from outside the site entrance. There is some noise from this road. The site has two swimming pools; the smaller is heated. a colourful themed paddling pool and outdoor spa are also here, behind tall hedges close to the entrance. A large terrace has sun loungers, and various entertainment aimed at young people is provided in season. The 366 flat pitches are shaded by mature trees, all with 5A electricity, in attractive gardens.

Facilities

Refurbished sanitary facilities are excellent with baby bath, dishwashing and laundry sinks. Facilities for disabled visitors. Washing machines. Gas supplies. Shop (1/7-31/8). Bar. Restaurant and snacks (1/7-31/8). Swimming pools, themed paddling pool and outdoor spa (1/7-31/8). New community room with giant satellite TV. Bicycle and road cart hire. Games room. Playground (3-12 yrs). Entertainment (1/7-30/8). Torches may be required. No pets allowed in Aug. Small wellness centre. WiFi. Bus from gate. Off site: Aquapark 300 m. Beach and fishing 400 m. Port Aventura 2.5 km.

Open: All year.

Directions

From A7 just southwest of Tarragona take exit 35 and follow signs to La Pineda and Port Aventura then campsite signs appear. GPS: 41.08921, 1.1837

Charges guide

Per unit incl. 2 persons	
and electricity (6A)	€ 29,00 - € 51,50
extra person	€ 5,40 - € 8,30
child (1-10 yrs)	€ 3,70 - € 6,20
dog	€ 3,90 - € 4,00

Llafranc
Kim's Camping
Font d'en Xeco 1, E-17211 Llafranc - Palafrugell (Girona) T: 972 301 156. E: info@campingkims.com
alanrogers.com/ES81200

This attractive, terraced site is arranged on the wooded slopes of a narrow valley leading to the sea and there are many trees including huge eucalyptus. There are 350 grassy and partly shaded pitches (70-120 sq.m), 240 used for touring units, all with electricity (5A). Many of the larger pitches are on a plateau from which great views can be enjoyed. The terraced pitches are connected by winding drives, narrow in places. This is a pleasant place for holidays where you can enjoy the bustling atmosphere of the village and beach, while staying in a quieter environment.

Facilities

All sanitary facilities are spotlessly clean and include excellent toilet facilities for disabled visitors. Laundry facilities. Motorcaravan services. Gas supplies. Shop. Bar. Bakery/croissanterie. Café/restaurant (15/6-15/9). Swimming pools. Play areas and children's club. TV room. Excursions arranged – bus calls at site. Visits arranged to sub-aqua schools (high season). Torches required. WiFi. Mobile homes to rent. Off site: Beach, fishing, sailing and bicycle hire 500 m. Llafranc 1 km. Riding 3.5 km.

Open: Easter - 2 October.

Directions

Llafranc is southeast of Palafrugell. Turn off the Palafrugell - Tamariu road at turn (GIV 6542) signed Llafranc. Site is on right 1 km. further on. GPS: 41.90053, 3.18935

Charges guide

Per unit incl. 2 persons	
and electricity	€ 18,15 - € 41,20
extra person	€ 2,65 - € 6,55

Lloret de Mar
Camping Tucan
Ctra de Blanes - Lloret, E-17310 Lloret de Mar (Girona) T: 972 369 965. E: info@campingtucan.com
alanrogers.com/ES82100

Situated on the busy Costa Brava near Lloret de Mar, Camping Tucan is well placed to access all the attractions of the area. Views over the mountains are mixed with views of the nearby town. Of the 300 good size pitches, 48 are fully serviced (60-100 sq.m) and most have electricity (3/6A). Laid out in a herringbone pattern, there are areas dedicated to singles, families with young children and couples who enjoy the quiet. Pitches are on terraces, flat surfaced with gravel and many are shaded. Tucan is a lively site with a variety of activities including an activities for children and modest entertainment at night.

Facilities

Two modern, clean toilet blocks have washbasins with hot water and facilities for disabled visitors (access can be difficult). Washing machines. Gas supplies. Shop. Busy bar and good restaurant. Takeaway. Swimming pools and indoor solarium. Playground and fenced play area. TV in bar. Bicycle hire. Entertainment in high season. Miniclub. Internet and WiFi (code). Off site: Town with supermarkets 500 m. Nearest beach 600 m. Riding 1 km. Golf 4 km.

Open: 1 April - 25 September.

Directions

From A7/E4, A19 or N11 Girona - Barcelona roads take an exit for Lloret de Mar. Site is 1 km. west of the town, well signed and is at the base of the hill off the roundabout. The entrance can get congested in busy periods. GPS: 41.6972, 2.8217

Charges guide

Per unit incl. 2 persons	
and electricity	€ 23,75 - € 38,95

For latest campsite news, availability and prices visit
alanrogers.com

Malgrat de Mar

Camping La Tordera

183

Cami de la Tordera s/n, E-08380 Malgrat de Mar (Barcelona) T: 937 612 778. E: camping@latordera.com
alanrogers.com/ES82330

Camping La Tordera has a seafront location and is adjacent to the natural reserve of the La Tordera delta. The site can be found close to Malgrat and Blanes, and around 50 km. from both Barcelona and Girona. Pitches are level, well shaded and all have 10A electricity. A number of mobile homes and chalets are available for rent. On-site amenities include a swimming pool (with large grassy sun terrace), a well stocked supermarket and a bar/restaurant. The site is lively in peak season with a varied programme of entertainment and activities for all ages.

Facilities

Swimming pool. Restaurant. Bar. Takeaway. Supermarket. Trampoline. Play area. Sports field. Motor caravan services. Activity and entertainment programme. Tourist information. Mobile homes for rent. Off site: Malgreat de Mar, Blanes 1.5 km. Watersports. Barcelona 63 km.

Open: 18 February - 13 November.

Directions

Approaching from Barcelona on C32, leave at the Malgrat-de-Mar exit and then head for the town centre (N11), from where the site is well signposted. GPS: 41.652304, 2.775483

Charges 2011

Per unit incl. 2 persons	€ 21,05 - € 36,00
extra person	€ 4,00 - € 6,40

Malgrat de Mar

Camping del Mar

Avenida Pomareda s/n, E-08380 Malgrat de Mar (Barcelona) T: 937 653 767. E: delmar@campingsonline.com
alanrogers.com/ES82340

With such a wide choice of campsites along this part of the coast, standards have to be kept high and that is just what the Sisa family achieve at Camping del Mar. Beautifully manicured lawns and a well designed site help to create a relaxed atmosphere. All the facilities are kept immaculately clean. The 120 flat, grassy pitches all have electricity (6A) and easy access to a water point. The site is surrounded by a high hedge providing privacy and some shade to those pitches alongside. In time the many young trees and shrubs on the site will give plenty of shade.

Facilities

Modern, clean sanitary facilities are in the central building. Showers in large cubicles, open style washbasins and controllable hot water. Laundry room. Shop. Bar with TV and separate restaurant with varied menu. Games room. Swimming pool with separate children's pool. Multisport court. Tennis. Large play area. Minigolf. Children's club and entertainment (July/Aug). Fishing. Internet access, WiFi. Off site: Boat launching 4 km. Riding 5 km. Golf 20 km. Watersports 4 km.

Open: 1 April - 28 November.

Directions

From Malgrat de Mar town centre follow signs to 'zona campings'. Cross railway line and head north along beach front. Site is the second campsite on the left. GPS: 41.64726, 2.76378

Charges guide

Per unit incl. 2 persons and electricity	€ 20,00 - € 34,00
extra person	€ 4,15 - € 5,85
child (4-10 yrs)	€ 2,95 - € 4,55

Mataró

Camping Barcelona

Ctra N-II km 650, E-08304 Mataró (Barcelona) T: 937 904 720. E: info@campingbarcelona.com
alanrogers.com/ES82450

Camping Barcelona has a pleasant Spanish flavour, evident in the restaurant which serves authentic food and tapas. Like other sites locally, it is on the beach road (N11) which means it is subject to train and traffic noise. However, the 180 touring pitches, which are separated from the permanent areas, do allow you to avoid the problem. Pitches vary in size and most have electricity (6/10A). An excellent pool is provided in which to cool off and reception will assist in arranging many off-site activities. There is a rocky coastline 100 m. away, but we recommend you to use the free shuttle to Mataró.

Facilities

Three clean sanitary blocks provide good facilities. Baby room. Facilities for disabled campers. Washing machines. Freezer. Motorcaravan service areas. Supermarket. Bar. Restaurant. Takeaway. Pool bar. Swimming pool with lifeguard (30/5-30/9). Pétanque. Playground. Children's farm. Miniclub and entertainment (high season). Disco. Internet access. WiFi (code). Picnic area. Electronic games. Daily bus to Barcelona (small charge Jul/Aug) and regular free shuttle to the site's Mataró beach club, train station and wellness centre. Night bus from Barcelona. Off site: Fishing 100 m. Bicycle hire 2 km. Golf 10 km. Riding 18 km. Historic town of Mataró. Watersports 2 km. Train to Barcelona 2 km.

Open: 4 March - 1 November.

Directions

Site is east of Mataró at the 650 km. marker on the N11. Leave the C-32 autoroute at exit 105 and follow signs for the sea and Mataró. Site is well signed on both carriageways. GPS: 41.55055, 2.48338

Charges 2011

Per unit incl. 2 persons and electricity	€ 25,95 - € 52,30
extra person	€ 5,50 - € 9,50
child (4-12 yrs)	€ 3,75 - € 6,50
dog	€ 2,00 - € 4,00

For latest campsite news, availability and prices visit
alanrogers.com

Miami-Playa
Camping Els Prats-Marius
Ctra N340 km 1137, E-43892 Miami-Playa (Tarragona) T: 977 810 027. E: info@campingelsprats.com
alanrogers.com/ES85330

This Costa Daurada beach resort now combines two sites, Campings Els Prats and Marius. This is a very popular area, not far from Tarragona and the Port Adventura theme park. There are now almost 450 pitches, all with electricity. They are fairly close together, mostly flat and shaded, and a few have access to the pleasant narrow, white sand/shingle beach. There are bungalows to rent and an apartment block in one corner. A feature is the tropical style beach bar. Attractive tropical plants adorn the site including many banana trees. There is some road and rail noise on the western side of the site.

Facilities

Two blocks, one for each sex, provide clean facilities. Separate unit for disabled campers. Children's bathroom. Washing machines. Motorcaravan services. Supermarket. Restaurant, takeaway and three bars. Swimming pool (3/4-17/10). Play area. Bicycle hire (organised trips). Windsurfing, canoeing and diving (free try dive Sat am). Activity programme and some evening entertainment in high season. Dogs are not accepted 1/7-31/8. Torches useful. Off site: Riding 3 km. Golf 5 km. Cambrils 7 km. Port Adventura 15 km.

Open: 5 March - 1 November.

Directions

Site is between Miami Playa and Cambrils on the N340. Take exit 37 from the A7 towards Cambrils, then 7 km. southwest of Cambrils at 1137 km. marker, take exit for Torre del Mar. Go under railway bridge and immediately right – site is 100 m. up this road. GPS: 41.03611, 0.975

Charges guide

Per person	€ 6,50 - € 7,00
child (under 10 yrs)	€ 1,00 - € 5,00
pitch incl. electricity (5A)	€ 11,00 - € 33,00

Montagut
Camping Montagut
Ctra Montagut - Sadernes km 2, E-17855 Montagut (Girona) T: 972 287 202. E: info@campingmontagut.com
alanrogers.com/ES91220

This is a delightful, small family site where everything is kept in pristine condition. Jordi and Nuria, a brother and sister team, work hard to make you welcome and maintain the superb appearance of the site. The 90 pitches are on attractively landscaped and carefully constructed terraces or on flat areas overlooking the pool. A tranquil atmosphere pervades the site and drinks on the pleasant restaurant terrace are recommended, along with sampling the authentic menu as you enjoy the views over the Alta Garrotxa. There is much to see in the local area between the Pyrenees and the Mediterranean.

Facilities

The modern sanitary block has free hot showers, washing and laundry facilities plus a modern section for babies and disabled campers; everything was spotless when seen. Motorcaravan services. Restaurant and bar (1/7-28/8; weekends only in low season). Supermarket. Medium sized swimming pool with large sunbathing area and children's pool (1/5-30/9). Playground. Pétanque. Barbecue area. WiFi area. Torches useful in some areas.

Open: 1 April - 16 October.

Directions

Going west from Figueres take the N260 Olot road which becomes the A26. Take exit 75, turn right towards Montagut. At end of village turn left towards Sadernes and site entrance is 3 km. GPS: 42.2469, 2.5971

Charges 2011

Per unit incl. 2 persons and electricity	€ 25,00 - € 33,00
extra person	€ 5,10 - € 7,10

Montblanc
Camping Caravaning Montblanc Park
Ctra Prenafeta km 1,8, E-43400 Montblanc (Tarragona) T: 977 862 544. E: info@montblancpark.com
alanrogers.com/ES85020

Montblanc Park may be described as a campsite of the future. Purpose designed, there are 200 terraced pitches for touring units and about 80 for wooden chalets, with more being developed on the upper terraces. The restaurant and terrace enjoy views of the lagoon-style pool and further across the valley, over the autoroute towards the town of Montblanc and the mountains of the Serra del Prades. The pitches are on terraces so take advantage of the mountain views and gentle cooling afternoon breezes. They vary in size, with hedging and trees, and are sloping (chocks useful).

Facilities

Two purpose built toilet blocks feature en-suite facilities including superb facilities for disabled campers and a well equipped baby room. Washing machines and dryers. Supermarket. Restaurant. Snack bar. Swimming pool and large paddling pool. Play areas. Boules. Bicycle hire. Entertainment for children (weekends and main holiday season). Barbecues may not be allowed in July/Aug. Tents for hire. Off site: Riding 4 km. Beach 30 km, golf 35 km. Mountain activities: climbing, caving, canyoning and orienteering. Quad biking and trips by 4x4.

Open: 1 March - 30 November.

Directions

Site is 3 minutes off the autopista. From the A2 (Barcelona - Lleida) take exit 9 and follow N240 (Reus - Tarragona), then road to Prenafeta and site stands out on the left. It is 1.8 km. out of Montblanc and signed in the town. GPS: 41.3787, 1.1826

Charges guide

Per unit incl. 2 persons and electricity	€ 22,00 - € 34,50
extra person	€ 4,50 - € 6,50

For latest campsite news, availability and prices visit
alanrogers.com

Montroig

Playa Montroig Camping Resort

Ctra N340 km 1136, E-43300 Montroig (Tarragona) T: 977 810 637. E: info@playamontroig.com
alanrogers.com/ES85300

What a superb site! Playa Montroig is about 30 kilometres beyond Tarragona set in its own tropical gardens with direct access to a very long, narrow, soft sand beach. The main part of the site lies between the sea, road and railway (some train noise) with a huge underpass. The site is divided into spacious, marked pitches with excellent shade provided by a variety of lush vegetation including very impressive palms set in wide avenues. There are 1,200 pitches, all with electricity and 564 with water and drainage. Some 48 pitches are directly alongside the beach. The site has many outstanding features: there is an excellent pool complex near the entrance with two pools (one heated for children). A new Espai Grill and bar with a rock and roll disco, plus a tasteful candlelit patio is just outside the gate. One restaurant serves good food with some Catalan fare (seats 150) and overlooks an entertainment area. A large terrace bar dispenses drinks or if you yearn for louder music there is a second disco with a smaller bar. There is yet another eating option in a 500 seat restaurant. Above this is the 'Pai-pai' Caribbean cocktail bar where softer music is provided in an intimate atmosphere. Activities for children are very ambitious – there is even a ceramics kiln (multi-lingual carers). 'La Carpa', a spectacular open air theatre, is an ideal setting for daily keep fit sessions and the professional entertainment provided. If you are five to eleven years old you can explore the 'Tam-Tam Eco Park', a 20,000 sq.m. forest zone where experts will teach about the natural life of the area. You can even camp out for a night (supervised) to study wildlife (a once weekly activity). This is an excellent site and there is insufficient space here to describe all the available activities. We recommend it for families with children of all ages and there is much emphasis on providing activities outside the high season. A member of Leading Campings Group.

Facilities

Fifteen sanitary buildings, some small, but very good quality with toilets and washbasins, others are excellent, air conditioned larger buildings with large showers, washbasins and separate WCs. Facilities for disabled campers and for babies. Launderettes. Motorcaravan services. Good shopping centre. Restaurants and bars. 250-seater 'Eurocentre' for entertainment. Fitness suite. Eco-park. TV lounges. Beach bar. Playground. Free kindergarten with multilingual staff. Skate-boarding. Jogging track. Sports area. Tennis. Minigolf. Organised activities including pottery and gardening classes. Sub aqua diving, windsurfing and water skiing courses. Surfboard and pedalo hire. Boat mooring. Bicycle hire. Internet café. Gas. Caravan storage. Internet café. WiFi in all bars. Dogs are not accepted. Off site: Public transport 100 m. from gate. Riding and golf 3 km.

Open: 1 April - 30 October.

Directions

Site entrance is off main N340 nearly 30 km. southwest from Tarragona. From motorway take Cambrils exit and turn west on N340 at 1136 km. marker. GPS: 41.03292, 0.96921

Charges guide

Per unit incl. 2 persons
and electricity € 11,00 - € 78,00
extra person € 6,00 - € 7,00
child (1-9 yrs) free - € 5,50
Discounts for longer stays and for pensioners.
See advertisement on the back cover.

Palamós

Camping Internacional de Palamós

Apdo 100, E-17230 Palamós (Girona) T: 972 314 736. E: info@internacionalpalamos.com
alanrogers.com/ES81500

This is an uncomplicated, comfortable site which is clean, welcoming and useful for exploring the local area from a peaceful base. traditional in style, it is open for a long season and has a range of facilities. It might have space when others are full and has over 453 moderate sized pitches. The majority are level and terraced with some less defined under pine trees on a gentle slope. All pitches have a sink and variable shade, with electrical connections (6A) available in most parts. Some access roads are gravel and may suffer in the case of heavy rain. The site's strong point is the large swimming pool, plus children's pool, with attractive palms. It has a grass sunbathing area and its own modest white-washed bar/terrace in season. Twenty pitches are used by a tour operator.

Facilities

Two refurbished toilet blocks and one smart new one are fully equipped. Some washbasins in cabins. Facilities for disabled visitors. Laundry room. Small shop. Bar (1/4-29/9). Snack bar serving simple food and takeaway (from 1/6). Swimming pool (36x16 m) with paddling pool. Play area. Car wash. ATM. Torches necessary. Off site: Nearest beach 400 m. Fishing 500 m. Town 1 km. with bus service. Bicycle hire or riding 1.5 km.

Open: 27 March - 30 September.

Directions

Central Palamós streets are too narrow for caravans which should turn off C255 road just outside Palamós. Continue north by large garage signed Kings Camping and La Fosca. Turn right just before Kings and follow Camping Internacional Palamós signs (not those for another site close by called Camping Palamós). GPS: 41.85722, 3.13805

Charges guide

Per unit incl. 2 persons
and electricity € 29,70 - € 51,35
extra person € 3,15 - € 3,85
No credit cards. Camping Cheques accepted.

For latest campsite news, availability and prices visit
alanrogers.com

Montroig
Kawan Village La Torre del Sol

Ctra N340 km 1136, E-43300 Montroig (Tarragona) T: 977 810 486. E: info@latorredelsol.com

alanrogers.com/ES85400

A pleasant banana tree-lined approach road gives way to avenues of palms as you arrive at Torre del Sol. This is a very large site occupying a good position in the south of Catalunya with direct access to the soft sand beach. The site is exceptionally well maintained by a large workforce. There is good shade on a high proportion of the 1,500 individual, numbered pitches. All have electricity and are mostly of about 70-80 sq.m. Strong features here are 800 m. of clean beach-front with a special Mediterranean type of pitch, and the entertainment that is provided all season. Part of the site is between the railway and the sea so there is some occasional train noise.The cinema doubles as a theatre to stage shows all season. A complex of three pools, thoughtfully laid out with grass sunbathing areas and palms has a lifeguard. There is wireless internet access throughout the site. There is usually space for odd nights but for good places between 10/7-16/8 it is best to reserve (only taken for a stay of seven nights or more). We were impressed with the provision of season-long entertainment and children were in the safe hands of the activities team who ensure they enjoy the novel Happy Camp and various workshops.

Facilities

Five very well maintained, fully equipped, toilet blocks include units for disabled visitors and babies. Washing machines. Gas supplies. Supermarket, bakery and souvenir shops at entrance, open to public. Restaurant. Takeaway. Bar with large terrace and daily entertainment. Beach bar. Coffee bar. Ice cream bar. Pizzeria. Open roof cinema with permanent seating for 520. Three TV lounges. Well soundproofed disco. Swimming pools (two heated). Solarium. Sauna. Two jacuzzis. Sports areas. Tennis. Squash. Language school (Spanish). Minigolf. Sub-aqua diving (first dive free!) Bicycle hire. Fishing. Windsurfing school. Playground, crèche and Happy Camp. Fridge hire. Library. Hairdresser. Business centre. WiFi. No animals permitted. No jet skis accepted. Off site: Buses on N340 close to site. Theme parks. Beach fishing. Riding 3 km. Golf 4 km.

Open: 15 March - 31 October.

Directions

Entrance is off main N340 road by 1136 km. marker, about 30 km. from Tarragona towards Valencia. From motorway take Cambrils exit and turn west on N340. GPS: 41.03707, 0.97478

Charges guide

Per unit incl. 2 persons and electricity	€ 19,70 - € 63,95
extra person	€ 3,25 - € 9,80
child (0-10 yrs)	free - € 7,75

Discounts in low season for longer stays.
Camping Cheques accepted.

For latest campsite news, availability and prices visit
alanrogers.com

Pals

Camping-Resort Mas Patoxas Bungalow-Park

Ctra C31 Palafrugell - Pals km 339, E-17256 Pals (Girona) T: 972 636 928. E: info@campingmaspatoxas.com
alanrogers.com/ES81020

This is a mature, lush and well laid out site for those who prefer to be apart from, but within easy travelling distance of, the beaches (five kilometres) and town (one kilometre). It has a very easy access and is set on a slight slope with wide avenues on level terraces providing 376 grassy pitches of a minimum 72 sq.m. All have 6A electricity and some share water taps. There are some very pleasant views and shade from a variety of mature trees. Both bar and restaurant terraces give views over the pools and distant hills. The air-conditioned restaurant/bar provides both waiter and self service meals. A good value takeaway operates close by (weekends only mid September-April) and entertainment takes place on a stage below the terraces during high season. The restaurant menu is varied and reasonable. We were impressed with the children's miniclub activity when we visited. There is a large, supervised irregularly shaped swimming pool with triple flume, a separate children's pool and a generous sunbathing area at the poolside and on the surrounding grass.

Facilities	Directions
Three modern sanitary blocks provide controllable hot showers, some washbasins with hot water. Baby bath and three cabins for children. No specific facilities for disabled visitors. Laundry facilities. Fridge rental. Gas supplies. Supermarket, restaurant/bar, pizzeria and takeaway (all 1/4-25/9). Swimming pool with a new bar (1/5-30/9). Tennis. Entertainment in high season. Fitness area with games. Massage. Bicycle hire. Internet access. WiFi throughout. Torches useful in some areas. Off site: Bus service from site gate. Bicycle hire and riding 2 km. Fishing or golf 4 km.	Site is east of Girona and about 1.5 km. south of Pals at km. 339 on the C31 Figueres - Palamós road, just north of Palafugel. GPS: 41.9568, 3.1573

Open: 14 January - 18 December.

Charges 2011

Per unit incl. 2 persons	
and electricity	€ 18,50 - € 50,00
extra person	€ 4,20 - € 6,80
child (1-7 yrs)	€ 3,60 - € 4,80
dog	€ 2,60 - € 4,00

Special low season offers.

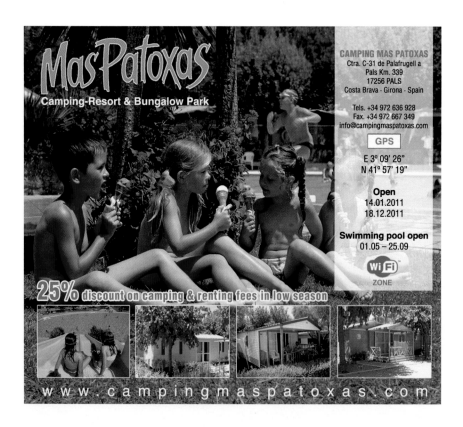

For latest campsite news, availability and prices visit
alanrogers.com

Pineda de Mar

Camping Caballo de Mar

Passeig Maritim 52-54, E-08397 Pineda de Mar (Barcelona) T: 937 671 706. E: info@caballodemar.com

alanrogers.com/ES82380

This is definitely a site for lovers of the seaside with its direct access to a lovely, sandy beach. Actually divided into two parts by the railway and dual-carriageway, the main part of the site is neatly arranged off a central access road with plenty of colourful shrubs and trees providing shade. In total there are 450 pitches, 300 taken by seasonal visitors and a few bungalows. On the beach side of the site the pitches are generally smaller (60-70 sq.m), all with shade, but there is a bar, snack bar and a toilet block on this side. All pitches have electricity (5/6A). A bar/restaurant fronts the main road (also open to the public) at the entrance. The site's rectangular pool is of a good size with lifeguards and an entertainment team organises activities (every day in high season, weekends at other times).

Facilities	Directions
Two toilet blocks, one in each area, are fully equipped and well maintained. En-suite units to rent (main side) with units for disabled visitors. Facilities for babies. Washing machines. Motorcaravan services. Shop and baker (15/6-31/8). Main bar and restaurant. Bar and snacks at the beach in high season. Swimming pool. Play area. Entertainment organised. Miniclub. Well equipped fitness room, massage and UVA machines. Internet access. ATM. Fishing. Off site: Beach activities. Town with bars and restaurants within walking distance or by road train. Bicycle hire 500 m. Riding 3 km. Barcelona 40 minutes by train. Riding 3 km. Golf 10 km.	Site is off the N11 coast road, southwest of Pineda de Mar. Leave the C32 at exit 122 and head for Pineda de Mar. Site is well signed off the beach road on the outskirts of the town. GPS: 41.61664, 2.64997

Open: 1 April - 30 September.

Charges guide

Per unit incl. 2 persons and electricity	€ 22,25 - € 36,65
extra person	€ 4,60 - € 7,95
child (1-9 yrs)	€ 3,20 - € 5,60

Platja de Pals

Camping Cypsela

Ctra de Pals - Platja de Pals, E-17256 Platja de Pals (Girona) T: 972 667 696. E: info@cypsela.com

alanrogers.com/ES80900

This impressive, de-luxe site with lush vegetation and trees is very efficiently run. The main part of the camping area is pinewood, with 637 clearly marked touring pitches of varying categories on sandy gravel, all with electricity and some with full facilities. The 228 'élite' pitches of 120 sq.m. are impressive. Cypsela is a busy, well administered site, only 2 km. from the sea, which we can thoroughly recommend, especially for families. The site has good quality fixtures and fittings, all kept clean and maintained to a high standard. All your needs will be catered for here. The site has many striking features, one of which is the sumptuous complex of sports facilities and amenities near the entrance.

Facilities	Directions
Four sanitary blocks are of excellent quality with regular cleaning schedules and solar heating. Three have washbasins in cabins and three have amazing children's rooms. Private sanitary facilities to rent. Superb facilities for disabled visitors. Serviced launderette. Supermarket and other shops. Restaurant, cafeteria and takeaway. Bar. Hairdresser. Swimming pools. Tennis. Squash. Minigolf. Skating rink. Fitness room. Solarium. Air conditioned social/TV room. Barbecue and party area. Comprehensive entertainment programme in season. Games room. Bicycle hire. Business centre. Internet access. WiFi (near reception). Gas supplies. ATM. Dogs are not accepted. Off site: Shuttle bus. Golf 1 km. Fishing 2 km.	Platja de Pals is southeast of Girona on the coast. From the AP7/E15 at Girona take exit 6 towards Palamós on the C66. This road changes number to the C31 near La Bisbal. 7.5 km. past La Bisbal, exit to Pals on the GI 652. Follow signs for Platja de Pals. At El Masos take the 6502 for 1 km. Main entrance for Cypsela is on the left between the white metal fencing. GPS: 41.98608, 3.18105

Open: 15 May - 14 September.

Charges 2011

Per unit incl. 2 persons and electricity	€ 36,60 - € 56,62
extra person	€ 6,31
child (2-10 yrs)	€ 4,81

For latest campsite news, availability and prices visit

alanrogers.com

Platja d'Aro

Camping Valldaro

Apdo de correos 57, Cami Vell 63, E-17250 Platja d'Aro (Girona) T: 972 817 515. E: info@valldaro.com

alanrogers.com/ES81700

Valldaro is 600 m. back from the sea at Platja d'Aro, a small, bright resort with a long, wide beach and plenty of amusements. It is particularly pleasant during off-peak weeks and is popular with Spanish, Dutch and British visitors. Valldaro has been extended and many pitches have been made larger, bringing them up to 85 sq.m. There are now almost 1,200 pitches with 544 for touring units. The site is flat, with pitches in rows divided up by access roads. You will probably find space here even at the height of the season. The newer section has its own vehicle entrance and can be reached via a footbridge; it is brought into use at peak times. It has some shade and its own toilet block, as well as a medium-sized swimming pool with a grassy sunbathing area and adjacent bar/snack bar and takeaway. The original pool is by an attractive Spanish-style restaurant which also offers takeaway fare.

Facilities

Four sanitary blocks are of a good standard and are well maintained. Child-size toilets. Washbasins (no cabins) and adjustable showers (temperature perhaps a bit variable). Two supermarkets and general shops. Two restaurants. Large bar. Swimming pools. New outdoor jacuzzi. Tennis. Minigolf with snack bar. Playgrounds. Sports ground. Children's club. Organised entertainment in season. Hairdresser. Internet. WiFi (code). Satellite TV. Gas supplies. Off site: Beach 1.5 km. Fishing and bicycle hire 1 km. Riding 4 km. Golf 5 km.

Open: 1 April - 25 September.

Directions

From Girona on the AP7/E15 take exit 7 to Sant Feliu on C65. On C65 at km. 313 take exit to Platja d'Aro (C31). In 200 m. at roundabout take GI662 towards Platja d'Aro. Site is at km. 4. If approaching from Palamós, access is via Platja d'Aro centre, exit on the GI662 as the GI662 cannot be accessed from the C31 southbound. GPS: 41.81427, 3.0437

Charges guide

Per unit incl. 2 persons	€ 20,00 - € 45,90
extra person	€ 4,10 - € 6,95

Discounts in low seasons. No credit cards.

resort de vacances
camping & bungalows
INTER PALS

Av. Mediterrània, Km. 4,5
E-17256 Platja de Pals · Girona
Tel. 972.63.61.79 · Fax 972.66.74.76
interpals@interpals.com
www.interpals.com

WiFi

resort de vacances
camping & bungalows
VALLDARO

C/ Cami Vell, 63
Apartado de correos 57
E-17250 PLATJA D'ARO · Girona
Tel. 972.81.75.15 · Fax 972.81.66.62
info@valldaro.com
www.valldaro.com

UNE-EN ISO 14001:2004
Nº 3.00.00013
TÜV

Two campsites with modern facilities. Entertainment for young and old. Campsites have ISO Environmental certificate. Rental of mobile homes, bungalows and tents. Reservation possible. Open from April to September.

Platja de Pals

Camping Inter-Pals

Avenida Mediterrania, E-17256 Platja de Pals (Girona) T: 972 636 179. E: interpals@interpals.com

alanrogers.com/ES81000

Set on sloping ground with tall pine trees providing shade and about 500 metres from the beach, Inter-Pals has 450 terraced pitches. It is sister site to no. ES81700 Valldaro. Arranged on level terraces, mostly with shade, some of the pitches have views of the sea through the trees. The main entrance and its drive resemble a pretty village street as the bungalows are set on both sides of the street, which is lined with traditional lamp posts. Continuing the village theme is a row of shops where you will find most campers' needs. The formal restaurant with good value menu and choice of takeaway overlooks the pools. The site is close to Platja de Pals which is a long sandy unspoilt stretch of beach, a discreet area, reached by a very hard climb, is now an official naturist beach.

Facilities

Three well maintained toilet blocks include facilities for disabled campers. Motorcaravan service point. Laundry facilities. Gas supplies. Fridge/TV rental. Shops. Restaurant/bar. Pizzeria with dancing and entertainment area. Café/bar. Swimming pool. Jacuzzi. Playground. Bicycle hire. Entertainment in high season. Excursions. Watersports arranged. Mini-adventure park. Medical centre. ATM. Internet access. WiFi. Torch useful. Off site: Fishing 200 m. Golf 1 km. Riding 10 km.

Open: 1 April - 25 September.

Directions

Site is on the road leading off the Torroella de Montgri - Bagur road north of Pals and going to Playa de Pals (Pals beach). GPS: 41.97533, 3.19317

Charges 2011

Per person	€ 4,40 - € 6,70
child (3-12 yrs)	€ 3,20 - € 4,00
pitch with electricity	€ 20,10 - € 35,50

Discounts for long stays in low season.
No credit cards. Camping Cheques accepted.

For latest campsite news, availability and prices visit
alanrogers.com

Platja de Pals

Camping Playa Brava

Avenida del Grau 1, E-17256 Platja de Pals (Girona) T: 972 636 894. E: info@playabrava.com

alanrogers.com/ES81010

This is an extremely pleasant site with an open feel, having direct access to an excellent soft sand beach and a freshwater lagoon where you can enjoy watersports and you may launch your own boat (charge). The ground is level and very grassy with shade provided for many of the 500 spacious pitches by a mixture of conifer and broad-leaf trees. All the pitches have 10A electricity and about a third have water and drainage. The spaciousness continues around the superb large swimming pool with its huge grass sunbathing areas, the whole being overlooked by the terrace of the restaurant and bar. The restaurant is very pleasant and offers a most reasonable 'menu of the day' including wine. An energetic entertainment programme runs during July and August. There are many interesting things to explore in the area including La Bisbal – famous for the ceramics, Dali's museum, the Roman ruins at Empuries Girona and many more. This is a clean, green and pleasant family site.

Facilities

Five modern, fully equipped toilet blocks include facilities for disabled visitors. Washing machines and dryers. Motorcaravan service point. Bar/restaurant. Takeaway. Supermarket. Swimming pool. Tennis. Minigolf. Beach volleyball. Football. Basketball. Play area on grass. Bicycle hire. Watersports on river and beach, including sheltered lagoon for windsurfing learners. New stage show. Internet access. WiFi. Satellite TV. Gas supplies. Torches required in some areas. Dogs are not accepted. Off site: Two 18-hole golf courses 300 m. (30% discount through reception). Riding 6 km. Fishing and sailing 300 m.

Open: 14 May - 11 September.

Directions

Platja de Pals is southeast of Girona on the coast. From the AP7/E15 at Girona take exit 6 towards Palamós on the C66. 7.5 km. past La Bisbal, exit to Pals on the GIV-6502. Follow signs for Platja de Pals - Golf Platja de Pals. Site is on left just before road ends at beach car park. GPS: 42.001130, 3.193800

Charges 2011

Per unit incl. 2 persons and electricity	€ 32,10 - € 53,80
extra person	€ 2,30 - € 3,40
child (3-9 yrs)	free - € 2,30

CÀMPING CARAVANING ★★★

Playa Brava

PLATJA DE PALS - COSTA BRAVA

GPS:
42.001130 N
3.193800 E

www.playabrava.com

Av. del Grau, 1 · 17256 PLATJA DE PALS (Girona) COSTA BRAVA
T. +34 972 63 68 94 · F. +34 972 63 69 52 · info@playabrava.com

Poboleda

Camping Poboleda

Placa de les Casetes s/n, E-43376 Poboleda (Tarragona) T: 977 827 197. E: poboleda@campingsonline.com

alanrogers.com/ES85080

Time stands still at this unique site hidden away in a corner of the village, watched over by La Morera de Montsant, a peak of the Serra del Montsant. Situated among olive groves, yet almost in the heart of the lovely old village of Poboleda, it is an idyllic site for tents, small caravans and motorcaravans. Large units may have problems negotiating the narrow village streets. The 151 pitches of 80 sq.m. are set under olive and almond trees. Fairly level and 70 with 4A electricity, they provide a peaceful haven broken only by the peal of church bells or bird song.

Facilities

One small block, open all year, is fully equipped, as is a larger block for high season. Shower for children. Facilities for disabled visitors (key). Laundry service. Breakfast can be ordered. Bar. Swimming pool (24/6-11/9). Tennis. Boules. Off site: Beach and Port Aventura 30 km. Bicycle hire 10 km. Fishing 12 km.

Open: All year.

Directions

Bypass Reus (west of Tarragona) on N420. After Borges del Camp pick up C242, signed Alforja. Continue over Coll d'Alforja. Watch for left turn (T702) for Poboleda. Continue for 6 km. to village. Watch for tent signs and follow carefully through narrow village streets. Not recommended for large units. GPS: 41.23231, 0.84316

Charges guide

Per person	€ 6,00
pitch incl. car	€ 11,00 - € 15,00
electricity	€ 5,50

For latest campsite news, availability and prices visit

alanrogers.com

Puigcerdá

Camping Stel

Ctra N152 Ramal - Llivia s/n, E-17520 Puigcerdá (Girona) T: 972 882 361. E: puigcerda@stel.es

alanrogers.com/ES91440

Sister site to ES84200 and ES91430, this is an extremely efficient, if pricey site. Part of a large, attractive building, the spacious entrance houses a modern reception (English is spoken). From here you will quickly be on your way to one of the flat, terraced pitches. Many of the pitches have shade and all are marked, clean and organized in rows with a water tap for each row. There is some road noise so, in order to avoid this and have views of the Cerdanya valley and the eastern Pyrenees, take one of the pitches on the upper terraces. It is worth the trouble.

Facilities

Sanitary facilities in the main building are of very high standard and are kept very clean. A small, smart block serves the upper terraces. Both can be heated. Separate modern unit with facilities for disabled campers. Laundry facilities. Shop. Bar/restaurant (all season). Swimming pool (June-Sept). Boules. Novel adventure style play frame (supervision needed). Adventure club (watersports and outdoor activities). Animation (high season). Off site: Riding 5 km. Fishing and golf 7 km.

Open: 3 June - 11 September.

Directions

From Perpignan take N116 to Prades and Andorra. At roundabout at the border crossing at Puigcerdá take first right for Llivia (almost a turn back on yourself). Site is on left after 1 km. GPS: 42.44153, 1.94128

Charges guide

Per unit incl. 2 persons and electricity	€ 40,90
extra person	€ 6,50

Camping Cheques accepted.

Roda de Bará

Camping Park Playa Bará

Ctra N340 km 1183, E-43883 Roda de Bará (Tarragona) T: 977 802 701. E: info@barapark.es

alanrogers.com/ES84100

This is a most impressive, family owned site near the beach, which has been carefully designed and developed. On entry you find yourself in a beautifully sculptured, tree-lined drive with an accompanying aroma of pine and woodlands and the sound of waterfalls close by. Considering its size, with over 850 pitches (fully serviced), it is still a very green and relaxing site with an immense range of activities. It is well situated with a 50 m. walk to a long sandy beach via a tunnel under the railway (some noise) to a new promenade with palms and a quality beach bar and restaurant.

Facilities

Excellent, fully equipped toilet blocks include private cabins and facilities for children, and new block for disabled visitors. Private facilities to hire. Launderette. Motorcaravan service points. Supermarket. Shops. Full restaurant. Large bar with simple meals and takeaway. Three other bars and bar/restaurant on beach. Swimming pools. Jacuzzi/hydro-massage. Windsurfing school. Gym. Massage. Fishing. Entertainment. Cocktail bar/disco (23.00 to 04.00). Bicycle hire. ATM. Hairdresser. Internet room. WiFi. Off site: Riding 6 km. Golf 8 km.

Open: 19 March - 26 September (with all amenities).

Directions

From the A7 take exit 31. Site entrance is at the 1183 km. marker on the main N340 just opposite the Arco de Bara Roman monument from which it takes its name. GPS: 41.17, 1.46833

Charges guide

Per unit incl. 2 persons and electricity	€ 17,60 - € 42,30
extra person	€ 3,00 - € 9,70
child (1-9 yrs)	€ 2,00 - € 6,80

No credit cards.

Roda de Bará

Kawan Village Stel

Ctra N340 km 1182, E-43883 Roda de Bará (Tarragona) T: 977 802 002. E: rodadebara@stel.es

alanrogers.com/ES84200

Camping Stel is situated between the pre-Littoral mountains and the sea. The rectangular site is between the N340 road and the excellent beach, with the railway running close to the bottom of the site. Beach access is gained through a gate and under the railway – there is rail noise on the lower pitches. The pitches are generally in rows with hedges around the rows but at the lower end of the site the layout is less formal. Many pitches have individual sinks. There is a separate area where no radio or TV is allowed ensuring peace and quiet.

Facilities

Four clean, fully equipped, sanitary blocks. One offers excellent facilities for children and disabled campers and four private cabins. Baby baths. Large launderette. Motorcaravan service area. Supermarket and tourist shop. Bar/restaurant and snack bar. Swimming pool, jacuzzi and paddling pool (4/4-28/9). Sport field. Bicycle hire. Miniclub and activities for adults (high season). Internet room. Hairdresser. ATM. Dogs are not accepted. Torches useful. Off site: Fishing from beach. Golf and riding 4 km.

Open: 25 March - 26 September.

Directions

Site is at 1182 km. marker on the N340 near Arc de Bara, between Tarragona and Vilanova. GPS: 41.16969, 1.46469

Charges guide

Per person	€ 7,35 - € 7,75
child (3-10 yrs)	€ 5,75 - € 6,05
pitch incl. electricity	€ 23,15 - € 28,45
incl. water and drainage	€ 27,90 - € 37,70

Camping Cheques accepted.

For latest campsite news, availability and prices visit

alanrogers.com

Roses
Camping Salatá
Port Reig s/n, Platja Salatá, E-17480 Roses (Girona) T: 972 256 086. E: info@campingsalata.com
alanrogers.com/ES80090

Situated in the heart of Roses, in one of the most attractive areas of the Costa Brava, Salata is a short walk from the magnificent seafront promenade with its bars, restaurants and shops. Opposite the site entrance there is a pretty landscaped sea inlet. There are 288 grass pitches with 16A electricity and some shade (80-110 sq.m). Buildings and amenities are very well maintained. The campsite is part of a complex that includes apartments and the Hotel Terraza where a spa centre, indoor pool and other amenities can be enjoyed by campers in low season (extra charge).

Facilities

Very clean toilet blocks wih British style toilets and good showers. Facilities for disabled visitors, babies and children. Washing machines. Gas supplies. Bar with snacks. Swimming pool. Playground. Entertainment programme (15/6-15/9). Internet. WiFi. Barbecue area. Bicycle hire. Minigolf. No pets in high season.
Off site: Extra facilities at hotel nearby (under the same ownership). Beach, bicycle hire 130 m. Boat launching 200 m. Tennis 300 m. Riding 3 km. Golf 15 km.

Open: 1 March - 30 November.

Directions

From the AP7/E15, take exit 3 south or exit 4 north (there is no exit 3 northbound) and then the N11 to the C260 and on to Roses. Site is well signed before you enter the town. GPS: 42.26588, 3.15762

Charges guide

Per person	€ 4,65 - € 7,75
child (3-10 yrs)	free - € 5,60
pitch	€ 10,00 - € 28,00
dog	free - € 2,75

Rupit
Camping Rupit
Ctra de Vic - Olot km 31,5, E-08569 Rupit (Barcelona) T: 938 522 153. E: info@rupit.com
alanrogers.com/ES83400

The approach road to the site from the coast is not for the faint hearted, but if a rural setting is what you're looking for, then this is the site for you – we loved it! The Morell family who own the site (and others on the coast) will welcome you warmly and speak English very well. The mostly level, grass pitches are slightly terraced and some have shade from mature trees. Long leads will be necessary as the electricity points are well spread out. There are two beautiful stone buildings, one housing the reception, bar and restaurant, the other a toilet block.

Facilities

The central toilet block provides open washbasins and shower cubicles with curtains only. Baby bath. Facilities for disabled visitors in the men's side only. Laundry room. No shop (essentials can be purchased from the bar). Bar and separate restaurant. Outdoor swimming pool and paddling pool overlooked by restaurant terrace. Games room. Play area. Communal barbecue area. Bicycle hire. Off site: Rupit town 1 km. Riding 5 km. Fishing 15 km.

Open: March - December.

Directions

From the AP7 exit 6 (Gerona), take the C66 to Olot. From Olot follow C153 for 31.5 km. This road is steep and winding in places. Site is 1 km. before the town of Rupit. The site entrance is on a sharp bend where extra care is required.
GPS: 42.02516, 2.45883

Charges guide

Per unit incl. 2 persons	€ 22,45 - € 31,75
extra person	€ 4,95 - € 6,95

Saldés
Camping Repos del Pedraforca
Ctra B-400 km 13.5, E-08697 Saldés (Barcelona) T: 938 258 044. E: pedra@campingpedraforca.com
alanrogers.com/ES91400

Looking up through the trees in this steeply terraced campsite in the area of the Cadi-Moixero Natural Parc, you see the majestic Pedraforca mountain. A favourite for Catalan climbers and walkers, its amazing rugged peak in the shape of a massive stone fork gives it its name. Access to the site is via a steep, curving road which could challenge some units. There are 200 pitches, including 100 for touring, all with electricity (3-10A) and 15 with connection to water and waste water. They vary in size and accessibility, although there are excellent pitches for larger units. The long scenic drive through the mountains to reach the site is breathtakingly beautiful.

Facilities

Two clean, modern sanitary blocks are fully equipped (at peak periods there may be queues). Facilities for disabled campers. Separate family room with baby baths. Washing machines and dryer. Shop and bar. Restaurant and takeaway (1/6-30/9). Heated indoor pool, gym and spa. Outdoor pool (15/6-30/9). Play areas. Entertainment in high season. Torches required. Off site: Mountain biking. Adventure park 5 km. Fishing 2 km. Riding 10 km.

Open: All year.

Directions

Site is about 90 minutes from Barcelona. Access to the site is gained from the C16 Berga road. 2 km. south of Guardiola de Berguedá turn north to Saldes and site is well signed. It is 13.5 km. to site from the C16. GPS: 42.23078, 1.75245

Charges guide

Per unit incl. 2 persons	€ 28,25 - € 34,70
extra person	€ 4,90 - € 6,05
Camping Cheques accepted.	

Salou
Camping & Bungalows Sanguli

Prolongacion Calle, Apdo 123, E-43840 Salou (Tarragona) T: 977 381 641. E: mail@sanguli.es

alanrogers.com/ES84800

Sanguli is a superb site boasting excellent pools and ambitious entertainment. Owned, developed and managed by a local Spanish family, it provides for all the family with everything open when the site is open. There are 1,067 pitches of varying size (75-90 sq.m) and all have electricity. About 100 are used by tour operators and 207 for bungalows. A wonderful selection of trees, palms and shrubs provides natural shade. The good sandy beach is little more than 100 metres across the coast road and a small railway crossing (a little noise). Although large, Sanguli has a pleasant, open feel and maintains a quality family atmosphere due to the efforts of the very keen and efficient staff. The owners are striving to achieve the 'Garden of Eden' that is their dream. There are three very attractive pool areas, one (heated) near the entrance with a grassy sunbathing area partly shaded and a second deep one with water slides that forms part of the excellent sports complex (with fitness centre, tennis courts, minigolf and football practice area). The third pool is the central part of the amphitheatre area at the top of the site which includes an impressive Roman style building with huge portals, containing a bar and restaurant with terraces. An amphitheatre seats 2,000 campers and treats them to very professional free nightly entertainment (1/5-30/9). All the pools have adjacent amenity areas and bars. A real effort is made to cater for the young including teenagers with a 'Hop Club' (entertainment for 13-17 year olds), along with an internet room. Located near the centre of Salou, the site can offer the attractions of a busy resort while still being private and it is only 3 km. from Port Aventura. This is a large, professional site providing something for all the family, but still capable of providing peace and quiet for those looking for it.

Facilities	Directions
The six quality sanitary facilities are constantly cleaned and are always exceptional, including many individual cabins with en-suite facilities. Improvements are made each year. Some blocks have excellent facilities for babies. Launderette with service. Motorcaravan services. Car wash (charged). Bars and restaurant with takeaway. Swimming pools. Jacuzzi. Fitness centre. Sports complex. Fitness room (charged). Playgrounds including adventure play area. Miniclub, teenagers club. Internet room. Upmarket minigolf. First-aid room. Gas supplies. Multiple internet options including WiFi. Security bracelets for children under 12 years. Well equipped medical centre. Off site: Bus at gate. Fishing and bicycle hire 100 m. Riding 3 km. Golf 6 km. Resort entertainment. Port Adventure 4 km.	On west side of Salou about 1 km. from the centre, site is well signed from the coast road to Cambrils and from the other town approaches. GPS: 41.075, 1.116

Charges guide

Per person	€ 6,00
child (4-12 yrs)	€ 4,00
pitch incl. electricity	€ 15,00 - € 52,00
incl. water and waste water	€ 17,00 - € 55,00

Reductions outside high season for longer stays. Special long stay offers for senior citizens.

Open: 19 March - 1 November.

Salou
Camping La Siesta

Calle Ctra Norte 37, E-43840 Salou (Tarragona) T: 977 380 852. E: info@camping-lasiesta.com

alanrogers.com/ES84700

The palm bedecked entrance of La Siesta is only 250 m. from the pleasant sandy beach and close to the life of the resort of Salou. The site is divided into 470 pitches which are large enough and have electricity (10A), with smaller ones for tents. Many pitches are provided with artificial shade and within some there is one box for the tent or caravan and a shared one for the car. There is considerable shade from the trees and shrubs that are part of the site's environment. In high season, the siting of units is carried out by the friendly management. Young campers are located separately to the rear of the site. The town is popular with British and Spanish holidaymakers and has just about all that a highly developed Spanish resort can offer. For those who do not want to share the busy beach, there is a large, free swimming pool which is elevated above pitch level.

Facilities	Directions
Three bright and clean sanitary blocks provide very reasonable facilities. Motorcaravan services. Supermarket. Various vending machines. Self-service restaurant and bar with cooked dishes to take away. Dancing some evenings until 23.00. Swimming pool (300 sq.m. open all season). Playground. Medical service daily in season. ATM point. Torches may be required. Off site: Shops, restaurants and bars nearby. Port Aventura is close. Bicycle hire 200 m. Fishing 500 m. Riding and golf 6 km.	Leave A7 at exit 35 for Salou. Site is signed off the Tarragona - Salou road and from the one way system in Salou. The site is in the town so look out for the small signs. GPS: 41.0777, 1.1389

Charges guide

Per person	€ 4,60 - € 8,80
child (4-9 yrs)	€ 3,40 - € 4,50
pitch	€ 3,40 - € 17,60
electricity	€ 3,25 - € 4,00

No credit cards.

Open: 14 March - 3 November.

For latest campsite news, availability and prices visit
alanrogers.com

Sant Antoni di Calonge

Eurocamping

Avinguda Catalunya 15, E-17252 Sant Antoni di Calonge (Girona) T: 972 650 879. E: info@euro-camping.com
alanrogers.com/ES81350

This large campsite on the Costa Brava near Girona is attractively landscaped, with lawns, flowers and pretty features around the site. It has 615 pitches of varying sizes, with 475 for touring, of which 100 are fully serviced. Older areas of the campsite are shaded by tall trees creating a cooler zone, while the new areas have good size trees but are not yet under the same shade canopy. There are two pool complexes, one near the entrance with an unusual feature where one large pool cascades into another at a slightly lower level. Alongside is a paddling pool, an outdoor chess game and a large grassy area.

Facilities

Four clean toilet blocks with mainly British style WCs (no seats) in cabins with shower and basin. Good facilities for disabled visitors. Family rooms. Washing machines. Gas supplies. Supermarket by gate. Pleasant bars and good restaurant. Swimming and paddling pools. Playgrounds. Tennis. TV in bar. Fitness room. Activity programme. Internet access and WiFi. ATM. Excursions. Beach train (July/Aug). Torches useful. Off site: Public transport from gate. Bicycle hire 100 m. Beach 300 m. Fishing 300 m.

Open: 16 April - 18 September.

Directions

The town of Sant Antoni de Calonge is southeast of Girona on the coast. Leave the AP7/E15 at exit 6. Take the C66 towards Palamós which becomes the C31. Use the C31 (Girona - Palamós) road to avoid Palamós town. Take the C253 coast road. Site well signed at northern end of Sant Antoni de Calogne. GPS: 41.8470, 3.0986

Charges 2011

Per person	€ 2,90 - € 7,25
pitch	€ 20,20 - € 33,75

Sant Feliu de Guíxols

Camping Sant Pol

Carrer del Doctor Fleming No.1, E-17220 Sant Feliu de Guíxols (Girona) T: 972 327269
E: info@campingsantpol.cat alanrogers.com/ES81800

Sant Pol is a small, family owned site and the owners have a firm understanding of campers' needs, as do the friendly staff. On the Costa Brava, this hillside site is on the edge of Sant Feliu, only 350 m. from the beach (there may be some road noise on one side of the site) and the resort town. An attractive solar-heated pool and a paddling pool, bar and restaurant are the central focus of the site. There are 100 pitches for tourers (19 fully serviced) and the pleasant small terraces take 37 tents.

Facilities

The clean and modern sanitary block has British style WCs and hot water throughout. WC for disabled campers, but no shower (terrain would be difficult for wheelchairs). Washing machines and dryer. Small supermarket. Pleasant restaurant/bar. Solar heated swimming pools. Play area. Entertainment for children in high season. Minigolf. Internet point and WiFi (code). Excursions. Torches needed in some areas. Off site: Large supermarket, restaurants 300 m. Beach 350 m. Riding, bicycle hire 1 km. Golf 5 km.

Open: 26 March - 12 December.

Directions

San Feliu is southeast of Girona and reached via the C65 (Girona - Palamós) road. Leave this at km. 312 signed to S'Agaró. Proceed towards Sant Feliu to outskirts of village. Site signed from first roundabout and is directly off third roundabout. Caution as entrance is up very steep slope marked with small green camping triangles. GPS: 41.78633, 3.04122

Charges guide

Per unit incl. 2 persons	€ 26,00 - € 53,00
extra person	€ 4,00 - € 7,00

Sant Pere Pescador

Camping La Gaviota

Ctra de la Platja s/n, E-17470 Sant Pere Pescador (Girona) T: 972 520 569. E: info@lagaviota.com
alanrogers.com/ES80310

La Gaviota is a delightful, small, family run site at the end of a cul-de-sac with direct beach access. This ensures a peaceful situation with a choice of the pleasant L-shaped pool or direct beach access to the fine clean beach and slowly shelving access to the water. Everything here is clean and smart and the Gil family are very keen that you enjoy your time here. There are 165 touring pitches on flat ground with shade and 6A electricity supply. A lush green feel is given to the site by many palms and other semi-tropical trees and shrubs. The restaurant and bar are very pleasant and have a distinct Spanish flavour.

Facilities

One smart and very clean toilet block is near reception. All WCs are British style and the showers are excellent. Superb facilities for disabled visitors. Family and baby rooms. Washing machine. Gas supplies. Supermarket (fresh bread), pleasant bar and small, delightful restaurant (all March-Oct). Swimming pool (May-Oct). Playground. Games room. Limited entertainment. Beach sports and windsurfing. Internet. Torches useful. ATM. Off site: Boat launching 2 km. Riding 4 km. Golf 15 km. Cycling routes.

Open: 25 March - 30 October.

Directions

From the AP7/E15 take exit 3 onto the N11 north towards Figueras and then the C260 towards Roses. At Castello d'Empúries take the GIV 6216 and continue to Sant Pere Pescador. Site is well signed in the town. GPS: 42.18901, 3.10843

Charges 2011

Per unit incl. 2 persons	€ 23,95 - € 51,95
extra person	€ 3,50 - € 4,50

No credit cards. Discounts for longer stays.

Sant Pere Pescador

Camping Riu

Ctra de la Platja s/n, E-17470 Sant Pere Pescador (Girona) T: 972 520 216. E: info@campingriu.com

alanrogers.com/ES80320

Camping Riu is an established campsite which has been purchased and upgraded by the Senia group. The pool and gym areas are brilliant for such a small site. There are 200 pitches of which 190 are for tourers with 5/10A electricity on flat ground and are shaded by mature trees. The bungalows are in a separate area away from the touring pitches. The pleasant bar/restaurant and terrace overlook the floodlit pool and children's area, where some entertainment is held in high season. Riu is on the Fluvia river, 1.5 km. from the sea.

Facilities

Two toilet blocks are clean and well positioned with good showers. Almost all WCs are British style. Facilities for disabled visitors. Baby room. Washing machines. Gas supplies. Supermarket. Pleasant bar and restaurant. Swimming pool and new pool for children. Adventure playground. Internet. Gym. Bicycle hire. Activities programme including entertainment for children (high season). Kayaking. Fishing. Barbecue area. Satellite TV in bar. Motorhome service point. Excursions. Torches useful. Pets welcome. Off site: Public transport 400 m. Golf 20 km. Road train to beach from site in high season.

Open: 1 April - 16 September.

Directions

Sant Pere Pescador is on the coast between Roses and L'Escala. From AP7/E15 exit 4 take N11 north towards Figueres and then the C31 towards Torroella de Fluvia. Take Vilamacolum road east and continue to Sant Pere Pescador. Site is well signed in the town. GPS: 42.18757, 3.08914

Charges guide

Per unit incl. 2 persons	
and electricity	€ 20,55 - € 42,65
extra person	€ 2,95 - € 4,45
child (1-9 yrs)	free - € 3,50

Sant Pere Pescador

Camping Las Palmeras

Ctra de la Platja, E-17470 Sant Pere Pescador (Girona) T: 972 520 506
E: info@campinglaspalmeras.com alanrogers.com/ES80330

A very polished site, the pleasant experience begins as you enter the palm bedecked site and are welcomed at the airy reception building. The 230 pitches are flat, very clean and well maintained, with some shade and 10A electricity. A few pitches are complete with water and drainage. Thirty smart mobile homes are placed unobtrusively around the site. A very pleasant pool complex has a lifeguard and the brightly coloured play areas are clean and safe. A great beach is just a 200 m. walk through a gate at the rear of the site. A full activities programme for children allows parents a break during the day and there is organised fun in the evenings in high season. Full recreational facilities include a gym. The very Spanish style restaurant serves high quality food.

Facilities

Two excellent, very clean, solar powered toilet blocks include first class facilities for disabled campers. Baby rooms. Facilities may become a little busy at peak periods. Washing machines. Motorcaravan services. Supermarket. Restaurant/bar (children's menu). Swimming pools (heated). Play areas. Tennis. 5-a-side. Fronton. Boules. Gym. Barbecue. Bicycle hire. Miniclub. Entertainment. Satellite TV. Internet access and WiFi. ATM. Torches useful. Off site: Beach and fishing 200 m. Sailing and boat launching 2 km. Riding 4 km. Golf 7 km.

Open: 27 March - 23 October.

Directions

From the AP7/E15 take exit 4 onto N11 north towards Figueres and then C31 towards Torroella de Fluvia. Take the Vilamacolum road east and continue to Sant Pere Pescador. Site well signed in town. GPS: 42.18805, 3.1027

Charges guide

Per unit incl. 2 persons	
and electricity	€ 23,80 - € 49,90
extra person	€ 3,00 - € 4,30
child (2-9 yrs)	€ 1,70 - € 2,50
No credit cards.	

49

For latest campsite news, availability and prices visit
alanrogers.com

Sant Pere Pescador

Kawan Village L'Amfora

Avenida Josep Tarradellas, 2, E-17470 Sant Pere Pescador (Girona) T: 972 520 540
E: info@campingamfora.com **alanrogers.com/ES80350**

This super, spacious site is family run and friendly. A Greek theme is evident, mainly in the restaurant and around the pool areas. The site is spotlessly clean and well maintained and the owner operates in an environmentally friendly way. There are 830 level, grass pitches (741 for touring units) laid out in a grid system, all with 10A electricity. Attractive trees and shrubs have been planted around each pitch. There is good shade in the more mature areas, which have 64 large pitches (180 sq.m), each with an individual sanitary unit (toilet, shower and washbasin). The newer area is more open with less shade and you can choose which you would prefer. Three excellent sanitary blocks (one heated) are fully equipped and have staff on almost permanent duty to ensure very high standards are maintained. Access is good for disabled visitors. At the entrance a terraced bar and two restaurants overlook a smart pool complex that includes three pools for children, one with two water slides. In high season (from July) there is ambitious evening entertainment and an activity programme for children. Alongside the site, the magnificent sandy beach on the Bay of Roses offers good conditions for children and a choice of high season watersports.

Facilities

Three main toilet blocks, one heated, provide washbasins in cabins and roomy free showers. Baby rooms. Laundry facilities and laundry service. Motorcaravan services. Supermarket. Terraced bar, self-service and waiter service restaurants. Pizzeria/takeaway. Restaurant and bar on the beach with limited menu (high season). Disco bar. Swimming pools (1/5-30/9). Pétanque. Tennis. Bicycle hire. Minigolf. Play area. Miniclub. Entertainment and activities. Windsurfing. Boat launching and sailing. Fishing. Exchange facilities. Games and TV rooms. Internet room and WiFi. Car wash. Torches required in beach areas.
Off site: Riding 4 km. Golf 15 km.

Open: 16 April - 30 September.

Directions

From the north on A17/E15 take exit 3 onto the N11 towards Figueres and then shortly onto the C260 towards Roses. At Castello d'Empúries turn right onto the GIV-6216 to Sant Pere. From the south on the A17 use exit 5 (L'Escala) and turn to Sant Pere in Viladamat. Site is well signed in the town towards the beach. GPS: 42.18147, 3.10405

Charges 2011

Per unit incl. 2 persons and electricity	€ 25,00 - € 54,70
extra person	€ 4,50 - € 6,20
child (2-9 yrs)	free - € 4,20
dog	€ 2,60 - € 4,95

No credit cards.
Camping Cheques accepted.

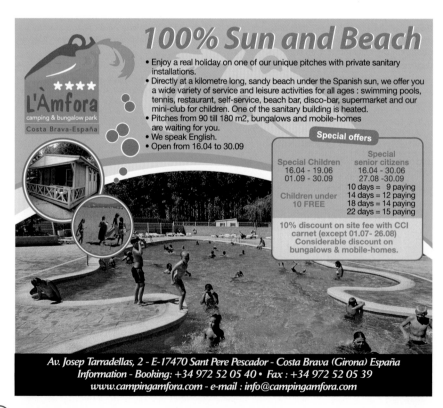

100% Sun and Beach

★★★★
L'Àmfora
camping & bungalow park
Costa Brava-España

- Enjoy a real holiday on one of our unique pitches with private sanitary installations.
- Directly at a kilometre long, sandy beach under the Spanish sun, we offer you a wide variety of service and leisure activities for all ages : swimming pools, tennis, restaurant, self-service, beach bar, disco-bar, supermarket and our mini-club for children. One of the sanitary building is heated.
- Pitches from 90 till 180 m2, bungalows and mobile-homes are waiting for you.
- We speak English.
- Open from 16.04 to 30.09

Special offers

Special Children 16.04 - 19.06 01.09 - 30.09	Special senior citizens 16.04 - 30.06 27.08 -30.09
	10 days = 9 paying
Children under 10 FREE	14 days = 12 paying
	18 days = 14 paying
	22 days = 15 paying

10% discount on site fee with CCI carnet (except 01.07- 26.08)
Considerable discount on bungalows & mobile-homes.

Av. Josep Tarradellas, 2 - E-17470 Sant Pere Pescador - Costa Brava (Girona) España
Information - Booking: +34 972 52 05 40 • Fax : +34 972 52 05 39
www.campingamfora.com - e-mail : info@campingamfora.com

For latest campsite news, availability and prices visit
alanrogers.com

Sant Pere Pescador

Camping Las Dunas

Ctra San Marti - Sant Pere, E-17470 Sant Pere Pescador (Girona) T: 972 521 717
E: info@campinglasdunas.com alanrogers.com/ES80400

Winner
2010 Awards

Las Dunas is an extremely large, impressive and well organised resort style site with many on-site activities and an ongoing programme of improvements. It has direct access to a superb sandy beach that stretches along the site for nearly a kilometre with a windsurfing school and beach bar. There is also a much used, huge swimming pool, plus a large double pool for children. Las Dunas has 1,700 individual hedged pitches (1,479 for tourers) of around 100 sq.m. laid out on flat ground in long, regular parallel rows. All have electricity (6/10A) and 180 also have water and drainage. Shade is available in some parts of the site. Pitches are usually available, even in the main season. Much effort has gone into planting palms and new trees here and the results are very attractive. The large restaurant and bar have spacious terraces overlooking the swimming pools and you can enjoy a very pleasant, more secluded, cavern styled pub. A magnificent disco club is close by in a soundproofed building (noise during the night can be a problem for pitches in the central area of the site). With free quality entertainment of all types in season and positive security arrangements, this is a great site for families with teenagers. Everything is provided on site so you don't need to leave it during your stay. A member of Leading Campings Group.

Facilities

Five excellent toilet blocks with electronic sliding glass doors (resident cleaners 07.00-21.00). British style toilets without seats, controllable hot showers and washbasins in cabins. Excellent facilities for youngsters, babies and disabled campers. Laundry facilities. Motorcaravan services. Large supermarket, boutique and other shops. Large bar with terrace. Large restaurant. Takeaway. Ice cream parlour. Beach bar in main season. Disco club. Swimming pools. Playgrounds. Tennis. Archery. Minigolf. Sailing/windsurfing school and watersports. Programme of sports, games, entertainment and excursions, partly in English (15/6-31/8). Exchange facilities. ATM. Safety deposit. Internet café. WiFi. Torches required in some areas. Off site: Riding and boat launching 5 km. Water park 10 km. Golf 30 km. Resort of L'Escala 5 km.

Open: 19 May - 2 September.

Directions

L'Escala is northeast of Girona on the coast between Palamós and Roses. From A7/E15 autostrada take exit 5 towards L'Escala on GI 623. Turn north 2 km. before reaching L'Escala towards Sant Marti d'Ampúrias. Site well signed.
GPS: 42.16098, 3.13478

Charges 2011

Per unit incl. 2 persons	
and electricity	€ 21,00 - € 59,20
extra person	€ 3,50 - € 5,75
child (3-10 yrs)	€ 3,00 - € 3,25
dog	€ 3,20 - € 4,50

Sant Pere Pescador

Camping Aquarius

Playa s/n, E-17470 Sant Pere Pescador (Girona) T: 972 520 003. E: camping@aquarius.es

alanrogers.com/ES80500

A smart and efficient family site, Aquarius has direct access to a quiet sandy beach that slopes gently and provides good bathing (the sea is shallow for quite a long way out). Watersports are popular, particularly windsurfing (a school is provided). One third of the site has good shade with a park-like atmosphere. There are 430 pitches with electricity (6/16A). Markus Rupp and his wife are keen to make every visitor's experience a happy one and even issue flags to denote the number of years they have stayed at the site. The site is ideal for those who really like sun and sea, with a quiet situation. Mr Rupp has a background in architecture and a wealth of knowledge on the whole Catalan area and culture. He has written a booklet of suggested tours (available from reception). The family is justifiably proud of their most attractive and absolutely pristine site which they continually upgrade and improve. The fountain at the entrance, the fishponds and the water features in the restaurant are soothing and pleasing. A small stage close to the restaurant is used for live entertainment in season. The spotless beach bar complex with shaded terraces, satellite TV and evening entertainment, has marvellous views over the Bay of Roses. The Surf Center with rentals, school and shop is ideal for enthusiasts and beginners alike.

Facilities

Attractively tiled, fully equipped, large toilet blocks provide some cabins for each sex. Excellent facilities for disabled visitors, plus baths for children. Superb new block has underfloor heating and features family cabins. Laundry facilities. Gas supplies. Motorcaravan services. Full size refrigerators. Supermarket. Pleasant restaurant and bar with terrace. Takeaway. Purpose built play centre for children (with qualified attendant), playground and separate play area for toddlers. TV room. Surf Center. Minigolf. Bicycle hire. Barbecue and dance once weekly when numbers justify. ATM. Internet access. WiFi. Dogs are accepted in one section. (Note: no pool). Off site: Beach 2 km. Fishing and boat launching 3 km. Riding 6 km. Golf 15 km.

Open: 15 March - 5 November.

Directions

Attention: SatNav take you a different route, but easier to drive is from AP7 exit 3 (Figueres Nord) direction Roses on C-68. At roundabout Castello d'Empuries take 2nd right to St. Pere Pescador, cross town and river bridge. From there site is well signed. GPS: 42.18092, 3.09425

Charges guide

Per person	€ 3,00 - € 4,00
child (under 12 yrs)	free - € 2,65
pitch incl. electricity	€ 8,80 - € 42,00
electricity	€ 3,70

Discounts for pensioners on longer stays.
No credit cards.

For latest campsite news, availability and prices visit

alanrogers.com

Sant Pere Pescador
Camping La Ballena Alegre

Ctra Sant Marti d'Empuries s/n, E-17470 Sant Pere Pescador (Girona) T: 902 510 520
E: infb2@ballena-alegre.com alanrogers.com/ES80600

La Ballena Alegre is partly in a lightly wooded setting, partly open, and has almost 2 km. of frontage directly onto an excellent beach of soft golden sand (which is cleaned daily). They claim that none of the 1,165 touring pitches is more than 100 m. from the beach. The grass pitches are individually numbered and there is a choice of size (up to 100 sq.m). Electrical connections (5/10A) are available in all areas and there are 481 fully serviced pitches. A recent addition is a resort village area within the site with holiday homes and its own small pool and play area. This is a great site for families. There are restaurant and bar areas beside the pleasant terraced pool complex (four pools including a pool for children). For those who wish to drink and snack late there is a pub open until 03.00. The well managed, soundproofed disco is popular with youngsters. A little train ferries people along the length of the site and a road train runs to local villages. Plenty of entertainment and activities are offered, including a well managed watersports centre, with sub-aqua, windsurfing and kite surfing, where equipment can be hired and lessons taken. You can also use a comprehensive open air fitness centre near the beach. A full entertainment programme is provided all season. An overflow area across the road provides additional parking and sports activities. The site has won Spanish tourist board awards and is keen on ecological fitness.

Facilities

Seven well maintained toilet blocks are of a very high standard. Facilities for children, babies and disabled campers. Launderette. Motorcaravan services. Gas supplies. Supermarket. 'Linen' restaurant. Self-service restaurant and bar. Takeaway. Pizzeria and beach bar in high season. Swimming pool complex. Jacuzzi. Tennis. Watersports centre. Fitness centre. Bicycle hire. Playgrounds. Sound proofed disco. Dancing twice weekly and organised activities, sports, entertainment, etc. ATM. In high season dogs only allowed in one zone (26/6-22/8). Internet access and WiFi. Torches useful in beach areas. Off site: Go-karting nearby with bus service. Fishing 300 m. Riding 2 km.

Open: 14 May - 26 September.

Directions

From A7 Figueres - Girona autopista take exit 5 to L'Escala GI 623 for 18.5 km. At roundabout take sign to Sant Marti d'Empúries and follow site signs. GPS: 42.15323, 3.11248

Charges 2011

Per unit incl. 2 persons and electricity	€ 25,60 - € 55,90
extra person	€ 3,80 - € 4,60
child (3-10 yrs)	€ 2,80 - € 3,30
dog	€ 2,30 - € 4,75

Discount of 10% on pitch charge for pensioners all season. No credit cards.

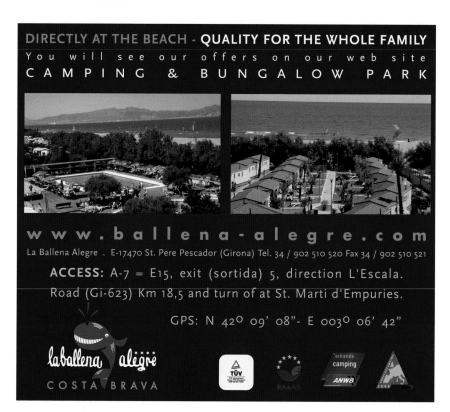
For latest campsite news, availability and prices visit
alanrogers.com

Santa Cristina d'Aro

Yelloh! Village Mas Sant Josep

Ctra Santa Cristina - Platja d'Aro km 2, E-17246 Santa Cristina d'Aro (Girona) T: 972 835 108
E: info@campingmassantjosep.com alanrogers.com/ES81750

This is a very large, well appointed, open site in two parts. There are 868 pitches with 200 for tourers in a separate area, with shade from established trees. These level pitches with some shade are in two sizes, access is good with well maintained gravel and tarmac roads. The main side of the site is centred around charming historic buildings, including a beautiful, but mysterious, locked and long unused chapel. Nearby is a huge, irregular lagoon-style pool with a bridge to a palm decorated island (lifeguards) and an excellent, safe paddling pool. A large complex including a bar, restaurant, takeaway and entertainment areas overlooks the pool. The sporting facilities and fitness areas across the minor road are superb. Here there is another swimming pool and all manner of sport and training is available on high quality facilities. There is a great miniclub for children and a huge games room (ten pool tables) There is entertainment in high season and reception can book excursions and visits to attractions.

Facilities

Two sound toilet blocks are here for tourers, ignore the block for the permanent pitches. Very good facilities for disabled visitors and pleasant baby rooms. Washing machines and dryers. Motorcaravan service point. Large supermarket. Bars, restaurant, snack bar and takeaway. Swimming pools. Playgrounds. Well equipped games room. Tennis. Squash. Minigolf. Spa room and gym. Entertainment programme. Hairdresser. Internet. WiFi (code). ATM. Bicycle hire. Torches useful. Dogs only in designated areas. Barbeques allowed. Off site: Riding 1 km. Beach 3 km. Fishing, boat launching, golf 3 km.

Open: 27 May - 11 September, weekends only 4 March - 8 December.

Directions

Site is at Santa Christiana d'Aro, 3 km. from the sea at San Feliu. From AP7 E15 (Girona - Barcelona) take exit 7 and C65 San Filiu road. Site is well signed at the Sant Christina d'Aro roundabout 3 km. from San Filiu. GPS: 41.811167, 3.018217

Charges guide

Per unit incl. 2 persons and electricity	€ 17,00 - € 46,00
extra person (over 1 yr)	€ 6,00 - € 8,00

Discounts for longer stays.

Camping

Mas Sant Josep

On route from Santa Cristina to Platja d'Aro, km.2
E-17246 • SANTA CRISTINA D'ARO
Tel.: (34) 972 83 51 08
Fax: (34) 972 83 70 18
Alle bungalows gerenoveerd
www.campingmassantjosep.com
info@campingmassantjosep.com

Costa Brava

ISO 14001-2004   yelloh! VILLAGE

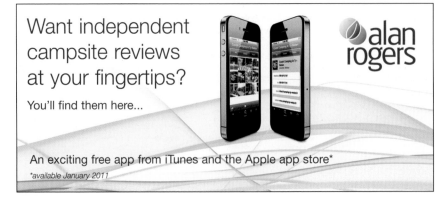

Santa Susana
Camping Bon Repos

Malgrat de Mar, E-08398 Santa Susana (Barcelona) T: 937 678 475. E: info@campingbonrepos.com

alanrogers.com/ES82350

If you enjoy the hustle and bustle of the Costa Brava in summer, then Bon Repos is ideal, if a little expensive. It is a long, narrow coastal site with many pitches along the length of the attractive fine sandy beach with direct access and no fence. The 500 pitches are of reasonable size, flat with a sand surface and lots of shade, and with 10A electricity. The railway runs close along one side of the site, which is good for train spotters but does create a noise problem. The beach is a strong point of the site having rocky outcrops and close by is the bar/restaurant with huge terrace.

Facilities

The two sanitary blocks are dated but clean. The number of showers is low and we suspect they are extremely busy at peak periods. Cold water at washbasins. Units for disabled campers. Baby room. Washing machines and dryers. Motorcaravan services. Supermarket. Restaurant. Chicken bar. Swimming pools (with lifeguard). Play area. Barbecue area. Tennis. Bicycle hire. Entertainment and happy hour. Internet access and WiFi. ATM. Torches useful. Off site: Public transport 500 m. Boat launching 200 m. Bicycle hire 1 km. Riding 3 km. Golf 5 km.

Open: All year.

Directions

From A7 exit 9 (A19 exit 22) take road to Malgrat de Mar. Then turn south on coast road for Santa Susanna. Follow obvious campsite signs – they lead to site through a high tunnel under the railway line on a minor beach road. GPS: 41.6314, 2.7199

Charges guide

Per unit incl. 2 persons and electricity	€ 16,41 - € 46,90
extra person	€ 1,82 - € 5,20
child	€ 1,43 - € 4,10
dog	€ 1,10 - € 3,15

Sitges
Camping El Garrofer

Ctra 246 km 39, E-08870 Sitges (Barcelona) T: 938 941 780. E: info@garroferpark.com

alanrogers.com/ES83920

This large pine covered site, alongside fields of vines, is 800 m. from the beach close to the pleasant town of Sitges. This is an attractive resort with seaside entertainments and is well worth exploring. The site has over 500 pitches of which 380 with 6A electricity are for tourers, including 28 with water used for large motorcaravans. Everything is kept clean and the pitches are tidy and shaded. The amenity buildings are along the site perimeter next to the road which absorbs most of the road noise. The permanent pitches are grouped in a completely separate area.

Facilities

Two of the three sanitary blocks have been refurbished and provide roomy showers and special bright facilities for children. Separate baby room with bath. Good facilities for disabled campers. Laundry. Bar/restaurant. Shop (reception in low season). Swimming pool (30/4-31/09). Tennis. Play area for older children and fenced play area for toddlers. Bicycle hire. Boules. Off site: Bus from outside site to Barcelona. Golf, riding and fishing 500 m.

Open: 28 January - 18 December.

Directions

From A16/C32 autopista take exit 26 towards Vilanova/St Pere Ribes. From Tarragona, go under autopista, around roundabout and back to roundabout on the other side to pick up site sign (towards Sitges). Follow C-246a to km. 39; site entrance is beside old large tree. Look for the flags. GPS: 41.23352, 1.78112

Charges 2011

Per unit incl. 2 persons and electricity	€ 23,75 - € 35,40

Solsona
Camping El Solsones

Ctra Sant Llorenc km 2, E-25280 Solsona (Lleida) T: 973 482 861. E: info@campingsolsones.com

alanrogers.com/ES91230

Situated on a hillside, two kilometres from Solsona, this all year site has pleasant views of the hills on three sides and lots of mature trees giving a pleasant green shady appearance. With a lovely Spanish feel, it would be a pleasant spot for a short stay during any season. There are many weekend units here, and although only 72 of the 269 pitches are for touring (22 for caravans or motorcaravans and 50 for tents), we were told that finding a pitch was unlikely to be a problem. They are in separate sections of the site and are slightly sloping, with shade and 6/10A electricity.

Facilities

Modern sanitary facilities with free hot water. Motorcaravan services. Supermarket. Restaurant and bar (24/6-15/9 and winter weekends). Swimming pool with lifeguard (24/6-12/9). Excellent sports complex. Minigolf. Tennis. Bicycle hire. Play area. Mini club. Pétanque. Aviary. Picnic area. WiFi over site. Dogs are not accepted. Off site: Golf, riding and skiing nearby. Solsona is interesting with good bars, restaurants and cafés.

Open: 8 January - 8 December.

Directions

Solsona is 45 km. northwest of Manresa, along the C55 and is on the C26 Lleida/Andorra - Barga road. Site is 2 km. out of town on the LV4241 signed to Sant Llorenc de Morunys and Ski Port del Comte. GPS: 42.01294, 1.51585

Charges guide

Per unit incl. 2 persons and electricity	€ 29,00 - € 37,60
extra person	€ 6,20

For latest campsite news, availability and prices visit
alanrogers.com

Tarragona
Camping Tamarit Park Resort

N340a km 1172, Tamarit, E-43008 Tarragona (Tarragona) T: 977 650 128. E: resort@tamarit.com

alanrogers.com/ES84830

This is a marvellous, beach-side site, attractively situated at the foot of Tamarit castle at one end of a superb one kilometre long beach of superb, fine sand. Landscaped with lush Mediterranean shrubs and studded with pines and palms, home to mischievous red squirrels. The 470 good sized pitches have 10A electricity (most have water). 50 are virtually on the beach and are very popular. On hard sand and grass, some are attractively separated by hedging and shaded by trees. The management and staff here are very keen to please and standards are very high. The charming restaurant and snack bar both serve typical Spanish dishes whilst enjoying superb views of the sandy beach and castle. The vast, attractively designed, lagoon-type swimming pool and paddling pool boasts a restaurant, snack bar, two bars, and sun terraces. It is excellent. The site boundary with the beach has three controlled accesses. Tamarit would be a good choice for watersport enthusiasts or a family holiday by the sea. The early morning sun shining on the blue sea and the golden stone of Tamarit castle high above is a memorable sight!

Facilities

The high quality sanitary blocks (two heated) are modern and tiled. Hot water is available throughout. Private bathrooms to rent. Laundry facilities. Motorcaravan services. Fridge hire. Gas supplies. Supermarket, boutique, bars, restaurant and takeaway. Bakery. Wellness area. Swimming pool (all season). Tennis courts. Pétanque. Bicycle hire. Minigolf. Playground. Sports zone. Club room with bar. Miniclub. Entertainment programme all season. Fishing. Internet access and WiFi (code). Pets allowed. Gas only barbecues. Off site: Village 1.5 km. along beach. Golf 8 km. Tarragona 9 km. Riding 15 km. Port Aventura 16 km.

Open: 8 April - 16 October.

Directions

From A7 take exit 32 towards Tarragona and continue for 4.5 km. At roundabout (km. 1172) turn back towards Atafulla/Tamarit and after 200 m. turn right to Tamarit (beside Caledonia Bungalow Park). Take care over railway bridge, then immediately sharp left. Site is on left after 1 km. having passed another campsite (Trillas Tamarit). GPS: 41.1316, 1.3610

Charges guide

Per unit incl. 2 persons	€ 12,00 - € 80,00
extra person	€ 6,00
child (6-12 yrs)	free - € 4,00
dog	free - € 5,00

Discounts for students, pensioners, large families and longer stays in low season. Minimum stay 7 nights 1/7-29/8.

5059

Special Offers! Midweek Pensioners Complete Week

First Class Family Seaside Campsite
Open from 08/04/11 to 16/10/11
www.tamarit.com

Platja Tamarit | Ctra N340a Km 1172 | 43008 Tarragona | Costa Daurada | España T. +34 977 650 128 | resort@tamarit.com

For latest campsite news, availability and prices visit
alanrogers.com

Tarragona
Camping Las Palmeras

Ctra N340 km 1168, E-43080 Tarragona (Tarragona) T: 977 208 081. E: laspalmeras@laspalmeras.com
alanrogers.com/ES84850

Situated amongst pine, poplar and palm trees, running parallel to a fine, white sandy beach, Camping Las Palmeras has a wonderful location. The final approach is under the railway (3.5 m) with a sharp turn into the parking area. The site is very long and thin (1.5 km. so bicycles are handy) along the shore. Most of the 700 pitches are on grass with plenty of shade. All have access to 5A electricity, although long leads may be necessary in places. For its beachside location alone, Las Palmeras is worthy of a visit and, with so many facilities on offer, it is a lively site offering something for the whole family. There is some noise from the frequent trains, which run 24 hours. The air-conditioned reception is smart and efficiently managed by helpful and welcoming staff.

Facilities

Four large toilet blocks attractively tiled in a traditional style, are evenly located and maintained to a high standard. Open style washbasins and good sized shower cubicles. Baby rooms. Laundry in each block. Shop. Bar and beach restaurant. Smaller bar and snack bar (high season only). Two swimming pools (June-Sept). Tennis. Two large play areas. Children's club in high season. Internet terminals and WiFi (code). Off site: Town 4 km. Riding 6 km. Golf 5 km.

Open: 15 March - 15 October.

Directions

Las Palmeras is easily accessed from the N340 (Barcelona - Tarragona) and is signed after the 1169 km. marker. Beware of the sharp bend at the entrance. GPS: 41.13019, 1.3117

Charges guide

Per unit incl. electricity	€ 12,00 - € 29,00
person	€ 6,00 - € 10,50
child (under 10 yrs)	€ 5,00 - € 7,50
dog	€ 3,00 - € 5,00

Tarragona
Camping Torre de la Mora

Ctra N340 km 1171, E-43080 Tarragona (Tarragona) T: 977 650 277. E: campmora@tinet.fut.es
alanrogers.com/ES84860

Located on a promontory in a pleasant corner of the Costa Daurada with a village like atmosphere, Torre de la Mora takes advantage of its wonderful location, offering some pitches with beautiful views over the white sandy beaches and rocky promontories of the coastline. The hinterland is pine forest and there are areas where you can pitch a tent, access electricity (6A) and feel close to nature. The 200 touring pitches vary in just about every way, some are on the lower flat area, including a few with beach frontage, others are on steep terraces around the promontory. Many of the higher pitches around the old coastal defence fort and building have amazing views. It is important to select a pitch related to your level of fitness as the higher pitches and some of the lower terraces require an energetic approach (children should be supervised). We spoke to some campers who enjoyed Torre de la Mora so much they had been happily returning to the site for years. Some areas of the site reflect its age, the sports area is across a small road, which has a pleasant large pool in a garden-like setting.

Facilities

Two large and three small sanitary blocks have been refurbished and are kept clean. There is a mixture of washing facilities, which have hot water, but this fades at peak periods. Facilities for disabled campers (careful selection of pitch is required). Washing machine. Motorcaravan services. Supermarket. Restaurant. Swimming pool and sports area. Play area. Entertainment. WiFi (code). Torches useful. Barbecues not permitted. Pets welcome. Off site: Pretty beach town outside the gate. Fishing. Bicycle hire 1 km. Golf 2 km. Riding 3 km. Boat launching 8 km.

Open: 18 March - 31 October.

Directions

From A7 (Barcelona - Tarragona) take exit 32, then N340 towards Tarragona. Turn off for Punta del la Mora and site is well signed approaching the village. The final approach is via some narrow streets so watch for one way signs and there is an unusual entry through a high wire fence alongside road. GPS: 41.128, 1.344

Charges guide

Per unit incl. 1 person and electricity	€ 20,35 - € 38,40
extra person	€ 4,60 - € 9,30
child (3-11 yrs)	€ 3,40 - € 5,35
dog	€ 1,80 - € 3,00

For latest campsite news, availability and prices visit
alanrogers.com

Torroella de Montgrí
Camping El Delfin Verde

Ctra de Torroella de Montgrí, E-17257 Torroella de Montgrí (Girona) T: **972 758 454**
E: info@eldelfinverde.com **alanrogers.com/ES80800**

A popular and high quality site in a quiet location, El Delfin Verde has its own long beach stretching along its frontage where activities such as scuba diving are organised. A prime feature of this site is an attractive large pool in the shape of a dolphin with a total area of 1,800 sq.m. This is a large site with 1,265 touring pitches and around 6,000 visitors at peak times. It is well managed by friendly staff. Level grass pitches are 100-110 sq.m. and marked, with many separated by small fences and hedging. All have electricity (5/6A) and access to water points. A stream runs through the centre of the site. There is shade in some of the older parts and a particularly pleasant area of pine trees in the centre provides marked but not separated pitches (sandy and not so level). The pool has two island areas, one containing a huge fountain which can be lit at night. In the main season an elevated area with a large bar, full restaurant and a separate takeaway give wonderful views over the huge pool. There is a further restaurant with slightly cheaper, good value food in the main complex with an open air arena for entertainment. El Delfin Verde is a large and happy holiday site with many good facilities, sports and a free family entertainment programme in season. It is well worth considering for a Costa Brava holiday. Used by British tour operators (60 pitches).

Facilities

Six excellent large and refurbished toilet blocks plus a seventh smaller block, all with resident cleaners, have showers using desalinated water and some washbasins in cabins. Laundry facilities. Motorcaravan services. Supermarket and shops. Swimming pools with lifeguard (from 1/5). Two restaurants, grills and pizzerias. Three bars. 'La Vela' barbecue and party area. Large sports area. 2 km. exercise track. Dancing and entertainment weekly in season. Excursions. Bicycle hire. Minigolf. Extensive new playground. Trampolines. Beach access. Scuba diving. Fishing. Hairdresser. Car servicing. Gas supplies. Internet café. WiFi. Dogs are not accepted in high season (11/7-14/8). Off site: Golf (20% discount) 4 km. Riding 4 km.

Open: 16 April - 25 September.

Directions

Torroella de Montgri is close to the coast, east of Girona. From A7/E15 take exit 6 and C66 (Palafrugell). Then the GI642 east to Parlava and turn north on C31 (L'Escala). Cross river Ter and turn east on C31 (Ulla and Torroella de Montgri). Site signed off the C31 and has a long approach road. Watch for white dolphin marker and flags on the left. GPS: 42.01197, 3.18807

Charges guide

Per unit incl. 2 persons and electricity	€ 30,50 - € 55,00
extra person	€ 4,75 - € 5,50
child (2-9 yrs)	€ 4,00 - € 5,00
dog (excl 10/7-14/8)	€ 4,00

Special offers on long stays in low season.

Tossa de Mar
Camping Cala Llevadó

Ctra GI-682 de Tossa a Lloret pk. 18,9, E-17320 Tossa de Mar (Girona) T: 972 340 314
E: info@calallevado.com alanrogers.com/ES82000

For splendour of position, Cala Llevadó can compare with almost any in this guide. A beautifully situated cliff-side site, enjoying fine views of the sea and coast below. It is shaped something like half a bowl with steep slopes. High up in the site with a superb aspect, is the attractive restaurant/bar with a large terrace overlooking the pleasant swimming pool directly below. There are terraced, flat areas for caravans and tents (with 10/16A electricity) on the upper levels of the two slopes, with a great many individual pitches for tents scattered around the site. Some of these pitches have fantastic settings and views. In some areas cars may be required to park separately. Many of the 577 touring pitches are available for caravans. There are a few tour operator pitches (45) and 26 bungalows. The steepness of the site would make access difficult for disabled visitors or those with limited mobility. One beach is for all manner of watersports within a buoyed area and has a subaqua diving school. Some other pleasant little coves can also be reached by climbing down (with care!).

Facilities

Four very well equipped toilet blocks are immaculately maintained and well spaced around the site. Baby baths. Laundry facilities. Motorcaravan services. Gas supplies. Fridge hire. Supermarket. Restaurant/bar (5/5-28/9). Swimming and paddling pools. Three play areas. Botanic garden. Entertainment for children (4-12 yrs). Sailing, water skiing and windsurfing school. Fishing. Excursions. Internet access and WiFi. Torches needed in some areas. Off site: Bicycle hire 3 km. Riding 10 km. Large complex adjacent for sports, activities and swimming.

Open: 1 May - 30 September.

Directions

Cala Llevadó is southeast of Girona. Leave AP7/E15 at exit 7 to the C65 Sant Feliu road then take C35 southeast to GI 681 to Tossa de Mare. Site is signed off the GI 682 Lloret - Tossa road at km. 18.9, about 3 km. from Tossa. Route avoids difficult coastal road. GPS: 41.71282, 2.90623

Charges guide

Per unit incl. 2 persons and electricity (6A)	€ 29,00 - € 49,30
extra person	€ 5,80 - € 9,75

Costa Brava
Tossa de Mar

Cala Llevadó
camping ★★★★

Choose sea and mountain
Choose **Cala Llevadó**

Cordenadas: 41° 42' 47" N - 2° 54' 23" E
41,713056 Latitud - 2,906389 Longitud
Ctra. GI-682 de Tossa a Lloret, km 18,9 - 17320 Tossa de Mar
Tel. (00-34) 972 34 03 14 - Fax. (00-34) 972 34 11 87
E-mail: info@calallevado.com
www.calallevado.com

Vilanova de Prades
Camping & Bungalow Park Serra de Prades

Sant Antoni s/n, E-43439 Vilanova de Prades (Tarragona) T: 977 869 050. E: info@serradeprades.com
alanrogers.com/ES85060

On the edge of the village of Vilanova, nestling in granite foothills with superb views from its elevation of 950 m, this is a welcoming and peaceful site. The 215 pitches are on terraces formed with natural stone and with good access. With 120 for touring units (all with 6A electricity), the remainder are occupied by seasonal units. The upper tent pitches have wonderful views although the sanitary facilities are on the lower level. Hedges and trees separate pitches providing a pleasant green environment and some shade, and 90 per cent of pitches have electricity. The site has won awards for its approach to ecology.

Facilities

The modern, heated, well equipped toilet block has washbasins in cabins and is well maintained. Facilities for disabled visitors and babies. Laundry facilities. Motorcaravan service point. Shop. Bar and good quality restaurant. Swimming pool (open and heated 24/6-5/9). Gym. Internet points. Archery. Quad bike and 4x4 hire. Paintball. Tennis. Riding with guided treks. Activities organised. Sports area. Entertainment in season. Safety deposit. Exchange facilities. Gas supplies. Torches required in some areas. WiFi. Off site: Golf 12 km.

Open: All year.

Directions

From Tarragona on the AP2 take exit 9 (Montblanc) and continue towards Lleida on N240. At km. 48 just west of Vimbodi, turn left towards Vallclara and Vilanova de Prades. Site on right after roundabout at entrance to village. From Lleida leave the AP2 at exit 8 towards Tarragona on N240, then as above from km. 48 just before Vimbodi. GPS: 41.3497, 0.95852

Charges guide

Per unit incl. 2 persons and electricity	€ 32,30

Camping Cheques accepted.

For latest campsite news, availability and prices visit
alanrogers.com

Vilanova i la Geltru

Camping Vilanova Park

185

Ctra de l'Arboc km 2.5, E-08800 Vilanova i la Geltru (Barcelona) T: 938 933 402. E: info@vilanovapark.es
alanrogers.com/ES83900

Sitting on the terrace of the bustling but comfortable restaurant at Vilanova Park, it is difficult to believe that in 1908 this was a Catalan farm and then, quite lacking in trees, it was known as 'Rock Farm'. Since then imaginative planting has led to there being literally thousands of trees and gloriously colourful shrubs making a most attractive, large campsite, with an impressive range of high quality amenities and facilities open all year. There are 344 marked pitches for touring units in separate areas. All have 6A electricity, 185 also have water and some larger pitches (100 sq.m) also have drainage. The terrain, hard surfaced and mostly on very gently sloping ground, has many trees and considerable shade. At present there are 786 pitches with a significant proportion occupied by bungalows and chalets carefully designed to fit into the environment. The site is used by tour operators (190 pitches). The really good amenities include a new second pool higher up in the site with marvellous views across the town to the sea and an indoor pool, sauna, jacuzzi and gym. Here there is also a second, more intimate restaurant for that special romantic dinner overlooking the twinkling evening lights. The original pool has water jets and a coloured floodlit fountain playing at night time, which complement the dancing and entertainment taking place on the stage in the courtyard overlooking the pool. An unusual attraction is a Nature Park and mini-zoo with deer and bird life, which has very pleasant picnic areas and views.

Facilities

All toilet blocks are of excellent quality, can be heated and have washbasins (over half in cabins) with free hot water, and others of standard type with cold water. Serviced laundry. Motorcaravan services. Supermarket. Souvenir shop. Restaurants. Bar with simple meals. Swimming pools (outdoor 1/4-15/10, indoor all year). Wellness centre including sauna, jacuzzi and gym. Play areas. Sports field. Games room. Bicycle hire. Tennis. ATM and exchange facilities. Off site: Fishing 4 km. Golf 5 km. Good train service from Vilanova to Barcelona, not so good the other way (to Tarragona and Salou). Bus service direct to Barcelona. Vilanova town and beach are 4 km. (local bus service).

Open: All year.

Directions

Site is 4 km. northwest of Vilanova i la Geltru towards L'Arboc (BV2115). From the A7 Tarragona - Barcelona take exit 29 onto C15 to Vilanova, then C31 El Vendrell road (Km. 153) then onto BV2115. GPS: 41.23237, 1.69092

Charges 2011

Per unit incl. 2 persons	
and electricity	€ 27,20 - € 46,70
extra person	€ 5,60 - € 10,20
child (4-12 yrs)	€ 3,20 - € 6,10
dog	€ 6,00 - € 12,00

Camping Cheques accepted.

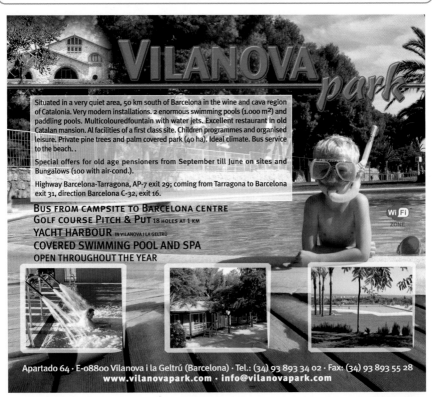

Situated in a very quiet area, 50 km south of Barcelona in the wine and cava region of Catalonia. Very modern installations. 2 enormous swimming pools (1.000 m²) and paddling pools. Multicoloured fountain with water jets. Excellent restaurant in old Catalan mansion. Al facilities of a first class site. Children programmes and organised leisure. Private pine trees and palm covered park (40 ha). Ideal climate. Bus service to the beach. .

Special offers for old age pensioners from September till June on sites and Bungalows (100 with air-cond.)

Highway Barcelona-Tarragona, AP-7 exit 29; coming from Tarragona to Barcelona exit 31, direction Barcelona C-32, exit 16.

BUS FROM CAMPSITE TO BARCELONA CENTRE
GOLF COURSE PITCH & PUT 18 HOLES AT 1 KM
YACHT HARBOUR IN VILANOVA I LA GELTRÚ
COVERED SWIMMING POOL AND SPA
OPEN THROUGHOUT THE YEAR

Apartado 64 · E-08800 Vilanova i la Geltrú (Barcelona) · Tel.: (34) 93 893 34 02 · Fax: (34) 93 893 55 28
www.vilanovapark.com · info@vilanovapark.com

For latest campsite news, availability and prices visit
alanrogers.com

Been to any good campsites lately?
We have

You'll find them here...

This Mediterranean region is famous for its magnificent orange groves and beautiful long, sandy beaches. Centuries of Moorish presence have resulted in a profound Hispano-Moorish heritage.

VALENCIANA IS MADE UP OF THE PROVINCES OF CASTELLON, VALENCIA AND ALICANTE

THE CAPITAL OF THE REGION IS VALENCIA

La Costa del Azahar (Orange-blossom Coast) stretches from Vinaros to Almanzora, with the great port of Valencia in the centre. Orange groves grow right down to the coast, particularly in the northern section. Good beaches can be found around Benicassim and Peñíscola. South of Valencia, the Costa Blanca derives its name from its 170 miles or so of silvery-white beaches – some of the best beaches are to be found on this coast, especially between Gandía and Benidorm. As a result, it is one of the most popular tourist areas in Spain. The capital city of Valencia boasts a great nightlife and plays host to numerous festivals held throughout the year, including the unique fiesta of Las Fallas de Saint Joseph, when enormous papier-mâché sculptures are set ablaze. Throughout it all are bullfights, music and fireworks. Alicante, the capital of the province of the same name, is dominated by the great Moorish castle of Santa Barbara, which offers marvellous views of the entire city. It also has several beaches in and around the town.

Places of interest

Castellón de la Plana: Santa Maria cathedral.

El Puig: monastery, Museum of Print and Graphics (world's smallest book).

La Albufera: vast lagoon, home to 250 species of bird.

Morella: medieval fortress town, dinosaur museum.

Oropesa: 16th-century Tower of the King.

Peñíscola: medieval castle.

Cuisine of the region

Rice is the dominant ingredient, grown locally in paddy fields; the most famous dish is the *Paella Valenciana*. Soups and stews known locally as *ollas* are popular and seafood is readily available. Tiger nut milk is a soft drink exclusive to this region, usually accompanied by *fartons* (local pastries).

Arnadí: dessert with pumpkin and sweet potato.

Arroz al horno: rice, baked with chickpeas.

Arroz con costra: meat-based paella topped with baked egg crust.

Arroz negro: rice cooked with squid.

Bajoques farcides: stuffed peppers.

Olla recapte: with potatoes and pork.

Turrón: made of nuts and honey, either soft and flaky or hard like nougat.

CATALUNYA

0.   25   50   75   100 kms

ARAGON

MORELLA

VINAROS

PENISCOLA

A7/E15

TERUEL

ALCOSSEBRE

RIBERA DE CABANES
OROPESA DEL MAR
BENICASIM

CASTELLON DE LA PLANA

NAVAJAS

MONCOFA

**CASTILLA-
LA MANCHA**

**COMUNIDAD
VALENCIANA**

VILLARGORDO DEL CABRIEL

A3/E901   VALENCIA

CULLERA

A7/E15

ALBACETE

GANDIA
OLIVA

CAMPELL   JAVEA

BOCAIRENT

MORAIRA

ALTEA
BENIDORM
VILLAJOYOSA
EL CAMPELLO
ALICANTE

MURCIA

A7/E15

CARAVACA DE LE CRUZ
MURCIA

LA MARINA
GUARDAMAR DEL SEGURA

A37

SAN MIGUEL DE SALINAS

PILAR DE LA HORADADA
SAN PEDRO DEL PINATAR

Comunidad Valenciana

For latest campsite news, availability and prices visit
alanrogers.com

Alcossebre

Camping Playa Tropicana

Playa Tropicana, E-12579 Alcossebre (Castelló) T: 964 412 463. E: info@playatropicana.com
alanrogers.com/ES85600

Playa Tropicana has been given a tropical theme with scores of 'Romanesque' white statues around the site including in the sanitary blocks. The site has 300 marked pitches separated by lines of flowering bushes under mature trees. The pitches vary in size (50-90 sq.m), most are shaded and there are electricity connections throughout (some need long leads). There are 50 pitches with shared water and drainage on their boundaries. The site has a delightful position alongside a good sandy beach.

Facilities

Three sanitary blocks delightfully decorated, fully equipped and of excellent standard, include washbasins in private cabins. Baby baths and facilities for disabled visitors. Washing machine. Motorcaravan services. Gas supplies. Large supermarket. Superb restaurant, a little expensive. (Easter-late Sept). Swimming pool (18x11 m) and children's pool. Playground. Bicycle hire. Children's club. Fishing. Torches necessary in some areas. No TVs allowed in July/Aug. Dogs are not accepted. Off site: Fishing and watersports on the beaches. Riding and boat launching 3 km. Golf 40 km.

Open: All year.

Directions

Alcoceber (or Alcossebre) is between Peníscola and Oropesa. Turn off N340 at 1018 km. marker towards Alcossebre on CV142. Just before entering town proceed through two sets of traffic lights and turn right immediately after the second set, follow the road to the coast and site is 2.5 km. Avoid narrow and uneven alternative route given by satnav. GPS: 40.222, 0.267

Charges guide

Per unit incl. 2 persons	€ 24,50 - € 52,50
extra person	€ 5,00 - € 7,00

Alcossebre

Camping Ribamar

Partida Ribamar s/n, E-12579 Alcossebre (Castelló) T: 964 761 163. E: info@campingribamar.com
alanrogers.com/ES85610

Camping Ribamar is tucked away within the National Park of the Sierra de Irta, to the north of Alcossebre, and with direct access to a rugged beach. There are two grades of pitches on offer here. A number of 'standard' pitches are available for small tents. These pitches of around 30 sq.m. have electrical connections. The majority of pitches are larger (90-100 sq.m) and are classed 'premium', with electricity and a water supply. A number of chalets (with air conditioning) are available for rent. Leisure facilities here include a large swimming pool plus delightful children's pool and a paddling pool. A main amenities building is adjacent and houses the site's slightly sterile bar/restaurant and shop. The Sierra de Irta is a magnificent landscape of intense colours. Although little over two hours' drive south of Barcelona, this is a very under populated region with some excellent long distance footpaths and cycle paths. Alcossebre is a delightful resort town which has retained its Spanish identity unlike some of the larger resorts to the north. The town has three Blue Flag beaches and a wealth of cafés and restaurants.

Facilities

One spotlessly clean toilet block with facilities for babies and campers with disabilities. Dishwashing and laundry facilities. Bar. Restaurant. Shop. Swimming pool. Paddling pool. Multisports terrain. Tennis. 5-a-side football. Boules. Paddle court. Cycle hire. Play area. Tourist information. Chalets for rent. Direct access to rocky beach. WiFi. Off site: Alcossebre 3 km. Golf. Fishing. Coastal walks.

Open: All year.

Directions

Leave the AP7 motorway at exit 44 and follow signs to Alcossebre using N340 and CV142. The site can be found to the north of the town. Follow signs to Sierra de Irta and then site, which is 2.5 km. along a dusty, gravel track. GPS: 40.270282, 0.306729

Charges guide

Per unit incl. 2 persons	
and electricity	€ 18,80 - € 44,30
extra person	€ 3,50 - € 5,00
child (3-12 yrs)	€ 2,60 - € 4,20

Altea

Camping Cap Blanch

Playa de Cap Blanch 25, E-03590 Altea (Alacant) T: **965 845 946**. E: capblanch@ctv.es

alanrogers.com/ES86870

This small site was untidy when seen, but it has direct access across a small but busy road to the pebble beach and is within a few hundred yards of all Albir's shops and restaurants. The 250 pitches on flat stone and gravel are of a good size with 5/10A electricity (extra charge for 10A). The site tends to be full in winter (January and February are the peak months) and is very popular with several nationalities as prices have not risen for four years. There is considerable traffic noise from the roads along two sides of the site and it is overlooked by the high-rise flats nearby.

Facilities

The neglected sanitary block can be heated and provides tired facilities including some washbasins in cabins, separate baby facilities and a room for disabled visitors (both these accessed by key). Motorcaravan services. Gas supplies. Laundry. Rustic bar and restaurant on seafront (open to public). Takeaway. Playground. Tennis. Boules. Fitness centre. Organised entertainment and courses. ATM. Off site: Restaurants, shops and commercial centre close. Golf 500 m. Bicycle hire 1 km. Riding 5 km.

Open: All year.

Directions

Site is on the Albir - Altea coast road and can be reached from either end. From N332, north or south, watch for sign Playa del Albir and proceed through Albir to the coast road. Site is on north side of Albir, well signed along one-way system alongside sea. GPS: 38.5777, -0.06461

Charges guide

Per person	€ 3,90 - € 6,00
pitch incl. car	€ 8,45 - € 13,00
electricity	€ 3,25 - € 5,00

Benicasim

Bonterra Park

Avenida de Barcelona 47, E-12560 Benicasim (Castelló) T: **964 300 007**. E: info@bonterrapark.com

alanrogers.com/ES85800

If you are looking for a town site which is not too crowded and has very good facilities, this one may be for you. It is a 300 m. walk to a good beach – and parking is not too difficult. The site has 320 pitches (70-90 sq.m), all with electricity (6/10A) and a variety of bungalows, some attractively built in brick. There are dedicated 'green' pitches for tents. Bonterra has a clean and neat appearance with tarmac roads, gravel covered pitches, palms, grass and a number of trees which give good shade. Overhead sunshades are provided for the more open pitches in summer. There is a little road and rail noise. The site has an attractive pool complex including a covered pool for the winter months. The beach is good for scuba diving and snorkelling (hire facilities available at Benicasim). This is a well run, Mediterranean style site with English spoken by reception staff. It is usefully located for visiting attractions such as the Carmelite monastery at Desierto de las Palmas, 6 km. distant or the historic town of Castellón.

Facilities

Four attractive, well maintained sanitary blocks provide some private cabins, washbasins with hot water, others with cold. Baby and dog showers. Facilities for disabled visitors. Laundry. Motorcaravan services. Restaurant/bar. Shop. Swimming and paddling pools. Swimming pool (heated Sept-June). Playground (some concrete bases). Tennis. Multisport court. Gym. Disco. Bicycle hire. Miniclub. Satellite TV. Internet access (WiFi). Dogs are not accepted in July/Aug. Off site: Town facilities. Sandy beach and fishing 500 m. Riding 3 km. Boat launching 4 km. Golf 12 km. Nature Park.

Open: All year.

Directions

Site is on the quiet old main road running through Benicasim. From either direction leave the N340 at km. 987. At roundabout turn left and travel for about 1.5 km. to site on the left (white painted walls). Site is well signed. GPS: 40.05708, 0.07432

Charges 2011

Per unit incl. 2 persons and electricity	€ 24,82 - € 52,08
extra person	€ 4,15 - € 6,05
child (0-9 yrs)	€ 3,53 - € 4,93

Less in low season and special long stay rates excl. July/Aug.

For latest campsite news, availability and prices visit

alanrogers.com

Benidorm

Camping Villasol

Avenida Bernat de Sarria no. 13., E-03503 Benidorm (Alacant) T: 965 850 422. E: info@camping-villasol.com
alanrogers.com/ES86810

Benidorm is increasingly popular for winter stays and Villasol is a genuinely good, purpose built modern site. Many of the 309 well separated pitches are arranged on wide terraces which afford views of the mountains surrounding Benidorm. All pitches (80-85 sq.m) have electricity and satellite TV connections, with 160 with full services for seasonal use. Shade is mainly artificial. Reservations are only accepted for winter stays of over three months (from 1 October).

Facilities

Modern toilet blocks provide free, controllable hot water to showers and washbasins and British WCs. Good facilities for disabled visitors. Laundry facilities. Good value restaurant. Bar. Shop. Swimming pools, outdoor and indoor. Satellite TV. Playground. Evening entertainment programme. Safes. Dogs are not accepted. Off site: Fishing and bicycle hire 1.3 km. Golf 8 km.

Open: All year.

Directions

From autopista exit 65 (Benidorm) and turn left at second set of traffic lights. After 1 km. at another set of lights turn right, then right again at next lights. Site is on right in 400 m. From northern end of N332 bypass follow signs for Benidorm Playa Levante. In 500 m. at traffic lights turn left, then right at next lights. Site is 400 m. on right.
GPS: 38.538, -0.119

Charges 2011

Per person	€ 5,50 - € 7,20
pitch incl. car	€ 11,20 - € 26,40
electricity	€ 4,15

Benidorm

Camping Benisol

Avenida de la Comunidad Valenciana s/n, E-03500 Benidorm (Alacant) T: 965 851 673
E: campingbenisol@yahoo.es alanrogers.com/ES86830

Camping Benisol is a well developed and peaceful site with lush, green vegetation and a mountain background. Mature hedges and trees afford privacy to each pitch and some artificial shade is provided where necessary. There are 298 pitches of which around 115 are for touring units (60-80 sq.m). All have electrical hook-ups (4/6A) and 75 have drainage. All the connecting roads are now surfaced with tarmac. Some daytime road noise should be expected. The site has an excellent restaurant serving traditional Spanish food at great prices, with a pretty, shaded terrace overlooking the pool.

Facilities

Modern sanitary facilities, heated in winter and kept very clean, have free, solar heated hot water to washbasins, showers and sinks. Laundry facilities. Gas supplies. Restaurant with terrace and bar (all year, closed one day a week). Shop. Swimming pool (Easter-Nov). Small, old style play area. Minigolf. Jogging track. Tennis. Golf driving range. ATM. WiFi. Off site: Riding 1 km. Bicycle hire 3 km. Fishing (sea) 3 km. Golf 14 km. Bus route.

Open: All year.

Directions

Site is northeast of Benidorm. Exit N332 at 152 km. marker and take turn signed Playa Levant. Site is 100 m. on left off the main road, well signed.
GPS: 38.559, -0.097

Charges guide

Per person	€ 4,95 - € 5,25
pitch	€ 13,25 - € 18,10
electricity	€ 2,80
No credit cards.	

Benidorm

Camping Caravaning El Raco

Avenida Doctor Severo Ochoa 35, E-03503 Benidorm (Alacant) T: 965 868 552. E: info@campingraco.com
alanrogers.com/ES86850

This purpose built site with good facilities provides about 597 pitches (90 for touring units). There is wide access from the Rincon de Loix road. The site is situated 1.5 km. from the town, Levante beach and promenade. It has wide tarmac roads and pitches of 80 sq.m. or more, separated by low cypress hedging and some trees which provide some shade. Satellite TV connections are provided to each pitch and there are 90 with all services including (10A) electricity.

Facilities

Four large toilet blocks are well equipped. Facilities for disabled visitors and babies. Dishwashing sinks. Laundry facilities. Gas supplies. Motorcaravan services. Large restaurant. Bar. Well stocked shop. Busy bar with TV also open to public and restaurant. Outdoor swimming pool, no slides or diving board (1/4-31/10). Indoor heated pool (1/11-31/3). Playground. ATM. WiFi. Off site: Beach 1 km. Bicycle hire 2 km. Golf 6 km. Theme parks.

Open: All year.

Directions

From autopista exit 65 (Benidorm, Levante) at second set of traffic lights turn left on N332 (Altea, Valencia). After 1.5 km. turn right (Levante Playa), then straight on at next lights for 300 m. to site on right. From north on N332 follow signs for Playa Levante (or Benidorm Palace). Left at lights (Playa Levante). Site well signed. GPS: 38.5487, -0.0991

Charges guide

Per person	€ 5,70 - € 6,60
pitch incl. electricity	€ 17,00 - € 19,00
No credit cards.	

For latest campsite news, availability and prices visit
alanrogers.com

Bocairent
Camping Mariola

Ctra Bocairent - Alcoi km 9, E-46880 Bocairent (Valencia) T: 962 135 160. E: info@campingmariola.com
alanrogers.com/ES86450

Situated high in the Sierra Mariola National Park, in a beautiful rural setting but only 12 km. from the old town of Bocairent, this is a real taste of Spain with hilltop views all around. Used mainly by the Spanish, the site is an undiscovered jewel with 170 slightly sloping pitches. These are well spaced and have shade from a mixture of young and mature trees. An orchard area well away from the main site (with no amenities close by) is used for more casual camping.

Facilities

Six identical small toilet blocks offer adequate facilities with British style WCs and showers with shared changing area. Open style washbasins. No facilities for disabled persons. Washing machine. Motorcaravan services. Small shop (weekends only). Bar/restaurant (weekends only in low season). Satellite TV. Outdoor pool with separate paddling pool (June-Sept). Two multisport pitches. Play area. Communal barbecue area. Children's club and entertainment (Aug. only). Off site: Riding and golf 12 km.

Open: All year.

Directions

From the CV40 take exit for Ontinyent and follow the CV81. Pass town of Bocairent heading west and in 2 km. look for camping sign (at textiles factory). Turn south on VV2031 to Alcoy. Turn right at first roundabout and straight on at next through small industrial estate. Persevere onwards and upwards for about 10 km. and site is a turn to left. GPS: 38.753317, -0.549402

Charges guide

Per person	€ 4,45
pitch	€ 4,45 - € 6,00
electricity	€ 4,20

Campell
Camping Vall de Laguar

Ctra Sant Antonio 24, la Vall de Laguar, E-03791 Campell (Alacant) T: 965 577 490
E: info@campinglaguar.com **alanrogers.com/ES86750**

Near the pretty mountain-top village of Campell, this new site is perched high on the side of a mountain with breathtaking views of hilltop villages, the surrounding hills and distant sea. With a wholehearted welcome from the owners, the well maintained site promises a real taste of Spain. The pitches, pool, terrace and restaurant all share the views. The 68 average size gravel pitches are on terraces and all have electricity and water. Trees and hedges have been planted and now give ample shade. This is a great place to get away from the coastal hustle, bustle and high rise of the beaches.

Facilities

Two new sanitary blocks have excellent clean facilities including some for disabled visitors. Washing machines and dryers. WiFi. Restaurant with pretty terrace (closed Sept). Bar. Swimming pool and small pool bar. Small entertainment programme in high season. Barbecue area with sinks. Torches useful. Off site: Attractive town close by. Golf and beach 18 km.

Open: All year.

Directions

Site is 20 km. west of Xabia/Javea. From the A7/E15 exit 62 head to Ondara/Valencia on the N332 and at the roundabout on the Ondara by-pass head to Benidoleig/Orba. At Orba turn right and follow the site signs. GPS: 38.7766, -0.105

Charges guide

Per unit incl. 2 persons and electricity	€ 21,75 - € 24,25
extra person	€ 5,00

Cullera
Camping Santa Marta

Ctra de Faro km 2, E-46400 Cullera (Alacant) T: 961 721 440. E: info@santamartacamping.com
alanrogers.com/ES86220

Santa Marta is beautifully located on the slopes of a mountain and is shaded by many old Mediterranean umbrella pine trees. Originally a municipal site, it was recently purchased by a group of four campsites and is being fully renovated and modernised. There are 250 small, terraced pitches, 235 for touring with 16A electricity. Access can be difficult due to the many trees. An olive grove has been bought to provide 18 motorcaravan pitches. During 2007/2008 the whole site was redeveloped to include better fire protection, new water points and better access to the pitches.

Facilities

Four toilet blocks, which are very well equipped (although shower cubicles have only one hook and no shelf or soap dish). Separate facilities for ladies and men. Facilities for campers with disabilities. Separate baby room. Small shop. Bar serving snacks with terrace. Swimming and paddling pools (23/6-16/9). Multisports field. Hiking trails. Barbecues are not permitted. Off site: Town of Cullera. Beach 100 m. Shop facing the site. Supermarkets at the outskirts of town. Kite surfing.

Open: All year excl. 16 December - 14 January.

Directions

From A7/N-332 (Valencia - Alicante) take exit for Cullera. Follow signs into Cullera and then signs to Faro or Far, through the centre of town. From the centre follow signs to site. GPS: 39.17694, -0.24333

Charges guide

Per unit incl. 2 persons and electricity (4A)	€ 30,00
extra person	€ 6,00
child (2-10 yrs)	€ 5,50

For latest campsite news, availability and prices visit
alanrogers.com

El Campello

Camping Costa Blanca

Calle Convento 143, N332 km 120,5, E-03560 El Campello (Alacant) T: 965 630 670
E: info@campingcostablanca.com **alanrogers.com/ES86900**

This small site has 80 pitches with 60 for tourers, some with views of the distant hills. Bungalows line three sides of the white walled rectangular site with a railway (not too busy) on the final side. Reception is efficient with keen staff members speaking several languages. The flat pitches are on gravel and all have 6A electricity. Some are small (40, 60 or 80 sq.m) and will be a challenge for large units. There is natural shade from trees and some artificial shade. A pleasant pool is the centre-piece with a bright poolside bar and a restaurant with a patio.

Facilities

Four clean refurbished sanitary units offer a variety of facilities including cabins with toilet and basin, toilet and bidet, washbasins with hot water, others with cold. Two baby baths in cabins. Facilities for disabled visitors. Washing machines and dryer. Motorcaravan services at entrance (€ 4 per token). Restaurant/bar (all year). Shop (1/7-1/9). Swimming pool. Basic play area (supervision required). Limited live entertainment in season. WiFi. Communal barbecue. Off site: Town facilities. Fishing, sailing and watersports 500 m. Riding 8 km. Golf 8 km. Boat launching 500 m. ATM 1 km.

Open: All year.

Directions

From the N332 take exit for El Campello Costa. Go through traffic lights onto the roundabout and take the first exit right. Site is visible from the roundabout although the name is behind the sliding gate! GPS: 38.43611, -0.38806

Charges 2011

Per unit incl. 2 persons	
and electricity	€ 23,93 - € 44,40
extra person	€ 4,11 - € 5,95
child (1-10 yrs)	€ 3,29 - € 4,75

Gandia

Camping L'Alqueria

Avenida del Grau 142, E-46730 Grau de Gandia (Valencia) T: 962 840 470. E: lalqueria@lalqueria.com
alanrogers.com/ES86200

Camping L'Alqueria is situated on the main Gandia to Grau road and, although in an urban location, it is 1 km. from the beaches of Gandia. The 137 touring pitches are of a good size and on level ground, all with 10A electricity and easy access to one of many water points. Some are separated by dividing hedges and there is plenty of shade from mature trees. An orchard area to the rear of the site is designated for casual camping and is adjacent to the football pitch. There is a large swimming pool (caps required) with a sliding cover and a small paddling pool, adjacent but outside. Below the pools are a steam room, hydro-bath, sauna and jacuzzi. When we visited a temporary structure provided a small bar and snack bar whilst a new building at the entrance is being completed. A wooden cabin houses a small shop that is reasonably well stocked.

Facilities

Four toilet blocks, three with British style toilets, placed evenly around the site. Mostly combined shower and washbasin cubicles. Laundry facilities (key from reception). Motorcaravan service point. Shop (all year) and snack bar (1/4-15/10). Covered swimming pool (all season) and outdoor paddling pool (1/6-15/10). Steam room and spa facilities. Fridge hire. Off site: Fishing, golf, bicycle hire, riding and boat launching 1 km. Beach 1 km. Shops, restaurant etc. within 1 km.

Open: All year.

Directions

From A7 (Valencia - Alicante) take exit 60 and follow signs to Gandia on the N332. Through the town follow signs for Grau and Platja de Gandia. Site is northwest of Gandia. GPS: 38.98627, -0.16365

Charges guide

Per unit incl. 2 persons	
and electricity	€ 21,52 - € 38,78
extra person	€ 3,48 - € 5,33
child (3-10 yrs)	€ 2,86 - € 4,23

Guardamar del Segura
Camping Marjal

Ctra N332 km 73,4, E-03140 Guardamar del Segura (Alacant) T: 966 727 070. E: camping@marjal.com
alanrogers.com/ES87430

Marjal is located beside the estuary of the Segura river, alongside the pine and eucalyptus forests of the Dunas de Guardamar natural park. The fine sandy beach can be reached through the forest (800 m). This is a very smart site with a huge tropical lake style pool wih bar and a superb sports complex. There are 212 pitches on this award winning site, all with water, electricity, drainage and satellite TV points. The ground is covered with crushed marble, making the pitches clean and pleasant. There is some shade and the site has an open feel with lots of room for manoeuvring. Reception is housed within a delicately coloured building complete with a towering Mirador, topped by a weather vane depicting the 'Garza Real' (heron) bird which frequents the local area and forms part of the site logo. The large restaurant overlooks the pools and the river that leads to the sea in the near distance. The bar has large terraces fringed by trees, palms and pomegranates. The impressive pool/lagoon complex (1,100 sq.m) has a water cascade, an island bar plus bridge, one part sectioned as a pool for children and a jacuzzi. The extensive sports area is also impressive. No effort has been spared here and facilities are of the highest quality. An extensive programme of entertainment is provided for adults and children in season by a professional team.

Facilities

Three excellent heated toilet blocks have free hot water, elegant separators between sinks, spacious showers and some cabins. Each block has high quality facilities for babies and disabled visitors, modern laundry and dishwashing rooms. Car wash. Well stocked supermarket. Restaurants. Bar. Large outdoor pool complex (1/6-31/10). Heated indoor pool (low season). Jacuzzi. Sauna. Solarium. Beaty Salon. Superb well equipped gym. Aerobics. Physiotherapy. All activities discounted for campers. Play room. Minigolf. Floodlit tennis and soccer pitch. Bicycle hire. Car rental. Games room. TV room. Full entertainment programme. Hairdresser. ATM. Business centre. Internet access and free WiFi. Off site: Beach 800 m. Riding and golf 4 km.

Open: All year.

Directions

On N332 40 km. south of Alicante, site is on the sea side between 73 and 74 km. markers.
GPS: 38.10933, -0.65467

Charges guide

Per unit incl. 2 persons and electricity	€ 27,00 - € 65,00
extra person	€ 5,00 - € 9,00
child (4-12 yrs)	€ 4,00 - € 6,00
dog	€ 1,50 - € 3,20

Low season discounts.

For latest campsite news, availability and prices visit
alanrogers.com

La Marina
Camping Internacional La Marina

Ctra N332 km 76, E-03194 La Marina (Alacant) T: 965 419 200. E: info@campinglamarina.com
alanrogers.com/ES87420

Very efficiently run by a friendly Belgian family, La Marina has 381 pitches of three different types and sizes ranging from 50 sq.m. to 150 sq.m. with electricity (16/25A), TV, water and drainage. Artificial shade is provided and the pitches are extremely well maintained on level, well drained ground with a special area allocated for tents in a small orchard. The huge lagoon swimming pool complex is fabulous and has something for everyone (with lifeguards). William Le Metayer, the owner, is passionate about La Marina and it shows in his search for perfection. A magnificent new, modern building which uses the latest architectural technology, houses many superb extra amenities. These include a relaxed business centre with internet access, a tapas bar decorated with amazing ceramics (handmade by the owner's mother) and a quality restaurant with a water fountain feature and great views of the lagoon. There is also a conference centre and an extensive computerised library. The whole of the lower ground floor is dedicated to children with a Marina Park play area and a 'cyber zone' for teenagers. With a further bar and a new soundproofed disco, the building is of an exceptional, eco-friendly standard. A superb fitness centre with attentive personal trainers and covered, heated pool (14x7 m) are incorporated. A pedestrian gate at the rear of the site gives access to the long sandy beach through the coastal pine forest that is a feature of the area. We recommend this site very highly. A member of Leading Campings Group.

Facilities

The elegant sanitary blocks offer the very best of modern facilities. Heated in winter, they include private cabins and facilities for disabled visitors and babies. Laundry facilities. Motorcaravan services. Gas. Supermarket. Bars. Restaurant and café. Ice cream kiosk. Swimming pools (1/4-15/10). Indoor pool. Fitness centre. Sauna. Solarium. Jacuzzi. Play rooms. Extensive activity and entertainment programme including barbecues and swimming nights. Sports area. Tennis. Huge playgrounds. Hairdresser. Bicycle hire. Road train to beach. Exclusive area for dogs. Internet café (charged) and free WiFi. Off site: Fishing 500 m. Boat launching 5 km. Golf 7 km. Riding 15 km. Hourly bus service. Theme parks.

Open: All year.

Directions

Site is 2 km. west of La Marina. Leave the N332 Guardamara de Segura - Santa Pola road at 75 km. marker if travelling north, or 78 km. marker if travelling south. Site is well signed. GPS: 38.129649, -0.649575

Charges 2011

Per unit incl. 2 persons and electricity	€ 33,28 - € 62,61
extra person	€ 5,35 - € 8,00
child (1-10 yrs)	€ 3,75 - € 5,50
dog	free - € 2,14

Good discounts for longer stays in low season.

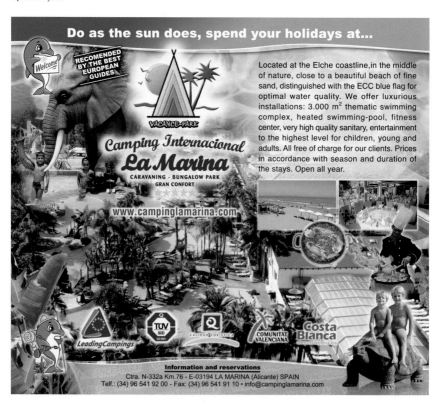

For latest campsite news, availability and prices visit
alanrogers.com

Jávea

Camping Jávea

Ctra Cami de la Fontana 10, Apdo 83, E-03730 Jávea (Alacant) T: 965 791 070. E: info@camping-javea.com
alanrogers.com/ES87540

The final approach to this site emerges from the bustle of the town and is decorated with palms, orange and pine trees, the latter playing host to a colony of parakeets. English is spoken at reception. The neat, boxed hedges and palms within the site, and its backdrop of hills dotted with villas present an attractive setting. Three hectares provide space for 214 numbered pitches with 183 for touring units. Flat, level and rectangular in shape, the pitches vary in size 60-80 sq.m. All pitches have a granite chip surface and 8A electricity. The restaurant provides great food, way above normal campsite standards.

Facilities	Directions
Two very clean, fully equipped, sanitary blocks include two children's toilets plus a baby bath. Facilities for disabled visitors. Two washing machines. Fridge hire. Extensive bar and restaurant with terraces where in high season you can purchase bread and milk. Large swimming pool with lifeguard and sunbathing lawns. Play area. Boules. Electronic barriers (deposit for card). Caravan storage. Five-a-side footaball. Basketball. Tennis. WiFi. Car rental. Off site: Old and New Jávea within easy walking distance with supermarkets and shops. Sandy beach, boat launching, fishing, bicycle hire all 1.5 km. Golf 3 km.	Exit N332 for Jávea on A134, continue in direction of port (road number changes to CV 734). In town the site is well marked with large orange indicators high on posts. Watch carefully for a sudden slip road sign! GPS: 38.78333, 0.16983

Charges guide

Per unit incl. 2 persons and electricity	€ 28,71 - € 31,40
extra person	€ 5,58 - € 6,20
child	€ 4,68 - € 5,20
dog	€ 1,50 - € 2,00

Open: All year.

Moncofa

Camping Monmar

Ctra Serratelles s/n, E-12593 Moncofa (Castelló) T: 964 588 592. E: campingmonmar@terra.es
alanrogers.com/ES85900

This purpose built, very neat site is in the small town of Moncofa, just 200 metres from the sea and right beside a water park with pools and slides. There are 170 gravel based pitches arranged in rows off tarmac access roads. The 100 touring pitches all have 6A electricity, water and a drain. Hedges have been planted to separate the pitches but these are still small so there is little shade (canopies can be rented in high season). The site's facilities and amenities are all very modern.

Facilities	Directions
Three modern toilet blocks are well placed and provide good, clean facilities. Free hot showers. Facilities and good access for disabled visitors. Laundry facilities. Shop (1/7-31/8). Bar and restaurant (weekends and high season). Swimming pool (all year). Good play area. Boules. New library. Internet (on payment). Animals are not accepted. Off site: Beach 200 m. Water complex. Local amenities within walking distance.	Turn off N340 Castellon - Valencia road on the CV2250 signed Moncofa. Follow sign for tourist information office in town and then signs for site. Pass supermarket and turn left to site in 600 m. GPS: 39.80884, -0.1281

Charges guide

Per unit incl. 2 persons and electricity	€ 11,00 - € 18,00

Open: All year.

Moraira

Camping Caravanning Moraira

Camino Paellero 50, E-03724 Moraira-Teulada (Alacant) T: 965 745 249
E: campingmoraira@campingmoraira.com alanrogers.com/ES87550

This neat hillside site with some views over the town and marina is quietly situated in an urban area amongst old pine trees and just 400 metres from a sheltered bay. Terracing provides shaded pitches of varying sizes, some small (access to some of the upper pitches may be difficult for larger units). Seventeen pitches are fully serviced (6/10A electricity). An attractive pool with large observation windows and paved sunbathing terrace is below the bar/restaurant and terrace.

Facilities	Directions
The high quality toilet blocks, with polished granite floors and marble fittings are built to a unique and ultra-modern design. Facilities for disabled visitors. Washing machines and dryers. Motorcaravan services. Bar/restaurant and shop (1/6-30/9). Bread and basics at the bar. Small swimming pool (all year). Sub-aqua with instruction. Tennis. Limited children's entertainment in high season. Torches may be required. WiFi code. Pets welcome. Off site: Shops, bars and restaurants within walking distance. Beach and fishing 400 m. Gym, ATM 600 m. Bicycle hire 1 km. Golf 8 km.	Best approach is from Teulada. From A7 exit 63 take N332 and in 3.5 km. turn right (Teulada and Moraira). In Teulada fork right to Moraira. At junction at town entrance turn right signed Calpe and in 1 km. turn right into road to site on bend immediately after Res. Don Julio. Do not take the first right, as the signs seem to indicate, otherwise you will go round in a loop. GPS: 38.692, 0.14

Charges guide

Per unit incl. 2 persons and electricity	€ 37,00
extra person	€ 7,50
child (4-10 yrs)	€ 5,35

Open: All year.

For latest campsite news, availability and prices visit
alanrogers.com

Navajas
Camping Altomira

Ctra CV213 Navajas km 1, E-12470 Navajas (Castelló) T: 964 713 211. E: reservas@campingaltomira.com
alanrogers.com/ES85850

Camping Altomira is a terraced site in a rural, hillside setting, on the outskirts of a quiet village and offers superb views across the valleys and hills. There are 80 touring pitches situated on the higher levels of the site with some shade (artificial awnings are allowed). Due to the nature of this site we would not recommend it for people with mobility problems. Access roads to the gravel pitches are steep with some tight turns. All pitches, although not separated, have electricity and share water points with a neighbour.

Facilities

Four modern toilet blocks (including a new one on the upper level) have showers in cubicles and open style washbasins. The larger block, also housing laundry facilities, is on the lowest level. The two smaller ones are accessed by stairways from the pitches. Shop. Bar/restaurant with small terrace next to play area. TV room. Outdoor swimming pool. Communal barbecue area. Internet WiFi. Off site: Village has a range of shops bars and restaurants. Lake fishing 2 km. Beach 20 km.

Open: All year.

Directions

From A23 (Sagunto - Teruel) road take exit 33 (Navajas). Follow CV213 to site which is 1 km. north of Navajas. GPS: 39.87471, -0.51051

Charges guide

Per unit incl. 2 persons and electricity	€ 19,56 - € 25,60
extra person	€ 4,76 - € 5,95
child (1-10 yrs)	€ 3,72 - € 4,65

Camping Cheques accepted.

Oliva
Camping Azul

No 1. Apartado 96, E-46780 Oliva (Valencia) T: 962 854 106. E: campingazul@ctv.es
alanrogers.com/ES86115

Found behind the beach and sand dunes, Camping Azul can best be described as rustic and relaxed, ideal for those who prefer a quiet, unregimented site. From reception the firm, sandy roads lead to sandy pitches with many low trees which have been sympathetically pruned to afford partial or full shade. Varying in size, some of the pitches are very compact, and pitching could be difficult. Food and drinks are served at the attractive bar/café area. Opposite this there is a small shop.

Facilities

Modern, heated sanitary block. Facilities for disabled visitors. Launderette. Motorcaravan services. Gas. Small shop selling basic items. Bar and snack bar. Play area. Bicycle and car hire. WiFi internet. Entertainment in high season. Direct beach access. Chalets for rent. Off site: Good restaurant providing menu of the day within 500 m. Oliva 3 km. with bars, restaurants, supermarkets and banks. Golf and tennis 1 km.

Open: 1 March - 1 November.

Directions

From the north leave the AP7 motorway at exit 61 (Oliva) and follow the N332 through Oliva. From the south take exit 62 onto the N332 and turn left for Oliva. At km. 213 (south) or km. 210.8 (north) turn for 'urbanisation' and follow signs to the site. GPS: 38.906944, -0.068611

Charges 2011

Per unit incl. 2 persons	€ 26,80 - € 28,80
extra person	€ 4,75

Oliva
Euro Camping

Partida Rabdells s/n, CN332 km210, E-46780 Oliva (Valencia) T: 962 854 098. E: info@eurocamping-es.com
alanrogers.com/ES86120

Approached through a new urbanisation, Euro Camping is a well maintained, British-owned site. Spacious and flat, it is set amidst high trees, mainly eucalyptus, with its own access to a sandy beach. From reception with its helpful English speaking staff and aviary opposite, wide tarmac or paved roads lead to 315 large, gravel based pitches which are either marked or hedged (most are for touring units). The main site road leads down to a beachside restaurant with superb views and a supermarket.

Facilities

One newly built and two mature sanitary blocks are well maintained. British type WCs, preset hot water in the showers. Toilet facilities for disabled visitors. Facilities for babies. Washing machines and dryer. Motorcaravan services. Well stocked supermarket and roast chicken takeaway. Restaurant/bar. Fridge hire. WiFi. Entertainment in high season. Gas. Bicycle hire. Off site: Golf, tennis and riding 1 km. Oliva is 3 km. with restaurants, cafés and supermarkets. Large street market on Fridays. Ideal area for cycling.

Open: All year.

Directions

From the north on the AP7 take exit 61 onto N332 and drive through Oliva. From the south exit 62 and left for Oliva. Exit at km. 213 (south) or 210 (north) signed 'urbanisation'. At roundabout take fourth (last) exit. Turn right immediately before narrow bridge. Continue along wide road, bearing right at end onto Carrer de Xeraco. Site is on the left at bottom of this road. GPS: 38.905, -0.066

Charges guide

Per unit incl. 2 persons and electricity	€ 30,20 - € 47,80
extra person	€ 4,50

Camping Cheques accepted.

For latest campsite news, availability and prices visit
alanrogers.com

Oliva
Kiko Park Oliva

Ctra Assagador de Carro 2, E-46780 Oliva (Valencia) T: 962 850 905. E: kikopark@kikopark.com

alanrogers.com/ES86150

Kiko Park is a smart site nestling behind protective sand dunes alongside a 'blue flag' beach. There are sets of attractively tiled steps over the dunes and a long boardwalk near the beach bar (good for prams and wheelchairs) to take you to the fine white sandy beach and the sea. From the central reception point (where good English is spoken) flat, fine gravel pitches and access roads are divided to the left and right. Backing onto one another, the 180 large pitches all have electricity and the aim is to progressively upgrade all these with full services. There are plenty of flowers, hedging and trees adding shade, privacy and colour. An outdoor pool complex provides a spa, whirlpool, solarium, gym and a pool bar. An award-winning restaurant and a tropical style beach bar, both overlook the marina, beautiful beach and sea. A wide variety of entertainment is provided all year and Spanish lessons are taught along with dance class and aerobics during the winter. The site is run by the second generation of a family involved in camping for 30 years and their experience shows. They are brilliantly supported by a friendly, efficient team who speak many languages. The narrow roads leading to the site can be a little challenging for very large units but it is worth the effort. Disabled visitors will find this site flat and convenient.

Facilities

Four mature, heated sanitary blocks include facilities for babies and for disabled visitors. Laundry facilities. Motorcaravan services. Gas supplies. Supermarket (closed Sundays). Restaurant. Bar with TV. Beach-side bar and restaurant. Swimming pools and gym. New spa with treatments and beauty programmes. Playground. Watersports facilities. Diving school in high season (from mid June). Pétanque. Entertainment for children from mid June. Internet access and WiFi. Bicycle hire. Off site: The footpath to the marina leads into the town. Golf 5 km.

Open: All year.

Directions

From the AP7 take exit 61. From the toll turn right at T-junction and continue to lights. Turn left then at roundabout turn right. At next roundabout (fountains) take third exit signed Platja and Alicante. Follow one way system to next roundabout then site signs. GPS: 38.9316, -0.0968

Charges guide

Per unit incl. 2 persons	€ 15,20 - € 34,00
extra person	€ 3,20 - € 6,40
child (under 10 yrs)	€ 2,60 - € 5,80
electricity (per kWh)	€ 0,40

Oliva
Camping Olé

Partida Aigua Morta s/n, E-46780 Oliva (Valencia) T: 962 857 517. E: campingole@hotmail.com

alanrogers.com/ES86130

Olé is a large, flat seaside holiday site south of Valencia and close to the modern resort of Oliva. Its entrance is only 250 m. from the pleasant sandy beach. For those who do not want to share the busy beach, a large swimming pool is opened in July and August. There are 308 small pitches of compressed gravel and with 6/10A electricity. Many are separated by hedges with pruned trees giving good shade to those away from the beach. There are a few unmarked pitches that are ideal for larger units.

Facilities

Three clean, well maintained sanitary blocks provide very reasonable facilities. The central one serves most of the touring pitches. Laundry facilities. Fridge rental. Well stocked supermarket (1/3-30/9). Various vending machines. Bar with TV and restaurant with daily menu, drinks and snacks (1/3-15/12). Takeaway. Swimming pool (1/7-1/9). Playground. Entertainment (July/Aug). Fishing off the beach. Off site: Oliva 5 km. Golf 800 m. Bicycle hire.

Open: All year.

Directions

From the north on AP7 (Alicante - Valencia) take exit 61 on N332 through Oliva. From the south take exit 62 and turn left for Oliva. Exit at km. 213 (south) or 210 (north) signed 'urbanisation'. At roundabout take third exit following signs to site. GPS: 38.8943, -0.0536

Charges guide

Per unit incl. 2 persons	€ 32,50 - € 37,15
extra person	€ 5,70

For latest campsite news, availability and prices visit

alanrogers.com

73

Oropesa del Mar

Camping Oasis

Carretera la Tall, s/n, E-12594 Oropesa del Mar (Castelló) T: 964 319 677. E: oasis@camping-oropesa.com

alanrogers.com/ES85750

Oasis is a fairly unsophisticated site with ambitious prices. Past the two large, plastic camels at the entrance, you will find that the vast majority of the site is made up of permanents and bungalows. The 30 (80 sq. m) flat touring pitches with hedges and 6A electricity are mainly in one area of the site near the pool, spa and services. A small bar with connected restaurant and terrace overlooks the pool with many plastic and stone animal figures. The beach is 200 metres away and very pleasant, as is the large pool on the site with its fountains; for an alternative to a cooling dip there is a heated outdoor spa in the pool area. Oasis is in a highly developed area of Oropesa del Mar and is overlooked by modern high rise flats. It is a mature site with around 30 pitches for tourers and some features which may appeal such as the library, reading room, gymnasium and large elaborate spa under an ornate roof. A paddling pool and two basic play areas are provided for children near reception. The site is recommended for transit visits rather than long stays and is open all year.

Facilities

Two traditional sanitary blocks have been renovated and are well maintained with facilities for disabled visitors, and a baby bath in the laundry room. Restaurant and bar (open all year). 10 washing machines. Dryer. Basic shop. Outdoor pool with separate paddling pool. Sports room with modern gym equipment. Limited entertainment programme in high season. Boules. Darts. WiFi. Internet access. Small dogs accepted. Bicycle hire in summer. Bus 200m. Torches useful. Off site: Fishing 200 m. Supermarket 400 m. Riding 3 km. Golf 20 km.

Open: All year.

Directions

From A7/E15 take exit 45 for Oropesa Del Mar on N340. Follow the road to Oropesa and then the many clear signs to the site.
GPS: 40.12161, 0.15563

Charges guide

Per unit incl. 2 persons and electricity	€ 31,00 - € 43,00
extra person	€ 5,00 - € 6,50
child (1-10 yrs)	€ 4,00 - € 5,50

Peñiscola

Spa Natura Resort

Ptda Villarroyos s/n, E-12598 Peñiscola (Castelló) T: 964 475 480. E: info@spanaturaresort.com

alanrogers.com/ES85590

Set inland from the popular coastal resort of Peñiscola, Spa Natura Resort (also known as Camping Azahar) is set amongst orange groves and vegetable fields. This unusual development of residential and holiday park homes provides 110 level touring pitches, with an increase planned for 2011. All pitches have electricity (6/10A) and access to water with wide, gravel roads. Amazingly, most are set on neat, artificial grass. Some shade is provided by young palms, pines and plane trees. The pitches are not separated and large units can be accommodated. Pitches are set between long rows of bungalows and there are very chunky elevated roofs over some. An impressive wellness centre is housed in a towering P&O-style building. A vehicle or bicycle is necessary as the site is rather remote. The sea and a 15 km. stretch of sandy beaches are 5 km. away.

Facilities

Two refurbished toilet blocks include showers, open washbasins and separate toilets. Facilities for disabled visitors. Washing machines and dryers. Shop. Bar/restaurant (all year). Small outdoor and indoor swimming pools (Easter-Oct). Spa centre offering steam room massage, jacuzzi, aquatic treatments, therapies. Gym. Indoor tennis court. Play area. Minigolf. Bicycle hire. Internet access. Activity programme (excursions, Spanish lessons, games, competitions). Dogs are not accepted in July/Aug. Cabins, mobile homes, apartments to rent. Off site: Costa Azahar shopping and entertainment complex 1 km. Irta mountains and nature reserve (hiking, cycling, riding) 3 km. Peñiscola 3 km. Fishing and golf 5 km. Beach, boat launching and sailing 5 km.

Open: All year.

Directions

From A7 (Barcelona - Valencia) take exit 43 and then the N340 towards Benicarlo. Immediately look for signs at the N340 1040 km marker to Camping Azahar on large boards steering you down a side road. You will be able to see the campsite with large elevated signs as you come down the slip road.
GPS: 40.40197, 0.38095

Charges guide

Per unit incl. 2 persons and electricity (10A)	€ 37,00 - € 50,00
extra person	€ 3,50 - € 5,00
child (0-10 yrs)	€ 3,00 - € 4,50
dog	€ 2,00 - € 3,00

For latest campsite news, availability and prices visit
alanrogers.com

Pilar de la Horadada

Camping Lo Monte

Avda. Comunidad Valenciana, no 157, E-03191 Pilar de la Horadada (Alacant)
E: info@campinglomonte-alicante.com alanrogers.com/ES87400

Lo Monte is a brand new, all year site which has been recommended by our Spanish agent. We plan to conduct a full inspection in 2011. There are 130 pitches , of which the majority are available for tourers. All have 16A electricity, water and drainage. Leisure facilities include a swimming pool (open May to September) and a wellness centre. Lo Monte is located at Pilar de la Horadada, the most southerly town on the Costa Blanca. This is a popular holiday destination, with a fine beach and a good range of facilities. For nature lovers, the areas around the town are rich in flora and fauna, the tidal sections support an incredible variety of creatures, with species such as pipefish, seahorses and wrasse. The birdlife is varied too, you are likely to spot curlew, grey herons, egrets, turnstones and plovers. There are a number of excellent golf courses in the vicinity, notably the three courses of the Orihuela Costa.

Facilities

Swimming pool. Wellness centre. Shop. Bar. Restaurant. Takeaway food. Children's play area. Tourist information. Mobile homes for rent. Off site: Pilar de la Horadada centre (shops and restaurants). Water sports. Fishing. Golf.

Open: June 2011 then all year.

Directions

Head south on AP7 motorway beyond Torrevieja and take the exit to Pilar de la Horadada. The site is well signposted. GPS: 37.86964, -0.77248

Charges 2011

Contact site.

Avda. Comunidad Valenciana, nº 157
E-03191 Pilar de la Horadada
(Alicante) SPAIN

www.campinglomonte-alicante.com • e-mail:info@campinglomonte-alicante.com

---

Ribera de Cabanes

Camping Torre La Sal 2

Cami l'Atall, E-12595 Ribera de Cabanes (Castelló) T: 964 319 744. E: camping@torrelasal2.com
alanrogers.com/ES85700

Torre La Sal 2 is a very large site divided into two by a quiet road, with a reception on each side with friendly, helpful staff. There are three pool complexes (one can be covered in cooler weather and is heated) all of which are on the west side, whilst the beach (of shingle and sand) is on the east. Both sides have a restaurant – the restaurant on the beach side has two air conditioned wooden buildings and a terrace. The 530 flat pitches vary in size, some have their own sinks, and most have shade. All have 10A electricity and a few have a partial view of the sea. There are 85 bungalows around the two areas. This is a high quality site offering a great choice to campers.

Facilities

Toilet facilities are of a good standard in both sections, four to the west and two to the east, with facilities for disabled visitors in both. Baby rooms. Hot water to some sinks. British style toilets. Washing machines. Motorcaravan services. Shop, bars, restaurants and takeaway (all year). Swimming pools – one heated and covered (a large new pool complex should be ready for the season). Jacuzzi and sauna (winter). Play park. Large disco. Sports centre. Tennis. Squash. Two football pitches. Pétanque. Outdoor gym. Games room. Bullring. Hairdresser. Varied programme of activities and entertainment. WiFi Internet access. Torches are useful. Off site: Village has a range of shops bars and restaurants. Bicycle hire. Riding 10 km. Golf 20 km.

Open: All year.

Directions

From A7/E15 take exit 45 for Oropesa Del Mar on N340. Follow road to Oropesa and then the many clear signs to the site. GPS: 40.127, 0.158

Charges guide

Per unit incl. 2 persons and electricity	€ 36,35
extra person	€ 6,80
child (2-9 yrs)	€ 6,25

Special prices for retired persons 1/9-30/6.

For latest campsite news, availability and prices visit
alanrogers.com

San Miguel de Salinas

Camping Florantilles

Ctra San Miguel de Salinas, Torrevieja, E-03193 San Miguel de Salinas (Alacant) T: 965 720 456
E: florantilles@terra.es alanrogers.com/ES87410

Florantilles is an excellent site situated 6 km. west of Torrevieja, 60 km. south of Alicante and occupying an elevated position overlooking orange groves and the famous salt lake nature reserve, Salinas de la Mata. The site is terraced and well lit, with gravel pitches of a good size and tarmac roads. All 268 pitches are separated by hedges and have 10A electricity (metered for long stays), water and waste water drainage. A third of the pitches are for touring (minimum stay seven nights) while the others are occupied by privately owned mobile homes and seasonal pitches in use by mainly retired British owners who spend the winter months here.

Facilities

Two, well kept toilet blocks with free hot water, plus another smaller block on each level with WCs and handbasins but no private cubicles. Good facilities for visitors with disabilities. Two laundry rooms. Well stocked shop (Mon-Sat), with freshly baked bread. Two unheated, linked swimming pools (15/6-30/9). Bar/café serving simple meals. TV room. Pétanque. Aerobics. Quiz/cards night. Line dancing. No vehicle movement on site between 23.00-07.00. Car washing area. Dogs are not accepted. Off site: Restaurant and shops 3 km. Golf 6 km. Sailing and fishing (licence required) 7 km.

Open: All year.

Directions

From south, leave motorway AP7 at exit 758. At roundabout, go under motorway, take exit for Los Montesinos. In 300 m, take first right (Los Montesinos). Site is on left through archway. From north, leave AP7 at exit 758. Take first exit (Los Montesinos), then as above. New arrivals (pre-booked only) should park to left of entrance so you do not obstruct barrier. GPS: 37.97721, -0.75424

Charges guide

Per unit incl. 2 persons and electricity	€ 15,50 - € 27,50
extra person	€ 3,00 - € 6,00
child (1-12 yrs)	€ 2,50 - € 5,00

Villajoyosa

Camping Playa Paraiso

Ctra Valencia - Alicante km 136, Partida Paraiso, 66, E-03570 Villajoyosa (Alacant) T: 966 851 838
E: jacinto@playaparaiso.com alanrogers.com/ES86880

This site has been reopened by new owners who lost one of their other sites to housing developers. Major works are underway to provide modern facilities. When we visited, work was being done on the upper levels of the site to provide serviced pitches and a fully refurbished toilet block. On the lower level, the main site road is of tarmac and the gravel pitches are on shallow terraces as the site slopes gently down to the sea which provides one of the boundaries. The views are pleasant and trees provide a degree of shade for some pitches, with overhead sunshades on others. Electricity connections are available (16A). Since the opening of a new bypass, the site has become very quiet with only local traffic passing the gate, so pitches nearer the sea will hear no traffic noise at all. Access to the shingle beach is fenced with a key available from reception to open large gates to facilitate boat launching.

Facilities

Two toilet blocks are old but are well maintained and very clean. Spacious showers. Facilities for disabled visitors. Separate building with facilities for babies. Washing machines and dryer. Bar and restaurant with limited menu. Indoor games and TV. Swimming pool (Easter-Oct). Off site: Beach. Bus stop 100 m. Riding and bicycle hire 15 km. Villajoysa with holiday attractions. Benidorm.

Open: 2 February - 31 December.

Directions

From the N332 take exit at km. 136 to Villajoysa Playa and site is 100 m. on the right. GPS: 38.50005, -0.24905

Charges guide

Per unit incl. 2 persons	€ 27,00 - € 43,00
Discounts of up to 50% in low season.	

For latest campsite news, availability and prices visit
alanrogers.com

Villargordo del Cabriel

Kiko Park Rural

Ctra Embalse Contreras km 3, E-46317 Villargordo del Cabriel (Valencia) T: 962 139 082
E: kikoparkrural@kikopark.com alanrogers.com/ES86250

Approaching Kiko Park Rural, you will see a small hilltop village appearing in a landscape of mountains, vines and a jewel-like lake. Kiko was a small village and farm and the village now forms the campsite and accommodation. Amenities are contained within the architecturally authentic buildings, some old and some new. The 76 generous pitches (mainly hardstanding and with 6A electricity and water) all have stunning views, as do the pools. Generous plantings have been made which already afford some privacy and hundreds of trees provide shade. The restaurant provides extremely good food in a pleasant, spacious setting overlooking the pools and their surrounding immaculate lawns. Kiko Rural is run by cousins from a family with 30 years of camping experience – a passionate and enthusiastic team with a vision of excellence. Kiko Rural is an ideal site for those folk, young and old, who enjoy adventurous activities, communing with nature, or relaxing with an occasional sightseeing excursion. A sister site to Kiko Park in Oliva, Valencia (ES8615), old and new have combined here to create an environment that is, within its category, outstanding. The new high speed Madrid-Valencia train line emerges from a tunnel approximately 500 m. from the site. However, noise moderating banks should eliminate any possible problems.

Facilities

Three excellent toilet blocks are well equipped, including excellent facilities for disabled visitors. Motorcaravan services. Gas. Well stocked shop. Pleasant bar. Excellent restaurant. Takeaway (Easter-Oct). Swimming and paddling pools. Very good playground. Bicycle hire. Entertainment in high season. Many adventurous activities can be arranged, including white-water rafting, gorging, orienteering, trekking, bungee and riding. Large families and groups catered for. Off site: Fishing, canoeing and windsurfing on the lake. Village 3 km.

Open: All year.

See advertisement on page 73.

Directions

From autopista A7/E15 on Valencia ring road (near the airport) take A3 (E901) to the west. Villargordo del Cabriel is 80 km. towards Motilla. Take village exit 255 and follow signs through village and over a hill – spot the village on a hill 2 km. away. That is the campsite! GPS: 39.552176, -1.47456

Charges guide

Per unit incl. 2 persons	
and electricity	€ 20,15 - € 29,95
extra person	€ 5,00 - € 6,25
child (under 10 yrs)	€ 3,80 - € 4,30
dog	€ 0,70

Vinaros

Camping Vinaros

Ctra N340 km 1054, E-12500 Vinaros (Castelló) T: 964 402 424. E: info@campingvinaros.com
alanrogers.com/ES85580

Taking its name from the nearby seaside town with its fishing harbour and marina, this pleasant site has 258 flat numbered pitches of average size on flat ground. Mature trees provide shade and neat hedges separate the pitches, all of which have an individual sink. The site entrance is directly off the N340, with a restaurant outside the main boundary. There is a spacious entrance with lots of outside parking, but there is traffic noise. A swimming pool has a sunbathing area and a paddling pool and a pleasant snack bar serves snacks all year. Large blocks of natural stone have been used for decoration around the site.

Facilities

Two exceptionally clean, fully equipped toilet blocks use marble and tiling to create a light environment enhanced by potted shrubs. Some washbasins are in cabins. Facilities for disabled visitors. Laundry facilities. Motorcaravan services. Milk and bread delivered daily. Restaurant, snack bar and bar (all year). Play area. Swimming pool (1/4-30/10). Pétanque. Musical and other entertainment in season. Large aviary and terrapin pool. Children's club (high season) and artistic activities for adults (all year). Off site: Beach and fishing 800 m. Bus service 500 m. Rail station close by. Vinaros 500 m. with extensive choice of bars and restaurants. Golf 7 km.

Open: All year.

Directions

Take exit 43 (Ulldecona) from the A7 and head to Vinaros. At the junction with the N340, turn left and head towards Barcelona. Site is at 1054 km. marker directly off the N340, opposite a large garden centre. GPS: 40.4931, 0.4838

Charges guide

Per unit, all inclusive	€ 11,00 - € 16,00

For latest campsite news, availability and prices visit
alanrogers.com

In the province of Murcia you'll find sandy beaches, dunes and unspoilt coves along the coast; inland hills and valleys plus the regional parks of Sierra de Carche, Sierra de la Pila, Sierra de Espuña, and Carrascoy and El Valle.

THE CAPITAL OF THE REGION IS THE CITY OF MURCIA

Murcia, the capital of the region, was founded in the ninth century by the Moors on the banks of the Río Segura. The square of Cardinal Belluga houses two of the town's architectural gems, the Episcopal Palace and the Cathedral, and there is a range of museums and exhibitions to visit. With narrow medieval streets, the characterful town of Cartagena has lots of bars and restaurants plus two nautical museums: the National Museum of Maritime Archaeology and the Naval Museum. Also on a nautical theme, the International Nautical Week is celebrated here in June. Along the coast there are numerous beaches offering a wide range of water sports: sailing, windsurfing, canoeing, water skiing and diving. And the area between the coastal towns of Águilas and Mazarrón is a breeding ground for tortoises and eagles. Inland are the historic towns of Lorca and Caravaca de le Cruz. The former is known as the 'baroque city' with its examples of baroque architecture, seen in the parish churches, convents, and houses; the latter too is home to beautiful churches, including El Santuario de Vera Cruz.

Places of interest

Águilas: seaside town with good beaches.

Moratalla: pretty village, castle offering stunning views of the surrounding countryside and forests.

Puerto de Mazarrón: Enchanted City of Bolnuevo - a small area of eroded rocks, nature reserve and lagoon at La Rambla de Moreras.

San Pedro del Pinatar: seaside resort, La Pagan beach is renowned for its therapeutic mud, which reputedly relieves rheumatism and is good for the skin.

Santiago de la Ribera: upmarket resort with sailing club.

Cuisine of the region

Vegetables are important and found in nearly every dish. Fish is also popular, cooked in a salt crust or *a la espalda* (lightly fried and baked), and usually accompanied by rice. Fig bread is a speciality of the region.

Bizcochos borrachos: sponge soaked in wine and syrup.

Cabello de Ángel: pumpkin strands in syrup.

Caldero: made of rice, fish and the hot ñora pepper.

Caldo con pelotas: stew made of turkey with meatballs.

Chuletas de cordero al ajo cabañil: suckling lamb chops served with a dressing of garlic and vinegar.

Tocino de cielo: dessert made with egg yolks and syrup.

Yemas de Caravaca: cake made with egg yolks.

Baños de Fortuna

Camping La Fuente

Camino de La Bocamina, E-30626 Baños de Fortuna (Murcia) T: **968 685 125**. E: info@campingfuente.com
alanrogers.com/ES87450

Located in an area known for its thermal waters since Roman and Moorish times and with just 87 pitches and 14 bungalows, La Fuente is a gem. Unusually winter is high season here. The main attraction here is the huge hydrotherapy centre where the water is constant at 36 degrees all year. The pool can be covered in inclement weather. The site is in two sections, one where pitches are in standard rows and the other where they are in circles around blocks. The hard, flat pitches are on shingle (rock pegs advised), have 10A electricity and 53 have their own mini sanitary unit. Some artificial shade has been added for 22 pitches. There is accommodation to rent on site but it is separate from the camping area. The site's buildings are a cheery yellow colour and the pool has a large terraced area and pool bar. Fed from thermal springs this is really good for old bones! Importantly there is a long gentle ramp into the pool, for the not so agile or where a bath chair could be lowered into the water. A daily charge applies for use of the pool and jacuzzis (€ 4.50 but well worth it). There is also a very good restaurant with terrace and separate bar.

Facilities

Some pitches have their own facilities including a unit for disabled visitors. Washing machines and dryers. High quality restaurant shared with accommodation guests. Snack bar by pool. Supermarket. Bicycle hire. Communal barbecues. Jacuzzi. Off site: Spa town, massage therapies, hot pools 500 m. Fortuna, shops, bars, restaurants 3 km. Golf and riding 20 km.

Open: All year.

Directions

From A7/E15 Alicante - Murcia road take C3223 to Fortuna then follow signs to Baños de Fortuna. The site with its bright yellow walls can be easily seen from the road and is very well signed in the town. GPS: 38.20682, -1.10732

Charges 2011

Per unit incl. 2 persons and electricity	€ 16,59
with individual sanitary facility	€ 18,70
extra person	€ 3,25
child (3-12 yrs)	€ 1,25
dog	€ 1,00
Pitch prices discounted after five days.	

For latest campsite news, availability and prices visit
alanrogers.com

Cartagena

Camping Naturista El Portus

El Portus, E-30394 Cartagena (Murcia) T: 968 553 052. E: elportus@elportus.com

alanrogers.com/ES87520

Set in a secluded south facing bay fringed by mountains, El Portus is a fairly large naturist site enjoying magnificent views and with direct access to a small sand and pebble beach. This part of Spain enjoys almost all year round sunshine. There are some 400 pitches, 300 for tourers, ranging from 60-100 sq.m, all but a few having electricity (6A). They are mostly on fairly level, if somewhat stony and barren ground. El Portus has a reasonable amount of shade from established trees and nearly every pitch has a view. Residential units are situated on the hillside above the site.

Facilities

Five acceptable, unisex toilet blocks are of varying styles, fully equipped and opened as required. Showers all with hot water. Unit for disabled visitors, key from reception. Washing machines. Motorcaravan services. Well stocked shop. Bar with TV and library. Restaurants. The beach restaurant is closed in low season. Swimming pools (June-Sept). Wellness centre. Play area. Tennis. Pétanque. Yoga. Scuba-diving club (high season). Windsurfing. Spanish lessons. Small boat moorings. Entertainment programme. Off site: Fishing from beach. Golf 28 km.

Open: All year.

Directions

Site is on the coast, 10 km. west of Cartagena. Follow signs to Mazarron then take E22 to Canteras. Site is well signed for 4 km. If approaching through Cartagena, exit the town on N332 following signs for Canteras. Site signed on joining the N332. GPS: 37.585, -1.06717

Charges guide

Per person	€ 7,00
child (3-9 yrs)	€ 5,00
pitch incl. electricity (6A)	€ 22,20

Isla Plana

Camping Los Madriles

Ctra de la Azohia km 4.5, E-30868 Isla Plana (Murcia) T: 968 152 151. E: camplosmadriles@terra.es

alanrogers.com/ES87480

An exceptional site with super facilities, Los Madriles is run by a hard working team, with constant improvements being made. Twenty kilometres west of Cartagena, the approach to the site and the surrounding area is fairly unremarkable, but the site is not. A fairly steep access road leads to the 313 flat, good to large size terraced pitches, each having electricity, water and a waste point. Most have shade from large trees with a number benefiting from panoramic views of the sea or behind to the mountains. The site has huge rectangular and lagoon style pools with water sprays and jacuzzis.

Facilities

Four sanitary blocks and one small toilet block provide excellent facilities, including services in one block for disabled visitors. Private wash cabins. Laundry facilities. Motorcaravan services. Car wash. Supermarket, restaurant/snack bar and bar (all open all season but hours are limited). Swimming pools with jacuzzi. Boules. Play areas. Animals are not accepted. Off site: Town close by. Beach 800 m. and fishing 800 m. (Licence required, purchase in Puerto Mazarron). Boat launching 3 km. Riding and bicycle hire 6 km. Golf 20 km.

Open: All year.

Directions

From E15/A7 take exit 845 and follow RM3 in direction of Cartagena, Fuente Alamo and Mazarron (do not turn into Mazarron). Continue towards Puerto Mazarron and take N332 (Cartagena). On reaching coast continue with N332 (Cartagena and Alicante). At roundabout turn right towards Isla Plana and La Azohia. Site is well signed and on the left in approx. 5 km. GPS: 37.5735, -1.19117

Charges guide

Per unit incl. 2 persons and electricity	€ 32,10

Moratalla

Camping La Puerta

Ctra de La Puerta s/n, E-30440 Moratalla (Murcia) T: 968 730 008. E: info@campinglapuerta.com

alanrogers.com/ES87440

Camping La Puerta is part of the Camping La Manga group. It is a typical Spanish weekend and holiday site and advance booking is essential for high season and most weekends. Set in the secluded hills above Moratalla, it provides a rural base from which to explore the surrounding countryside. It is a place where you can relax and forget about the hustle and bustle of city life whilst relaxing around the magnificent swimming pool complex. Most of the 159 touring pitches are rather small and large units could have difficulty in manoeuvring due to randomly growing trees. Limited English is spoken on site.

Facilities

Three fully fitted sanitary blocks provide toilets, washbasins and shower cubicles. Facilities for disabled visitors. Washing machines. Shop. Bar and terrace. Caféteria and restaurant serving a variety of local dishes. Play area. Tennis. Fishing. Barbecues are not permitted. Off site: Riding 5 km.

Open: All year.

Directions

From the A7 (Murcia - Lorca) exit at 651 km. onto the C415 in the direction of Mula and Caravaca. Follow signs to Moratalla and then on to site which is well signed. GPS: 38.20555, -1.91975

Charges guide

Per unit incl. 2 persons	€ 20,20 - € 23,20
extra person	€ 4,05
Camping Cheques accepted.	

For latest campsite news, availability and prices visit

alanrogers.com

La Manga del Mar Menor

Caravaning La Manga

Autovia Cartagena - La Manga Salida 11, E-30386 La Manga del Mar Menor (Murcia) T: 902 021 352
E: lamanga@caravaning.es alanrogers.com/ES87530

This is a very large well equipped 'holiday style' site with its own beach and both indoor and outdoor pools. With a good number of typical Spanish long stay units, the length of the site is impressive (1 km) and a bicycle is very helpful for getting about. The 1,000 regularly laid out, gravel touring pitches (100 or 110 sq. m) are generally separated by hedges which also provide a degree of shade. Each has 10A electricity supply, water and the possibility of satellite TV reception. This site's excellent facilities are ideally suited for holidays in the winter when the weather is very pleasantly warm. If you are suffering from aches and pains try the famous local mud treatment. Reception will assist with bookings. November daytime temperatures usually exceed 20 degrees. La Manga is a 22 km. long narrow strip of land, bordered by the Mediterranean on one side and by the Mar Menor on the other. There are sandy bathing beaches on both sides and considerable development in terms of hotels, apartments, restaurants, night clubs, etc. in between – a little reminiscent of Miami Beach! The very end of the southern part is great for 'getting away from it all' (take a picnic for the beach and be sure to go over the little bridge for privacy). The campsite is situated on the approach to 'the strip' enjoying the benefit of its own semi-private beach with impressive tall palm trees alongside the Mar Menor which provides shallow warm waters, ideal for families with children. Here you will find a sailing, canoeing and windsurfing school, and an excellent restaurant/bar serving traditional Spanish tapas and meals. In winter, when British occupancy exceeds 60%, typical British meals are available including Sunday roast and full breakfasts.

Facilities

Nine clean toilet blocks of standard design, well spaced around the site, include washbasins (all with hot water). Laundry. Gas supplies. Large well stocked supermarket. Restaurant. Bar. Snack bar. Swimming pool complex (April-Sept). Indoor pool, gymnasium (April-Oct), sauna, jacuzzi and massage service. New outdoor fitness course for adults. Open air family cinema (July/Aug). Tennis. Pétanque. Minigolf. Play area. Watersports school. Internet café (also WiFi). Winter activities including Spanish classes. Pet washing area. Max. 2 dogs. Off site: Buses to Cartagena and Murcia from outside site. Golf, bicycle hire and riding 5 km.

Open: All year.

Directions

Use exit (Salida) 11 from MU312 dual carriageway towards Cabo de Palos, signed Playa Honda (site signed also). Cross road bridge and double back on yourself. Site entrance is clearly visible beside dual carriageway with many flags flying.
GPS: 37.62445, -0.74442

Charges guide

Per unit incl. 2 persons and electricity	€ 19,75 - € 34,50
extra person	€ 4,00 - € 5,00
child	€ 3,50 - € 4,00
dog	€ 1,25

Discounts and special prices for low season and long winter stays.
Camping Cheques accepted.

For latest campsite news, availability and prices visit
alanrogers.com

Famous for its sun, its beautiful traditions, its poets, original folklore, age-old history and magnificent heritage left behind by the Moors, Andalucía is one of the most attractive regions in Spain.

THIS COMPRISES EIGHT PROVINCES: ALMERIA, CADIZ, CORDOBA, GRANADA, HUELVA, MALAGA, JAEN AND SEVILLE

THE REGIONAL CAPITAL IS SEVILLE

With the River Guadalquivir running through it, the charming city of Seville is one of the most visited places in the region. The old city, with its great monuments; the Giralda tower, Cathedral and the Alcázar, plus the narrow, winding streets of Santa Cruz, is particularly popular. Also on the Guadalquivir, Cordoba is located northeast of Seville. It too has a picturesque Jewish Quarter along with a rich Moorish heritage. Indeed, the Mezquita is one of the grandest mosques ever built by the Moors in Spain. Located further east on the foothills of the Sierra Nevada mountain range, Granada is home to the impressive Alhambra, a group of distinct buildings including a Royal Palace, splendid gardens, and the fortress of Alcazaba. The Sierra Nevada, Spain's highest range, offers good skiing and trekking. Further south, you'll find the fine beaches and tourist areas of the Costa Tropical and the Costa del Sol, including the developed resort of Malaga. There are more beaches on the west coast plus one of the oldest settlements in Spain, the bustling port of Cádiz.

Places of interest

Almeria: preserved Moorish heritage with greatest purity. Located on a beautiful bay.

Casa-Museo Pablo Ruiz Picasso: art museum including collection of originals by Pablo Picasso.

Jaen: medieval fortress, Renaissance cathedral, 11th century Moorish baths, Santa Catalina castle.

Jerez de la Frontera: birthplace of sherry and Spanish brandy, site of renowned equestrian school.

Mijas: enchanting village, with narrow streets bordered by brilliantly white-washed houses.

Parque Natural de las Sierras de Cazorla y Segura: largest park in Spain with mountains, river gorges, forests and wildlife.

Ronda: beautiful town on the edge of an abrupt rocky precipice.

Cuisine of the region

Andalucía has more tapas bars than anywhere else in Spain. Sea food in abundance, fresh vegetables and fruit: oranges from Cordoba; persimmons, pomegranates, figs, strawberries from Alpujarra; avocados, mangos, guavas, papayas from the coast of Granada and Malaga. Locally produced wine and sherry.

Alboronía: vegetable stew.

Alfajors: almond and nut pastry.

Gazpacho ajoblanco: cold soup with garlic and almond.

Gazpacho salmorejo: much thicker and made with tomatoes only.

Pestiños: honey coated pastries.

Tocinillo de cielo: pudding made with egg yolks and syrup.

For latest campsite news, availability and prices visit

alanrogers.com

Alcalá de los Gazules

Camping Los Gazules

Ctra de Patrite km 4, E-11180 Alcalá de los Gazules (Cádiz) T: 956 420 486

E: camping@losgazules.e.telefonica.net alanrogers.com/ES88900

The site is set in the beautiful surroundings of the Los Alcornocales natural park and has 135 touring pitches with 10A electricity. Although basic, this would make an ideal site for a quiet, relaxing holiday in the countryside. The main building complex, consisting of the shop and restaurant has been newly painted outside and improved and the well furnished restaurant/bar is a pleasant place to eat. The sanitary facilities have also been improved and there is an inviting swimming pool.

Facilities

A circular sanitary block offers clean facilities, including facilities for disabled visitors. Washing machine in supervised room. Bar/restaurant. Shop in bar sells basic supplies. Swimming pool (June-Sept). Playground. Off site: Site is well placed for exploring the local area and excursions to Cádiz.

Open: All year.

Directions

From A381 Algecieras - Jerez road take exit to Alcalá de los Gazules onto A375(C440). Continue around village on A375 to Ubrique and proceed to 42 km. marker. Then turn onto the road to Patrite, the site is on the right at the 4 km. marker. GPS: 36.463, -5.664

Charges guide

Per unit incl. 2 persons and electricity	€ 18,00 - € 19,00
extra person	€ 4,50 - € 5,00

Almayate

Camping Naturista Almanat

Carril de la Torre Alta s/n, E-29749 Almayate (Málaga) T: 952 556 462. E: info@almanat.de

alanrogers.com/ES87830

With direct access to a one kilometre grey sand and shingle naturist beach, this established all year naturist site, set amongst agricultural land with mountain backdrop, is proving a firm favourite with many British seeking winter sun. The facilities on site are to a very high standard. The entire two-hectare site is flat with a fine shingle surface. A large number of mature trees provide much needed shade in the summer months. The 194 touring pitches with 16A electricity, vary in size and shape with the majority demanding physical manoeuvring of a touring caravan.

Facilities

The large, unisex toilet block is fully equipped, regularly cleaned and all under cover. Good facilities for disabled visitors near reception. Small shop. Bar/restaurant with terrace. Large unheated swimming pool. New indoor pool with jacuzzi (closed 15/6-15/9). Sauna and gym. Cinema (56 seats). Social room. Play area. Minigolf. Weather permitting, one is expected to be nude which is obligatory in the pool area and bar during the day. Off site: Torre del Mar is 2 km. Regular bus service 1 km. Fishing, riding nearby.

Open: All year.

Directions

Approaching from the east (Torre del Mar) it is necessary to turn left to access the 600 m. single track access to the site. It is illegal to make that left turn. From east or west on N340 autovia take exit 265 signed Cajiz Iznate and Costa 340a. Follow Costa direction and on reaching the coast turn left on 340a toward Torre del Mar. Site well signed in 5 km. on right. GPS: 36.72703, -4.11334

Charges guide

Per person	€ 4,80
pitch incl. electricity	€ 8,50 - € 22,70

Almeria

Camping La Garrofa

Ctra N340 km 435,4, direccion a Aguadulce via Litoral, E-04002 Almeria (Almería) T: 950 235 770

E: info@lagarrofa.com alanrogers.com/ES87650

One of the earliest sites in Spain (dating back to 1957), La Garrofa nestles in a cove with a virtually private beach accessed only by sea or through the campsite. It is rather dramatic with the tall mountain cliffs behind. Many of the rather small 100 flat and sloping sandy pitches are shaded, with some very close to the beach and sea. Eighty have 6/10A electricity. An old fortress looks down on the campsite – you can walk to it via a valley at the back of the site and across an old Roman bridge. Other walks directly from the site include a Roman road providing fine coastal views.

Facilities

Sanitary facilities are mature but clean. Facilities for disabled visitors. Restaurant/snack bar. Shop. Play area. Torches useful. Fishing. Off site: Town close by. Walks. Sub-aqua diving. Bicycle hire 2 km. Golf 8 km. Excursions – tickets to attractions sold. Bus stop nearby to Almeria and Aguadulce.

Open: All year.

Directions

Site is west of Almeria. Take the 438 exit from the N340 and follow the camping signs. The site is below the minor road on the beach side. GPS: 36.8257, -2.5161

Charges 2011

Per unit incl. 2 persons and electricity	€ 24,28 - € 27,90
extra person	€ 5,50
child	€ 4,86

For latest campsite news, availability and prices visit
alanrogers.com

Almonte

Camping La Aldea

El Rocio, E-21750 Almonte (Huelva) T: 959 442 677. E: info@campinglaaldea.com
alanrogers.com/ES88730

This impressive site lies just on the edge of the Parque Nacional de Donana, southwest of Sevilla on the outskirts of El Rocio. The town hosts a fiesta at the end of May with over one million people attending the local shrine. They travel for days in processions with cow drawn or motorized vehicles to attend. If you want to stay this weekend book well in advance! The well planned, modern site is well set out and the 246 pitches have natural shade from trees or artificial shade and 10A electricity. There are 52 serviced pitches with water and drainage. There are also pitches for tents and bungalows for rent.

Facilities

Two sanitary blocks provide excellent facilities including provision for disabled visitors. Motorcaravan service point. Swimming pool (May-Oct). Restaurant and bar in separate new complex. Shop. Internet connection. Playground. Off site: Bus stop 5 minutes walk. Huelva and Sevilla are about an hour's drive. Beach 15 km.

Open: All year.

Directions

From main Huelva - Sevilla road E1/A49 take exit 48 and drive south through Almonte to outskirts of El Rocio. Site is on left just past 25 km. marker. Go down to the roundabout and back up to be on the right side of the road to turn in. GPS: 37.1428, -6.491164

Charges guide

Per unit incl. 2 persons and electricity	€ 23,00 - € 26,00
extra person	€ 5,50
child (0-10 yrs)	€ 4,50
dog	€ 3,00

Barbate

Camping Pinar San José

Carretera de Vejer - Caños de Meca km 10,2, Los Caños de Meca, E-11159 Barbate (Cádiz) T: 956 437 030
E: info@campingpinarsanjose.com alanrogers.com/ES88570

Pinar San José is a new site, first opened in 2008. The site is located in the La Breña natural park and has been developed to reflect the natural beauty that surrounds it. The nearest beaches on the Costa de la Luz are around 1 km. distant. On site amenities are modern and well designed and include two swimming pools, tennis and a sports court. Pitches are grassy and all have electrical connections. There is a good provision of water points and many pitches also have drainage and internet connections. A number of brick built chalets are available for rent. Cabo de Trafalgar (Cape Trafalgar) is very close and, of course, gave its name to the famous battle several kilometres to the west. The nearest village to the site is Zahora and the great cities of Cádiz and Jerez, as well as Gibraltar are all accessible in less than an hour. La Breña natural park was formerly a massive sand dune and is now a large, forested area, criss-crossed with cycle tracks and footpaths. Riding is also possible in the park.

Facilities

Bar. Restaurant. Shop. Two swimming pools. Tennis. Sports court. Play area. Games room. Chalets for rent. Dogs are not accepted in high season. Off site: Nearest beach 1 km. Cádiz 50 km. Fishing. Golf. Watersports.

Open: All year.

Directions

Heading south from Cádiz on the A48 motorway at the Vejer de la Frontera exit and head west on A2230 and then south on A2233 to Zahora. Site is well signed from here. GPS: 36.19998, -6.034627

Charges guide

Per unit incl. 2 persons and electricity	€ 21,50 - € 32,00
extra person	€ 4,50 - € 6,00
child (2-11 yrs)	€ 3,00 - € 4,00
dog	€ 2,00

For latest campsite news, availability and prices visit
alanrogers.com

Cabo de Gata

Camping Cabo de Gata

Ctra Cabo de Gata s/n, E-04150 Cabo de Gata (Almería) T: 950 160 443. E: info@campingcabodegata.com
alanrogers.com/ES87630

Cabo de Gata is situated on the Gulf of Almeria, a pleasant, all year campsite offering facilities to a good standard. Popular with British visitors through the winter, and within the Cabo de Gata-Nijar nature park and set amongst fruit farms, it is only a 1 km. walk to a fine sandy beach. The 250 gravel pitches are level and of a reasonable size, with 6/16A electricity and limited shade from maturing trees or canopies. There are specific areas for very large units with very high canopies for shade and 7 chalets for rent.

Facilities

Two, well maintained, clean toilet blocks provide all the necessary sanitary facilities. including British type WCs, washbasins and free hot showers. Facilities for disabled visitors. Restaurant, bar and shop (all year). Swimming pool. Football. Pétanque. Tennis. Small playground. Library. Bicycle hire. English spoken. Entertainment programme. Internet access (charged). WiFi throughout site. Off site: Nearest beach 1 km. Bus from gate. Fishing 1 km. Golf 10 km. Riding 15 km.

Open: All year.

Directions

From A7-E15 take exit 460 or 467 and follow signs for Retamar via N344 and for Cabo de Gata. Site is on the right before village of Cabo de Gata. The final stretch of road is in a poor state of repair due to restrictions imposed within the natural park. GPS: 36.80188, -2.24471

Charges 2011

Per unit incl. 2 persons and electricity	€ 29,45 - € 30,10
extra person	€ 5,95
child (2-10 yrs)	€ 5,40

Conil de la Frontera

Camping La Rosaleda

Ctra del Pradillo km 1,3, E-11140 Conil de la Frontera (Cádiz) T: 956 443 327. E: info@campinglarosaleda.com
alanrogers.com/ES88580

The owner of this excellent site in Andalucia has many years of experience and has listened to what campers want and has then delivered. Much money has been spent and will continue to be spent to make this an even better site. Great care has been taken with the planning to ensure campers have an enjoyable holiday, with many top class facilities and a first class service. There are 335 well kept pitches of three different sizes, the smallest just for tents, the largest with electricity and water.

Facilities

Four modern, fully equipped sanitary blocks include facilities for campers with disabilities and were spotless when seen. Motorcaravan services. Gas supplies. Excellent supermarket. Bar/restaurant. Swimming pool complex (large with stunning views). Large play area. Massage, sauna, gym, yoga room, hairdressing. Wooden bungalows with good facilities and own gardens. No barbecues on pitches between 15/6 and 15/10. Dogs are not accepted in high season. Off site: Water based activities at beach 1.5 km. Conil town with bars restaurants and shops. Excursions. Bicycle hire 1 km. Riding 1.5 km. Golf 15 km.

Open: All year.

Directions

Follow signs to Conil from N340, then signs to site around several roundabouts. Site is 1 km. from centre on Ctra del Pradillo, on the side of this road with a car park in front and a large campsite sign high in the air. GPS: 36.29317, -6.09547

Charges guide

Per person	€ 4,72 - € 8,00
child (3-10 yrs)	€ 3,24 - € 5,50
pitch incl. electricity	€ 11,80 - € 21,00

Conil de la Frontera

Camping Roche

N340 km 19,5, Carril de Pilahito, E-11140 Conil de la Frontera (Cádiz) T: 956 442 216
E: info@campingroche.com alanrogers.com/ES88590

Camping Roche is situated in a pine forest near white sandy beaches in the lovely region of Andalucia. It is a clean and tidy, welcoming site. English is spoken but try your Spanish, German or French as the staff are very helpful. A family site, it offers a variety of facilities including a sports area and swimming pools. A recently built extension provides further pitches, a new toilet block and a tennis court. There are now 335 pitches which include 104 bungalows to rent. The touring pitches all have electricity (10A), and 76 also have water and waste water.

Facilities

Three toilet blocks are traditional in style and provide simple, clean facilities. Washbasins have cold water only. Washing machine. Supermarket. Bar and restaurant. Swimming and paddling pools. Sports area. Tennis. Play area. Off site: Bus stops 3 times daily outside gates. Cadiz. Cape Trafalgar. Baelo Claudia archaeological site.

Open: All year.

Directions

From the N340 (Cádiz - Algeciras) turn off to site at km. 19.5 point. From Conil, take El Pradillo road. Keep following signs to site. From CA3208 road turn at km. 1 and site is 1.5 km. down this road on the right. GPS: 36.31089, -6.11268

Charges guide

Per unit incl. 2 persons and electricity	€ 33,00
extra person	€ 6,50

For latest campsite news, availability and prices visit
alanrogers.com

Conil de la Frontera
Camping Fuente del Gallo

Apdo 48, E-11149 Conil de la Frontera (Cádiz) T: 956 440 137. E: camping@campingfuentedelgallo.com
alanrogers.com/ES88600

Fuente del Gallo is well maintained with 229 pitches allocated to touring units. Each pitch has 6A electricity and a number of trees create shade to some pitches. Although the actual pitch areas are generally a good size, the majority are long and narrow. This could, in some cases, prevent the erection of an awning and your neighbour may feel close. In low season it is generally accepted to make additional use of an adjoining pitch. Good beaches are relatively near at 300 m.

Facilities	Directions
Two modernised and very clean sanitary blocks include excellent services for babies and disabled visitors and hot water at all facilities. Laundry facilities. Motorcaravan services. Gas supplies. Shop. Bar and restaurant (breakfast served). Swimming pool (1/6-30/9 with lifeguard) with paddling pool. Play area. TV and games machines in bar area. Safety deposit boxes. Excursions. Torches useful. Picnic area with playground and games. Off site: Watersports on beach. Fishing 300 m. Riding 1 km. Bicycle and motor scooter hire 2 km. Golf 5 km.	From the Cadiz - Algeciras road (N340) at km. 23.00, follow signs to Conil de la Frontera town centre, then shortly right to Fuente del Gallo and 'playas', following signs. GPS: 36.2961, -6.1102

Open: 18 March - 30 September.

Charges guide

Per unit incl. 2 persons and electricity	€ 27,00
extra person	€ 6,00
child (3-10 yrs)	€ 5,00
dog	€ 3,00

Less 11-30% for longer stays (except Jul/Aug).

Córdoba
Camping Los Villares

Parque Periurbano, avenida de I Fuen Santa 8, E-14071 Córdoba (Córdoba) T: 957 330 145
alanrogers.com/ES90780

This is a site with a difference. Unusually it is part of one of Spain's natural parks and the environmental rules must be strictly followed. For peaceful, simple camping with no frills, there is an area with electricity for 30 units about five minutes walk from a toilet block, restaurant and reception. The 170 tent pitches are delightfully informal. Bountiful pine, olives, gums and other trees provide shade and the setting is absolutely natural. Thoughtfully some natural stone tables and benches are scattered around.

Facilities	Directions
The single toilet facility is centrally located, provides free hot water and is of good quality. Washing machines. Shop. Restaurant/bar. Off site: Natural Parque (protected) with walks and wildlife.	Site is 7 km. north of Córdoba on the north side of the river which bisects the city. Go to the centre to find the small access road to Parque and site. Follow signs for Parador or Parque Periurbano and also for municipal camping. These bring you past the municipal camping. Look for a major right turn and follow signs out of city. Site is a stiff climb. GPS: 37.95738, -4.81033

Open: All year.

Charges guide

Per person	€ 3,75
pitch incl. car	€ 7,00 - € 8,00

No credit cards.

Córdoba
Camping Municipal El Brillante

Avenida del Brillante 50, E-14012 Córdoba (Córdoba) T: 957 403 836. E: elbrillante@campings.net
alanrogers.com/ES90800

Córdoba is one of the hottest places in Europe and the superb pool here is more than welcome. If you really want to stay in the city, then this large site is a good choice. It has 120 neat pitches of gravel and sand, the upper pitches covered by artificial and natural shade but the lower, newer area has little. The site becomes very crowded in high season. The entrance is narrow and may be congested so care must be exercised – there is a lay-by just outside and it is easier to walk in initially. All pitches have electricity (6/10A) plus the newer area has 32 fully serviced pitches and an area for a few large motorhomes.

Facilities	Directions
The toilet blocks include facilities for babies and disabled visitors. Motorcaravan services. Gas supplies. Shop (all year). Bar and restaurant (1/7-15/9). Swimming pool (1/6-10/9). Play area. Off site: Bus service to city centre from outside site. Commercial centre 300 m. (left out of site, right at traffic lights).	From the NIV/E25 road from Madrid, take exit at km. 403. Follow signs for Mosque/Cathedral to city centre. Pass it (on right) and turn right onto main avenue. Continue, taking right fork where road splits. Follow signs for site and/or district of El Brillante. Site on right up slight hill. GPS: 37.899975, -4.787319

Open: All year.

Charges guide

Per unit incl. 2 persons	€ 25,00 - € 28,00

No credit cards.

For latest campsite news, availability and prices visit
alanrogers.com

Dilar

Camping Los Avellanos de Sierra Nevada

Ctra de la Fábrica s/n, E-18152 Dilar (Granada) T: 958 596 016. E: Avellano@Teleline.es

alanrogers.com/ES92750

This is a fascinating tiny business with a philosophy of peace and tranquillity, a world apart from other sites in southern Spain. This has been achieved by Pilar and her brother Idvier. The site is also called Camping Cortijo, which loosely translates from the Spanish as a 'big house in grounds with animals, birds and produce where people work towards people'. There is a fabulous old house and 20 beautifully terraced pitches (mainly for tents) with amazing views enjoying the sound of water tinkling through the ancient irrigation channels on its way to the crops (cars are parked separately).

Facilities

Toilet facilities are modern and clean. Pretty bar/restaurant serves typical local fare and sells basic supplies (very limited in low season). Kitchen for hire. Restaurant/bar. Swimming pool (high season only). Bicycle hire. Riding. Fishing in river Dilar. Details of walks from reception. Torches essential. Excellent rooms to let. Off site: Tours of Granada (20 minutes away), especially the Alhambra, organised. Site also useful for skiing in Sierra Nevada in season.

Open: All year.

Directions

Heading south from Granada on (E902) A44 exit 139 (Otura). Heading north exit 144. Head towards Otura on GR 5025. Proceed through town and right at roundabout (Dilar/Rio Dilar) on through village. In 2 km. site on right, very steep climb. Not suitable for American RVs. GPS: 37.068, -3.581

Charges guide

Per unit incl. 2 persons and electricity	€ 22,77
extra person	€ 4,28

No credit cards.

El Puerto de Santa Maria

Camping Playa Las Dunas

Paseo Maritimo, Playa de la Puntilla s/n, E-11500 El Puerto de Santa Maria (Cádiz) T: 956 872 210
E: info@lasdunascamping.com alanrogers.com/ES88650

This site lies within the Parque Natural Bahia de Les Dunes and is adjacent to the long and gently sloping golden sands of Puntilla beach. This is a pleasant and peaceful site (though very busy in August) with some 539 separate marked pitches, 260 for tourers, with much natural shade and ample electrical connections (10A). Motorcaravans park in an area called the Oasis which is very pretty. The tent and caravan pitches, under mature trees, are terraced and separated by low walls. This is a spacious site with a tranquil setting and it is popular with people who wish to 'winter over' in peace.

Facilities

Immaculate modern sanitary facilities with separate facilities for disabled visitors and a baby room. Laundry facilities are excellent. Gas supplies. Bar/restaurant (all year). Supermarket (high season). Very large swimming pool and paddling pool (1/7-31/8). Night security all year. Barbecues not permitted 15/5-15/10. Off site: Beach 100 m. Fishing 500 m. Bicycle hire, riding and golf 2 km. Municipal sports centre. Local buses for town and city visits and a ferry to Cadiz.

Open: All year.

Directions

Site is 5 km. north of Cadiz off the N443. Take road to Puerto Santa Maria, site is very well signed throughout the town. From south, turn left into town just after large bridge. Keeping sea inlet on your left, follow road for about 1 km. Site on right opposite beach. GPS: 36.5890, -6.2384

Charges 2011

Per unit incl. 2 persons and electricity	€ 21,28 - € 26,28
extra person	€ 4,65 - € 5,17
child (3-10 yrs)	€ 3,98 - € 4,42

Fuente de Piedra

Espacios Rurales Fuente de Piedra

Ctra La Rábita s/n, E-29520 Fuente de Piedra (Málaga) T: 952 735 294. E: info@camping-rural.com

alanrogers.com/ES87900

In a remote area of Andalucia, this tiny campsite with just 30 touring pitches looks over the salty lakes and marshes of the Laguna de Fuente. The average size pitches are on a sloping, terraced hillside, with some having a view of the lake. With a gravel surface and good shade, many pitches slope so chocks would be useful. There is a separate grassy area for tents near the pool and bungalows (cars are not permitted here). Unusually for a site of this size there is a pool and a huge restaurant.

Facilities

Sanitary facilities are in one block and are looking a little tired. Facilities for disabled visitors. Washing machines. Shop. Restaurant. Bar with TV. Snack bar. Swimming pool. Pool bar. Electronic games. Bicycle hire. Off site: Lake with flamingos. Bicycle hire 1 km. Fishing 5 km. Riding 10 km. Golf 40 km. Excursions organised in July and August.

Open: All year.

Directions

Site is 20 km. northwest of Antequera. From Antequera take A92 and exit at 132 km. point and follow road to the town. Site is well signed from the town but the signs are small. GPS: 37.1292, -4.7334

Charges guide

Per person	€ 5,40 - € 6,00
child (0-12 yrs)	€ 3,60 - € 4,00
pitch	€ 3,60 - € 8,00
electricity	€ 5,00

For latest campsite news, availability and prices visit

alanrogers.com

Granada
Camping Suspiro del Moro

Ctra Bailén - Motril km 144, Puerto Suspiro del Moro, E-18630 Granada (Granada) T: 958 555 411
E: campingsuspirodelmoro@yahoo.es alanrogers.com/ES92700

Suspiro Del Moro is small family run site with 64 pitches which packs a big punch with its associated Olympic size swimming pool and huge bar and restaurant. It is cool and peaceful with great views from the site perimeter. The flat pitches are shaded by mature trees and there are no statics here. The whole site is neat, clean and well ordered and great for visiting the area and the famous Alhambra (connecting buses from the gate). The site also has its own small bar and restaurant serving snacks.

Facilities

Clean and tidy, the small toilet blocks are situated around the camping area with British style WCs and free hot showers. Laundry and dishwashing facilities. Small basic shop. Small simple restaurant/bar (high season). Small play area on gravel. WiFi. Off site: Swimming pool and restaurant adjacent. Sierra Nevada and Granada within reasonable distance to explore. Public transport 50 m. from gate.

Open: All year.

Directions

Leave Granada to Motril road (E902/A44) at exit 144 (from south) or 139 (from north) and follow un-named campsite signs. At roundabout go towards Suspiro, then left (signed after turn). Site is about 600 m. on right on A4050 beside large restaurant. GPS: 37.0852, -3.6348

Charges guide

Per person	€ 4,00 - € 4,80
pitch incl. car	€ 9,00 - € 9,50
electricity	€ 3,00 - € 3,30

Granada
Camping Sierra Nevada

Avenida Juan Pablo II no.23, E-18014 Granada (Granada) T: 958 150 062. E: campingmotel@terra.es
alanrogers.com/ES92800

This is a good site either for a night stop or for a stay of a few days while visiting Granada, especially the Alhambra, and for a city site it is surprisingly pleasant. Quite large, it has an open feeling and, to encourage you to stay a little longer, a smart, irregular shape pool with a smaller children's pool open in high season. There is some traffic noise around the pool as it is on the road boundary. With 148 pitches for touring units (10/20A electricity), the site is in two connected parts with more mature trees and facilities to the northern end.

Facilities

Two modern sanitary blocks, with good facilities, including cabins, very good facilities for disabled visitors and babies. Washing machines. Motorcaravan services. Gas. Shop (15/3-15/10). Swimming pools with lifeguards and charge of € 1.80 (15/6-15/9). Bar/restaurant by pool. Tennis. Pétanque. Playground. Off site: Supermarket. Bus station 100 m. Fishing 10 km. Golf 12 km.

Open: 1 March - 31 October.

Directions

Site is just outside the city to north, on road to Jaén and Madrid. From autopista, take Granada North - Almanjayar exit 123 (close to central bus station). Follow road back towards Granada and site is on the right, well signed. From other roads join the motorway to access the correct exit. GPS: 37.20402, -3.61703

Charges 2011

Per person	€ 6,00
child (3-10 yrs)	€ 5,10
pitch incl. electricity (10A)	€ 18,00

Güéjar-Sierra
Camping Las Lomas

Ctra de Sierra Nevada, E-18160 Güéjar-Sierra (Granada) T: 958 484 742. E: laslomas@campings.net
alanrogers.com/ES92850

This site is high in the Güéjar-Sierra and looks down on the Patano de Canales reservoir. After a wonderful drive to Güéjar-Sierra, you are rewarded with a site boasting excellent facilities. It is set on a slope but the pitches have been levelled and are quite private, with high separating hedges and many mature trees giving good shade (some pitches are fully serviced, with sinks and most have electricity). The large bar/restaurant complex and pools have wonderful views over the lake.

Facilities

Pretty sanitary blocks (heated in winter) provide clean facilities. First class facilities for disabled visitors and well equipped baby room (key at reception). Spa for hire. Good supermarket. Restaurant/bar. Motorcaravan services. Swimming pool. Play area. Minigolf. Many other activities including parascending. Barbecue. Internet access. Torches useful. Off site: Buses to village and Granada (15 km). Tours of the Alhambra organised. Useful site for winter skiing.

Open: All year.

Directions

Heading south towards Granada on A44 (E902 Jaén - Motril) take exit 132 onto A395 (Alhamba - Sierra Nevada). After 4 km. marker, exit 5B (Sierra Nevada). At 7 km. marker, exit right onto slip road. At junction turn left (Cenes de la Vega - Güéjar-Sierra). In 200 m. turn right on A4026. In 1.6 km. turn left (Güéjar-Sierra). Drive uphill, past dam and site is on right in 2.8 km. GPS: 37.16073, -3.45388

Charges guide

Per person	€ 4,00 - € 6,00
child (2-10 yrs)	€ 3,50 - € 4,50
pitch	€ 12,00 - € 14,00

For latest campsite news, availability and prices visit
alanrogers.com

Isla Cristina

Camping Giralda

Ctra Provincial 4117, E-21410 Isla Cristina (Huelva) T: 959 343 318. E: campinggiralda@infonegocio.com
alanrogers.com/ES88710

The fountains at the entrance and the circular 'thatched' reception building set the tone for this very large site. The 587 pitches are quite spacious on sand, most benefiting from the attractive mature trees which abound on the site. Most pitches have electricity (142 are for tents). Access to the excellent beach is gained by a short stroll, crossing the minor road alongside the site and passing through attractive pine trees. This is a quiet site out of the main tourist areas, with good leisure and adventure facilities.

Facilities	Directions
Four large, modern, semi-circular thatched sanitary blocks are clean and fully equipped. Laundry. Shop and bar (all year). Restaurant and snacks (June-Sept). Swimming pools. Archery. Pétanque. Mountain biking. Beach games. Watersports school. Play area. Organised activity area for groups low season. Excursions booked. Off site: Beach and fishing 200 m. Bicycle hire 1.5 km. Golf 4 km. Riding 7 km. Open: All year.	Leave E1/A49 at exit 113 signed Lepe on N444. Turn right on N431, use Lepe bypass, then left to Le Antilla and then on to Isla Cristina. Site is on right (signed) just as you reach Isla Christina (this route avoids Pozo del Camino and many speed bumps). GPS: 37.19998, -7.30087

Charges guide

Per person	€ 5,80
child (2-10 yrs)	€ 4,20
caravan and car	€ 10,95
motorcaravan	€ 9,00
electricity	€ 5,25

Iznate

Camping Iznate

Ctra Benamocarra - Iznate km 2,7, E-29792 Iznate (Málaga) T: 952 535 613. E: info@campingiznate.com
alanrogers.com/ES87850

This brand new site is situated amid beautiful scenery 1 km. away from the picturesque village of Iznate. It is surrounded by avocado and olive trees and is on the wine route – the region is the centre of Spain's Muscadet production. The site is well thought out and immaculately maintained. The large swimming pool is an ideal spot for cooling off after a walk and the next door restaurant serves excellent food at very reasonable prices. This is a small site and we would recommend booking during high season. There are wonderful views all round the site and eagles, wild boar and black squirrels can be seen in the surrounding countryside.

Facilities	Directions
The modern toilet block has hot showers and facilities for disabled visitors. Laundry facilities under a covered area. Fridge hire. Small shop. Bar/restaurant with terrace adjoining the site. Swimming pool (15/5-15/9). Summer entertainment. Pétanque. Play area. TV room. Barbecues not permitted in high season. Off site: Beach 20 minutes drive. Towns of Sayalonga and Frigeliana nearby. Open: All year.	From A7/E15 take exit 265 and head towards Cajiz and Iznate. Site is on left 1 km. past Iznate. GPS: 36.79219, -4.17131

Charges guide

Per person	€ 4,30
child (2-10 yrs)	€ 3,70
pitch incl. car	€ 8,30 - € 9,30
electricity	€ 3,00 - € 3,50

La Carlota

Camping Carlos III

Ctra Madrid - Cadiz km 430, E-14100 La Carlota (Córdoba) T: 957 300 338. E: camping@campingcarlosiii.com
alanrogers.com/ES90850

This rural site lies 25 km. south of Córdoba, just off the main Córdoba - Sevilla road and may be a good alternative to staying in the city. A very large, busy site especially at weekends, it has many supporting facilities including a good swimming pool and a pool, play area and animal corner for children. With the catering services open all year, the site has a more open feel than the bustling municipal site in Córdoba. The touring areas are canopied by trees which offer considerable shade for the 338 separated pitches. On sandy, gently sloping ground, around two-thirds have 5/10A electricity.

Facilities	Directions
Modern toilet blocks provide a mix of British and Turkish WCs, with hot showers in the block near reception. Laundry service. Motorcaravan services. Bar/restaurant, shop (all year). Swimming pools (1/6-15/9). Aviary. Boules. Minigolf. Play area. Hairdressers. Off site: Bus service outside site. Riding 500 m. Village 2 km. Open: All year.	From NIV Córdoba-Seville motorway take La Carlota exit (at km. 429 point northbound or exit 432 southbound). Site is 500 m. and well signed. GPS: 37.67664, -4.93329

Charges 2011

Per unit incl. 2 persons and electricity	€ 24,50 - € 24,85
extra person	€ 5,35
child (3-12 yrs)	€ 4,00

For latest campsite news, availability and prices visit
alanrogers.com

La Zubia

Camping Reina Isabel

Ctra Granada - La Zubia km 4, E-18140 La Zubia (Granada) T: 958 590 041. E: info@reinaisabelcamping.com
alanrogers.com/ES92760

Reina Isabel can be found just 3 km. from the centre of Granada and just 1 km. from the entrance to the spectacular Sierra Nevada National Park. The site is open for an extended season and is well located for winter sports holidays in the Sierra Nevada. There are 51 shady touring pitches here (each around 70 sq.m), all with electrical connections. There are also 11 bungalows available for rent. A regular bus service operates to the city centre and to other places of interest, notably the Alhambra palace.

Facilities

The single toilet block is clean but the toilet and shower cubicles have large frosted glass panels which are revealing at night. Used paper goes into baskets and not into the toilet. Shop in reception. Swimming pool. Play area. Bungalows for rent. Excursions available. Off site: Bus stop with regular service to the city centre. Sierra Nevada ski resort 29 km.

Open: All year.

Directions

Site is south of Granada. Leave A44 motorway at exit 132 and head east on A395. Follow signs to La Zubia, joining the southbound Calle de Laurel de la Reina. Site is clearly signed from here.
GPS: 37.12456, -3.58625

Charges 2011

Per unit incl. 2 persons and electricity	€ 29,00
extra person	€ 5,90
child	€ 4,35

Marbella

Camping Marbella Playa

Ctra N340 km 192,8, E-29600 Marbella (Málaga) T: 952 833 998. E: recepcion@campingmarbella.com
alanrogers.com/ES88000

This large site is 12 kilometres east of the internationally famous resort of Marbella with public transport available to the town centre and local attractions. A sandy beach is about 150 metres away with direct access. There are 430 individual pitches of up to 70 sq.m. with natural shade (additional artificial shade is provided to some), and electricity (10/20A) available throughout. Long leads may be required for some pitches. The site is busy throughout the high season but the high staff/customer ratio and the friendly staff approach ensures a comfortable stay.

Facilities

Four sanitary blocks of mixed ages, are fully equipped and well maintained. Three modern units for disabled visitors. Laundry service. Large supermarket with butcher and fresh vegetable counter. Bar, restaurant and café (all open all year). Supervised swimming pool (free Apr-Sept). Playground. Children's activities. Torches advised. Off site: Bus service 150 m. Fishing 100 m. Golf and bicycle hire 5 km. Riding 10 km. Beach 200 m.

Open: All year.

Directions

Site is 12 km. east of Marbella with access close to the 193 km. point on the main N340 road. Signed Elviria, then follow camping signs.
GPS: 36.49127, -4.76325

Charges guide

Per person	€ 3,42 - € 5,67
child (1-10 yrs)	€ 2,96 - € 4,98
pitch	€ 3,40 - € 13,50
electricity	€ 4,17 - € 7,17

Reductions (up to 50%) for long stays and senior citizens outside 1/6-16/9.

Marbella

Kawan Village Cabopino

Ctra N340 km 194,7, E-29604 Marbella (Málaga) T: 952 834 373. E: info@campingcabopino.com
alanrogers.com/ES88020

This large, mature site is alongside the main N340 Costa del Sol coast road, 12 km. east of Marbella and 15 km. from Fuengirola. The Costa del Sol is also known as the Costa del Golf and fittingly there is a major golf course alongside the site. The site is set amongst tall pine trees which provide shade for the sandy pitches (there are some huge areas for large units). The 300 touring pitches, a mix of level and sloping (chocks advisable), all have electricity (10A), but long leads may be required for some. There is a separate area on the western side for groups of younger guests.

Facilities

Five mature but very clean sanitary blocks provide hot water throughout (may be under pressure at peak times). Washing machines. Bar/restaurant and takeaway (all year). Shop. Outdoor pool (1/5-15/9) and indoor pool (all year). Play area. Some evening entertainment. Excursions can be booked. ATM. Torches necessary in the more remote parts of the site. Only gas or electric barbecues are permitted. Off site: Beach and golf 200 m. Fishing, bicycle hire and riding within 1 km.

Open: All year.

Directions

Site is 12 km. from Marbella. Approaching Marbella from the east, leave the N340 at the 194 km. marker (signed Cabopino). Site is off the roundabout at the top of the slip road. GPS: 36.49350, -4.74383

Charges 2011

Per unit incl. 2 persons and electricity	€ 22,20 - € 34,82
extra person	€ 4,55 - € 6,97
child (2-11 yrs)	€ 2,93 - € 5,80
dog	€ 1,72

Camping Cheques accepted.

For latest campsite news, availability and prices visit
alanrogers.com

Marbella

Camping La Buganvilla

Ctra N340 km 188,8, E-29600 Marbella (Málaga) T: 952 831 973. E: info@campingbuganvilla.com
alanrogers.com/ES88030

This site has 250 touring units, mostly on terraces so there are some views across to the mountains and hinterland of this coastal area. La Buganvilla is a large, uncomplicated site with mature trees providing shade to some pitches. The terrain is a little rugged in places and the buildings are older in style but all were clean when we visited. A pool complex near the bar and restaurant is ideal for cooling off after a day's sightseeing. This is an acceptable base from which to explore areas of the Costa del Sol and it is an easy drive to the picturesque Ronda Valley.

Facilities

Three painted sanitary blocks are clean and adequate. Laundry facilities (not all sinks have hot water). Well stocked small supermarket. Bar/restaurant with basic food. Play area. Tennis (high season). Dogs are not accepted in July/Aug. Off site: Bus service close to site entrance. Fishing and watersports 400 m. Bicycle and scooter hire 1 km. Golf 5 km. Resort type entertainment close.

Open: All year.

Directions

Site is between Marbella and Fuengirola off the N340. Access at 188.8 km. marker is only possible when travelling west, i.e. from Fuengirola. From the other direction, continue to the 'cambio de sentido' signed Elviria and turn back over the dual carriageway. Site is signed. GPS: 36.5023, -4.804

Charges 2011

Per unit incl. 2 persons and electricity	€ 22,82 - € 33,82
extra person	€ 3,00 - € 7,50

Maro

Nerja Camping

Ctra N340 km 297, E-29787 Maro (Málaga) T: 952 529 714. E: info@nerjacamping.com
alanrogers.com/ES87110

This site is set on the lower slopes of the Sierra Laminar, some five kilometres from Nerja and two kilometres from the excellent beaches. Nerja Camping is a small site of 55 pitches with impressive views of the surrounding mountains and the Mediterranean. There are 25 touring pitches (15A electricity) and four new mobile homes to rent. The pitches are on the small side and set on slopes with some terracing along with some artificial shade. The roads, although sloping, should present few problems for siting units. A new motorway will be close, but extensive sound barriers have been installed.

Facilities

The single sanitary block has been refurbished and tiled; all washbasins and showers have hot water. Laundry facilities. Small restaurant/bar (Mar-Sept). Essentials from the bar. Small swimming pool (Mar-Sept). Accommodation to rent. Weekend activities in Spring and Summer. Off site: Beach 2 km. Nerja limestone caves 1 km. Fishing 3 km. Bicycle hire and riding 5 km. Sub-aqua diving, parascending and watersports. Day trips to Granada and Gibraltar. Sierra Nevada 100 km. (1.5 hours in winter).

Open: All year excl. October.

Directions

Site signed from main N340 coast road about 5 km. east of Nerja after 296 km. marker. If coming from Nerja, go 500 m. past site entrance (opposite radio masts) to cross very busy main road. GPS: 36.7605, -3.83475

Charges 2011

Per unit incl. 2 persons and electricity	€ 20,00 - € 24,25
extra person	€ 3,50 - € 5,50
No credit cards.	

Mojacar

Camping Sopalmo

Apdo 761, Sopalmo, E-04638 Mojacar (Almería) T: 950 478 413. E: info@campingsopalmoelcortijillo.com
alanrogers.com/ES87490

This is a tiny, homely site run by the cheerful Simon and his charming wife Macu (both speaking some English) who are determined that you will enjoy your stay. The site is on three levels (with a slightly steep gravel track to the gates) with space for 29 tents, caravans or medium sized motorcaravans. All the pitches are marked, level and on gravel with electricity. The site is unspoilt and has much rustic charm with the family house providing the focal point. Attractive trees and shrubs around the site include olives, figs, mimosa and cacti. Some pitches near the road may experience a small amount of traffic noise.

Facilities

The small sanitary block is very clean and fully equipped. Hot showers assisted by solar power. Facilities for disabled visitors. Basic laundry and dishwashing facilities. Bar. Breakfast available in summer and the baker calls at 10.30 daily. Torch useful. Internet access. Off site: Bus to Mojacar from site. Beach 1.5 km. Nearest serious shops 5 km. Riding 6 km. Golf 10 km.

Open: All year.

Directions

Exit from main coast road (N340) at junction 520 (northeast of Almeria). Take the AL152 (formerly A150) to Mojacar Playa and continue south towards Carboneras. Site is 6 km. south of Mojacar Playa, signed off the road GPS: 37.06533, -1.86881

Charges guide

Per unit incl. 2 persons and electricity (6A)	€ 20,20
extra person	€ 2,45 - € 4,65
No credit cards.	

For latest campsite news, availability and prices visit
alanrogers.com

Mojacar

Camping Cueva Negra

Camino Lotaza 2, Frenta - Playa Macenas, E-04638 Mojacar (Almería) T: 950 475 855
E: info@campingcuevanegra.es **alanrogers.com/ES87560**

This tiny jewel of a site, just 9 km. south of Mojacar is approached by a short, steep and winding road with passing places. There are only 40 pitches, all 100 sq.m. and 30 have electricity, water and drainage, with artificial shade provided in summer. The elevated site is attractively laid out with views to the nearby sea. The superb covered swimming pool has four jacuzzis and a large, partly covered terrace with an open air shower for disabled visitors. There are facilities for tennis and pétanque and a play area for children. A small bar serving drinks and tapas is open all year and a restaurant should now be open.

Facilities

Modern toilet block with facilities for disabled visitors. Laundry with washing machine and dryer. Well stocked shop and small bar (all year). Takeaway (high season). Covered swimming pool (1/5-31/10). Tennis. Pétanque. Play area. Apartment and bungalow for rent. Off site: Beach 400 m. Five golf courses nearby. Towns of Mojacar, Aguilas Nijar and Almeria within easy reach.

Open: All year.

Directions

Site is 9 km. south of Mojacar on the Mojacar - Carboneras road, on the right when travelling south. There is a small sign at the entry road. GPS: 37.08674, -1.85396

Charges guide

Per unit incl. 2 persons and electricity	€ 19,19 - € 29,60
extra person	€ 2,58 - € 5,57
dog	€ 1,04 - € 1,86

Motril

Camping Don Cactus

Ctra N340 km 343, Playa de Carchuna, E-18730 Carchuna-Motril (Granada) T: 958 623 109
E: camping@doncactus.com **alanrogers.com/ES92950**

Situated between the main N340 and the beach, this family run campsite is pleasantly surprising with clever planning and ongoing improvements. It is a comfortable site of 320 pitches (280 for touring). The flat pitches vary in size with electricity (5/12A), some providing water and satellite TV connections, and are arranged along avenues with eucalyptus trees (which keep the mosquitoes away apparently) for shade. This quieter section of the coast is beautiful with coves and access to larger towns if wished. The friendly reception staff are very helpful with tourist advice and can arrange trips for you if needed.

Facilities

The large toilet block is dated but clean and provides British style WCs, showers and plenty of washbasins. Laundry facilities. Beach showers. Well stocked shop. Bar, restaurant and takeaway (all year). Swimming pool (in high season € 1.50 per day). Tennis. Play area. Summer activities for children. Outdoor fitness centre for adults. Pets corner. ATM. Internet point. Dogs are not accepted in July/Aug. Barbecues only in special area. Caravan storage. Off site: Bus service 500 m.

Open: All year.

Directions

From Motril - Carchuna road (N340/E15) turn towards the sea at km. 343. (site signed, but look at roof level for large green tent on the top of the building!). Travel about 600 m. then turn east to site on left. GPS: 36.70066, -3.44032

Charges guide

Per person	€ 6,00
child (4-10 yrs)	€ 5,70
pitch incl. electricity (5A)	€ 18,30

Nijar

Camping Los Escullos

Paraje de los Escullos s/n, E-04118 San Jose-Nijar (Almería) T: 950 389 811. E: info@losescullossanjose.com
alanrogers.com/ES87620

This efficient, well maintained, medium sized site has 171 pitches (60-80 sq.m). They are divided by hedges and trees and 100 pitches have 10A electric supply and some have artificial shading. Specific taps about the grounds provide drinking water. The pool has an overlooking bar and restaurant which is kept busy serving excellent typical Spanish 'menu del dia' food at very low prices. It is a popular site with British tourists seeking the sun. The salinas on the approach to Cabo de Gata are famous for bird life (including flocks of pink flamingo).

Facilities

The main sanitary block is large, clean and fully equipped with hot showers and facilities for disabled visitors. Second small sanitary block close to reception. Small supermarket. Bar/restaurant. Large outdoor pool (15/5-1/10) and jacuzzi (1/7-1/10). Hairdresser. Massage. Gym. Internet access. Multisport court. Scuba diving. TV room. Bicycle hire. Gas or electric barbecues only. Entertainment programme in high season. Free WiFi. Off site: No public transport (a vehicle is required here). Fishing 1 km. Riding 7 km. Golf 25 km. Walking track to the nearest beach (stony) 1 km.

Open: All year.

Directions

From A7/E15 autovia exit at either exit 479 or 471 in direction of San Jose. On approach to San Jose left turn toward Los Escullos. Site is well signed. GPS: 36.80288, -2.07756

Charges guide

Per unit incl. 2 persons and electricity	€ 23,50 - € 35,60
extra person	€ 5,50 - € 7,25
child (2-14 yrs)	€ 4,50 - € 6,25
Camping Cheques accepted.	

We can book this site for you! Call 01580 214000

alan rogers travel

For latest campsite news, availability and prices visit
alanrogers.com

Orgiva

Camping Puerta de La Alpujarra

Ctra Lanjarón - Orgiva (Las Barreras), E-18400 Orgiva (Granada) T: 958 784 450

E: puertadelaalpujarra@campings.net **alanrogers.com/ES92920**

You will receive a warm welcome from the family who run this site and nothing is too much trouble. The site overlooks the Sierra Nevada with lovely panoramic views. There are 77 pitches, terraced and with plenty of shade (43 with electricity connections). This is an area that is becoming more popular with tourists and is an ideal spot from which to explore the mountain villages. Orgiva, steeped in history, is just 1.5 km. from the site and there are many interesting walks from here.

Facilities

Three central sanitary blocks are clean and provide open washbasins and roomy shower cubicles. Toilet for disabled visitors (no shower). Laundry facilities. Shop (baker delivers daily). Bar, restaurant and takeaway (closed Mondays-Wednesdays). Outdoor swimming and paddling pools (mid June-mid Oct). Play area. Torches useful. No barbecues in summer. Off site: Orgiva 1.5 km. Pampaneria, Bubion and Capileira (steep and winding with many bends so time and care should be taken).

Open: All year.

Directions

Head south from Granada on A44 (E902) and exit 164 signed Lanjaron onto A348. Alpujarra is signed with Orgiva. Site is on right on outskirts of Orgiva (signed). GPS: 36.90375, -3.43891

Charges guide

Per person	€ 4,00 - € 5,00
child	€ 2,50 - € 4,00
pitch	€ 8,00 - € 10,00
electricity	€ 3,00 - € 4,00

Orgiva

Camping Orgiva

Ctra A348 km 18,9, E-18400 Orgiva (Granada) T: 958 784 307. E: campingorgiva@descubrelaalpujarra.com

alanrogers.com/ES92930

Set in the high slopes of the Sierra Nevada and only 2 km. from Orgiva, this is a small and well managed site that offers the opportunity to escape into rural Spain. It is open all year and is an ideal place to relax. For those who feel more energetic, there are facilities for climbing, horse riding and canoeing, all within close proximity of the site. The 40 touring pitches are well defined and separated by shrubs and small trees and all have views of the surrounding countryside. Access to the site is good but being high in the mountains it is not suitable for large units.

Facilities

One centrally placed sanitary block provides toilets, washbasins and shower cubicles. Facilities for disabled visitors. Washing machine and dryer. Very good swimming pool with adjacent small pool for children (June-Sept). Shop. Terrace bar. No barbecues allowed on site. Off site: Fishing 10 km. Golf 35 km.

Open: All year.

Directions

From A44-E902 Granada - Motril road, exit at 164 km. and take A348 east to Lanjaron and Orgiva. Continue past Orgiva and the site is well signed on left. GPS: 36.88708, -3.41754

Charges guide

Per person	€ 4,74
child	€ 3,42
pitch incl. car	€ 8,45
electricity	€ 3,64

Palomares

Camping Cuevas Mar

Cuevas del Almanzora, E-04618 Palomares (Almería) T: 950 467 382. E: cuevasmar@arrakis.es

alanrogers.com/ES87510

This is a popular, well established and traditional campsite, busy during the warm winter months with 180 pleasant pitches with shrubs and trees providing pitch dividers and shade. A few pitches are quite close to the road but it is not busy with traffic. All the pitches are flat and are of an acceptable 80-100 sq.m. with a clean stone chip surface and 6/10A electricity supply. During the hot summer months overhead shade canopies are erected on several pitches. A pleasant and uncomplicated site with a peaceful atmosphere and a spa.

Facilities

The well designed sanitary blocks provide sufficient showers and toilets for all. Washing machines and dryer. Water to the taps is to European standard, however a single tap near reception provides high quality water from a nearby mountain spring source. Daily fresh bread, emergency provisions and gas from reception. Open air unheated swimming pool and jacuzzi (May-Sept). Caravan storage. WiFi (weekly charge). Off site: Public transport 100 m. from gate. Many restaurants in the near vicinity. Fishing 200 m. Bicycle hire 3 km. Golf 4 km. Riding 12 km. Beach 600 m. Naturist beach 800 m.

Open: All year.

Directions

From E15/A7 take exit 537 passing under autovia following signs in general direction of Cuevas Del Almanzora. At T-junction turn right toward Palomares and Vera. In 1 km. on right hand bend turn left towards Palomares. Continue to roundabout, take first exit and site is on left in 2 km. To avoid left turn continue 500 m. to next roundabout and return. GPS: 37.237, -1.798

Charges guide

Per unit incl. 1 or 2 persons	€ 8,60 - € 17,90
extra person	€ 4,20
electricity (6A)	€ 3,00
No credit cards.	

For latest campsite news, availability and prices visit

alanrogers.com

Pitres
Camping El Balcon de Pitres
Ctra Orgiva - Ugijar km 51, E-18414 Pitres (Granada) T: 958 766 111. E: info@balcondepitres.com
alanrogers.com/ES92900

A simple country site perched high in the mountains of the Alpujarras, on the south side of the Sierra Nevada, El Balcon de Pitres has its own rustic charm. Many thousands of trees planted around the site provide shade. There are stunning views from some of the 175 level grassy pitches (large units may find pitch access difficult). The garden is kept green by spring waters, which you can hear and sometimes see, tinkling away in places. The Lopez family have transformed this site from barren mountain top to cool oasis in the mountains in just 15 years.

Facilities

Two toilet blocks provide adequate facilities but the steeply sloping site is unsuitable for disabled visitors and thus there are no facilities for them. Snack bar. Bar. Shop (closed Tuesdays). Swimming pools (extra charge, € 2.40 adult € 1.50 child). Bicycle hire. Torches useful. Off site: Fishing. Canyoning. Trekking. Parascending. Quad bikes. Sports centre for football.

Open: All year.

Directions

Site is about 30 km. northeast of Motril. Heading south on A44 (E902) exit 164 (Lanjaron) onto E348 towards Orgiva. Fork left at sign (A4132) Pampaneira 8 km. Continue to Pitres (7 km). Site signed (steep and winding roads). GPS: 36.9323, -3.3334

Charges guide

Per person	€ 5,00
child	€ 3,50
pitch incl. car	€ 9,50 - € 11,50
electricity (2A)	€ 3,00

Ronda
Camping El Sur
Ctra Ronda - Algeciras km 1,5, Apdo 127, E-29400 Ronda (Málaga) T: 952 875 939. E: info@campingelsur.com
alanrogers.com/ES88090

The delightfully decorated entrance with generous manoeuvring area at this site are a promise of something different which is fulfilled in all respects. The very friendly family who run the site have worked hard for many years combining innovative thinking with excellent service. The 125 terraced pitches have electricity and water, and are partially shaded by olive and almond trees. Levels vary so chocks are recommended. Most have relaxing views of the surrounding mountains but at an elevation of 850 m. the upper pitches (the very top 45 pitches are for tents only) allow a clear view of the town of Ronda.

Facilities

The immaculate sanitary block is fully equipped. Laundry facilities in a separate block. Gas supplies. Bar and very large, high quality restaurant (1/2-31/10). Kidney shaped pool (1/6-30/9). Playground and adventure play area. Separate camping area for groups. Minigolf. Off road bicycle hire. Internet terminal. Off site: Riding 1.5 km. Bicycle hire 2.5 km. The famous town of Ronda with all its attractions. The coast is about an hour's drive (50 km).

Open: All year.

Directions

Site is on the A369 Ronda - Algerciras road at the 3 km. point south of Ronda (which now has a ring road so one does not have to go through the town). GPS: 36.7211, -5.1716

Charges guide

Per unit incl. 2 persons and electricity (6/10A)	€ 23,00 - € 28,00
extra person	€ 4,80
child (under 10 yrs)	€ 4,30
dog	€ 1,60

No credit cards (except in restaurant).

Roquetas de Mar
Camping Roquetas
Ctra Los Parrales s/n, E-04740 Roquetas de Mar (Almería) T: 950 343 809. E: info@campingroquetas.com
alanrogers.com/ES87680

This level, very well maintained site is conveniently situated 9 km. from the A7 motorway within easy reach of Roquetas de Mar and 400 m. from a stony beach. It is a family run site and English is spoken. There are excellent facilities including two swimming pools and the site is within easy reach of the popular resort of Almeria and the Cabo de Gata nature park. There are 731 quite small pitches (60 sq.m), although during the winter months two pitches are allocated for the price of one. There are 18 pitches for longer units with water, electricity and waste connections.

Facilities

Five well equipped toilet blocks spread throughout the site. Two units for disabled visitors are close to the pools, as well as a baby room. Spanish restaurant with excellent menu and reasonable prices. Shop. Two swimming pools, one with paddling pool. Tennis. Pétanque. Off site: Towns of Roquetas de Mar and Almeria nearby. Mojacar, Nijar, 'Mini Hollywood' and the Tabernas desert are within easy reach.

Open: All year.

Directions

From A7/E15 exit 429 head towards Roquetas de Mar. Site is well signed and is about 9 km. from the motorway. GPS: 36.797814, -2.590992

Charges guide

Per unit incl. 2 persons and electricity	€ 30,32 - € 33,54
extra person	€ 4,87
child (1-12 yrs)	€ 4,76
dog	€ 2,25

For latest campsite news, availability and prices visit
alanrogers.com

San José

Camping Tau de San José

Cua de Cala Hibuera s/n, E-04118 San José (Almería) T: 950 380 166. E: tau@parquenatural.com

alanrogers.com/ES87580

This attractive and quiet site was originally part of an old farm, typical of this region. It is well shaded and is particularly suitable for tents and low units. There is limited space for caravans and motorcaravans and phoning ahead is strongly advised. Electricity hook-ups are provided (6/16A) but long leads may be required. A level site, it is set in a nature park and is about 300 m. from the beach and the unspoilt village of San José. There is a new toilet block and the small bar/restaurant has a Spanish atmosphere with a large shady terrace outside, ideal for that relaxing drink.

Facilities

Large modern toilet block with extra unisex showers. Facilities for disabled visitors. Laundry. Small, well stocked shop. Covered barbecue area. A further covered area has pool and electronic games. Play area. Dogs are not accepted. Off site: Village of San José where fish restaurants are a speciality, beach and harbour 300 m. Almeria, and the white villages of Nijar and Mojacar are close by. Further afield is the Tabernas desert.

Open: Easter - 1 October.

Directions

From E15 exit 471 or 479 follow signs for San José. Site is north of the village on left hand side (keep the white buildings to your right). Follow made up road to site. GPS: 36.76757, -2.10532

Charges guide

Per person	€ 4,75
pitch incl. car	€ 9,50 - € 13,00
electricity	€ 3,50 - € 5,50
Credit cards accepted for a minimum €100.	

Santa Elena

Camping Despeñaperros

Ctra Infanta Elena, E-23213 Santa Elena (Jaén) T: 953 664 192. E: info@campingdespenaperros.com

alanrogers.com/ES90890

This site is on the edge of Santa Elena in a natural park with shade from mature pine trees. This is a good place to stay en route from Madrid to the Costa del Sol or to just explore the surrounding countryside. The 116 pitches are fully serviced including a satellite TV/internet link. All rubbish must be taken to large bins outside the site gates (a long walk from the other end of the site). The site is run in a very friendly manner where nothing is too much trouble. Reception has a monitor link with tourist information and access to the region's sites of interest.

Facilities

Two traditional, central sanitary blocks have Turkish style WCs and well equipped showers. One washing machine (launderette in town). Shop. Excellent bar (all year) and charming restaurant (12/3-20/10). Swimming pools (15/6-15/9). Tennis. Caravan storage. Night security. Off site: Walking, riding and mountain sports nearby. The main road gives good access to Jaén and Valdepeñas.

Open: All year.

Directions

Travelling north towards Madrid on A4 (E5) take exit 259 (Santa Elena). Drive through town and site is on right up steep slope (alternative entrance for tall vehicles – ask reception). Travelling south towards Bailén take exit 257 and as above. GPS: 38.34307, -3.53528

Charges 2011

Per unit incl. 2 persons	
and electricity	€ 20,90 - € 23,20
extra person	€ 3,20 - € 4,70

Santaella

Camping La Campiña

Ctra A-379 km 46,2 La Guijarrosa, E-14547 Santaella (Córdoba) T: 957 315 303

E: info@campinglacampina.com alanrogers.com/ES90840

A charming site amongst the olive trees and set high on a hill to catch cool summer breezes. Matilde, the daughter of the Martin-Rodriguez family, runs this site with enthusiasm and hard work, making a visit here a delightful experience. Everything is immaculately kept and we rarely see sites of this size with such excellent amenities and standards. The 35 pitches are level and most have shade, the surface is gravel and there are views over the olive fields to the surrounding hills. There is a large pool in a garden setting and the restaurant has a menu of homemade food. Breakfast is included in pitch prices.

Facilities

Two small traditional sanitary blocks (heated in winter) have clean services including facilities for disabled visitors (key at reception). Washing machines. Restaurant. Snack bar. Shop. Outdoor swimming pool (Apr-Oct). Bicycle hire. Yoga lessons. Torches useful. Walks and excursions arranged. Off site: Bus from gate to Córdoba. Town 2 km. Riding 15 km. Golf 40 km.

Open: All year.

Directions

From the NIV/A4 (Sevilla - Córdoba) take exit 441 (La Rambla - Montilla) or 424 (La Victoria). Continue past Santaella towards La Victoria. La Campiña is tucked off this road behind high hedging. From the A92 use exit 109 (Fuente-Genil) or from the A45 (Malaga - Córdoba), exit 27 (La Rambla) and on towards Santaella. GPS: 37.623, -4.8587

Charges guide

Per unit incl. 2 persons	
and electricity	€ 19,00 - € 25,50
extra person	€ 4,50 - € 5,00

For latest campsite news, availability and prices visit

alanrogers.com

Sevilla

Camping Villsom

Ctra Sevilla - Cadiz km 554,8, E-41700 Sevilla (Sevilla) T: 954 720 828

alanrogers.com/ES90810

This city site was one of the first to open in Spain and it is still owned by the same friendly family. The administrative building consists of a peaceful and attractive bar with patio and satellite TV (where breakfast is served) and there is a pleasant, small reception area. It is a good site for visiting Seville with a frequent bus service to the centre. Camping Villsom has around 180 pitches which are level and shaded. A huge variety of trees and palms are to be seen around the site and there are bright flowers in summer. Not suitable for large motorhomes and there are few places for large caravans, but book.

Facilities	Directions
Sanitary facilities require modernisation in some areas. Some washbasins have cold water only. Laundry facilities. Small shop selling basic provisions. Bar with satellite TV (open July/Aug). Swimming pool (June-Sept). Putting. Drinks machine. Off site: Bus stop close. Most town facilities including restaurant, supermarket, cinema and theatre.	On main Seville - Cadiz NIV road travelling from Seville take exit at km. 553 (Dos Hermanos - Isla Meno). Go under road bridge and immediately right (Isla Mentor) to site 80 m. on right. From Cadiz take same signed exit. At roundabout take fourth exit to go over main road and down a slip road to go under bridge, then as above. GPS: 37.27735, -5.93683

Open: 10 January - 23 December.

Charges guide

Per person	€ 4,45
pitch incl. car	€ 9,40 - € 11,50
electricity	€ 3,05

Tarifa

Camping Paloma

Ctra Cadiz - Malaga km 70, E-11380 Tarifa (Cádiz) T: 956 684 203

alanrogers.com/ES88500

This spacious, neat and tidy, family orientated site is popular with Spanish families and young people of all nations in high season. Paloma is well established and the many tall palms around the site remind one of how close are Africa and the romance of Tangier. The site has 337 pitches on mostly flat ground, although the westerly pitches are sloping. They are of average size with some places for extra large units, some are separated by hedges and most are shaded by mature trees; around 150 pitches have electrical connections (10A).

Facilities	Directions
Two sanitary blocks, one of a good size, although a long walk from the southern end of the site. The other block is smaller and open plan. British style WCs with some Turkish, washbasins have cold water. Facilities for disabled visitors in the smaller block. Washing machine. Gas supplies. Shop. Busy bar and good restaurant. Swimming pool with adjacent bar (high season only). Play area. Excursions (June-Sept). Dogs are not accepted in high season. Off site: Beach 700 m. Bicycle hire 5 km. Riding 10 km. Tarifa 12 km. Golf 25 km.	Site is signed off N340 Cadiz road at Punta Paloma, about 10 km. northwest of Tarifa, just west of km. 74 marker. Watch carefully for the site sign (there is no advance notice). Be sure to use the slip road to turn left if coming from Tarifa. Follow signs down the road for 300 m. GPS: 36.0776, -5.694

Open: All year.

Charges guide

Per person	€ 2,70 - € 5,50
pitch	€ 5,00 - € 10,00
electricity	€ 3,00

Tarifa

Camping Tarifa

Ctra N340 km 78,87, E-11380 Tarifa (Cádiz) T: 956 684 778. E: camping-tarifa@camping-tarifa.com

alanrogers.com/ES88550

The long, golden sandy beach adjacent to this site is a good feature being ideal for windsurfing and also clean and safe for swimming. The site has a pleasant, open feel and is reasonably sheltered from road noise. It has been thoughtfully landscaped and planted out with an amazing variety of shrubs and flowers and is clean. The 265 level pitches are of varying sizes and are surrounded by pine trees which provide ample shade. All have electricity (5/10A) and there are adequate water points.

Facilities	Directions
Two modern, fully equipped sanitary blocks include facilities for campers with disabilities and baby room. All spotless when seen. Motorcaravan services. Gas supplies. Supermarket and excellent bar/restaurant (fast food only), all open all year with patio. Swimming pool complex with bar. Large play area. Dogs are not accepted. Off site: Fishing 100 m. Riding 300 m. Bicycle hire 5 km. Excursions.	Site is on main N340 Cádiz road at 78.87 km. marker, 7.5 km. northwest of Tarifa. Large modern signs well ahead of the site with a deceleration lane if approaching from the Tarifa direction. GPS: 36.0613, -5.6692

Open: All year.

Charges guide

Per person	€ 4,17 - € 6,95
pitch	€ 2,24 - € 6,95
electricity	€ 2,24 - € 3,74

Camping Cheques accepted.

For latest campsite news, availability and prices visit

alanrogers.com

Torre del Mar

Camping Caravaning Laguna Playa

Prolongacion Paseo Maritimo, E-29740 Torre del Mar (Málaga) T: 952 540 631. E: info@lagunaplaya.com
alanrogers.com/ES87820

Laguna Playa is a pleasant and peaceful site run by a father and son team (the son speaks excellent English) and they give a personal service, alongside one of the Costa del Sol beaches. Trips are organised to the famous Alhambra Mosque in Granada on a weekly basis and the site is well placed for visits to Malaga and Nerja. The 142 touring pitches are flat, of average size and with good artificial shade supplementing that provided by the many established trees on site. All pitches have electricity (10A). The busy restaurant with a terrace offers good value for money and many locals use it.

Facilities	Directions
Two well equipped, modern, sanitary blocks, both recently refurbished, can be heated. Baby baths. Good facilities for disabled visitors. Laundry facilities. Supermarket. Bar and busy restaurant also used by locals (closed for two weeks in both May and Oct). Swimming pools (high season). Play area. Children's entertainment. Spanish classes in low season. Dancing classes. Off site: Beach promenade 200 m. Bicycle hire 500 m. Regular bus service 700 m. outside site. Golf 1.5 km. Riding 2 km.	Site is on the sea front west of the town of Torre del Mar. Go to the end of the 'paseo' on the west side of the town. Site is on the right. GPS: 36.72433, -4.10133

Open: All year.

Charges guide

Per person	€ 5,05
child (2-10 yrs)	€ 4,10
pitch and car	€ 10,10 - € 10,75
electricity	€ 4,00

Special offers for longer stays in low season.

Torrox

Camping El Pino

Ctra Nacional 340 km 285, Urb. Torrox Park s/n, E-29793 Torrox-Costa (Málaga) T: 952 530 006
E: info@campingelpino.com alanrogers.com/ES87810

El Pino is located in the Axarquia region of the Costa del Sol, east of Malaga and is surrounded by avocado groves. The site enjoys some fine views of the surrounding countryside. There are 425 pitches here, mostly well shaded, and a further 47 mobile homes and chalets for rent. Most pitches have electrical connections and vary in size from 60-100 sq.m. The site is open all year and has some impressive facilities including a swimming pool, supermarket and bar/restaurant. The nearest beach is 800 m. distant – a bus service runs there from the site. The site can be found close to Torrox Costa, an area claiming to have the best climate in Europe. The old village of Torrox, like many in the area, has traces of its Arabic origins, with narrow, winding streets and whitewashed houses. Torrox Costa is quite different and has been extensively but attractively developed with a lighthouse at one end and a fine sandy beach, the Playa Ferrara.

Facilities	Directions
Toilet block with hot showers and individual cabins. Facilities for disabled visitors. Laundry facilities. Bar, restaurant and shop (all year). Swimming pool with new children's pool (1/6-15/9). Play area. Games room. Pétanque. Children's club. WiFi (free). Mobile homes and chalets for rent. Only gas or electric barbecues are permitted. Off site: Nearest beach 800 m. Fishing 1 km. Riding 8 km. Golf 9 km. Malaga 45 km.	Leave the A7 Autovia del Mediterraneo at exit 285 (Torrox) and follow signs to Torrox Park. Site is well signed from here. GPS: 36.739245, -3.949713

Open: All year.

Charges 2011

Per unit incl. 2 persons and electricity	€ 16,80 - € 21,80
extra person	€ 3,00 - € 4,25
child (under 10 yrs)	€ 2,00 - € 3,00
dog	€ 1,50 - € 2,50

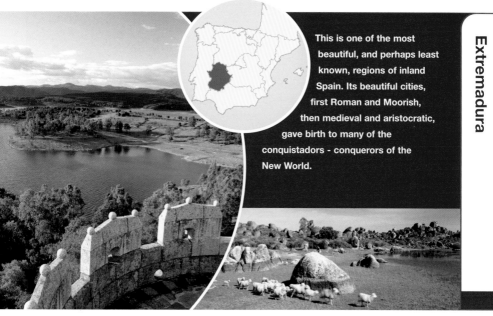

This is one of the most beautiful, and perhaps least known, regions of inland Spain. Its beautiful cities, first Roman and Moorish, then medieval and aristocratic, gave birth to many of the conquistadors - conquerors of the New World.

EXTREMADURA HAS TWO PROVINCES: BADAJOZ AND CÁCERES

Extremadura is a large and sparsely populated region in the west of Spain, bordering central Portugal and consisting of two provinces, both of which bear the name of their main town. Cáceres, to the north, has a fascinating old quarter, ringed by old Moorish walls and superb watchtowers. Nearby Plasencia is home to a splendid Gothic cathedral, old medieval walls and beautiful Baroque and Renaissance palaces. And the attractive town of Trujillo, birthplace of Pizzaro, the conqueror of Peru, has palaces, churches and a bustling town square. To the south is Badajoz, the second province and the largest in Spain. With its fortified main town and Alcazaba (citadel), the city of Badajoz is located on the Vía de la Plata (Silver Route), an old pilgrimage route to Santiago de Compostela used during the Middle Ages. Located on this route, Mérida is one of the best preserved archaeological sites in Spain. Indeed, the city boasts more Roman remains than any other city, including a Roman theatre and amphitheatre, a Roman bridge spanning over 800 metres long, with 60 arches, Roman villas and the Museum of Roman Art.

Places of interest

Alcántara: six-arched Roman bridge, castle, mansions.

Corio: quiet old town enclosed by 4th century Roman walls, cathedral.

Cuacos de Yuste: town with 15th-century Jeronimos Monastery.

Guadalupe: old pilgrimage centre, church and monastery.

Jerez de los Caballeros: birthplace of various conquistadores.

Olivenza: town with strong Portuguese influence, castle, ethnographic museum, 17th-century church.

Pedroso de Acim: Convento del Palancar – said to be the smallest monastery in the world.

Cuisine of the region

Local cuisine includes Iberian cured ham and a variety of cheeses; *Torta del Casar, La Serena, Ibores, Gata* and *Cabra del Tietar.* Game abounds in this region (partridge, pigeon, turtledove, rabbit, hare, wild boar, deer) served with wild mushrooms, truffles or wild asparagus. Honey, thyme, heather, rosemary, lavender, lime and eucalyptus are used to prepare a great variety of desserts.

Alfeñiques: caramel dessert.

Nuégados: egg yolk and orange buns.

Perrunillas: small round cakes.

Rosquillas: ring-shaped biscuits.

Técula-mécula: cinnamon, almond and tea.

CASTILLA Y LEON

AVILA

GUARDA

BEIRAS &
CENTRE
(PORTUGAL)

A66/E803

GATA

N110

CUACOS DE YUSTE

PLASENCIA

CORIO

MALPARTIDA DE PLASENCIA

CASTILLA-
LA MANCHA

NAVALMORAL DE LA MATA

A5/E90

ALCANTARA

CÁCERES

N521

TRUJILLO

GUADALUPE

A66/E803

ALENTEJO
(PORTUGAL)

EXTREMEDURA

A5/E90

N430

MERIDA

ELVAS

BORBA

BADAJOZ   A5/E90

A66/E803

OLIVENZA

N432

A66/E803

ANDALUCIA

CORDOBA

0   25   50   75   100 kms

For latest campsite news, availability and prices visit
alanrogers.com

Cáceres
Cáceres Camping
Ctra N630 km 549,5, E-10005 Cáceres (Cáceres) T: 927 233 100. E: info@campingcaceres.com
alanrogers.com/ES90860

Cáceres Camping is quite a small site, located to the west of the interesting city of Cáceres, a World Heritage site. There are 130 pitches here, and, unusually, each has a chalet providing a shower, washbasin and toilet. The pitches are of a reasonable size (80 sq.m) and are well shaded. A range of leisure facilities is provided, including a swimming pool and a separate children's pool. Cáceres is a city with much interest, and a fascinating history. Cave paintings on the city outskirts date back 30,000 years! The city is capital of High Extremadura and close by, the Montanchez mountain range offers many opportunities for walking and cycling.

Facilities	Directions
Individual toilet blocks. Bar, restaurant, cafeteria and takeaway meals. Supermarket. Swimming pool. Off site: City centre 2 km. Golf, walking and cycling opportunities. Open: All year.	From the east (E90 motorway) take the N521 to Cáceres. Continue on this road to the west of the city. At the large roundabout sign for 'Campo de Futbol Principe Felipe' is the entrance to the site. GPS: 39.489, -6.4128

Charges guide

Per unit incl. 2 persons and electricity	€ 20,00 - € 22,00
child	€ 3,00
extra person	€ 4,00 - € 4,50

Ctra. N-630, km. 549,5
E-10005 CÁCERES
Tel/Fax: 927 233 100

www.campingcaceres.com
info@campingcaceres.com

Fantastic site in the town of Caceres, open throughout the year and with installations of the first category.Private individual sanitary install. on each site - equipped wooden bungalows – studio's for 2 p. – Wi-Fi service in install. –social room w. TV - launderette – supermarket – cafeteria and restaurant with terrace – 2 swimming pools and large green areas with children's playground and sports zone.

Offer Sept. 08/June 09 except Easter week: 1 week 99 €; 15 days 175 €; 1 month 275 € including private bathroom on site, electr., hot water, 1 car and 2 adults.

Gata
Camping Sierra de Gata
Ctra Ex109 a Gata km 4,100, E-10860 Gata (Cáceres) T: 927 672 168. E: sierradegata@campingsonline.com
alanrogers.com/ES94000

For a taste of the real, rural Spain this very Spanish site (no English was spoken when we visited) is situated just before the tiny village of Sierra de Gata, south of Ciudad Rodrigo and northwest of Plasencia. Situated in beautiful countryside with a small stream alongside the site, the pitches are on grass with plenty of shade from trees. This site is undergoing refurbishment with the addition of 12 beautiful new bungalows to sleep four to six people. A special area with huts for groups of children to stay is positioned in one corner of the site. We suspect that it is a popular site with Spanish people which would give the opportunity to practise the language.

Facilities	Directions
Two toilet blocks with British style toilets also include child size toilets, a laundry room and dishwashing facilities. Medium sized shop for necessities in summer. Smart restaurant/bar complex provides good food. Two swimming pools. Tennis. Play area. Fishing. Riding. Bicycle hire. Off site: Restaurant near site entrance. Open: 18 March - 3 November.	Approach ONLY from the southwest from the 109 Ciudad Rodrico - Coria road. Where the 205 meets the 109 take turn 20-30 m. north signed Gata 10. Travel along this road until km. 4. Turn left (near restaurant and small bridge) and site is ahead through gate. GPS: 40.21195, -6.64224

Charges guide

Per person	€ 3,75 - € 4,25
child (3-12 yrs)	€ 3,25 - € 3,75
pitch	€ 4,50 - € 8,00
electricity	€ 3,75 - € 4,25

Guadalupe

Camping Las Villuercas

Ctra Villanueva, E-10140 Guadalupe (Cáceres) T: 927 367 139
alanrogers.com/ES90280

This rural site nestles in an attractive valley northwest of Guadalupe. The 50 pitches (25 with 10A electricity) are level and of a reasonable size; although large units may experience difficulty in getting into the more central pitches. With an abundance of mature trees most pitches offer some degree of shade. A river runs alongside the site and the ground can be muddy in very wet periods. The site is co-located with hostel accommodation. The restaurant provides excellent food at low prices.

Facilities	Directions
The single toilet block is older but very clean, with one area for women and one for men, providing British type WCs, washbasins and showers (hot water is from a 40 litre immersion heater which could be overwhelmed in busy periods). Facilities for disabled visitors. Laundry facilities. Restaurant. Bar. Swimming pools. Shop. Tennis. Small playground. Barbecue area. No English spoken. Off site: Riding 2 km. Fishing 3 km.	From NV/E90 Madrid - Mérida exit at Navelmoral de la Mata. Follow south to Guadalupe on the CC713 (83 km). Site is 2 km. from Guadalupe (near Monastery). From further southwest take exit 102 off main E90/NV (northeast of Mérida). Follow signs (Guadalupe). Go through a few villages and near 72 km. marker turn left to site, 100 m. on right. GPS: 39.441228, -5.322

Open: 1 March - 30 November.

Charges guide

Per person	€ 3,21
pitch	€ 4,28 - € 5,88
electricity	€ 2,67
No credit cards.	

Malpartida de Plasencia

Camping Parque Natural de Monfrague

Ctra Plasencia - Trujillo km 10, E-10680 Malpartida de Plasencia (Cáceres) T: 927 459 233
E: contacto@campingmonfrague.com alanrogers.com/ES90270

Situated on the edge of the Monfrague National Park, this well managed site owned by the Barrado family, has fine views to the Sierra de Mirabel and delightful surrounding countryside. Many of the 130 generous grass pitches are on slightly sloping, terraced ground. Scattered trees offer a degree of shade, there are numerous water points and 10A electricity. Created as a National Park in 1979, Monfrague is now recognised as one of the best locations in Europe for those interested in birdwatching.

Facilities	Directions
Large modern toilet blocks, fully equipped, are very clean. Facilities for disabled visitors and baby baths. Laundry. Motorcaravan service point. Supermarket/shop. Restaurant, bar and coffee shop. TV room with recreational facilities. WiFi. Swimming and paddling pools (June-Sept). Play area. Tennis. Entertainment for children in season. Barbecue areas. Guided safaris into the Park for birdwatching. Off site: Large supermarket at Plasencia. Bicycle hire 2 km. Riding 6 km.	On the N630, from the north take EX-208 (previously C524) Plasencia - Trujillo; site on left in 6 km. From the south turn right just south of Plasencia on EX-108 (previously C511) in direction of Malpartida de Plasencia. Right at main junction onto EX-208 to site. GPS: 39.9395, -6.084

Open: All year.

Charges guide

Per unit incl. 2 persons and electricity	€ 20,10 - € 20,40
extra person	€ 3,80 - € 4,20
Camping Cheques accepted.	

Mérida

Camping Mérida

Ctra NV Madrid - Portugal km 336,6, E-06800 Mérida (Badajoz) T: 924 303 453. E: proexcam@jet.es
alanrogers.com/ES90870

Camping Mérida is situated alongside the main NV road to Madrid, the restaurant, café and pool complex separating the camping area from the road where there is considerable noise. The site has 80 good sized pitches, most with some shade and on sloping ground, with ample electricity connections (long leads may be needed) and hedges with imaginative topiary. No English is spoken, but try out your Spanish. Reception is open until midnight. Camping Mérida is ideally located to serve both as a base to tour the local area or as an overnight stop en route when travelling either north/south or east/west.

Facilities	Directions
The central sanitary facility includes hot and cold showers, British style WCs. Gas supplies. Small shop for essentials. Busy restaurant/cafeteria and bar, also open to the public. Medium sized swimming and paddling pools (May-Sept). Bicycle hire. Play area (unfenced and near road). Caravan storage. Torches useful. Off site: Town 5 km.	Site is alongside NV road (Madrid - Lisbon), 5 km. east of Mérida, at km. 336.6. From east take exit 334 and follow camping signs (doubling back). Site is actually on the 630 road that runs alongside the new motorway. GPS: 38.9348, -6.3043

Open: All year.

Charges guide

Per person	€ 4,06
pitch incl. car and electricity	€ 22,74

For latest campsite news, availability and prices visit

alanrogers.com

This region is located south of Madrid and occupies what was the southern part of the ancient kingdom of Castille, including the area known as La Mancha, universally famous as the setting for Miguel de Cervantes great novel 'Don Quijote de la Mancha'.

CASTILLA-LA MANCHA HAS FIVE PROVINCES: ALBACETE, CIUDAD REAL, CUENCA, GUADALAJARA AND TOLEDO

THE CAPITAL OF THE REGION IS TOLEDO

The terrain can be divided into two distinct parts: the plateau, an extensive, flat land with very few mountains, and the mountainous areas, which encircle the plateau around the region's borders, including the foothills along the massifs of the Central mountain range, the Iberian mountain range and the Sierra Morena. Toledo is crammed with monuments and nearly all the different stages of Spanish art are represented with Moorish-Mudejar-Jewish buildings; Gothic structures, such as the splendid cathedral; and Renaissance buildings. Toledo was also home to El Greco and many of his paintings are displayed in the Museum of El Greco. The region of Cuenca is surrounded by mountainous, craggy countryside, with the city itself home to extraordinary houses which hang over the cliff tops of the deep gorges. One of these has been converted into the Museum of Abstract Art. In the heartland of La Mancha, through the region of Ciudad Real, you can follow the Ruta de Don Quixote and see the famous windmills at Campo de Criptana.

Places of interest

Almagro: home of international theatre festival.

Albacete: renowned for its knife-making industry, 16th-century cathedral.

Guadalajara: preserved Moorish walls, 10th-century bridge, Santa Maria la Mayor, 15th-century Duque del Infantado Palace.

Cuisine of the region

Local produce features heavily: aubergines, garlic, peppers, tomatoes, olive oil, meat, including both game and farm animals. Wine from La Mancha, Valdepeñas, Méntrida, Almansa, Dominio de Valdepusa and Finca de Elez.

Alajú: an almond and nut pastry.

Bizcochás de Alcázar: a tart soaked in milk with sugar, vanilla and cinnamon.

Caldereta manchega: lamb stew.

Morteruelo: pâté made of pork and game birds.

Pisto manchego: a type of ratatouille with tomatoes, red and green peppers, courgettes, served either hot or cold.

Tiznao: filleted cod which is flame-grilled in an earthenware dish with pepper, tomatoes, onions and garlic.

Fuencaliente

Camping de Fuencaliente

Ctra N420 km 105,8, E-13130 Fuencaliente (Ciudad Real) T: **926 698 170**. E: raquel@campingfuencaliente.es
alanrogers.com/ES90880

This quiet site nestles in an attractive valley between the Sierra Modrona and the Sierra Morena. It is ideal for getting away from it all and sampling the peaceful mountain beauty. It could be a useful stopover if crossing Spain coast to coast, or visiting the fascinating historic town of Córdoba. With very few other desirable sites in this region of Castilla - La Mancha, this one is spacious with 91 generously sized pitches (over 100 sq.m) all with electricity (6A) and water. There is natural shade from pine trees and beautiful, restful views. Areas are also allocated for tents. The large swimming pool with separate children's area is most welcome in summer, as this part of Spain gets very hot. The site has a good restaurant overlooking the pools, with reasonable prices. The local village of Fuencaliente is 5 km. south and has the usual village facilities including some very good Spanish restaurants and bars.

Facilities

The large, modern toilet block has reasonable facilities. Laundry sinks. Washing machine. Swimming pool (1/6-15/9; free). Restaurant/bar. Supermarket. Playground. Barbecue area with table and benches overlooking the countryside Off site: Fuencaliente 5 km.

Open: Easter - 30 September.

Directions

From the N420 road (Cuidad Real - Córdoba) turn by 105 km. marker (about 5 km. north of Fuencaliente) onto unmade road signed Camping San Isidro to site. GPS: 38.442, -4.32

Charges guide

Per person	€ 4,00 - € 4,50
child (2-10 yrs)	€ 3,50 - € 4,00
pitch	€ 7,50 - € 11,00

Electricity included. Min. price per pitch
€ 18-21 according to season.

For latest campsite news, availability and prices visit
alanrogers.com

Horcajo de Los Montes
Camping El Mirador de Cabaneros

Canada Real Segoviana s/n, E-13110 Horcajo de Los Montes (Ciudad Real) T: **926 775 439**
E: info@campingcabaneros.com **alanrogers.com/ES90960**

With panoramic views all around of the Sierra de Valdefuertes mountains, Camping El Mirador is set in the Cabaneros National Park. This is a well cared for, landscaped site with 80 terraced pitches on gravel and all with electricity. Although you will be level once sited, the approach is via a steep slope which may cause difficulties for larger units. Run by a very helpful and friendly family, this site is in a peaceful location where you can just sit and relax or visit the many attractions that the National Park has to offer. It is an ideal base for walking and birdwatching.

Facilities

One spotlessly clean central toilet block with solar heating includes open washbasins and cubicle showers. Facilities for disabled visitors and babies. Laundry facilities. Motorcaravan services. No shop but bread and gas from reception. Bar and restaurant (15/6-15/9, weekends in low season). Outdoor swimming pool. Games room. Basic (unfenced) play area. Off site: Village of Horcajo de los Montes 200 m.

Open: All year.

Directions

From north head towards Toledo (southwest from Madrid). At Toledo, take CM4013 to Cuerva and pick up CM403 to El Molinillo. Turn right onto CM4017 to Horcajo de los Montes. Through village onto the CM4016 towards Alcoba de los Montes, past garage and up hill for 2 km. Site is on left (narrow approach). GPS: 39.3219, -4.6495

Charges 2011

Per person	€ 4,80 - € 5,20
child	€ 3,70 - € 3,90
pitch	€ 7,70 - € 9,90
electricity	€ 4,20

Molinicos
Camping Rio Mundo

Ctra Comarcal 412 km 205, Mesones, E-02449 Molinicos (Albacete) T: **967 433 230**
E: riomundo@campingriomundo.com **alanrogers.com/ES90980**

This uncomplicated and typically Spanish site is situated in the Sierra de Alcaraz (south of Albacete), just off the scenic route 412 between Elche de la Sierra and Valdepenas. The drive to this site is most enjoyable through beautiful scenery and from the west the main road is winding in some places. Shade is provided by mature trees for the 80 pitches and electricity (6/10A) is supplied to 70 (long leads are useful). It is in a beautiful setting with majestic mountains and wonderful countryside which begs to be explored. This is a brilliant place to relax and enjoy the beauty of nature and is ideal for those wanting to experience true rural Spain.

Facilities

One toilet block has been upgraded and provides clean modern facilities. Basic toilet facilities for disabled visitors. Washing machine. Small shop for basics. Outside bar serving snacks with covered seating area. Takeaway. Another bar by the swimming pool. Playground. Pétanque. Barbecue area. Off site: Riding 7 km.

Open: 18 March - 12 October.

Directions

Site is just off the 412 road which runs west to east between the A30 and 322 roads south of Albacete. Turn at km. 205 on the 412, 5 km. east of village of Riopar and west of Elche de la Sierra. From here follow signs to site. The road narrows to one lane for a few hundred yards but keep straight on for 1-2 km. to site. GPS: 38.48917, -2.34639

Charges guide

Per person	€ 4,00 - € 5,25
child	€ 2,75 - € 3,60
pitch incl. electricity	€ 13,10 - € 16,30

For latest campsite news, availability and prices visit
alanrogers.com

Ossa de Montiel
Camping Los Batanes

Ctra Lagunas de Ruidera km 8, E-02611 Ossa de Montiel (Albacete) T: 926 699 076
E: camping@losbatanes.com alanrogers.com/ES90970

This large campsite is in a lovely setting at the side of one of the many lakes in this area. The route to get here is beautiful and it is well worth the trip, but careful driving was necessary in parts with our large motorhome. A smaller, older part of the campsite houses reception, a small shop and a bar/restaurant. Here are medium sized pitches, shaded by pine trees with a small river running through. Over a wooden bridge is the main, newer part of the site with over 200 level, gravel and sand pitches of mixed sizes, shaded again by pine trees. There is a new toilet block (cleaner and more modern than the one the other side) plus two barbecue areas. Another small stream runs towards the lake which can be seen from a few of the pitches. Towards one end of this new site is the swimming pool complex with two pools surrounded by hedges and grass for sunbathing, more toilets and places to eat, drink and have fun. In summer, children's club activities are run from here and this is definitely the part of the campsite with a lot going on. The site is increasingly popular with Spanish campers who come to relax and enjoy watersport activities in a beautiful area. Because of its popularity it is being extended and should develop into a good large place to stay.

Facilities

One old toilet block and a newer, more spacious one. If cleaning is maintained they should cope in high season. Small shop. Simple restaurant, snacks and bar. Swimming pools (16/6-9/9). Play area. Children's activities. Off site: Beautiful walks and many lakes to explore. Watersports in summer. Tourist information either at reception or 9 km. at nearest village. Bus stop in village.

Open: All year.

Directions

On E5/NIV Córdoba - Madrid road (south of Madrid) take 430 road towards Albacete. Coming into Ruidera turn right (just after lake on the right) signed Lagunas de Ruideria. Drive 8 km. along this country road to site on right. GPS: 38.93717, -2.84744

Charges guide

Per person	€ 4,60 - € 5,60
child (1-13 yrs)	€ 3,80 - € 4,70
pitch	€ 18,50 - € 27,00
electricity (5A)	€ 3,40 - € 3,50

Discounts for longer stays.

Toledo
Camping El Greco

Ctra CM4000 km 0,7, Puebla de Montalban, E-45004 Toledo (Toledo) T: 925 220 090
E: campingelgreco@telefonica.net alanrogers.com/ES90900

Toledo was the home of the Grecian painter and the site that bears his name boasts a beautiful view of the ancient city from the restaurant, bar and superb pool. The friendly, family owners make you welcome and are proud of their site which is the only one in Toledo (it can get crowded). The 150 pitches are of 80 sq.m. with electrical connections (5/10A) and shade from strategically planted trees. Most have separating hedges that give privacy, with others in herringbone layouts that make for interesting parking in some areas. The river Tagus stretches alongside the site which is fenced for safety. There is an attractive, tree-lined approach to the site. Ivy clad pergolas run down each side of the swimming pool (also fenced for safety) and a large shaded terrace offers shelter from the sun which can be very hot here. This site makes a relaxing base to return to after a hard day visiting the amazing sights of the old city of Toledo or for something different visit the Warner Brothers theme park.

Facilities

Two sanitary blocks, both modernised, one with facilities for disabled campers and everything is of the highest standard and kept very clean. Laundry. Motorcaravan services. Swimming pool (15/6-15/9, charged). Restaurant/bar (1/4-30/9) with good menu and fair prices. Small shop in reception. Playgrounds. Ice machine. Off site: Fishing in river. Golf 10 km. Riding 15 km. An hourly air-conditioned bus service runs from the gates to the city centre, touring the outside of the walls first.

Open: All year.

Directions

Site is on the C4000 road on the edge of the town, signed towards Puebla de Montelban; site signs also in city centre. From Madrid on N401, turn off right towards Toledo city centre but turn right again at the roundabout at the gates to the old city. Site is signed from the next right turn. GPS: 39.865, -4.047

Charges 2011

Per unit incl. 2 persons and electricity	€ 29,70
extra person	€ 6,45
child (3-10 yrs)	€ 5,60

For latest campsite news, availability and prices visit
alanrogers.com

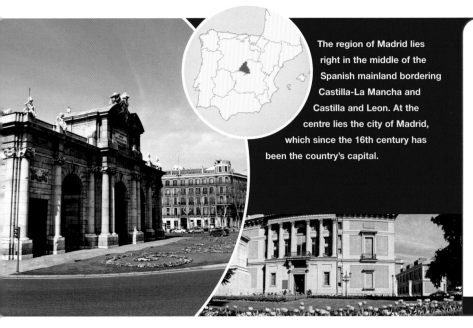

The region of Madrid lies right in the middle of the Spanish mainland bordering Castilla-La Mancha and Castilla and Leon. At the centre lies the city of Madrid, which since the 16th century has been the country's capital.

THE REGION OF MADRID IS A ONE PROVINCE AUTONOMY, ALSO CALLED MADRID

The mountainous region of Madrid can be divided into two areas: the Sierra, in the north and west of the region, which includes part of Somosierra and Guadarrama; and the central and southern parts, where the area is flatter and forms part of the plateau of La Mancha and La Alcarria. Founded by the Moors in the ninth Century, Madrid is now a modern, vibrant city offering innumerable attractions to the visitor. Its architectural heritage is immense. Some of the oldest parts of Madrid lie around the Puerta del Sol; a good starting place for exploring the city. Full of outdoor restaurants and bars, Plaza Mayor is considered to be one of the finest in Spain, and in summer becomes an outdoor theatre and music stage. The city also has a large number of parks and gardens, among them el Retiro, the Botanical Gardens, the Parque del Oeste and the Casa de Campo; and numerous museums and art galleries. Outside the capital, the Sierra de Madrid is ideal for winter sports and the beautiful town of Aranjuez, home to the Royal Palace and glorious gardens, is a popular retreat from the city.

Places of interest

Alcala de Henares: university town, birthplace of Cervantes, author of Don Quixote, Cervantes House Museum, Archepiscopal Palace Cathedral.

Chinchón: 15th-century castle, beautiful medieval square, 19th-century church with painting by Goya, home of Alchoholera de Chinchón – aniseed liqueur!

Parque Natural de la Cumbre: mountain park, the highest mountains in the Madrid region.

San Lorenzo de El Escorial: town in heart of Guadarrama Mountains, Monastery of El Escorial, Royal Pantheon.

Cuisine of the region

Tapas is popular with typical dishes including seafood: steamed mussels, anchovies in vinegar and pickled bonito plus croquettes and mini-casseroles. Sea bream and cod is used a lot. Local produce includes beef from the Guadarrama Mountains, olives from Campo Real, aniseed from Chinchón and asparagus from Aranjuez. Madrid is also a good place to experience every regional style of Spanish cooking.

Buñuelos: a type of fritter which is filled with custard, chocolate and cream.

Cocido: meat, potato and chickpea stew.

Con gabardina: prawns cooked in beer.

Torrijas: bread pudding.

El Escorial

Caravanning El Escorial

Apdo 8, Ctra M600 km 3,5, E-28280 El Escorial (Madrid) T: 902 014 900. E: info@campingelescorial.com
alanrogers.com/ES92000

There is a shortage of good sites in the central regions of Spain, but this is one. El Escorial is very large, there are 1,358 individual pitches of which about 600 are for touring, with the remainder used for permanent or seasonal units, but situated to one side of the site. The pitches are shaded (ask for a pitch without a low tree canopy if you have a 3 m. high motorcaravan). There are another 250 pseudo 'wild' spaces for tourists on open fields, with good shade from mature trees (long cables may be necessary for electricity). The general amenities are good and include three swimming pools (unheated), plus a paddling pool in a central area with a bar/restaurant with terrace and plenty of grassy sitting out areas. At weekends in high season the site can be noisy. It is well situated for sightseeing visits especially to the magnificent El Escorial monastery (5 km). Also, the enormous civil war monument of the Valle de los Caidos is very close plus Madrid and Segovia both 50 km. away.

Facilities

One large toilet block for the touring pitches, plus two smart, small blocks for the 'wild' camping area, are all fully equipped with some washbasins in cabins. Baby baths. Facilities for disabled campers. The blocks can be heated. Supermarket, restaurant/bar and snack bar/takeaway (all year; w/ends only in low season). Disco-bar. Swimming pools (15/5-15/9). Three tennis courts. Two well equipped playgrounds on sand. ATM. Off site: Town 3 km. Riding or golf 7 km.

Open: All year.

Directions

From the south go through town of El Escorial, and follow M600 Guadarrama road. Site is between the 2 and 3 km. markers north of the town on the right. From the north use A6 autopista and exit 47 to M600 towards El Escorial town. Site is on the left. GPS: 40.62400, -4.099

Charges 2011

Per person	€ 6,85
child (3-10 yrs)	€ 6,75
pitch incl. electricity	€ 20,55

No credit cards.

Aranjuez

Camping Internacional Aranjuez

Soto del Rebollo, s/n antigua NIV km 46,8, E-28300 Aranjuez (Madrid) T: 918 911 395
E: info@campingaranjuez.com alanrogers.com/ES90910

Aranjuez, supposedly Spain's version of Versailles, is worthy of a visit with its beautiful palaces, leafy squares, avenues and gardens. This useful, popular and unusually well equipped site is therefore excellent for enjoying the unusual attractions or for an en-route stop. It is 47 km. south of Madrid and 46 km. from Toledo. The site is alongside the River Tajo in a park-like situation with mature trees. There are 162 touring pitches, all with electricity (16A), set on flat grass amid tall trees. The site was bought by the owners of La Marina (ES87420) who have worked hard to improve the pitches and the site. Two little tourist road trains run from the site to the palaces daily. You can visit the huge, but slightly decaying Royal Palace or the Casa del Labrador (translates as farmer's cottage) which is a small neo-classical palace in unusual and differing styles. It has superb gardens commissioned by Charles II. Canoes may be hired from behind the supermarket and there is a lockable moat gate to allow access to the river. There is good security backed up with CCTV around the river perimeter.

Facilities

The largest of three modern, good quality sanitary blocks is heated in winter and well equipped with some washbasins in cabins. Laundry facilities. Gas supplies. Small shop, bar and restaurant (all year) with attractive riverside patio (also open to the public). Takeaway. TV room. Swimming and paddling pools, (1/5-15/9). New play area. Pétanque. Bicycle hire. Canoe hire. Torch useful. Off site: Within easy walking distance of palace, gardens and museums. Riding and golf 2 km.

Open: All year.

Directions

From the M305 (Madrid - Aranjuez) look for 8 km. marker on the outskirts of town. Then follow campsite signs – these lead back onto the M305 (going north now) and the site is signed off right at 300 m. on the first left bend. Follow signs down the narrow road for 400 m. If coming from the south ensure that you have the M305 to Madrid (other roads are signed to Madrid). If in doubt ask as it is very confusing if the M305 road is missed. GPS: 40.0426, -3.5995

Charges guide

Per unit incl. 2 persons and electricity	€ 20,87 - € 33,82
extra person	€ 4,28 - € 5,89
child (3-10 yrs)	€ 3,21 - € 4,82

Discounts for groups or long stays.

For latest campsite news, availability and prices visit
alanrogers.com

Gargantilla de Lozoya

Camping Monte Holiday

Ctra Rascafria - Lozoya km 9, E-28739 Gargantilla de Lozoya (Madrid) T: 918 695 278
E: monteholiday@monteholiday.com alanrogers.com/ES92120

The Somosierra offers spectacular scenery and is very popular with Spanish skiers. This site is situated in an open, sunny lower valley, in the Madrid area's only beech forest near a large nature reserve. The area is ideal for anglers and walkers and also offers many opportunities for outdoor sports enthusiasts. The site is on terraces and has 308 small pitches with 100 for touring (electricity 7A; long leads required in some areas). These pitches are mainly flat with grass or gravel surfaces and shade from mature trees but unfortunately are very uneven. The upper area is taken by permanent units. The site has an attractive swimming pool with sunbathing areas. The bar/restaurant offers a limited range of meals including some regional dishes. The strength of this site is the range of adventure and outdoor activities in the nearby mountains. There is horse riding in the area within the site and skiing on the nearby slopes in winter. On site, less arduous activities are also organised for children (high season). From here it is possible to enjoy the wonderful Somosierra mountains or even to make a short trip to Spain's exciting capital, Madrid.

Facilities

The modern, heated and well equipped toilet block is well maintained. Facilities for disabled visitors and babies. Laundry facilities. Motorcaravan services. Shop. Bar and fair quality restaurant (15/6-15/9 and weekends). Swimming pool (mid June-mid Sept). Shop. Multisports court. Tennis. Play area. Gas supplies. Barbecues are not permitted in summer. Bicycle hire. Off site: Mountain trips, guided climbs. Skiing 20 minutes. Boat launching and riding 8 km. Fishing 1 km.

Open: All year.

Directions

From A1 motorway (Burgos - Madrid) take exit 69 towards Rascafria. Turn right after passing under a railway tunnel and site is on left after 800 m. GPS: 40.949917, -3.729267

Charges guide

Per unit incl. 2 persons and electricity	€ 26,70 - € 29,40
extra person	€ 6,30
child (3-10 yrs)	€ 5,80

Camping Cheques accepted.

La Cabrera

Camping Pico de la Miel

Ctra. A-1, Salida 57, E-28751 La Cabrera (Madrid) T: 918 688 082. E: info@picodelamiel.com
alanrogers.com/ES92100

Pico de la Miel is a very large site 60 km. north of Madrid. Mainly a long-stay site for Madrid, there is a huge number of very well established, fairly old statics. There is a small separate area with its own toilet block for touring units. The pitches are on rather poor, sandy grass, some with artificial shade. Others, not so level, are under sparse pine trees and there are yet more pitches for tents (the ground could be hard for pegs). The noise level from the many Spanish customers is high and you will have a chance to practise your Spanish! Electricity connections are available. Tall hedges abound and with the trees, make it resemble a giant maze. No internal signs are provided and the long walk to the pool can be a challenge. The site is well signed and easy to find, two or three kilometres southwest off the main N1 road, with an amazing mountain backdrop.

Facilities

Dated but clean tiled toilet block, with some washbasins in cabins. It can be heated. En-suite unit with ramp for disabled visitors. Motorcaravan services. Gas supplies. Shop. Restaurant/Bar and takeaway (1/6-30/9). Excellent swimming pool complex (15/6-15/9). Tennis. Playground. Off site: Bicycle hire and riding 500 m. Fishing 6 km.

Open: All year.

Directions

Site is well signed from the N1. Going south or north use exit 57 and follow site signs. When at T-junction, facing a hotel, turn left. (Exit 57 is closer to site than exit 60). GPS: 40.85797, -3.6158

Charges guide

Per person	€ 6,00
child (3-9 yrs)	€ 5,20
pitch with electricity	€ 10,45 - € 16,45

Less 10-25% for longer stays.

For latest campsite news, availability and prices visit
alanrogers.com

The large region of Castilla y León is located inland, bordering Portugal to the west. It has a rich legacy dating back to the Romans, with an extraordinary wealth of castles, cathedrals and mansions, historic cities and towns.

THE REGION IS MADE UP OF THE FOLLOWING PROVINCES: AVILA, BURGOS, LEON, PALENCIA, SALAMANCA, VALLADOLID, ZAMORA, SEGOVIA AND SORIA

Steeped in history and architectural sights, the major towns and cities of the provinces all have something to offer. In the south, the town of Ávila is set on a high plain, surrounded by 11th-century walls; and the graceful city of Salamanca was once home to one of the most prestigious universities in the world. Its grand Plaza Mayor is the finest in Spain. In the east, Segovia is well known for its magnificent Roman aqueduct, with 163 arches and 29 metres at its highest point; the cathedral; and the fairy-tale Alcázar, complete with turrets and narrow towers. And the attractive city of Soria still retains a Romanesque legacy in its network of medieval streets. Burgos in the north, is the birthplace of El Cid and has a Gothic cathedral of exceptional quality. The lively university city of Leon boasts a Royal Pantheon, decorated by Romanesque wall paintings, and also an impressive Gothic cathedral. There too is a Gothic cathedral in Palencia plus an archaeology museum. South of Leon, the old walled quarters of Zamora have a retained medieval appearance, with a dozen Romanesque churches. And in the centre of the region, Valladolid is famous for its extravagant and solemn processions during the Holy Week celebrations.

Places of interest

Astorga: city of Roman origin, chocolate museum, cathedral.

Ciudad Rodrigo: Renaissance mansions, cathedral, 12th-century walls.

Coca: impressive Mudejar castle, birthplace of the famous Roman emperor Theodosius the Great.

Pantano de Burgomillodo: reservoir, great for birdwatchers.

Parque Natural del Cañón del Río Lobos: park created around the canyon of the River Lobos with rock formations, cave and good walking tracks.

Parque Natural del Lago de Sanabria y alrededores: mountainous area with deep valleys and glacier lagoons, variety of flora and fauna including 76 types of birds and 17 large mammals.

Cuisine of the region

The region is best known for its roast pork and lamb which has earned it the nickname *España del Asado* (Spain of the Roast). Other local products include trout from León and Zamora, and a variety of pulses: white, red and black beans, Castilian and *Pedrosillano* chickpeas, and various types of lentils. Soups feature a lot in winter: trout soup, typical of Órbigo de León; garlic soup; Zamora soup, a garlic soup with ripe tomatoes and hot chilli peppers.

Bizcochos de San Lorenzo: sponge cakes.

Farinatos: sausages made from breadcrumbs, pork fat and spices.

Hornazos: sausage and egg tarts.

Judias del barco con chorizo: haricot beans with sausage.

Yemas: a sweet made with egg yolks and sugar.

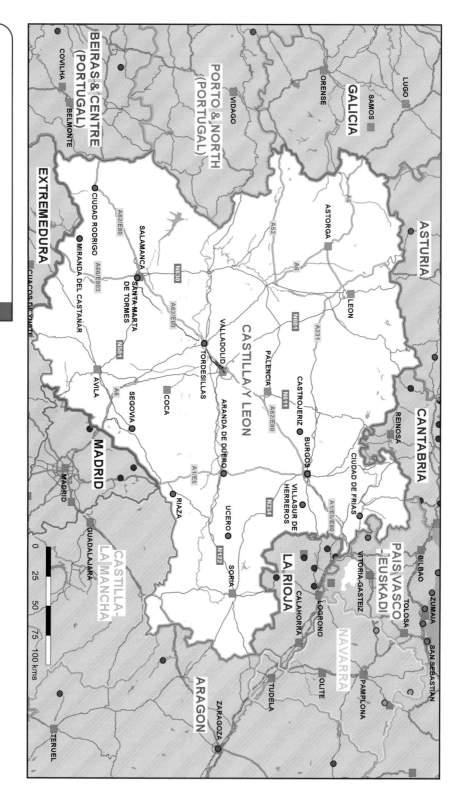

For latest campsite news, availability and prices visit

alanrogers.com

Aranda de Duero

Camping Costajan

Ctra NI E-5 km 164-165, E-09400 Aranda de Duero (Burgos) T: 947 502 070
E: costajan@camping-costajan.com alanrogers.com/ES92500

This site is well placed as an en-route stop for the ferries, being 80 km. south of Burgos. This is the capital of the Ribera del Duero wine region that produces many fine wines competing with the great Riojas. With 225 unmarked pitches, all with electricity available, there are around 100 for all types of tourer. Large units may find access to the 225 unmarked, variably sized pitches a bit tricky among dense olive and pine trees and on the slightly undulating sandy ground but the trees provide good shade. There are 115 electricity connections.

Facilities

Good, heated, modern sanitary facilities have hot and cold water. Facilities for disabled visitors. Washing machine. Gas supplies. Shop with essentials (all year). Bar serving simple meals (all year). Free access to adjacent large swimming pool (June-Sept). Tennis. Minigolf. WiFi throughout (charged). Torch useful. If reception is unmanned, choose a pitch and book in later.
Off site: Public transport 1 km. Riding 2 km. Fishing and river beach 3 km. Golf 30 km.

Open: All year.

Directions

From A1/E5 take exit at 164,5 km. and turn south on N1 towards Aranda de Duero. The site is on the right at the 162 km. mark. GPS: 41.702, -3.68803

Charges guide

Per person	€ 5,40 - € 5,60
child	€ 5,10 - € 5,30
pitch	€ 8,90 - € 11,50
electricity	€ 5,00
dog	€ 2,40

Burgos

Camping Municipal Fuentes Blancas

Ctra Cartuja - Miraflores km 3,5, E-09193 Burgos (Burgos) T: 947 486 016. E: info@campingburgos.com
alanrogers.com/ES90210

Fuentes Blancas is a comfortable municipal site on the edge of the historical town of Burgos and within easy reach of the Santander ferries. There are around 350 marked pitches of 70 sq.m. on flat ground, 250 with electrical connections (6A) and there is good shade in parts. The site has a fair amount of transit trade and reservations are not possible for August, so arrive early. Burgos is an attractive city, ideally placed for an overnight stop en-route to or from the south of Spain. The old part of the city around the cathedral is quite beautiful and there are pleasant walks along the river banks just outside the site.

Facilities

Clean, modern, fully equipped sanitary facilities in five blocks with controllable showers and hot and cold water to sinks (not all are always open). Facilities for babies. Washing machine/dryer. Motorcaravan service point. Small shop (high season). Bar/snack bar and restaurant (high season). Swimming pool (1/7-30/8). Playground. English is spoken. Off site: Fishing and river beach 200 m. Bus service to city or a fairly shaded walk. Golf 30 km.

Open: All year.

Directions

From the north (Santander) continue on the N623 through city centre to km. 0. Follow signs for E5/A1 Madrid. After crossing river take slip road for N120/A231 Leon but then turn left towards Fuentes Blancas and Cartuja de Miraflores for 3 km. Site is well signed on left. GPS: 42.34125, -3.65762

Charges guide

Per person	€ 4,65
child (2-10 yrs)	€ 3,20
pitch incl. electricity	€ 13,30

Castrojeriz

Camping Camino de Santiago

Avenida Virgen del Manzano s/n, E-09110 Castrojeriz (Burgos) T: 947 377 255. E: info@campingcamino.com
alanrogers.com/ES90230

This tranquil site lies to the west of Burgos on the outskirts of Castrojeriz. In a superb location, almost in the shadow of the ruined castle high on the hillside. The 50 marked pitches are level, grassy and divided by hedges, with electricity (10A). Mature trees provide shade and there is a pretty orchard in one corner of the site. This site is a birdwatcher's paradise – large raptors abound – and the owner takes visitors out on birdwatching trips currently on an ad hoc basis.

Facilities

Older style sanitary block with hot showers, washbasin with cold water and British and Turkish style WCs. No facilities for disabled visitors. Washing machine. Bar/restaurant and takeaway with traditional cuisine. Bicycle hire. Library. WiFi (free). Games room. Tennis. Play area. Barbecue area. Ad hoc guided birdwatching. Off site: Fishing and riding 17 km.

Open: 1 March - 30 November.

Directions

Castrojeriz is 45 km. west of Burgos. From the N120/A231 (Leon - Burgos), turn on Bu404 (Villasandino, Castrojeriz), then left at crossroads on southwest side of town, then left at site sign. From A62 (Burgos - Valladolid) turn north at Vallaquirán on Bu400/401 to Castrojeriz. Turn sharp right at filling station and as above. GPS: 42.2913, -4.1448

Charges guide

Per unit incl. 2 persons and electricity	€ 19,50 - € 24,00
extra person	€ 4,75 - € 5,00
child (under 14 yrs)	€ 3,25 - € 3,50

Ciudad de Frias
Camping Frias
E-09211 Ciudad de Frias (Burgos) T: 947 357 198. E: info@campingfrias.com
alanrogers.com/ES92570

Located in a natural park northeast of Burgos, on the edge of the old, small Spanish town of Frias, much of this site is taken up with static units. However, an area at the end is reserved for touring caravans and motorcaravans. A beautiful river runs alongside, about 20 feet below the campsite but with access for fishing, and the level, numbered pitches (30 for touring) have views across the really beautiful scenery surrounding the campsite. A little shade is provided from a few trees. This is a very Spanish site (no English was spoken when we visited) and it may be noisy in summer with lively Spanish visitors.

Facilities
One toilet block provides basic facilities with British style WCs, washbasins with cold water only and coin operated showers. Washing machine and dryer. Shop with good range of produce (from 1/6). Bar and restaurant (from 1/6). Two swimming pools (22/6-15/9) and paddling pool. Off site: Transport would be needed to visit any interesting places.

Open: 1 April - 30 September.

Directions
Site is on the north side of Frias – approach only from this side. From A1 exit 5 onto A2122 (Quintana Martin Galindez), with a few tunnels (turn right on 625 then left to Quintana). After 16 km. turn left (Frias). Site is 3 km. on right. Or on A1 from exit 4 on N232 then 629 to Trespaderne. Turn right (Miranda) and drive east for 10 km. then turn right to Frias. GPS: 42.77098, -3.29686

Charges guide
Per person	€ 4,00
pitch incl. electricity	€ 11,00

Ciudad Rodrigo
Camping La Pesquera
Ctra de Caceres - Arrabal, E-37500 Ciudad Rodrigo (Salamanca) T: 923 481 348
alanrogers.com/ES90190

This modest site has just 54 pitches and is located near the Rio Agueda looking up to the magnificent fortress ramparts of Ciudad Rodrigo. Entry to the site is through a municipal park with a large play area. Whilst the site is small it can take even the largest units, the centrally located facilities have all been refurbished to a high standard, the pitches are flat and grassy and the roads are well maintained gravel. The pitches are shaded by trees and there is site lighting at night, but you may find torches useful.

Facilities
Attractive ochre stone sanitary building with British style WCs and free hot showers. Facilities for disabled campers. Washing machine. Basics sold from bar in high season. Bar/snacks (Apr-Sept). Playground and barbecue area outside gates. Torches useful. Off site: River fishing 1 km. Riding 5 km. Superb walking area.

Open: 25 April - 30 September.

Directions
Site is southwest of Salamanca close to Ciudad Rodrigo. From the E80 N260, any direction, take the 526 to Coria. Site is alongside river directly off the road and well signed. GPS: 40.599, -6.533

Charges guide
Per person	€ 3,20
pitch	€ 3,20 - € 6,40
electricity	€ 3,00

Miranda del Castañar
Camping El Burro Blanco
Camino de las Norias s/n, E-37660 Miranda del Castañar (Salamanca) T: 923 161 100
E: camping.elburroblanco@gmail.com alanrogers.com/ES90260

Set on a hill side, within the Sierra Peña de Francia and with views of the romantic walled village of Miranda del Castañar and its charming, crumbling castle, this site is run by a Dutch couple, Jeff and Yvonne, and their friend Paul. You are welcomed at the gate and are walked around the facilities. There is a total of 31 level touring pitches (all 80 to 120 sq.m), 25 with electricity. They are beautifully set in 3.5 hectares of the most attractive natural woodland. Owners of large caravans and motorhomes should contact the site first due to the restricted number of suitable pitches.

Facilities
One central modern sanitary facility, fully equipped includes a baby bath. Two washbasins have hot water. Out of season part of the unit is closed and therefore facilities are unisex. Launderette. Gas supplies. Library with book swap and small bar. Off site: Restaurants, bars, shops and ATM in village 600 m. Municipal swimming pool nearby. River swimming and fishing 1.5 km. Riding 15 km.

Open: 1 April - 1 October.

Directions
From north - south direction take Salamanca - Coria road southwest for about 70 km. through Vecinos, Linares de Rio Frio towards Coria (keeping on main road). From east-west direction take Bejar - Ciudad Rodrigo road south towards Cepeda/Coria. Road to Miranda del Castañar is 7 km. northeast of Cepeda. Turn off main road (Miranda). After 1.2 km. downhill towards town look for left turn on concrete road. In 1.1 km. site is on right. GPS: 40.4748, -5.99885

Charges 2011
Per unit incl. 2 persons	€ 20,63 - € 24,19

No credit cards.

For latest campsite news, availability and prices visit
alanrogers.com

Riaza

Camping Riaza

Ctra de la Estacion s/n, E-40500 Riaza (Segovia) T: 921 550 580. E: info@campingriaza.com
alanrogers.com/ES90245

We visited this beautiful site shortly after its inauguration in 2007. It is situated in the province of Segovia, a hundred or so kilometres north of Madrid, making an ideal spot for a few days rest en-route north or south. Of the 350 spacious pitches 213 are for touring, all with electricity (8A), water, drainage and sewerage. The pitches are divided by hedges and oak trees giving some shade. The buildings on the site are sympathetically built of local stone housing a large clubroom, bar and welcoming restaurant lit by chandeliers, a good place to relax and enjoy the excellent menu.

Facilities

Two excellent, centrally located toilet blocks with underfloor heating. Shop. Bar, restaurant and clubroom (all year). Swimming pool (1/6-31/8). Two natural pools in the river bordering site. Large modern play area. Wellness centre with all year heated indoor pool, gym, massage room, jacuzzi and sauna. Minigolf. New sports area. Tennis. Archery. Children's club (summer only). Off site: Village of Riaza 2 km. with restaurant and some shopping. Riding 2 km. Golf 9 km.

Open: All year.

Directions

From the A1 (Burgos - Madrid) take exit 104 and the N110 towards Soria. Leave the N110 signed Riaza and follow camping signs. At roundabout follow signs for 'Estacion' and site is 50 m. on left. GPS: 41.26944, -3.49749

Charges guide

Per unit incl. 2 persons	
and electricity	€ 22,00 - € 25,80
extra person	€ 5,90

Santa Marta de Tormes

Camping Regio

Ctra de Madrid km 4, E-37900 Santa Marta de Tormes (Salamanca) T: 923 138 888
E: recepcion@campingregio.com alanrogers.com/ES90250

Salamanca is one of Europe's oldest university cities, and this beautiful old sandstone city has to be visited. This is also a useful staging post en-route to the south of Spain or central Portugal. The site is 7 km. outside the city on the old road to Madrid, behind the Hôtel Regio where campers can take advantage of the hotel facilities. The 129 pitches (with a large area for tents) are clearly marked on slightly sloping ground, with some shade in parts and plentiful electricity points (10A). Access to those pitches not on the wide central road can be difficult for caravans.

Facilities

Very large, fully equipped sanitary block is very clean. Good facilities for disabled campers. Washing machines. Gas supplies. Motorcaravan services. Bar. Supermarket (1/6-30/9). The hotel restaurant, café and swimming pool may be used by campers (discounts at the café and restaurant). Play area. Tennis. Internet and WiFi (both within hotel area). English is spoken. Off site: Bus to town terminates at hotel carpark. Fishing 2 km. Bicycle hire 4 km. Town centre 7 km. Golf 14 km.

Open: All year.

Directions

Take the main N501 route from Salamanca towards Avila, then to St Marta de Tormes 7 km. east of the city. Hôtel Regio is on the right just outside the town at the 90 km. marker. There are yellow hotel and camping signs through the city and on the roads to the east. GPS: 40.9471, -5.614

Charges 2011

Per unit incl. 2 persons	
and electricity	€ 19,40 - € 21,70

Segovia

Camping El Acueducto

Avenida D Juan de Borbón 49, E-40004 Segovia (Segovia) T: 921 425 000
E: informacion@campingacueducto.com alanrogers.com/ES92420

Located right on the edge of the interesting city of Segovia with lovely views across the open plain with mountains in the background, this is a family run, typically Spanish site. The grass pitches are mostly of medium size, although a few pitches near the gate would have room for larger motorcaravans. An uncomplicated site, reception is small, but efficient and the owner is helpful and speaks good English. El Acueducto is about 5 km. from the city. Segovia is deeply and haughtily Castilian, with plenty of squares and mansions from its days of Golden Age grandeur, when it was a royal resort.

Facilities

Two traditional style toilet blocks provide simple, clean facilities. Laundry room. Small shop for essentials. Bar. Two swimming pools. Large play area. WiFi in reception. Car wash. Motorcaravan services. Off site: Large restaurant nearby. Bus service into city centre. Madrid is within reasonable driving distance.

Open: 1 April - 30 September.

Directions

From the north on N1 (Burgos - Madrid) take exit 99 on N110 towards Segovia. On outskirts of city take third exit onto N603 signed Madrid. Pass one exit to Segovia and take second signed Segovia and La Granja. At roundabout turn right towards Segovia. Site is 500 m. on right beside the dual-carriageway. GPS: 40.93125, -4.09243

Charges guide

Per person	€ 5,00 - € 5,60
pitch incl. electriciy (5A)	€ 11,70 - € 19,50

For latest campsite news, availability and prices visit
alanrogers.com

Tordesillas

Kawan Village El Astral

Camino de Pollos 8, E-47100 Tordesillas (Valladolid) T: 983 770 953. E: info@campingelastral.es

alanrogers.com/ES90290

The site is in a prime position alongside the wide River Duero (safely fenced). It is homely and run by a charming man, Eduardo Gutierrez, who has excellent English and is ably assisted by brother Gustavo and sister Lola. The site is generally flat with 154 pitches separated by thin hedges. The 144 touring pitches, 132 with electricity (6/10A), vary in size from 60-200 sq.m. with mature trees providing shade. The new toilet block has been designed with environmental awareness, including solar heated water.

Facilities

One attractive new sanitary block with fully equipped, modern facilities designed to include energy saving measures and to be easily cleaned. Showers for children and baby room. Facilities for disabled campers. Washing machines. Motorcaravan services. Supermarket. Bar and restaurant, frequented by locals, plus a takeaway service all 1/4-30/9. Swimming and paddling pools (1/6-15/9). Playground. Tennis (high season). Minigolf. Internet point and WiFi. English speaking staff. Local bus service. Torches are useful. Off site: River fishing 100 m. Golf 10 km. Riding 20 km.

Open: 1 April - 30 September.

Directions

Tordesillas is 28 km. southwest of Valladolid. From all directions, leave the main road towards Tordesillas and follow signs to campsite or 'Parador' (a hotel opposite the campsite). GPS: 41.495305, -5.005222

Charges 2011

Per person	€ 4,50 - € 6,75
child (3-12 yrs)	€ 3,50 - € 5,60
pitch incl. car	€ 8,40 - € 12,35
electricity (5A)	€ 3,60 - € 5,00

Discounts in low season and for longer stays.
Camping Cheques accepted.

Ucero

Camping Cañon del Rio Lobos

Ctra Burgos de Osma - San Leonardo, E-42317 Ucero (Soria) T: 975 363 565

alanrogers.com/ES92510

This is a delightful site with 83 neat pitches and vast amounts of flowers, set among attractive limestone cliffs of the Burgos canyons. The site is pricey but facilities are excellent and there are few others in the area. Reception is purpose built and control of the security barrier is from within – everything here is very organised. The camp logo depicts a bird of prey and many raptors continuously wheel above the site. The very attractive swimming pool is within a secure walled area, which again has many flowers and shrubs and is private from the road that runs alongside the site (some traffic noise).

Facilities

Two fully equipped toilet blocks (only one opened when site is quiet). Bar serving a 'menu del día' and smart restaurant. Basic shopping from bar. Swimming pool (charge). Two excellent tennis courts (charged). Play area. Bicycle hire. Fishing. Football pitch. Torch useful. Dogs are not accepted. Off site: Local bus service 1 km. on Wed./Sat. for town. Walking, climbing, caving, fishing in nearby 'Parque Natural'. Riding 10 km. Golf 35 km.

Open: Easter - 30 September.

Directions

From N234 (Burgos - Soria) turn south in San Leonado de Yagüe on SO690. Turn left after village on SO920 signed El Burgo de Osma. Site is on left in 18 km. just before Ucero. From N122/A11 (Valladolid - Soria) turn north in El Burgo de Osma on SO920 signed San Leonardo, 16 km. to Ucero. From San Leonardo cross Rio Lobo on El Burgo de Osma road. Site is 400 m. GPS: 41.7293, -3.0475

Charges guide

| Per unit incl. 2 persons | € 23,00 |

Villasur de Herreros

Camping Puerta de la Demanda

Ctra de Pineda km 2, E-09199 Villasur de Herreros (Burgos) T: 983 796 819. E: info@puertadelademanda.com

alanrogers.com/ES92540

This site on flat ground, is overlooked on three sides by the hills and mountains of the Sierra de la Demanda which give the site its name. There is little shade over 50 well marked large pitches all of which have electricity (3-6A) and drainage. The modern buildings are of local stone and wood in sympathy with the quiet surroundings, yet providing an excellent set of facilities. The whole site is securely fenced. A river is very close for swimming and fishing, as is the trail of the pilgrims to Santiago de Compostella.

Facilities

Sanitary building with British WCs and free hot showers. Washing machine. Facilities for disabled campers. Shop (April-Sept). Bar serving meals and selling basics (all season). Bicycle hire. Torches useful. Pets are not accepted. Off site: River fishing 1 km. Sailing on nearby reservoir. Shop, restaurants and bars in attractive village 1 km. Superb walking area.

Open: 1 February - 30 November.

Directions

From the N120 (Burgos - Logroño), turn east at Ibeas de Juarros (about 13 km. east of Burgos) on Bu-P8101/Bu820 through Arlanzon to Villasur de Herreros. Site is beyond village after km. 13. GPS: 42.306, -3.375

Charges guide

Per person	€ 3,70
child (up to 12 yrs)	€ 2,60
pitch incl. car and electricity	€ 9,50 - € 10,40

For latest campsite news, availability and prices visit

alanrogers.com

With a coastline of inlets and wide, rocky estuaries, sheltering traditional old fishing villages and fine beaches, Galicia is perhaps best known for Santiago de Compostela, the place where the famous pilgrims' route comes to an end.

THIS REGION IS MADE UP OF FOUR PROVINCES: OURENSE, LUGO, A CORUÑA AND PONTEVEDRA

The obvious highlight in the region has to be the beautiful medieval city of Santiago de Compostela, capital of Galicia and world famous centre of the old European pilgrimage. Now a World Heritage Site, the city boasts an impressive Romanesque cathedral with more churches, convents and monasteries dotted around. One of the best times to go to Santiago de Compostela is during the Festival of St James on 25 July, which has also been designated Galicia Day. Following the route into the city, are the towns of Portomarín and Samos. Near Samos, the Lóuzara valley and the Sierra do Oribio are ideal for those interested in hiking and wildlife. The Galician coastline is characterised by high cliffs and estuaries collectively known as the Rías Atlas and Rías Baixas with the Costa da Morte or Coast of Death separating them; so called because of the hundreds of shipwrecks that litter the cliffs and rocks. It was also once considered by the pilgrimages to be the 'end of the world'. Along the coast are medieval towns and villages including Noia, Muros, A Coruña and Finisterre. Corcubión, Camariñas and Corme-Laxe are other rias with fishing villages and home to some of the best barnacles in the region.

Places of interest

A Coruña: medieval quarters, Romanesque churches, Roman lighthouse.

Baiona: one of the region's best resorts.

Camariñas: town on the 'end of the world', good barnacle hunting ground, lacemaking traditions.

Lugo: town completely enclosed within preserved Roman walls, along which are 85 towers.

Malpica: seaside harbour, jumping off point for nearby islands.

Pontevedra: picturesque old town with lively atmosphere.

Vigo: fishing port, beaches.

Viveiro: beaches, old town surrounded by Renaissance walls.

Cuisine of the region

Local cuisine features heavily in fiestas and throughout the region are numerous markets. Good quality seafood is found in abundance; *percebes* (barnacles) are a favourite. *Pulpo* (octopus) is also popular and special *pulperías* will cook it in the traditional way. Vegetable dishes include the Galician broth, made with green beans, cabbage, parsnip, potatoes and haricot beans. *Aguardiente gallego*, a regional liqueur, is used to make the traditional mulled drink known as *queimada*, where fruit, sugar and coffee grains are added and then set alight.

Caldeirada: fish soup.

Caldo gallego: thick potato and cabbage stew.

Empanada: light-crusted pastries often filled with pork, beef, tuna or cod.

Lacon con grelos: ham boiled with turnip greens.

Bayona
Camping Bayona Playa
Ctra Vigo - Bayona km 19, E-36393 Bayona (Pontevedra) T: 986 350 035
E: campingbayona@campingbayona.com alanrogers.com/ES89360

Situated on a narrow peninsula with the sea and river estuary all around it, this large and well maintained campsite is great for a relaxing break. The 450 pitches, 358 for touring, benefit from the shade of mature trees whilst still maintaining a very open feel. All have 5A electricity and 50 are fully serviced. It is busy here in high season so advance booking is recommended. Sabaris is a short walk away and Bayona is a 20-minute walk along the coast, where you can find a variety of shops, supermarkets, banks, bars and eating places. Maximum unit length is 7.5 m. From the moment you arrive at the well appointed reception, the staff, all of whom speak good English, make every effort to ensure that you have a memorable stay. You can also visit a replica of the 'Pinta', the ship that bought back the news of Christopher Columbus' discovery of America, which is moored here. The surrounding countryside has plenty of attractions and a variety of water sports are available, including the site's own school of windsurfing. Buses run from Sabaris to Vigo and to A Guarda.

Facilities

Three well maintained modern toilet blocks (one open low season), washbasins and shower cubicles. No washing machines but site provides a service wash. Facilities for visitors with disabilities. Large well stocked supermarket and gift shop (June-Sept). Terrace bar, cafeteria, restaurant. Excellent pool complex with slide (small charge, redeemable in shop and restaurant). Play area. Organised activities July/Aug. Off site: Fishing 100 m. Bicycle hire 5 km. Riding 8 km. Golf 20 km.

Open: All year.

Directions

From Vigo leave AG57, exit 5 Bayona North. Follow signs to site at Sabaris, 2 km. east of Bayona. GPS: 42.113978, -8.826013

Charges guide

Per person	€ 6,30
child (3-12 yrs)	€ 3,95
pitch	€ 3,95 - € 13,05
electricity	€ 3,95

For latest campsite news, availability and prices visit
alanrogers.com

Muros
Camping San Francisco

Camino do Convento 21, Louro, E-15291 Muros (A Coruña) T: 981 826 148. E: ofmlouro@yahoo.es
alanrogers.com/ES89300

Situated 400 m. from the coast, this small and attractive touring site with 104 small pitches occupies a clearing on a hillside that is undoubtedly a magnet for Spanish holidaymakers. Advance booking is recommended. The neatly laid out and numbered pitches are on level grass, divided by trees but with little shade. All have 10A electricity and 74 pitches are fully serviced. The surrounding countryside is scenic and unspoilt by development and the superb white sandy beaches and rocky coves provide endless hours of fun or relaxation for the whole family. Bars and restaurants, together with a few small shops, are all within 300 m. of the site but for everything else, the small town of Muros is only 3.5 km. There is a promenade along the sea front which passes the marina and the small working harbour where you can take a selection of boat trips into the sheltered bays around this coastline.

Facilities	Directions
One modern spotlessly clean toilet block is centrally positioned with all necessary facilities. A family shower room with facilities for disabled visitors is provided in both male and female areas. Washing machines, dryers and a first aid point are housed in separate rooms. Well stocked shop. Café/bar. Restaurant with terrace. Play area. Tennis and multisport court. Off site: Sandy beach, fishing 400 m. Bicycle hire 500 m. Boat launching, sailing 3.5 km.	From Santiago de Compostela take AC543 to Noia. Just before Noia turn right onto road signed Muros and continue on AC550. Site well signed 3.5 km. past Muros on right, up a narrow road. GPS: 42.761975, -9.072701

Open: 21 June - 7 September.

Charges guide

Per person	€ 5,50
child	€ 4,00
pitch incl. car	€ 10,75 - € 11,25
electricity	€ 3,90

Santa Cruz
Camping Los Manzanos

Avenida de Emilia Pardo Bazan, E-15179 Puerto de Santa Cruz (A Coruña) T: 981 614 825
E: informacion@campinglosmanzanos.com alanrogers.com/ES89420

Los Manzanos has a steep access drive down to the site, which is divided by a stream into two sections linked by a bridge. Pitches for larger units are marked and numbered, 85 with electricity (12A) and, in one section, there is a fairly large, unmarked field for tents. Some aircraft noise should be expected as the site is under the flight path to La Coruña (but no aircraft at night). The site impressed us as being very clean, even when full, which it tends to be in high season. Some interesting huge stone sculptures create focal points and conversation pieces. This site is to the east of the historic port of La Coruña, not far from some ria (lagoon) beaches and with good communications to both central and north Galicia – it is only an hours drive from Santiago de la Compostela, for example.

Facilities	Directions
One good toilet block provides modern facilities including free hot showers. Small shop with fresh produce daily (limited outside June-Sept). High quality restaurant/bar (July/Aug). Swimming pool with lifeguard, free to campers (15/6-30/9). Playground. Barbecue area. Bungalows for rent. Off site: Bus service at end of entrance drive. Beach and fishing 800 m. Bicycle hire 2 km. Golf and riding 8 km.	From western end of the AP-9 take exit 3, signed. GPS: 43.34908, -8.33567

Open: April - 30 September.

Charges 2011

Per unit incl. 2 persons and electricity	€ 29,20 - € 29,90
extra person	€ 6,00
child	€ 5,00

For latest campsite news, availability and prices visit
alanrogers.com

Portonovo

Camping Paxarinas

Ctra San Xenxo - O'Grove, E-36979 Portonovo (A Coruña) T: **986 723 055**. E: info@campingpaxarinas.com
alanrogers.com/ES89380

Paxarinas is a family-owned and managed coastal site open all year, set on a gently sloping area of hillside overlooking Ria de Pontevedra. Of the 260 very small pitches only 60 are for touring, in the centre of the site. All pitches are numbered and have 3A electricity, there is very little shade. It gets very busy in high season and advance booking is recommended. Care is needed with larger units at busy times. The site is situated in a most attractive area of Galicia and with access to two excellent beaches it makes a good stop-over whilst visiting the area. Although open all year, facilities are very limited in low season.

Facilities	Directions
Two well maintained modern sanitary blocks. Private cabins. Facilities for visitors with disabilities. Washing machine and dryer. Play area. Shop, bar and snacks (20/6-5/9). Separate restaurant in adjacent hotel. Off site: Two beaches adjacent. Riding 4 km. Golf 8 km.	From AP9, exit 129 Pontevedra, follow signs to Sanxenxo. Follow coast road PO308 for 22 km. Site poorly signed on left hand side, behind hotel, 3 km. past Sanxenxo and just before a bend. GPS: 42.392481, -8.844069

Open: All year.

Charges guide

Per unit incl. 2 persons and electricity	€ 26,95 - € 31,05
extra person	€ 6,20

Santiago de Compostela

Camping As Cancelas

Rue do 25 de Xullo 35, E-15704 Santiago de Compostela (A Coruña) T: **981 580 476**
E: info@campingascancelas.com alanrogers.com/ES90240

The beautiful city of Santiago has been the destination for European Christian pilgrims for centuries and they now follow ancient routes to this unique city, the whole of which is a national monument. The As Cancelas campsite is excellent for sharing the experiences of these pilgrims in the city and around the magnificent cathedral. It has 125 marked pitches (60-90 sq.m), arranged in terraces and divided by trees and shrubs. On a hillside overlooking the city, the views are very pleasant, but the site has a steep approach road and access to most of the pitches can be a challenge for large units. Electrical hook-ups (5A) are available, the site is lit at night and a security guard patrols. There are many legendary festivals and processions here, the main one being on July 25th, especially in holy years (when the Saint's birthday falls on a Sunday). Examine for yourself the credibility of the fascinating story of the arrival of the bones of St James at Compostela (Compostela translates as 'field of stars'), and also discover why the pilgrims dutifully carry a scallop shell on their long journey. There are many pilgrims' routes, including one commencing from Fowey in Cornwall.

Facilities	Directions
Two modern toilet blocks are fully equipped, with ramped access for disabled campers. The quality and cleanliness of the fittings and tiling is good. Laundry with service wash for a small fee. Small shop. Restaurant. Bar with TV. Well kept, unsupervised swimming pool and children's pool. Small playground. Internet access. Off site: Regular bus service runs into the city from near football ground 200 m. from site. Huge commercial centre (open late and handy for off season use) 20 minutes, walk downhill (uphill on the return!).	From motorway AP9-E1 take exit 67 and follow signs for 'Casco Historico' and 'Centro Ciudad' then follow site signs. GPS: 42.88939, -8.52418

Charges guide

Per person	€ 4,50 - € 5,90
child (up to 12 yrs)	€ 2,70 - € 4,50
pitch	€ 4,50 - € 19,00
electricity	€ 4,10

Open: All year.

For latest campsite news, availability and prices visit

alanrogers.com

Like its neighbouring province, Cantabria, Asturias also has a beautiful coastline, albeit more rugged and wild, with the Picos range separating them. In the south the Cantabrian mountains form a natural border between Asturias and Castilla-León.

THIS IS A ONE PROVINCE REGION

THE CAPITAL IS OVIEDO

Situated between the foothills of the Picos mountains and the coast is the seaside town of Llanes, in the east. It has several good beaches, beautiful coves and given its location, is a good base for exploring the Picos del Europa. Along the coast towards Gijón are more seaside resorts including Ribadesella, with its fishing harbour and fine beach. The cities of Gijón and, in particular, Avilés are renowned for their Carnival festivities, a national event which takes place in late February. This week-long party involves dancing, live music, fireworks and locals who dress up in elaborate fancy-dress costumes. South of here towards the centre of the province is the capital, Oviedo. The city boasts a pedestrian old quarter with numerous squares and narrow streets, a cathedral, palaces, a fine arts museum, an archaeological museum plus various remarkable churches that date from the ninth century. There are also plenty of sidrerías (cider houses). The west coast of Asturias is more rugged. One of the most attractive towns along here is Luarca, built around a cove surrounded by sheer cliffs. With a fishing harbour and an array of good restaurants and bars, the town's traditional character is reflected in its chigres – old Asturian taverns – where visitors can learn the art of drinking cider.

Places of interest

Avilés: 14th- and 15th-century churches and palaces.

Cudillero: small, charming fishing port.

Gijón: 18th-century palace, beaches, museums.

Villahormes: seaside town with excellent swimming coves.

Villaviciosa: atmospheric old town, 13th-century church, cider factory.

Cuisine of the region

Local specialities include *fabada,* a type of stew made with haricot beans called *fabes*, *potes* (soups) and of course cider, which can be drunk in *sidrerías.* The customary way to serve cider is to pour it from a great height, a practice known as *escanciar*, into a wide-mouthed glass only just covering the *culín* or bottom. Rice pudding is the traditional dessert and *frixuelos* (crepe), *huesos de santo* (made from marzipan) and *tocinillo de cielo* (syrup pudding) are eaten during festivals.

Brazo de gitano: a type of Swiss roll.

Carne gobernada: beef in white wine with bacon, eggs, peppers and olives.

Fabada asturiana: haricot beans, chorizo, cabbage, cured pork shoulder and potatoes.

Pastel carbayón: almond pastry.

Arbón

Camping La Cascada

Arbón Villayón, E-33718 Arbón (Asturias) T: 985 625 081. E: campinglacascada@hotmail.com
alanrogers.com/ES89440

Located in a clearing of the attractive Arbon Valley this friendly, family run site offers the chance to experience the delights of rural Spain. There are 74 very small pitches (60 for touring units), all sited on gently sloping grass with electricity (4A), long leads are required. The beaches and small villages of the Costa Verde are only 12 km. away and the site has information about this spectacular region. Access to the site is not difficult but a 3500 kg. weight restriction on the small bridge at the site entrance makes it unsuitable for larger units. The focal point of this small and well maintained site is its traditional style restaurant. It is open during July and August and serves a variety of home cooked, locally grown produce. The unheated, fenced swimming pool is open all season and provides a good sunbathing area. Open from Easter to the end of September, this is a quiet site but it can get busy in high season and advance booking is advised.

Facilities

Well maintained and modern toilet block. No specific facilities for visitors with disabilities. No washing machine. Shop, bar and snacks (all season). Restaurant (July/Aug). Swimming pool with sun terrace (all season). Play area. Fishing. Off site: Bicycle hire 500 m. Beaches 12 km.

Open: Easter - September.

Directions

From A8 (direction of La Coruña) exit, Navia onto N634. Turn left, AS25 (direction of Arbón). Site is 10 km. on right, well signed. Note: sign at site entrance refers to it as Camping Arbón. GPS: 43.47993, -6.70261

Charges guide

Per person	€ 3,21
child	€ 3,00
caravan and car	€ 7,50
electricity	€ 2,68

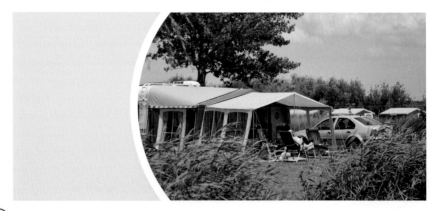

For latest campsite news, availability and prices visit
alanrogers.com

Avín-Onís
Camping Picos de Europa
E-33556 Avín-Onís (Asturias) T: 985 844 070. E: info@picos-europa.com
alanrogers.com/ES89650

This delightful site is, as its name suggests, an ideal spot from which to explore these dramatic limestone mountains on foot, by bicycle or on horseback. The site itself is continuously developing and the dynamic owner, José or his nephew who helps out when he is away, are both very pleasant and nothing is too much trouble. The site is in a valley beside a pleasant, fast flowing river. The 160 marked pitches are of varying sizes and have been developed in three avenues, on level grass mostly backing on to hedging, with 6A electricity. An area for tents and apartments is over a bridge past the fairly small, but pleasant, round swimming pool. Local stone has been used for the L-shaped building at the main entrance which houses reception and a very good bar/restaurant. The site can organise caving activities, and has information about the Cares gorge along with the many energetic ways of exploring the area, including by canoe and quad-bike! The Bulnes funicular railway is well worth a visit.

Facilities

Toilet facilities include a new fully equipped block, along with new facilities for disabled visitors and babies. Pleasant room with tables and chairs for poor weather. Washing machine and dryer. Shop (July-Sept). Swimming pool (Feb-Sept). Bar and cafeteria style restaurant (all year) serves a good value 'menu del dia' and snacks. WiFi in restaurant area. Play area. Fishing. Torches necessary in the new tent area. Off site: Riding 12 km. Bicycle hire 15 km. Golf 25 km. Coast at Llanes 25 km.

Open: All year.

Directions

Avín is 15 km. east of Cangas de Onís on the AS114 road to Panes and is probably best approached from this direction especially if towing. From A8 (Santander - Oviedo) use km. 326 exit and N634 northwest to Arriondas. Turn southeast on N625 to Cangas and join AS114 (Covodonga/Panes) by-passing Cangas. Site is just beyond Avín after 16 km. marker. GPS: 43.3363, -4.94498

Charges guide

Per person	€ 5,02
child (under 14 yrs)	€ 4,01
pitch incl. car	€ 8,57 - € 9,64
electricity	€ 3,75

Caravia Alta
Camping Caravaning Arenal de Moris
A8 Salida 337, E-33344 Caravia Alta (Asturias) T: 985 853 097. E: camoris@desdeasturias.com
alanrogers.com/ES89550

This smart, well run site is close to three fine sandy beaches so gets very busy at peak times. It has a backdrop of the mountains in the nature reserve known as the Sueve which is important for a breed of short Asturian horse, the 'Asturcone'. The site has 330 grass pitches (269 for touring units) of 40-70 sq.m. and with 200 electricity connections available (10A). With some shade, the pitches are terraced, while others are on an open, slightly sloping field with limited views of the sea. The restaurant with a terrace serves local dishes and overlooks the pool and hills and woods beyond. The mountains of 'Picos de Europa' are only 35 km. away, Covadonga and its lakes are near and Ribadesella is 12 km. It is an ideal area for sea and mountain sports, horse riding, walking, birdwatching and cycling. A new motorway viaduct curves its way across the valley inland from the site and there was some traffic noise when we visited.

Facilities

Three sanitary blocks provide comfortable, controllable showers (no dividers) and vanity style washbasins, laundry facilities and external dishwashing (cold water). Supermarket. Bar/restaurant. Swimming pool. Tennis. Play area in lemon orchard. English is spoken. WiFi in restaurant area. Off site: Fishing 200 m. Golf 5 km. Riding, bicycle hire and sailing 10 km. Bar and restaurants in village 2 km. Beach 200 m. Bus 1 km. from gate.

Open: 1 June - 17 September.

Directions

Caravia Alta is 50 km. east of Gijón. Leave the A8 Santander - Oviedo motorway at km. 337 exit, turn left on N632 towards Colunga and site is signed to the right in the village, near 16 km. marker. GPS: 43.47248, -5.18332

Charges guide

Per person	€ 5,50
child	€ 4,40
pitch incl. car	€ 9,70 - € 14,00
electricity	€ 4,50

For latest campsite news, availability and prices visit
alanrogers.com

Colunga

Camping Costa Verde

Playa de la Griega, E-33320 Colunga (Asturias) T: 985 856 373

alanrogers.com/ES89500

This uncomplicated coastal site has a marked Spanish flavour and is just 1.5 km. from the pleasant town of Colunga. Although little English is spoken, the cheerful owner and his helpful staff will make sure you get a warm welcome. The great advantage for many is that, 200 m. from the gate, is a spacious beach by a low tide lagoon with a recently constructed marine parade, ideal for younger children. Some of the 200 pitches are occupied on a seasonal basis, but there are 155 for tourers. These are flat but with little shade and electricity (6A) is available (long leads needed in places). The site is very busy in high season.

Facilities

The single toilet block is of a high standard with a mixture of British and Turkish style toilets (all British for ladies), large showers and free hot water throughout. Laundry. Well stocked shop. Bar/restaurant is traditional and friendly. Play area. Torches needed. Off site: Nearby towns of Ribadesella, Gijón and Oviedo. Excellent beaches. Fishing in river alongside site. Bicycle hire 2 km. Sailing 4 km. Golf and riding 18 km.

Open: Easter - 1 October.

Directions

Colunga is 45 km. east of Gijón. Leave the A8 Santander - Oviedo motorway at km. 345 exit and take N632 towards Colunga. In village, turn right on As257 towards Lastres; site is on right after 1 km. marker. GPS: 43.49662, -5.26447

Charges guide

Per person	€ 4,70
pitch incl. car	€ 8,50 - € 9,85
electricity	€ 3,50 - € 5,20

Cudillero

Camping l'Amuravela

El Pito, E-33150 Cudillero (Asturias) T: 985 590 995

alanrogers.com/ES89480

This very well maintained, family run site, is close to the quaint old town of Cudillero and it is an ideal stop over when visiting 'green Spain'. Nearby is some of the most attractive mountain scenery in the region and if you stay here for one night it can easily extend to a much longer visit. There are 70 good sized touring pitches on level or gently sloping grass with easy access. Some pitches can accommodate large units. Mature trees give some shade and all pitches have 5A electricity. The excellent swimming pool and separate children's pool provide an area for relaxation.

Facilities

One modern and very well maintained toilet block is close to all pitches and includes washbasins and shower cubicles. There are no specific facilities for visitors with disabilities. Washing machines and dryers. Well stocked shop. Café/bar and restaurant area (20/6-10/9). Swimming pool (June-Sept). Play area. Very little English is spoken. Off site: Fishing, beach 2 km. Golf 28 km.

Open: June - September.

Directions

From A8 take N632 towards Cudillero. After 120 km. marker turn right onto CU2 signed El Pito. Site is well signed on right in 2 km. On no account take caravans into Cudillero. GPS: 43.554391, -6.144581

Charges guide

Per unit incl. 2 persons and electricity	€ 21,80 - € 27,00
extra person	€ 4,90 - € 5,50
child	€ 4,50 - € 5,20

Luarca

Camping Los Cantiles

Ctra N634 km 502,7, E-33700 Luarca (Asturias) T: 985 640 938. E: cantiles@campingloscantiles.com

alanrogers.com/ES89400

Luarca is a picturesque little place with a pretty inner harbour and two sandy beaches, and Los Cantiles is two kilometres to the east of town on a cliff top that juts out into the sea, giving excellent views from some pitches and the sound of the waves to soothe you to sleep. The site is well maintained and is a pleasant place to stop along this under-developed coastline. The 150 pitches, 105 with electricity, are mostly on level grass, divided by huge hedges of hydrangeas and bushes. Some pitches have gravel surfaces. There is a separate area for late arrivals in high season.

Facilities

Two modern, fully equipped sanitary blocks (one in low season which is heated in winter) are kept very clean. Facilities for disabled visitors and babies. Laundry. Freezer service. Gas supplies. Small shop (open all year for basics). Bar with hot snacks (1/7-15/9). Backpackers' day room with tables, chairs and cooking facilities (own gas). Small playing field. Torches helpful after midnight. English is spoken. WiFi (on payment). Off site: Indoor swimming pool, sauna and fitness centre, plus a bar/restaurant and shop 300 m. Luarca 2 km. Beach and fishing 700 m. Riding 4 km.

Open: All year.

Directions

Luarca is 85 km. west of Gijón. From A8 Oviedo - La Coruña exit at 467 onto N634 for Luarca. After km. 502 east of Luarca, turn right at petrol station and follow signs to site for 2.5 km. Last 150 m. is narrow. GPS: 43.54998, -6.51665

Charges 2011

Per unit incl. 2 persons and electricity	€ 18,80 - € 21,00
extra person	€ 4,30
child (under 10 yrs)	€ 3,70
dog	free

No credit cards.

For latest campsite news, availability and prices visit

alanrogers.com

Somiedo
Camping Lagos de Somiedo

Valle de Lago, E-33840 Somiedo (Asturias) T: 985 763 776. E: campinglagosdesomiedo@hotmail.com
alanrogers.com/ES89450

This is a most unusual site in the Parque Natural de Somiedo. Winding narrow roads with challenging rock overhangs, hairpin bends and breathtaking views (for 8 km) finally bring you to the campsite at an elevation of 1,200 m. This is a site for 4x4s, powerful small campervans and cars – not for medium or large motorhomes, and caravans are not accepted. It is not an approach for the faint hearted! The friendly Lana family make you welcome at their unique site, which is tailored for those who wish to explore the natural and cultural values of the Park without the 'normal' campsite amenities. There are 210 pitches (just four with electric hook-up), undefined in two open meadows. In this extraordinary glacial valley you can leave reality behind in the exploration of the marvels of nature including bears, wolves, capercailles and a unique wild goat which frequent these mountains. A building, in keeping with the area, provides the amenities and contains many items of natural interest. A small bar/restaurant set tight into the vertical rock face offers traditional Asturian food, but watch out for the local's stilted wooden clogs scattered in the entrance hall. There is a cool wind here most of the time and a torch is essential at night. Cars are parked away from the pitches here.

Facilities

There are British style toilets and free hot water to clean hot showers and washbasins. Facilities for babies and children, and for disabled visitors. Washing machine. Combined reception, small restaurant with takeaway food, bar and reference section. Shop for bread, milk and other essentials, plus local produce and crafts. Horses for hire, trekking. Lectures on flora, fauna, history and culture. Fishing (licence required). Barbecue area. Small play area. Gas supplies. Off site: The very small village is 500 m. and it maintains the Spanish customs and traditions of this area.

Open: 1 April - 30 September.

Directions

From N634 via Oviedo turn left at 442 km. marker on AS-15 signed Parque Natural de Somiedo. At 9 km. marker past village of Longoria, turn left on AS-227. At 38 km. marker, turn left into Pol de Somiedo, signed Centro Urbano. Follow signs for Valle de Lago and El Valle; 8 km. of hairpin bends from Pola, passing Urria on the left, brings you to the valley. Site is signed on the right. GPS: 43.072018, -6.198885

Charges guide

Per person	€ 5,35
child	€ 4,28
tent and car	€ 11,23
motorhome with electricity	€ 11,77

Vidiago-Llanes
Camping La Paz

Ctra N634 Irun - Coruña km 292, E-33597 Vidiago-Llanes (Asturias) T: 985 411 235
E: delfin@campinglapaz.com alanrogers.com/ES89600

This site occupies a spectacular location. The reception building is opposite a solid rock face and many hundred feet below the site and the climb to the upper part of the site is quite daunting but staff will place your caravan for you, although motorcaravan drivers will have an exciting drive to the top, especially to the loftier pitches. Once there, the views are absolutely outstanding, both along the coast and inland to the Picos de Europa mountains. There are 434 pitches, 350 with 10/15A electricity. There is also a lower section in a shaded valley to which access is easier, if rather tight in places. The upper area is arranged on numerous terraces, many of which require you to park your car by the roadside and climb the hill to your tent. The way down to the attractive beach is quite steep; from the lower area there is an easy walk to a smaller beach. The cliff-top restaurant and bar has commanding views over the ocean and beach. The site is very popular in high season so it does get crowded.

Facilities

Four good, modern toilet blocks are well equipped and include an interesting mix of electronic hot water and cold water from a tap for the showers. They are kept very clean even at peak times. Baby bath. Full laundry facilities. Motorcaravan services. Restaurant and bar/snack bar with small shop (all season). Watersports. Games room. Fishing. Torches useful in some areas. English spoken. WiFi in the restaurant. Off site: Shop, bar and restaurant in nearby village. Golf, riding, sailing and boat launching all 8 km.

Open: Easter - 30 September.

Directions

Vidiago is 85 km. west of Santander. Site is signed from A8/N634 Santander - Oviedo/Gijón road near km. 292 marker (on non-motorway section). Site approach road is just east of the village of Vidiago, marked by campsite signs (not named) and flags. Cross the railway track and exercise caution on bends. GPS: 43.39957, -4.65149

Charges guide

Per person	€ 6,15
child	€ 5,55
pitch incl. car	€ 13,20 - € 15,95
electricity	€ 4,25

For latest campsite news, availability and prices visit
alanrogers.com

The region of Cantabria in the north of Spain offers the best of both worlds. On the one hand there is the glorious coastline with beautiful beaches and pretty fishing villages; while inland there are a number of national parks including the mountainous, Picos de Europa.

CANTABRIA IS A ONE PROVINCE REGION

THE CAPITAL IS SANTANDER

The capital, Santander, is an elegant city which extends over a wide bay with views of the Cantabrian Sea. Its historic quarter is situated against a backdrop of sea and mountains, although the town is best known for its beaches; the Playa de la Magdalena, which has a summer windsurfing school, and the popular El Sardinero beach. There is also a Maritime Museum and Museum of Prehistory and Archaeology, plus a small zoo housed in the gardens of the old royal palace. A short distance from the city is the pretty medieval village of Santillana del Mar and the prehistoric caves of Altamira. Despite being closed indefinitely for restoration work, the adjacent Altamira Museum houses a replica of these caves and their impressive prehistoric drawings. Also on the outskirts of the capital is the Cabárceno Nature Park with more protected areas scattered around the region, including those at Oyambre, Peña Cabarga and Saja-Besaya. The largest is the mountain range of Picos de Europa, a national park which shares its territory with Asturias and Castilla-León. With river gorges, valleys, woodlands and an abundance of wildlife, it is popular with walkers, trekkers and climbers.

Places of interest

Castro Urdiales: beaches, Gothic church, Roman bridge, old quarter.

Comillas: rural town, beaches, Gaudí-designed villa.

Laredo: lively seaside resort, 13th-century church, 5 km. long sandy beach.

Lienganes: 17th- and 18th-century architecture, spa.

Potes: on east side of Picos de Europa, mountain bike hire, paragliding available.

San Vicente de la Barquera: picturesque fishing port.

Cuisine of the region

Seafood is used a lot, including fresh shellfish, sardines, *rabas* (fried squid), *bocartes rebozados* (breaded whitebait). Cheese is produced throughout the region; *queso de nata* (cream cheese), *picón* from Treviso Bejes, and smoked cheeses from Áliva and Pido. A typical dish of the region is the Cantabrian stew, which contains haricot beans, cabbage, rice and sausage. Desserts include the traditional cheesecakes of the Pas Valley and pastries. The local tipple is *orujo*, a strong liquor.

Maganos encebollados: squid with onion.

Quesada: cheesecake.

Sobaos pasiegos: sponge cakes.

Sorropotún: type of fish stew.

Cabuérniga

Camping El Molino de Cabuérniga

Sopeña de Cabuérniga, Ctra C625 km 42, E-39510 Cabuérniga (Cantabria) T: 942 706 259
E: cmcabuerniga@campingcabuerniga.com **alanrogers.com/ES89640**

Located in a peaceful valley with magnificent views of the mountains, beside the Saja river and only a short walk from the picturesque and unspoiled village of Sopeña, this gem of a site is on an open, level, grassy meadow with trees. Wonderful stone buildings and artefacts are a feature of this unique site. There are 102 marked pitches, all with 6A electricity, although long leads may be needed in places. This comfortable site is very good value and ideal for a few nights (or you may well choose to stay longer once there) whilst you explore the Cabuérniga Valley which forms part of the Reserva Nacional del Saja. The area is great for just relaxing or for indulging in active pursuits with opportunities for mountain biking, climbing, walking, swimming or fishing in the river, horse riding, hunting, paragliding and 4x4 safaris. Although little English is spoken, you will receive a warm welcome here with friendly advice on how best to enjoy your stay. Sopeña Fiesta is in mid July each year.

Facilities

A superb, spotless sanitary block provides spacious, controllable showers and hot and cold water to washbasins. Washing machines and free ironing. Unit for disabled campers. Baby and toddler room. Bar serving breakfasts and 'bocadillos' (sandwiches) includes small shop section. Wonderful playground in rustic setting – supervision recommended. Fishing. Bicycle hire. Attractive stone cottages and apartments for rent. Off site: Bus service 500 m. Restaurant in village 1 km. Riding and bicycle hire 3 km. Golf 20 km. Beach 20 km. Skiing 50 km.

Open: All year.

Directions

Sopeña is 55 km. southwest of Santander. From A8 (Santander - Oviedo) take km. 249 exit and join N634 to Cabezón de la Sal. Turn southwest on CA180 towards Reinosa for 11 km. to Sopeña (site signed to left). Turn into village (watch out for low eaves/gutters on buildings), continually bearing right following small site signs. GPS: 43.22594, -4.29034

Charges guide

Per unit incl. 2 persons	
and electricity	€ 26,00 - € 34,00
extra person	€ 6,00
child	€ 5,00

For latest campsite news, availability and prices visit
alanrogers.com

Isla

Camping Playa de Isla

Ctra Arnadal no. 1, E-39195 Isla (Cantabria) T: 942 679 361. E: bernac@teleonica.net

alanrogers.com/ES89980

This well maintained site is set on a headland, overlooking the sea on one side and the village of Quejo on the other. The 200 well defined small pitches (100 for touring) with little shade are on two levels. All have 6A electricity and some have sea views. Large units may experience difficult access to some pitches. There is direct access via a short flight of steps to the superb beach with its golden sand and rocky pools. The site has an illuminated 500 m. footpath to the village where there are restaurants, shops and bars.

Facilities	Directions
One modern spotless toilet block is centrally positioned. Family shower room. Washing machines and dryers. Well stocked shop (Easter-Sept). Café/bar (July-Sept), with terrace overlooking the sea. Play area. Fishing from adjacent beach. Dogs are not accepted. Off site: Boat launching 500 m. Golf, bicycle hire 5 km. Riding 6 km.	From A8 (Santander - Bilbao) take exit at 185 km. marker onto N634 towards Beranga. Almost immediately turn right, CA147 (Noja). At roundabout turn left, CA141, towards Somo/Santander. Turn right, CA449 signed Isla. Site is 5 km. through village. GPS: 43.5016, -3.54292

Open: Easter - 30 September.

Charges guide

Per person	€ 5,13 - € 5,35
pitch	€ 11,55 - € 12,30
electricity	€ 4,28

Isla

Camping Punta Marina

Playa de la Arena s/n, E-39195 Isla (Cantabria) T: 942 679 349. E: puntamarina@ceoecant.es

alanrogers.com/ES89990

This well maintained site is open from Easter to the end of September. It has 98 pitches with only 28 for touring, on grass with little shade and all with 3A electricity, water and drainage. Most have sea views. The site comes alive at weekends and in the high season, when it can become very busy. Advanced booking is advisable. The small holiday village of Isla, with its many shops, restaurants and bars is only 1 km. away, and here there is also an excellent beach, rocky coves and a boat launching slipway. Care is needed with large units when approaching the site.

Facilities	Directions
One modern, very clean toilet block with family shower room and good facilities for visitors with disabilities. Washing machine and dryers. Well stocked shop (July/Aug). Separate restaurant, bar and takeaway (June-Sept). Swimming pools (July/Aug). Play area. Children's club (July/Aug). Tennis. Bicycle hire. Games room. TV room. Dogs are not accepted. Off site: Fishing, boat launching 1 km. Golf 5 km. Riding 6 km.	Exit A8 at 185 km. marker and take N634 towards Beranga. Turn right, CA147, in towards Noja. At roundabout turn left, CA141 (Somo/Santander). Turn right, CA449 to Isla. Turn left CA448 to Playa la Arena. In 1.6 km. turn right to site. GPS: 43.49741, -3.57631

Open: Easter - 30 September.

Charges guide

Per person	€ 4,00 - € 4,30
child	€ 3,40 - € 3,70
pitch incl. car	€ 13,40 - € 14,50
electricity	€ 2,70 - € 3,00

Laredo

Camping Playa del Regaton

El Regaton 8, E-39770 Laredo (Cantabria) T: 942 606 995. E: recepcion@campingplayaregaton.com

alanrogers.com/ES89930

Situated a short distance from the bustling seaside town of Laredo and easily accessible from Santander and Bilbao, Camping Playa del Regaton is an ideal stopover for those en-route to the ferries. The site has direct access to the beach and the estuary of the Ria del Ason and is an important marsh area for migrating birds. Of the 128 small pitches, 100 are for touring and have 6/10A electricity and a sink. All are on level grass, with mature trees providing separation and a degree of shade. The site is popular with Spanish holidaymakers. Only limited English is spoken outside high season.

Facilities	Directions
One modern, heated toilet block. Baby bath. Facilities for visitors with disabilities. Washing machine and dryer. Small shop (1/4-25/9) sells most essentials. Café/bar (1/4-25/9) with snacks (1/7-31/8). Play area. Children's club in high season. Games room. Dogs are not accepted. Off site: Fishing 200 m. Riding 500 m. Boat launching 3 km. Golf 20 km. Beaches in Larado.	From the A8 (Santander - Bilbao) take exit 172 to Laredo. Straight on at roundabout signed hospital and beaches. Do not go into Laredo. At traffic lights turn left, site is well signed on left, 500 m. past hospital. GPS: 43.41319, -3.45039

Open: 1 April - 25 September.

Charges guide

Per person	€ 4,20
child (3-10 yrs)	€ 3,70
pitch incl. electricity (10A)	€ 15,45

For latest campsite news, availability and prices visit

alanrogers.com

Noja

Camping Los Molinos

Ctra La Ria s/n, E-39180 Noja (Cantabria) T: 942 630 426. E: losmolinos@ceoecant.es

alanrogers.com/ES89950

Camping Los Molinos is close to the village of Noja, a seaside resort that gets very busy in high season. It is on the coast of Cantabria, a ten minute walk from the Playa del Ris beach which has fine sand and clear water. The site is divided into two main areas, both with a large number of permanent units, some of which look a little run down. There are 100 (60 sq.m) touring pitches for caravans and motorcaravans on level ground, but with little shade; 42 have 3A electricity. A separate large area without electricity is used for tents.

Facilities

Six fully equipped toilet blocks, two new and two recently refurbished, are kept clean. Facilities for disabled campers. Washing machines. Supermarkets and butcher. Restaurant (July/Aug). Bars and café bar serving tapas and pizzas. Swimming and paddling pools with lifeguard (20/6-7/9). Play area. ATM. Torch useful. Off site: Beach and fishing 400 m. Indoor pool and bicycle hire 500 m. Golf 9 holes 1 km, 18 holes 20 km. Riding 10 km. Free bus to the beach and town in high season.

Open: Easter, then 1 June - 30 September.

Directions

From A8 (Bilbao - Santander) take exit at km. 185 and join N634 towards Beranga, almost immediately turn right on CA147 to Noja. In 10 km. turn left and go down through town. At beach roundabout turn left and then left again just before Camping Playa Joyel at large sign for site. GPS: 43.48516, -3.53807

Charges 2011

Per unit incl. 2 persons	€ 22,60 - € 30,60
extra person	€ 5,00 - € 6,50
No credit cards.	

Noja

Camping Playa Joyel

Playa de Ris, E-39180 Noja (Cantabria) T: 942 630 081. E: playajoyel@telefonica.net

alanrogers.com/ES90000

This very attractive holiday and touring site is some 40 kilometres from Santander and 80 kilometres from Bilbao. It is a busy, high quality, comprehensively equipped site by a superb beach providing 1,000 well shaded, marked and numbered pitches with 6A electricity available. These include 80 large pitches of 100 sq.m. Some 250 pitches are occupied by tour operators and seasonal units. This well managed site has a lot to offer for family holidays with much going on in high season when it gets crowded. The swimming pool complex (with lifeguard) is free to campers and the superb beaches are cleaned daily in high season.

Facilities

Six excellent, spacious and fully equipped toilet blocks include baby baths. Large laundry. Motorcaravan services. Gas supplies. Freezer service. Supermarket. General shop. Kiosk. Restaurant and takeaway (1/7-31/8). Bar and snacks. Swimming pools, bathing caps compulsory (20/5-15/9). Entertainment and soundproofed pub/disco (July/Aug). Tennis. Playground. Riding. Fishing. Natural animal park. Hairdresser (July/Aug). Animals are not accepted. Off site: Sailing and boat launching 10 km.

Open: 15 April - 1 October.

Directions

From A8 (Bilbao - Santander) take km. 185 exit and N634 towards Beranga. Almost immediately turn right on CA147 to Noja. In 10 km. turn left at multiple campsite signs and go through town. At beach follow signs to site. GPS: 43.48948, -3.53700

Charges 2011

Per unit incl. 2 persons	€ 28,20 - € 47,40
extra person	€ 4,40 - € 6,70
child (3-9 yrs)	€ 3,10 - € 5,00

Pechón

Camping Las Arenas-Pechón

Ctra Pechón - Unquera km 2, E-39594 Pechón (Cantabria) T: 942 717 188. E: info@campinglasarenas.com

alanrogers.com/ES89700

This site is in a very quiet, but rather spectacular location bordering the sea and the Tina Mayor estuary, with views to the mountains and access to an attractive little beach. Taking 350 units, half the site has grassy pitches (60 sq.m) in bays or on terraces with stunning sea and mountain views, with electricity available (5A) and connected by asphalted roads. There are some quite steep slopes to tackle – reception is at the top, as are the bar and restaurant; the latter has a terrace with fantastic views of the estuary and of the mountains beyond.

Facilities

Clean, well tiled sanitary facilities are in the older, simple style. Various blocks include showers (no divider; add hot water to the cold by pushing a switch). Washing machines. Well stocked supermarket. Restaurant/bar and snack bar (all season). Small playground. Riding arranged (collected from site). River and sea fishing and swimming. Torches helpful. English is spoken. Off site: Shops, bars, restaurants and bar/disco in Pechón 1 km. Golf 28 km.

Open: 1 June - 30 September.

Directions

On A8 from Santander, take km. 272 exit for Unquera (N621) at end of motorway section. Take first exit CA380 signed Pechón and site which is 2 km. on left. From Oviedo/Gijón (A8/N634 at km. 272) take N621 slip-road for Unquera (do not join motorway), then as above. GPS: 43.39093, -4.5106

Charges guide

Per person	€ 6,25
pitch incl. car and electricity	€ 14,60 - € 17,90

For latest campsite news, availability and prices visit

alanrogers.com

Potes
Camping La Viorna

Ctra Santo Toribio, E-39570 Potes (Cantabria) T: 942 732 021. E: info@campinglaviorna.com
alanrogers.com/ES89630

The wonderful views of the valley below from the open terraces, with its spectacular backdrop of mountains, make this smart and sophisticated site an attractive base from which to tour this region or to relax by the excellent swimming pool. It is very popular with both families and couples. There are beds of flowers everywhere and the trees provide shade on many pitches. Access is good for all sizes of unit to the 115 pitches of around 70 sq.m, all of which have electricity (6A). In high season, however, tents may be placed on less accessible, steeply sloping areas.

Facilities	Directions
Single, clean and modern sanitary block of very high standard. Washbasins have cold water only. Facilities for disabled visitors double as unit for babies (key). Laundry facilities. Shop. Restaurant/bar with terrace. Swimming pool and paddling pool (25/6-30/9; caps compulsory). Play area. Games room. Many sporting activities can be arranged. WiFi. Off site: Potes 1.5 km. Bicycle hire 1 km. Fishing and riding 1.5 km. Toribio Monastery close.	From A8/N634 (Santander - Oviedo) take km. 272 exit for Unquera (end of motorway section). Take N621 south to Panes and up spectacular gorge (care needed if towing) to Potes. After town take left fork signed Toribio de Liébana and site is on right after 800 m. GPS: 43.15435, -4.64348

Open: Easter/1 April - 31 October.

Charges guide

Per person	€ 3,90 - € 4,40
pitch incl. electricity (3/6A)	€ 13,00 - € 14,70

Potes
Camping La Isla Picos de Europa

Picos de Europa, E-39570 Potes-Turieno (Cantabria) T: 942 730 896. E: campicoseuropa@terra.es
alanrogers.com/ES89620

La Isla is beside the road from Potes to Fuente Dé, with many mature trees giving good shade and glimpses of the mountains above. Established for over 25 years, a warm welcome awaits you from the owners (who speak good English) and a most relaxed and peaceful atmosphere exists here. All the campers we spoke to were delighted with the family feeling of the site. The 106 unmarked pitches are arranged around an oval gravel track under a variety of fruit and ornamental trees. Electricity (6A) is available to all pitches, although some need long leads. A brilliant small bar and restaurant are located under dense trees where you can enjoy the relaxing sound of the river which runs through the site.

Facilities	Directions
Single, clean and smart sanitary block retains the style of the site. Washbasins with cold water. Washing machine. Gas supplies. Freezer service. Small shop. Restaurant/bar (all season). Small swimming pool (caps compulsory; 1/5-30/9). Play area. Barbecue area. Fishing. Bicycle hire. Riding. WiFi. Off site: Bus from gate in high season. Shops, bars, restaurants and Monday morning market in Potes 4 km. Fuente Dé and its spectacular cable car ride 18 km.	Potes is 110 km. southwest of Santander. From A8/N634 (Santander - Oviedo) take km. 272 exit for Unquera (end of motorway section). Take N621 south to Panes and up spectacular gorge (care needed if towing) to Potes. Take CA165 to Fuente Dé and site is on the right, 3 km. beyond Potes. GPS: 43.14999, -4.69997

Open: 1 April - 30 October.

Charges guide

Per person	€ 3,75 - € 4,05
pitch incl. car and electricity	€ 9.15 - € 11.50

Ramales de la Victoria
Camping La Barguilla

E-39800 Ramales de la Victoria (Cantabria) T: 942 646 586
alanrogers.com/ES89910

Located in a rural setting on the outskirts of the small Spanish town of Ramales de la Victoria, this small site provides an opportunity to sample traditional Spanish life. Access to the town is via an easy 1 km. walk. There are 79 small pitches with 50 for touring, all with 3/6A electricity. Some pitches have shade, whilst others enjoy views of the nearby Sierra del Hornijo mountains. Facilities are minimal but the site is well maintained and offers a comfortable stay. Advance booking in high season is recommended. Be sure to sample the on site Periguena restaurant which serves a variety of cuisine, popular with the locals.

Facilities	Directions
One heated toilet block provides WCs, washbasins and shower cubicles. No facilities for disabled visitors. Washing machines. Shop. Terrace bar, cafeteria, restaurant (all season). Fenced play area. Games room. Barbecues are not permitted. Off site: Fishing 200 m. Riding 10 km. Golf 20 km. Beaches in Laredo.	From A8, take exit 173 and N629 to Ramales de la Victoria. At entry to town, turn right, CA261 signed Arredondo. In 1.6 km. turn left over bridge into Parque Publico. Campsite is on right behind Restaurant Perigena. Sharp incline to site so care is needed for those with larger units. GPS: 43.25918, -3.47151

Open: All year (except November).

Charges guide

Per person	€ 4,82
pitch incl. electricity	€ 7.50 - € 11.78

For latest campsite news, availability and prices visit
alanrogers.com

Ruiloba

Camping El Helguero

Ctra Santillana - Comillas, E-39527 Ruiloba (Cantabria) T: 942 722 124. E: reservas@campingelhelguero.com
alanrogers.com/ES89610

This site, in a peaceful location surrounded by tall trees and impressive towering rock formations, caters for 240 units (of which 100 are seasonal) on slightly sloping ground. There are many marked pitches on different levels, all with access to electricity (6A), but with varying amounts of shade. There are also attractive tent and small camper sections set close in to the rocks and 22 site owned chalets. The site gets very crowded in high season, so it is best to arrive early if you haven't booked. The reasonably sized swimming pool and children's pool have access lifts for disabled campers.

Facilities

Three well placed toilet blocks, although old, are clean and include controllable showers and hot and cold water to all basins. Facilities for children and disabled visitors. Washing machines and dryers. Motorcaravan services. Small supermarket (July/Aug). Bar/snack bar. Separate restaurant. Swimming pool (caps compulsory). Playground. Activities and entertainment (high season). ATM. WiFi (charged). Off site: Bus 500 m. Bar/restaurants in village (walking distance). Beach, fishing, sailing, golf and riding, all 3 km. Santillana del Mar 12 km.

Open: 1 April - 30 September.

Directions

From A8 (Santander - Oviedo) take km. 249 exit (Cabezón and Comillas) and turn north on CA135 towards Comillas. At km. 7 turn right on CA359 to Ruilobuca and Barrio la Iglesia. After village turn right up hill on CA358 to site on right (note: signs refer to 'Camping Ruiloba'). GPS: 43.38288, -4,24800

Charges 2011

Per unit incl. 2 persons and electricity	€ 24,55 - € 34,40
extra person	€ 4,55 - € 5,50

Camping Cheques accepted.

San Vicente de la Barquera

Camping Caravaning Playa de Oyambre

Finca Peña Guerra, E-39547 San Vicente de la Barquera (Cantabria) T: 942 711 461
E: camping@oyambre.com alanrogers.com/ES89710

This exceptionally well managed site is ideally positioned to use as a base to visit the spectacular Picos de Europa or one of the many sandy beaches along this northern coast. Despite its name, it is one kilometre from the beach on foot. The 100 touring pitches all have 10A electricity (long leads needed in places). The fairly flat central area is allocated to tents while caravans are mainly sited on wide terraces (access to some could be a little tight for larger units) and there is some shade. There may be some traffic noise on the lower terraces.

Facilities

Good, clean sanitary facilities are in one, well kept block. Showers are spacious but have a frustrating mixture of pushbutton hot and ordinary cold controls. Facilities for babies and disabled visitors. Washing machines. Motorcaravan services. Restaurant. Shop in bar (all season). Takeaway. Swimming pools with lifeguard (1/6-15/9). Playground. WiFi. Off site: Bus service at site entrance. Fishing and superb beach 1 km. Golf 2 km. Riding 5 km. San Vicente de la Barquera 5 km.

Open: Easter/1 April - 30 September.

Directions

From A8 take exit at km. 258 (signed Caviedes) and join N634. Turn towards San Vicente. Site is signed at junction to Comillas, at km. 265 on the E70, 5 km. east of San Vicente de la Barquera. The entrance is quite steep. Another 'Camping La Playa' at Oyambre within 500 m. (on the beach) is not recommended. GPS: 43.38332, -4.39998

Charges guide

Per person	€ 5,08
pitch incl. electricity	€ 14,70

Santillana del Mar

Camping Santillana

Ctra de Comilias s/n, E-39330 Santillana del Mar (Cantabria) T: 942 818 250
E: complejosantillana@cantabria.com alanrogers.com/ES89730

This is an attractive site on a hill above the charming medieval village of Santillana del Mar and five to ten kilometres from some of Costa Verde's good beaches. There are 400 pitches, all with access to electricity (5A), some primarily for tents, informally arranged on a slope, with others for caravans and motorcaravans on the lower part of the site. Where the pitches are numbered but unmarked some overcrowding may occur in high season, and those alongside the road will experience some noise.

Facilities

Toilet blocks are modern, well placed, fully equipped and have facilities for disabled campers. Washing machines and irons. Supermarket and souvenir shop. Bar/restaurant and self-service café. Swimming and paddling pools (1/5-30/9). Play areas. Minigolf. Games room. Tennis. Bicycle hire. Library. Security lockers. Entertainment in high season. Off site: Bus 500 m. from gate. Riding 300 m. Fishing 5 km. Boat launching 16 km. Golf 20 km.

Open: All year.

Directions

Santillana is 30 km. west of Santander. From A8 (Santander - Oviedo) take km. 234 exit west of Torrelavega and follow CA133 north to Santillana. Turn left at T-junction (busy) towards Comillas and site is on right in 300 m. GPS: 43.39258, -4.11334

Charges guide

Per person	€ 5,00 - € 5,61
pitch incl. electricity	€ 10,00 - € 18,04

No credit cards. Camping Cheques accepted.

For latest campsite news, availability and prices visit
alanrogers.com

Located in northern Spain, this is a region steeped in Basque traditions, which is reflected in the architecture, native language, local sports and cuisine.

THERE ARE THREE PROVINCES: ALAVA, GIPUZKOA AND BIZKAIA

THE REGIONAL CAPITAL IS VITORIA

The province of Gipuzkoa adjoins France in the east. Its capital, San Sebastian, is a bustling, picturesque seaside town with a strong Basque identity. Overlooking La Concha Bay and enclosed by rolling low hills, this popular resort boasts four good beaches, including the celebrated La Concha Beach. As cider production is one of the oldest traditions in Basque country there are also plenty of sidrerías (cider houses) to visit. Heading along the rocky fringe of Costa Vasca towards Bilbao in Bizkaia are more excellent beaches and pretty fishing villages including Orio, Zarautz and Getaria. The biggest attraction in Bilbao is the famous Guggenheim Museum. Opened in 1997 this spectacular building is completely covered with titanium sheets and houses a collection of modern and contemporary art from around the world. The city also boasts a beautiful old quarter with a Gothic cathedral, the Plaza Nueva and a museum. Further inland in Alava is Vitoria, the region's capital. Its medieval streets intermingle with Renaissance Palaces and fine churches and are lined with lively bars and tavernas. In the summer the city plays host to a jazz festival. Elsewhere in the province are several nature reserves.

Places of interest

Encartanciones: one of the world's largest cave chambers Torca del Carlista, wildlife sanctuary.

Hondarribia: fishing port, beaches, charming walled old town.

Laguardia: old walled town with cobbled streets, historic buildings, in wine-growing district of Rioja Alavesa.

Oñati: Baroque architecture, old university.

Tolosa: impressive old town square, carnival in February.

Zarautz: seaside town, famous for production of *txakoli.*

Zumaia: beaches, good coastal walks, July fiesta with Basque sports, dancing and bull racing.

Cuisine of the region

Basque cuisine is considered to be the finest in Spain. Tapas or *pintxos* is readily available in bars, served with the local white wine *txakolí.* Fish is popular, especially *bacalao* (cod) and seafood is often used to make casseroles and sauces. Lots of milk based desserts. Founded in the 19th century, the tradition of dining clubs or *txokos* are unique to the Basque country.

Alubias pochas: white haricot bean stew.

Chipirones en su tinta: squid cooked in its ink.

Goxua: sponge cake with whipped cream and caramel.

Intxaursalsa: milk pudding with cinnamon and walnuts.

Marmitaco: fish and potato stew.

Pantxineta: custard slice.

133

For latest campsite news, availability and prices visit
alanrogers.com

Itziar-Deba

Camping Itxaspe

Ctra Nacional 634 km 38, E-20829 Itziar-Deba (Bizkaia) T: 943 199 377

alanrogers.com/ES90380

Set on a hill, surrounded by farmland and with views of the mountains, this site is ideal for a stopover or a couple of days rest. A fifteen-minute walk through the woods leads to a rocky beach and the sea. Pitches are of medium size, flat and on grass, with plenty of water and 5A electrical connections. There is a comfortable bar, restaurant and swimming pool open in July and August. Offering plenty of rural walks, this site will appeal to those wanting peace and quiet but with little entertainment and some unfenced areas, children will need supervision.

Facilities

The single traditional style sanitary block is basic but clean. Recently refurbished, new showers have been installed and more modernisation is gradually being undertaken. Facilities for disabled visitors. Washing machine. Well stocked shop. Restaurant and bar. Swimming pool (1/7-31/8). WiFi. Toddlers' play area. Barbecue and solarium area. Off site: Fishing 1 km. Golf 15 km. Riding and bicycle hire 7 km. Beach 7 km.

Open: 1 April - 30 September.

Directions

From the A8 take exit 13 and follow signs for Itziar. At junction turn left. In 150 m. take right slip road for immediate turn left onto GI3291 (i.e. to cross main road). Site is signed and at end of road. GPS: 43.29398, -2.32978

Charges guide

Per person	€ 4,75
pitch	€ 10,40
electricity	€ 3,00

Mendexa

Camping Leagi

Calle Barrio Leagi s/n, E-48289 Mendexa (Bizkaia) T: 946 842 352. E: leagi@campingleagi.com

alanrogers.com/ES90340

This site is perched high above Lekeitio and has commanding views of the town, sea and surrounding areas. A steep road leads up to the site, but upon arriving at the car park and reception, the area becomes flat. There are 111 touring pitches on open, level grass with good mountain views. All have electricity (5A). There is little shade and the pitches are not defined. This is a quiet site, suitable for couples and families with small children and for those wishing to explore the attractive local towns or the many rural walks in the area. Transport is essential.

Facilities

Two modern, clean sanitary blocks are well equipped and there are separate facilities for those with disabilities. Excellent laundry. Motorcaravan services. Shop (1/7-10/9). Restaurant, bar and takeaway (all year, closed Tues/Wed). Dog washing area. Small toddlers' play area in car park. Off site: Fishing, sailing and beach 1.5 km.

Open: All year.

Directions

From Lekeitio cross bridge heading East. Immediately turn right onto BI4449 to Mendexa. Continue up hill for 800 m. Site is signed on bend. Immediately turn sharp right and access is via a steep and narrow road. GPS: 43.35163, -2.49203

Charges guide

Per person	€ 4,60 - € 5,50
child	€ 4,00 - € 4,60
pitch incl. electricity	€ 14,50 - € 17,50

Mundaka

Camping Portuondo

Ctra Gernika - Bermeo, E-48360 Mundaka (Bizkaia) T: 946 877 701. E: recepcion@campingportuondo.com

alanrogers.com/ES90350

This site has a lovely restaurant, bar and terrace taking full advantage of the wonderful views across the ocean and estuary. Set amongst gardens, the pitches are mainly for tents and smaller vans, but there are eight large pitches at the lower levels for caravans and motorhomes. The access to these is a little difficult as the road is very steep and there is no turning space. In high season it is essential to ring to book your space. With its mostly small pitches, the site is popular in high season with surfers and young people without children. English is spoken and the friendly owner Imanol and his staff are keen to help.

Facilities

Two toilet blocks include mostly British WCs and a baby room. A reader reports poor cleaning and maintenance during their visit. Washing machines and dryers. Shop (15/6-15/9). Bar and two restaurants, all open to public (28/1-14/12). Takeaway (15/6-15/9). Swimming pools (15/6-15/9). Barbecue area. Torches may be useful. Off site: Fishing 100 m. Beaches 500 m. bracing walk. Surfing on Mundaka beach 500 m. Boat launching 1 km. Shops, bars and restaurants 2 km. Riding 8 km. Bicycle hire 1 km. Golf 40 km. Buses to Bilbao and Gernika (every 30 mins) 300 m.

Open: 25 January - 15 December.

Directions

Mundaka is 35 km. northeast of Bilbao. From A8 (San Sebastián - Bilbao) take exit 18 and follow signs for Gernika on BI635. Continue on BI2235 towards Bermeo. Site is on right approaching Mundaka. Care is needed as a wide approach may be necessary as this is a sharp right turn with a steep access. Road signs do not permit turning left to site. GPS: 43.39918, -2.69610

Charges 2011

Per unit incl. 2 persons and electricity	€ 30,05 - € 32,40
extra person	€ 6,35 - € 7,00

For latest campsite news, availability and prices visit

alanrogers.com

San Sebastian

Camping Igueldo

Paseo Padre Orkolaga no. 69, Barrio de Igueldo, E-20008 San Sebastian (Gipuzkoa) T: 943 214 502
E: info@campingigueldo.com **alanrogers.com/ES90300**

A five kilometre drive from the city takes you to this terraced campsite, high above San Sebastian, between the mountains and the sea. It offers mostly level, shaded, small (max. 70 sq.m.) grass pitches with electricity and drainage. The restaurant and bar are open all year and a sun terrace looks toward the mountains. An excellent bus service to and from San Sebastian runs every 30 minutes (all year). There are 25 attractive chalets to rent at the entrance to the site. With few sporting facilities, this site is for those wishing to mix quiet surroundings with city life. English is spoken in reception.

Facilities

Three traditional toilet blocks are clean and light. Facilities for disabled visitors and babies (accessed by key). Adequate covered dishwashing and laundry facilities. Motorcaravan service point. Shop for basics (20/6-15/9). Bar/restaurant (all year, Wed-Sun in early/late season, every day in summer). Play area. Off site: Igueldo is within walking distance with shops, restaurants and bars. Bicycle hire and fishing 5 km. Beach 5 km. Golf 9 km.

Open: All year.

Directions

From A8 take exit 8 for San Sebastian West. Head for Ondarreta. At Playa de Ondarreta, follow beach road on Avda de Satrustegui. At T-junction turn left. Keep right on Pase O De Igueldo. Continue up hill for 5 km. to site on left. GPS: 43.3046, -2.04605

Charges 2011

Per unit incl. 2 persons	
and electricity	€ 21,40 - € 32,10
extra person	€ 3,95 - € 5,10

Villanañe

Camping Angosto

Ctra Villanane - Angosto no. 2, E-01425 Villanañe (Araba) T: 945 353 271. E: info@camping-angosto.com
alanrogers.com/ES90450

This is a smart eco-friendly site with good facilities surrounded by wooded hills near the Valderejo National Park. Opened in 1999, the facilities are improving every year and a keen young team run things efficiently, gearing the site towards families. Most of the pitches are seasonal and in high season it is bustling and very Spanish! The limited number of touring pitches are flat and of average size. There is a large area for tents. Young trees have been planted around the site and are beginning to provide a little shade. The attractive new, heated pool has a sliding roof for inclement weather. A phone call before arriving is essential to establish availabilty.

Facilities

Fully equipped and well maintained toilet block with facilities for disabled campers. Washing machine and drier. Good shop (1/3-30/9). Stylish bar with takeaway and separate restaurant (15/2-30/11; weekends only in low season). Indoor and outdoor swimming pools (1/4-30/11). Sauna. Small fenced play area close to entrance and grass toddler play area. Activities for children (high season). Mountain bike hire. Fishing. Ice machine. Off site: Many outdoor activities arranged locally. Riding 30 km. Sailing 40 km. Golf 45 km. Sea 60 km.

Open: 15 February - 12 December.

Directions

Villanañe is 25 km. northwest of Miranda de Ebro. From Miranda de Ebro, take A1 towards Burgos, leave at exit 5 and take A2122 to Puentelarrá and on to Espejo. From N1 Burgos - Victoria road, turn north on A2625 (west of Ameyugo) to Sta Gadea and Espejo. Site is just after village, clearly signed. GPS: 42.84221, -3.06867

Charges guide

Per unit incl. 2 persons	
and electricity	€ 23,80 - € 28,20
extra person	€ 5,60

Zarautz

Gran Camping Zarautz

Monte Talai-Mendi, Ctra N634 San Sebastian - Bilbao, E-20800 Zarautz (Gipuzkoa) T: 943 831 238
E: info@grancampingzarautz.com **alanrogers.com/ES90390**

This friendly site sits high in the hills to the east of the Basque town of Zarautz and has commanding views over the bay and the island of Getaria. Of the 400 pitches, 300 are for touring units, with 5A electricity; 10 also have water and drainage. The remaining pitches are for tents and seasonal caravans. The grass pitches are of average size, shaded by mature trees and are reasonably level; those on the perimeter have superb sea views. Between the site and the sea is a protected public area where flora and fauna flourish and you can enjoy watching the birds and wildlife.

Facilities

Three well-equipped toilet blocks. Facilities for disabled campers. Washing machines. Bar/snack bar with TV plus terrace. Play area. Restaurant with menu del día and à la carte meals. Well stocked shop (all facilities open all year). Off site: Beach, fishing and golf (9 holes) 1 km. Bicycle hire 2 km. Boat launching 4 km. Shops, restaurants, bars, indoor pool plus bus/train services in Zarautz 2 km.

Open: All year.

Directions

Zarautz is 20 km. west of San Sebastian. From the A8 take exit 11 for Zarautz and straight on through two roundabouts and follow signs to site. If using the N634 coast road, site is signed near km. 17 marker. GPS: 43.28958, -2.14603

Charges 2011

Per unit incl. 2 persons and electricity	€ 26,10
extra person	€ 5,40
Camping Cheques accepted.	

For latest campsite news, availability and prices visit
alanrogers.com

This small region located in the north eastern part of the country is the most outstanding wine-growing area in Spain. Its production, Rioja wine, figures among the finest wines in the world.

THIS IS A ONE PROVINCE REGION

THE CAPITAL IS LOGROÑO

The capital of the region, Logroño, did not gain importance till the 11th century, when the rise in popularity of the Pilgrims' Route to Santiago de Compostela attracted people. Indeed the 12th-century Codex Calixtinus, the first guide to the route, mentions the city. And throughout the region, every town along the way has a church dedicated to the saint. Pilgrimages aside, La Rioja is best known for its wine. At the centre of the region's wine production is Haro, a stately town northwest of Logroño, and obviously a good place to stock up on a bottle or two! For those interested in the wine processes the Museum of Wine is worth a visit; admission includes cheese and wine tasting. During the last week of June the town comes alive with festivities. With free outdoor concerts, costumed characters on giant stilts, wine tastings and bargain buys, the climax of these fiestas is the Battle of the Wine, where thousands of people happily gather to be drenched in wine.

Places of interest

Calahorra: main town in Lower Rioja, Cathedral Museum.

Ezcaray: in the Sierra de la Demanda mountains, the surrounding area is made up of streams, forests and peaks over 2,000 metres high.

Nájera: monastery of Santa María la Real, built in 1032, History and Archaeological Museum.

San Millán de la Cogolla: traditional town, Monasteries of Suso and Yuso where the first texts written in Spanish are preserved.

Santo Domingo de la Calzada: last great staging post of the Pilgrims' Route in La Rioja, Cathedral of San Salvador.

Cuisines of the region

Asparagus, beans, peppers, garlic, artichokes and other vegetables and pulses are the basic ingredients of a long list of dishes such as vegetable stew, potatoes a la riojana, lamb cutlets with vine shoots or stuffed peppers. Traditional desserts include pears in wine, almond pastries from Arnedo and marzipan from Soto.

Camerano Cheese: cheese made from goat's milk, typical of La Rioja, usually eaten as a dessert with honey.

Fardelejo: pastry cake filled with marzipan.

Riojan-style potatoes: prepared with chorizo, peppers, garlic and lamp chops (optional).

Berceo

Camping Berceo

Ctra de Nájera - Sto Domingo dir. San Millán, E-26227 Berceo (La Rioja) T: 941 373 227
alanrogers.com/ES92280

Camping Berceo would ideally suit those looking for a quiet break at a site with limited facilities. It sits low in the San Millán valley in the heart of the Sierra de la Demanda and a steep walk of about 20 minutes will take you into the village. Here you will find several bars and restaurants, but little English is spoken. The 30 touring pitches are varied in size and separated by hedges. Some have shade and there are views of the green valley and mountains. Apart from the swimming pool which is open in peak season, there are few activities provided.

Facilities

One main toilet block providing sufficient facilities, but none for disabled visitors. Laundry area. Shop for basic supplies. Bar/restaurant. Takeaway on request. TV in bar and games area. Swimming and paddling pools. Play area. Off site: Berceo village 20 minute uphill walk. San Millán monasteries.

Open: All year.

Directions

From A68 head west until N120 exit. Turn left onto N120 (Najera). Turn left onto LR113 (Bobadilla). Within 5 km. turn right onto 205 (Cárdenas) until Berceo village. In village centre follow site arrow down steep hill. Site is on left within 500 m.
GPS: 42.33497, -2.85328

Charges guide

Per person	€ 4,28 - € 4,81
child	€ 3,75 - € 4,30
pitch	€ 3,00 - € 9,50
electricity	€ 4,17

For latest campsite news, availability and prices visit
alanrogers.com

Castanares de Rioja
Camping de La Rioja

Ctra de Haro - Sto Domingo de la Calzada, E-26240 Castanares de Rioja (La Rioja) T: 941 300 174
E: info@campingdelarioja.com **alanrogers.com/ES92250**

This site is situated just beyond the town of Castanares de Rioja. This is a busy site during the peak season with many sporting activities taking place. In low season it becomes rather more quiet with limited facilities available. There are 30 level, grass touring pitches, out of a total of 250, and these are separated by hedges and trees allowing privacy. Each has their own water, drainage and electricity connection. To the rear of the site is the Oja River which is ideal for fishing and there are views of the Obarenes mountains in the distance. Some noise from the main road is possible.There are many historic places worth visiting and naturally, being in Rioja, plenty of local wine to taste. A walk or cycle into the town of Castanares will enable you to sample the local cuisine.

Facilities
The central sanitary facilities are old and traditional in style but clean. Open style washbasins and controllable showers. Laundry and dishwashing facilities. Shop, bar, restaurant, takeaway (on request) all open 20/6-20/9. Outdoor swimming pool (20/6-20/9 supervised). Multisport court. Football. Tennis. River fishing. Riding. Children's cycle circuit. Play area. No individual barbecues. Off site: Town centre 1.5 km. The Guggenheim Museum in Bilbao. City of San Sebastian with beaches and aquarium.

Open: 1 January - 9 December.

Directions
Head west on N120. Turn right onto LR111 signed Castanares de Rioja. Continue through town towards Haro. Site is on left, 800 m. after leaving town speed restriction. GPS: 42.52911, -2.92243

Charges guide
Per person	€ 4,60 - € 5,75
child	€ 4,00 - € 5,00
pitch	€ 10,00 - € 12,50
electricity	€ 3,60

Haro
Camping de Haro

Avenida Miranda 1, E-26200 Haro (La Rioja) T: 941 312 737. E: campingdeharo@fer.es
alanrogers.com/ES90400

This quiet riverside site is on the outskirts of Haro, the commercial centre for the renowned Rioja wines. It is a family run site with excellent pools. Staff in the modern reception are helpful and you may well get a cheery welcome from Carlos, the owner's son, who speaks excellent English. All 236 pitches are on level ground and of reasonable size. Approximately 50% are occupied on a seasonal basis. Many of the touring pitches have some shade, a few have a great deal. Electricity connections (5A) are provided, although long leads may be required on some pitches. The river Tirón running alongside the site can provide fishing, and there is secure fencing. Reception provides information on the jewel of a town, and on tastings at the 'Bodegas' close by – CUNE and Muga are just two of those within easy walking distance. The famous Paternina is a few minutes drive away.

Facilities
Two toilet blocks, one heated in winter, the other with facilities for disabled campers. Laundry. Bar/snack bar with small counter selling basic provisions and adjacent swimming pool (15/6-15/9). Play area and entertainment for children in season. WiFi. Fishing. Torch useful. Off site: Large municipal pool complex nearby. Shops, bars, restaurants within walking distance. Bicycle hire 1 km. Riding 3 km. Boat launching 6 km. Golf 25 km.

Open: All year excl. 9 December - 14 January.

Directions
Haro is between Miranda de Ebro and Logroño. From AP68 (Bilbao - Logroño) take exit 9 to Haro. Keep to LR-111 (Vitoria) bearing left, crossing lights and over river where site is signed to left. From N124 (Vitoria - Logroño) leave at exit north of Haro onto LR-111 towards town and turn right before bridge (site signed). Avoid other turnings into town centre! GPS: 42.57894, -2.85157

Charges 2011
Per unit incl. 2 persons and electricity	€ 20,60 - € 24,80
extra person	€ 4,15 - € 5,20
child (3-10 yrs)	€ 3,35 - € 4,20
dog	€ 2,10 - € 2,60

Camping Cheques accepted.

For latest campsite news, availability and prices visit
alanrogers.com

Najera

Camping El Ruedo

Paseo San Julián 24, E-26300 Najera (La Rioja) T: 941 360 102
alanrogers.com/ES92290

Camping El Ruedo is situated 500 metres from the town of Najera and the river Rio Najerilla runs close by. There are numerous walks possible and seating provided along the riverbank. This is a small site with a total of 20 touring pitches on level ground, unmarked and with no separation. You can pitch at your own discretion. The traditional style sanitary block is kept clean and tidy with ample provision for the small amount of visitors. Extremely quiet and with very basic facilities, this site would suit those looking for peace and tranquillity. The site is not suitable for large units. No English is spoken.

Facilities

One immaculate toilet block with washbasins and showers. No facilities for disabled visitors. Washing machines (rather old). No shop, but provisions in town. Swings. No site lighting so torches useful. Off site: Town 500 m. (10 minutes walk).

Open: 1 April - 10 September.

Directions

From Logroño head west on AP68 until sign for N120 Najera. Turn left onto LR113 signed Najera. At traffic lights turn sharp left immediately before cobbled bridge. Site on left within 500 m. It is poorly signed after the A12. GPS: 42.41068, -2.73284

Charges guide

Per unit incl. 2 persons and electricity	€ 22,80
extra person	€ 4,00

Navarrete

Camping Navarrete

Ctra de Entrena km 1, E-26370 Navarrete (La Rioja) T: 941 440 169. E: campingnavarrete@fer.es
alanrogers.com/ES92270

Camping Navarrete is a spotlessly clean site in which the owners take great pride. Ideal as a base for exploring the surrounding countryside and sampling wonderful wines as it is located in the heart of La Rioja. Many of the 180 pitches are taken up by static caravans but a designated grassy area has been set aside for 40 unmarked, spacious touring pitches with 5A electricity. Some have shade and there are good views of the Rioja valley. Facilities on site are limited until the height of the season but the area is surrounded by many villages and places of artistic and historical importance. Noise is possible from the main road.

Facilities

One modern central sanitary block with heating is clean and provides communal washbasins and separate shower cubicles. Facilities for disabled visitors, one unisex cabin. Laundry facilities. Motorcaravan services. Shop (15/6-15/9). Bar, restaurant and takeaway (weekends only in low season). Outdoor swimming and paddling pools (15/6-15/9). Tennis. Bicycle hire. Unfenced play area. Off site: Large town of Logroño 10 km.

Open: 12 January - 10 December.

Directions

From Logroño proceed west along AP68. Take exit 11 signed Navarrete. At town centre turn left onto LR137 signed Entrena. Site is on the right in 800 m. GPS: 42.41614, -2.55172

Charges guide

Per person	€ 4,50 - € 5,35
child (under 10 yrs)	€ 4,15 - € 4,90
pitch	€ 4,50 - € 9,75
electricity	€ 4,25

Villoslada de Cameros

Camping Los Cameros

Ctra de la Virgen de Lomos de Orios km 3, E-26125 Villoslada de Cameros (La Rioja) T: 941 747 021
E: info@camping-loscameros.com **alanrogers.com/ES92260**

Situated 3 km. from the small town of Villoslada de Cameros, this site is in a quiet location, in a valley surrounded by tree covered mountains. The area provides the opportunity for plenty of hill walking and a footpath from the site takes you into the town. Of the 173 pitches, 40 are available for touring. They are open with some shade and have 5A electricity. This is a simple site with limited facilities available but it is well kept and has character; it is ideal for relaxation. A large playing field allows children to play ball games and bicycles can be hired from reception.

Facilities

One heated sanitary block provides WCs, washbasins with cold water only (one with hot water) and cubicle showers. No facilities for disabled visitors. Cold water only for washing machine and dishwashing. Shop. Bar with games. Restaurant with comprehensive menu and takeaway to order. Playing field and play area. Picnic area. Off site: Town 3 km. with shops, bars and restaurants and swimming pool.

Open: 20 January - 21 December.

Directions

From Logroño (AP68) turn left onto the N111 heading south towards Soria and Madrid. At sign for Villoslada de Cameros turn right, pass the centre and turn left by camping sign (LR448). Site on left in 3 km. Road bumpy and uneven, drive carefully and watch for animals on road. GPS: 42.08068, -2.67723

Charges guide

Per unit incl. 2 persons and electricity	€ 22,52 - € 25,30
extra person	€ 4,86 - € 5,20

The region of Navarra lies in the north of Spain, separated from France by the Pyrenees. With mountain retreats, beautiful valleys and an array of attractive towns and historic buildings, it is also popular for those wishing to follow the Pilgrim's Route to Santiago de Compostela.

THERE IS ONLY ONE PROVINCE ALSO KNOWN AS NAVARRA

THE CAPITAL IS PAMPLONA

Founded by the Roman general Pompey in 75 BC, the region's capital Pamplona is perhaps best known for the Fiestas de San Fernmín (July), when the encierro takes place – a tradition which involves people running through the streets in front of bulls. The city also boasts its fair share of sights including the old town, with its ancient churches and elegant buildings. Outside the city is the Sierra de Aralar, with well-marked paths of all grades. A wander through here will take you past waterfalls and caves and in Excelsis you'll come across Navarra's oldest church, the Sanctuario de San Miguel, a popular pilgrimage destination. In the south, the historic medieval town of Olite is home to an outstanding 15th-century castle, with turrets galore, and a Romanesque and Gothic church. To the west is the Urbasa and Andía Nature Reserve. Further north and in the east, the villages and valleys of the Pyrenees provide some of the most beautiful landscapes in the province and offer the perfect place to relax. Of particular note are the Valle de Baztán and the Valle de Salazar. For the more active, the Valle de Roncal is a good place to explore the mountains as is the Pirenaico National Park.

Places of interest

Andía Nature Reserve: forests, ponds, wildlife including the golden eagle, wild boar and wildcat.

Camino de Santiago: ancient Pilgrims' route. There are variants but the most popular point of entry into Spain was the pass of Roncesvalles, in the Pyrenees. It then continues south through Navarra via Sangüesa, Puente La Reina and Estella, then west through the provinces of La Rioja and Castilla-León till it reaches Santiago in the Galicia province.

Orreaga-Roncesvalles: a town established as a sanctuary and hospital in 1132 and first staging post for pilgrims, museum with exhibition on Pilgrims' Route.

Sangüesa: small town, 14th-century churches, medieval hospital.

Ujué: medieval defensive village, Romanesqe church.

Cuisine of the region

Typical products found in abundance in this area include asparagus grown on the river banks, small red peppers and artichokes from Tudela, pork from Estella, cherries from Ciriza, cheese made in the Roncal Valley and *chorizo* from Pamplona.

Ajoarriero: cod cooked with garlic, potato, 'choricero' peppers and tomatoes.

Canutillos de Sumbilla: sweet pastry made with aniseed, filled with lemon flavouring.

Chorizo: shaped like a candle, stuffed in thick tripe with pork and beef, seasoned with salt, paprika, garlic and sugars.

Cordero al chilindrón: lamb stew.

Cuajada: made from sheep's milk and natural curd, sweetened by honey or sugar.

Pacharán: traditional aniseed liquor.

Erratzu

Camping Baztan

Ctra Francia s/n, E-31714 Erratzu (Navarra) T: 948 453 133. E: campingbaztan@campingbaztan.com
alanrogers.com/ES90490

When driving through the small town of Erratzu extreme caution is required due to the narrowness of the streets and it is not advised at all for large units. This site's rural setting and the mountain views make this a retreat for those who enjoy camping in quiet surroundings. It consists of a main building housing reception, a shop, a bar and a small restaurant and above, 14 tidy apartments. There are also ten timber cottages for rent. Tarmac roads lead to the grass touring pitches which are supplied with water and electricity (10A). Shady and of a good size, most of the pitches are level. In early and late season the campsite is open, but a telephone call is necessary to gain access. You may be the only occupants. The one toilet block is open and cleaned but facilities are minimal.

Facilities	Directions
The single sanitary block is clean and has facilities for disabled visitors. Shop, bar and restaurant (weekends only outside 1/6-20/9). Swimming pool (1/6-20/9). Squash court. In April, May and 20/9-1/11 the site is only open at weekends. If you wish to stay on weekdays, entry can be obtained by dialling a number displayed at reception (sanitary block will be open). Off site: River fishing 50 m. Village (5 mins walk) with a small supermarket, bars and restaurant. Riding 2 km. Excursions arranged to activity centre (riding, kayaking, rafting) 15 km. away. Buses run to Pamplona and San Sebastian (3 per day, all year). Bicycle hire 15 km. Golf (in France) 20 km.	From Hendaye head south on the N121A. Turn east on N121B. Continue north to the junction with NA2600. Turn right to Erratzu. Proceed through village, bear left at sign 'Francia NA2600' and site is on the right. GPS: 43.18067, -1.45139

Charges 2011

Per unit incl. 2 persons and electricity	€ 23,90 - € 34,50

Open: 1 April - 30 October.

For latest campsite news, availability and prices visit
alanrogers.com

Espinal

Camping Urrobi

Ctra Pamplona - Valcarlos km 42 N135, E-31694 Espinal (Navarra) T: 948 760 200. E: info@campingurrobi.com
alanrogers.com/ES90480

This large site is in a beautiful location with mountain views. At the entrance is a lively bar, a reasonably priced restaurant and a well stocked shop. The site is popular with Spanish families and there are many mobile homes, so it can be busy at holiday times and weekends. However, there is plenty of room on the 150 unmarked grass pitches. All have electricity points (6A) and there are plenty of water taps. Water activities of all types are catered for with both a swimming pool and an area of the river sectioned off for safe bathing and paddling. This is a suitable site for families.

Facilities	Directions
Clean sanitary blocks include facilities for disabled visitors (key from reception). Laundry facilities. Motorcaravan service point. Shop, bar and restaurant (all season). Swimming pool. Games room with TV (Spanish). Internet access. Minigolf. Tennis. Playing field. Play area. Off site: Village 1 km. with shops, restaurant and bars. Forest of Irati 15 mins. Bicycle hire 15 km. Golf and riding 40 km. Beach 70 km. One bus per day to and from Pamplona.	From Pamplona take N135 northeast for 42 km. After village of Auritzberri turn right onto NA172. Site is on the left. GPS: 42.97315, -1.351817

Open: 1 April - 31 October.

Charges 2011

Per unit incl. 2 persons and electricity	€ 24,00 - € 25,50
extra person	€ 5,00
child (2-12 yrs)	€ 4,00

Etxarri-Aranatz

Camping Etxarri

Paraje Dambolintxulo s/n, E-31820 Etxarri-Aranatz (Navarra) T: 948 460 537. E: info@campingetxarri.com
alanrogers.com/ES90420

Situated in the Valle de la Burundi, this site is a peaceful oasis with superb views of the 1,300 m. high San-Donator Mountains. The approach to this improving site is via a road lined by huge 300-year-old oak trees, which are a feature of the site. Reception is housed in the main bulding beside the pool with a restaurant above (access also by lift). There are 108 pitches of average size on flat ground (50 for tourers) with 6A electricity to all and water to 25. The site is well placed for fascinating walks in unspoilt countryside and is close to three recognised nature walks. The site gets very crowded during the Fiestas de San Ferm'n (bull-running) in Pamplona early in July. It is essential to make a reservation if you wish to stay. A visit to Pamplona is recommended. Parking is difficult – try to the west of the bullring, then wander down to Plaza de Toros (renamed Plaza Hemingway), to savour the atmosphere. It is common to use dual-naming of places and roads (one in the Spanish language, the other in Basque and it can be confusing) – ask for advice if in doubt.

Facilities	Directions
Toilet facilities are good and include a baby bath and facilities for disabled visitors. Laundry. Motorcaravan service point. Gas supplies. Essential supplies kept in high season. Bar (1/4-30/9). Restaurant and takeaway (1/6-15/9). Swimming and paddling pools (15/6-15/9) also open to the public and can get crowded. Bicycle hire. Minigolf. Play area. Entertainment for children (high season). WiFi (charged). Tennis and squash courts. Off site: Buses and trains nearby to Pamplona (40 km). Restaurants and shops 2 km. Golf, fishing, riding all 20 km.	Etxarri-Aranatz is 40 km. northwest of Pamplona. From A8 (San Sebastian - Bilbao) take A15 towards Pamplona, then 20 km. northwest of Pamplona, take A10 west towards Vitoria/Gasteix. At km. 19 take NA120 to and through town following site signs. Turn left after crossing railway to site at end of road. GPS: 42.913031, -2.079924

Open: 1 April - 3 October.

Charges 2011

Per unit incl. 2 persons and electricity	€ 23,60 - € 27,60

(143)

For latest campsite news, availability and prices visit
alanrogers.com

Mendigorría
Camping Caravanning Errota el Molino

E-31150 Mendigorría (Navarra) T: 948 340 604. E: info@campingelmolino.com

alanrogers.com/ES90430

This is an extensive site set by an attractive weir near the town of Mendigorría, alongside the river Arga. It takes its name from an old disused water mill (molino) close by. The site is split into separate permanent and touring sections. The touring area is a new development with good-sized flat pitches with electricity and water for tourers, and a separate area for tents. Many trees have been planted around the site but there is still only minimal shade. The friendly owner Anna Beriain will give you a warm welcome. Reception is housed in the lower part of a long building along with the bar/snack bar which has a cool shaded terrace, a separate restaurant and a supermarket. The upper floor of this building is dormitory accommodation for backpackers. The site has a sophisticated dock and boat launching facility and an ambitious watersport competition programme in season with a safety boat present at all times. There are pedaloes and canoes for hire. The site is very busy during the festival of San Fermín (bull running) in July in Pamplona (28 km). Tours of the local bodegas (groups of ten) to sample the fantastic Navarra wines can be organised by reception.

Facilities

The well equipped toilet block is very clean and well maintained, with cold water to washbasins. Facilities for disabled campers. Washing machine. Large restaurant, pleasant bar. Supermarket. Superb new swimming pools for adults and children (1/6–15/9). Bicycle hire. Riverside bar. Weekly entertainment programme (July/Aug) and many sporting activities. Squash courts. Internet access. River walk. Torches useful. Off site: Bus to Pamplona 500 m. Riding 15 km. Golf 35 km.

Open: All year (excl. 23 December - 4 January).

Directions

Mendigorría is 30 km. southwest of Pamplona. From A15 San Sebastian - Zaragoza motorway, leave Pamplona bypass on A12 towards Logon. Leave at km. 23 on NA601 to hill top town of Mendigorría. At crossroads turn right towards Larraga and down hill to site. GPS: 42.62423, -1.84259

Charges guide

Per person	€ 4,70 - € 5,00
child	€ 3,95 - € 4,22
pitch incl. car and electricity	€ 12,90 - € 13,80

Discounts outside high season.
Camping Cheques accepted.

Your first class site next to Pamplona!

With a capacity for 1.500 campers, many pitches divided by hedges; all with connection for electricity, water and waste water.
Bungalows and mobile homes for hire. Hostal with bunk beds and special prices for fll- and half board. Free hot water. Situated in the centre of Navarra, ideal for excursions to the Pyrenees, the Irati forest (second largest forest of Europe) and the Bardenas Reales (half-desert): all declared protected nature reseves. Open throughout the year. Special offers in low season.

Dual carriageway A-12 (Pamplona-Logroño)
Exit-24 Mendigorria
Tel. (34) 948 34 06 04 • Fax (34) 948 34 00 82
info@campingelmolino.com • www.campingelmolino.com

camping ERROTA-EL MOLINO
MENDIGORRIA

ISO and 14001 environmentally managed

In the north eastern part of Spain, Aragón borders France with the Pyrenees lying between them. It is a region rich in folklore, with rural, mountainside villages renowned for their Romanesque architecture, beautiful valleys and awe-inspiring peaks.

ARAGÓN IS MADE UP OF THREE PROVINCES: HUESCA, ZARAGOZA AND TERUEL

THE CAPITAL OF THE REGION IS ZARAGOZA

The region can be separated into three different areas: the central area consisting of the Ebro basin, a vast flat lowland, the northern Pyrenees, and the area made up of the Iberian mountain range in the northwest and southeast of the region. The northern-most province of Huesca is located in the foothills of the Pyrenees mountains, a beautiful area with plenty of picturesque towns and villages to visit. It is also good walking country with numerous trails offering anything from short day-walks in the valleys to long-distance treks in the mountains. Skiing is popular too. Bordering Huesca, the province of Zaragoza is home to the region's capital, also of the same name. Zaragoza is a lively town with plenty of bars and restaurants, plus numerous museums and architectural treasures. Outside the capital you'll find more villages, countryside, and vineyards where the best of the region's wine is produced; the mapped out Ruta del Vino will take you through the area. The third province of Teruel is largely comprised of the Iberian mountain range, with attractive towns, medieval sights and more dramatic scenery to admire.

Places of interest

Aljafería Palace: spectacular Moorish monument.

Basílica de Nuestra Señora del Pilar: Baroque temple from the 17th and 18th centuries.

Benasque: attractive alpine town, gateway to Pyrenees.

Casa-Museo de Goya: art museum, including engravings by Goya.

Jaca: home of the country's oldest Romanesque cathedral.

Monasterio de San Juan de la Peña: 17th-century Baroque monastery and 10th-century Old monastery in Romanesque style.

Parque Nacional de Ordesa y Monte Perdido: alpine national park.

Cuisine of the region

Specialities include lamb, locally-produced ham and sausages; fruit is also used a lot in desserts.

Chilindrones: sauce of tomato and pepper.

Frutas de Aragón: sugar-candied fruits covered in chocolate.

Pollo al chilindrón: chicken (or lamb) stew with onions, tomatoes and red peppers.

Salmorrejos: cold soup.

Suspiros de amante: dessert with cheese and egg.

Ternasco: roast lamb.

Tortas de alma: dessert made with pumpkin, honey and sugar.

Trenza de Almudévar: dessert with nuts and raisins soaked in liqueur.

ORREAGA-RONCESVALLES

FRANCE

PAMPLONA

GAVÍN

BENASQUE

NAVARRA

SANTA CILIA DE JACA

LABUERDA N260

OLITE

BOLTANA

BONANSA

LA RIOJA

RODELLAR

LIGUERRE DE CINCA

HUESCA

LA PUEBLA DE CASTRO

TUDELA

N123

A23/E7

ARAGON

CASTILLA Y LEON

A68/E804

ZARAGOZA

LLEIDA/ LERIDA

A2/E90

N234

CATALUNYA

A2/E90

N330

NUEVALOS

N232

LA FRESNEDA

N232

N234

MORELLA

ALBARRACIN

TERUEL

COMUNIDAD VALENCIANA

N330

CASTILLA-LA MANCHA

CUENCA

CASTELLON DE LA PLANA

0   25   50 kms

For latest campsite news, availability and prices visit

alanrogers.com

Albarracin

Camping Ciudad de Albarracin

Junto al Polideportivo, Camino de gea, E-44100 Albarracin (Teruel) T: 978 710 197

alanrogers.com/ES90950

Albarracin, in southern Aragon is set in the Reserva Nacional de los Montes Universales and is a much frequented, fascinating town with a Moorish castle. The old city walls towering above date from its days when it attempted to become a separate country within Spain. This neat and clean family site is set on three levels on a hillside behind the town, with a walk of 1 km. to the centre. It is very modern and has high quality facilities including a superb building for barbecuing. There are 140 pitches (70 for tourers), all with electricity and separated by trees. Some require cars to be parked separately.

Facilities	Directions
The two spotless, modern sanitary buildings provide British style WCs, quite large showers and hot water throughout. Baby bath. Washing machines. Bar/restaurant (all season). Essentials from bar. Special room for barbecues with fire and wood provided. Play area. Torches required in some areas. Off site: Municipal swimming pool 100 m. (high season). Town shops, bars and restaurants 500 m. Fishing 1 km.	From Teruel north on the N330 for about 8 km. then west onto A1512 for 30 km. From the A23 use exit 124 then the A1512, from the N235 take exit for Albarracin and the A1512. Site is well signed in the town. GPS: 40.41655, -1.43332

Open: 1 March - 2 November.

Charges guide

Per unit incl. 2 persons and electricity	€ 18,05 - € 18,75
extra person	€ 3,80

Boltaña

Camping Boltaña

Ctra N260 km 442, E-22340 Boltaña (Huesca) T: 974 502 347. E: info@campingboltana.com

alanrogers.com/ES90620

Nestled in the Rio Ara valley, surrounded by the Pyrenees mountains and below a tiny but enchanting, historic, hill top village, is the very pretty, thoughtfully planned Camping Boltaña. Generously sized, 190 grassy pitches (all with 10A electricity) have good shade from a variety of trees and a stream meanders through the campsite. The landscaping includes ten charming rocky water gardens and a covered pergola doubles as an eating and play area. A stone building houses the site's reception, social room and supermarket. Angel Moreno, the owner of the site, is a charming host and has tried to think of everything to make his guests comfortable.

Facilities	Directions
Two modern sanitary blocks include facilities for disabled visitors and laundry facilities. Supermarket. Bar, restaurant and takeaway (1/7-31/8). Swimming pools (1/6-15/9). Playground. Barbecues. Entertainment for children (high season). Pétanque. Guided tours, plus hiking, canyoning, rafting, climbing, mountain biking and caving. Torches useful in some parts. Off site: Local bus service.	South of the Park Nacional de Ordesa, site is about 50 km. from Jaca near Ainsa. From Ainsa travel northwest on N260 toward Boltana (near 443 km. marker) and 1 km. from Boltana turn south toward Margudgued. Site is well signed and is 1 km. along this road. GPS: 42.43018, 0.07882

Open: 15 January - 15 December.

Charges guide

Per unit incl. 2 persons and electricity	€ 35,40
extra person	€ 6,50
Camping Cheques accepted.	

Bonansa

Camping Baliera

Ctra N260 km 355,5, E-22486 Bonansa (Huesca) T: 974 554 016. E: info@baliera.com

alanrogers.com/ES90580

With its wonderful location in a quiet river valley with views of the surrounding mountains all around, Camping Baliera is an excellent site for enjoying this beautiful area. Combining camping with timber chalets and apartments, the site has 133 well kept grass touring pitches (80-120 sq.m) all with electricity (5/7/10A). The pitches are mostly located close to the attractive, stone built reception building which also houses a comfortable bar and shop. The approach to this site is by narrow and winding mountain roads and it is 5 km. from the nearest village. However, for all but the largest units, the trip is well worth making.

Facilities	Directions
Two toilet blocks, one part of the apartment block near the entrance, the other in the reception building (this is closed in low season). Heated, they are good with well equipped showers, vanity style washbasins. Laundry room and drying room. Motorcaravan services. Shop (1/7-31/8). Bar (automatic). Takeaway (1/7-31/8). Swimming pool (15/7-15/9). Fitness equipment. Play area. Entertainment in high season. Communal barbecue. WiFi. Off site: National parks and activities. Nearest village 5 km.	On N230, 34 km. south of Vielha, turn on N260 for 2-3 km, then onto A1605 signed Graus for 100 m. to site on left. Reception is 200 m. through the site. Approach roads are narrow and winding, but navigable. GPS: 42.43958, 0.69918

Open: All year excl. November.

Charges 2011

Per unit incl. 2 persons and electricity	€ 29,00 - € 30,00
Camping Cheques accepted.	

For latest campsite news, availability and prices visit

alanrogers.com

Gavín

Camping Gavín

Ctra N260 km 503, E-22639 Gavín (Huesca) T: 974 485 090. E: info@campinggavin.com

alanrogers.com/ES90640

Camping Gavín is set on a terraced, wooded hillside and you will find a friendly welcome. The site offers 150 pitches of 90 sq m. in size and with electricity available to all (6A). In some areas the terracing means that some pitches are quite small. The main site buildings are built of natural stone. There are also 24 mobile homes, 13 new bungalows and 11 superb, balconied apartments. At about 900 m. the site is surrounded by towering peaks at the portal of the Tena Valley. One can enjoy the natural beauty of the Pyrenees and venture near or far along the great Pyrenean footpaths.

Facilities

Excellent shower and toilet facilities in three main buildings with subtle, tasteful décor include facilities for babies and disabled visitors. Laundry facilities. Bar and snacks. Well stocked supermarket. Swimming and paddling pools (15/6-15/9). Tennis. Playground. Barbecues are not permitted at some times of the year. Off site: Windsurfing, rafting, fishing, walking and climbing in the vicinity. Bicycle hire 2 km. Riding 6 km. Golf 15 km. Day excursions to the Monastery of San Juan de la Pena.

Open: All year.

Directions

Site is off the N260, 2 km. from Biescas at km. 503. GPS: 42.61940, -0.30408

Charges guide

Per unit incl. 2 persons and electricity	€ 29,92 - € 37,37
extra person	€ 4,97 - € 6,80

Camping Cheques accepted.

La Fresneda

Camping La Fresneda

Partida Vall del Pi, E-44596 La Fresneda (Teruel) T: 978 854 085. E: info@campinglafresneda.com

alanrogers.com/ES91100

La Fresneda is a great little campsite, situated on three terraces at the foot of a wooded escarpment and overlooking the huge valley of the National Reserve of Los Puertos de Beceite. Everything is in line with the natural beauty of the area and the very clean, very well equipped, toilet block is partly underground. There are 25 pitches with grass and gravel surfaces, all used for touring and with 6A electricity. The site is quite new and the enthusiastic Dutch owners, Jet Knijn and her partner Joost Leeuwenberg, built it from scratch, recently adding a shady garden atrium with a terrace and plunge pool for guests to enjoy.

Facilities

Toilet block with hot water throughout. Washing machine. Bar with terrace where meals are served a few times a week. Fresh bread daily. Garden atrium with terrace and plunge pool. Bicycle hire. Information on walking and cycling routes. Gas barbecue for hire. Pets not accepted. Off site: Baker, grocery and butcher in the village. Alcañiz 30 minutes drive. Riding 10 km. Fishing 20 km.

Open: 1 April - 1 October.

Directions

From the N232 (Alcañiz - Vinaros/Castellón) turn off just east of Valdealgorfa (at Restaurant Las Ventas) onto A231 to Valjunquera/Valderrobres, then La Fresneda. GPS: 40.90695, 0.061667

Charges guide

Per person	€ 5,00
child (0-1 yrs)	free
pitch incl. electricity	€ 12,00

La Puebla de Castro

Camping Barasona

Ctra N123a km 25, E-22435 La Puebla de Castro (Huesca) T: 974 545 148. E: info@lagobarasona.com

alanrogers.com/ES91250

This site, alongside its associated ten room hotel, is beautifully positioned on terraces across a road from the shores of the Lago de Barasona (a large reservoir), with views of hills and the distant Pyrenees. The very friendly, English speaking owner is keen to please and has applied very high standards throughout the site. The grassy, fairly level pitches are generally around 100 sq.m. with 35 high quality pitches of 110 sq.m. for larger units. All have electricity (6/10A), many are well shaded and some have great views of the lake and/or hills. Water skiing and other watersports are available in July and August.

Facilities

Two toilet blocks in modern buildings have high standards and hot water throughout including cabins (3 for ladies, 1 for men). Bar/snack bar and two excellent restaurants (all season). Shop (1/4-30/9). Swimming pools (1/6-30/9). Tennis. Mountain bike hire. Canoe, windsurfing motor boat and pedalo hire. Miniclub (high season). Lake swimming, fishing, canoeing, etc. Walking (maps provided). Money exchange. Minidisco. WiFi. Wellness centre with sauna, jacuzzi and gym. Off site: Riding 4 km.

Open: All year.

Directions

Site is on the west bank of the lake, close to km. 25 on the N123A, 6 km. south of Graus (about 80 km. north of Lleida/Lerida). Travelling from the south, the site is on the left from a newly built roundabout and slip road. GPS: 42.14163, 0.31525

Charges guide

Per unit incl. 2 persons and electricity	€ 23,00 - € 35,00
extra person	€ 4,50 - € 6,50
child (2-10 yrs)	€ 3,50 - € 5,50

Camping Cheques accepted.

For latest campsite news, availability and prices visit

alanrogers.com

Labuerda

Camping Peña Montañesa

Ctra Ainsa - Francia km 2, E-22360 Labuerda (Huesca) T: 974 500 032. E: info@penamontanesa.com
alanrogers.com/ES90600

A large site situated quite high up in the Pyrenees near the Ordesa National Park, Peña Montañesa is easily accessible from Ainsa or from France via the Bielsa Tunnel (steep sections on the French side). The site is essentially divided into three sections opening progressively throughout the season and all have shade. The 288 pitches on fairly level grass are of about 75 sq.m. and 10A electricity is available on virtually all. Grouped near the entrance are the facilities that make the site so attractive, including a fair sized outdoor pool and a glass-covered indoor pool with jacuzzi and sauna. Here too is an attractive bar/restaurant with an open fire and terrace, with a supermarket and takeaway opposite. There is an entertainment programme for children (21/6-15/9 and Easter weekend) and twice weekly for adults (July/August). This is quite a large site which has grown very quickly and as such, it may at times be a little hard pressed, although it is very well run. The site is ideally situated for exploring the beautiful Pyrenees. The complete town of Ainsa is listed as a national monument of Spain and should be explored while you are here, along with the national park.

Facilities

A newer toilet block, heated when necessary, has free hot showers but cold water to open plan washbasins. Facilities for disabled visitors. Small baby room. An older block in the original area has similar provision. Washing machine and dryer. Bar, restaurant, takeaway and supermarket (all 1/1-31/12). Outdoor swimming pool (1/4-31/10). Indoor pool (all year). Playground. Boules. Bicycle hire. Riding. Rafting. Only gas barbecues are permitted. Torches required in some areas. Off site: Fishing 100 m. Skiing in season. Canoeing.

Open: All year.

Directions

Site is 2 km. from Ainsa, on the road from Ainsa to France. GPS: 42.4352, 0.13618

Charges guide

Per unit incl. 2 persons
and electricity   € 24,60 - € 33,30

Ligüerre de Cinca
Camping Ligüerre de Cinca
Ctra A-138 km 28 de Barbastro a Ainsa, E-22393 Ligüerre de Cinca (Huesca) T: 974 500 800
E: info@liguerredecinca.com **alanrogers.com/ES90610**

Ligüerre de Cinca, a medieval village abandoned when the El Grado reservoir was constructed, is now being regenerated for tourism. It is situated near the Ordesa National Park in a beautiful region of the Pyrenees mountains and has the advantage of being open all year. Attractive traditional style buildings house the reception, bar, restaurant and takeaway. The swimming and paddling pools are surrounded by grass sunbathing areas with wonderful mountain views. There are 150 small, terraced, level pitches marked out and shaded by tall trees. These include 110 for touring units, all with 10A electricity. Access is easy for large outfits.

Facilities

Adequate central toilet block, heated in winter, with smaller one on periphery. No facilities for disabled campers. Shop (July/Aug). Bar, restaurant, takeaway. Swimming and paddling pools (July/Aug). Miniclub (July/Aug). Multisports court. Tennis. Boules. Playground. Fishing, watersports, boat storage. Organised watersports including courses. Internet access. ATM. Barbecues are not allowed. Off site: Bus to Huesca. Riding 18 km. Rafting, canyoning, climbing, biking, hiking.

Open: All year.

Directions

Site is between El Grado and Ainsa on the N138. From the Tunnel de Bielsa at the French/Spanish border, go south on N138, through Ainsa. Site is on left in about 20 km. GPS: 42.28111, 0.19638

Charges guide

Per person	€ 4,85
child (2-10 yrs)	€ 4,25
pitch	€ 5,75 - € 7,05

Low season and long stay discounts.

Nuevalos
Camping Lago Park
Ctra Alhama de Aragon - Nuevalos, E-50210 Nuevalos (Zaragoza) T: 976 849 038
alanrogers.com/ES91050

Lago Park is situated in an attractive area which receives many visitors for the Monasterio de Piedra just 3 km. distant and it enjoys pleasant views of the surrounding mountains. This site is suitable for transit stops or if you wish to visit the monasterio as it is the only one hereabouts and appears to make the most of that fact. It is not recommended for extended stays. Set on a steep hillside, the 280 pitches (260 for tourers) are on terraces. Only the lower rows are suitable for large caravans. These pitches are numbered and marked by trees, most having electricity (10A).

Facilities

The single very clean sanitary block has British style WCs. washbasins with hot water and controllable hot showers (no dividers). Restaurant/bar. Shop (all season). Swimming pool (late June-Sept). Play area. Gas supplies. Torches needed in some areas. Off site: Fishing 300 m. Riding 2 km.

Open: 1 April - 30 September.

Directions

From Zaragoza (120 km) take fast A2/N11/E90 road and turn onto C202 road beyond Calatayud to Nuévalos (25 km). From Madrid, exit A2 at Alhama de Aragón (13 km). Follow signs for Monasterio de Piedra from all directions. GPS: 41.21800, -1.792

Charges guide

Per unit incl. 2 persons and electricity	€ 19,00

Rodellar
Camping El Puente
Ctra N-Z40, E-22144 Rodellar (Huesca) T: 974 318 312. E: info@campingelpuente.com
alanrogers.com/ES90630

Situated in the world famous Parc de la Sierra y los Canyons de Guara in Aragon, this specialised site is a must for those who wish to experience canyoning and climbing. There are 78 rather dusty pitches which are shaded by mature trees, just 12 with 6A electricity. The site is set on a hillside although any views are restricted by trees. A pleasant restaurant serves excellent food at no nonsense prices. A professional team of guides is here to hire, as is all the necessary equipment for you to experience the thrills of around 100 superb canyons in the area.

Facilities

One sanitary block with mature but clean facilities. Good hot showers. Cold water at washing sinks, hot for dishwashing. Motorcaravan service point. Washing machines. Well stocked shop. Excellent restaurant. Snack bar. Barbecue areas. River swimming. Fishing. Canyon guides and canyoning and climbing equipment for hire. Tourist information. Off site: Village of Rodella 1 km. with all facilities. Adventurous sports: canyoning, swimming, hiking, climbing, caving, cycling, riding (and river crossing by horse), 'Route Ferrata' climbing (using embedded metal 'ladders').

Open: Easter - 1 November.

Directions

From the N240 (Lleida - Huesca), 15 km. west of Barbastro take the A1229 towards Abiego, then the A1227 to Abiego and Bierge. Finally take the HU341 to Las Aluminas and continue to Rodellar. Site is well signed 1 km. before the village. Do not try to take caravans and motorcaravans into the village as the roads are too narrow, park outside and walk. GPS: 42.274104, -0.073222

Charges guide

Per unit incl. 2 persons	€ 19,20 - € 19,60
extra person	€ 4,80 - € 5,00
electricity	€ 4,40 - € 4,60

For latest campsite news, availability and prices visit
alanrogers.com

Santa Cilia de Jaca
Centro de Vacaciones Pirineos

Ctra N240 km 300, E-22791 Santa Cilia de Jaca (Huesca) T: **974 377 351**. E: pirineos@pirinet.com

alanrogers.com/ES90700

This pretty site which is open most of the year, is directly on the pilgrimage route to Santiago. The area has a mild climate, being near the River Aragon, not too high and it is convenient for touring the Pyrenees. This is a friendly site which is useful for transit stops and off-season camping on the large, mostly level wooded area which can accommodate 250 units (no marked pitches), with electric points throughout. The trees provide good shade and the attractive swimming pool is being rebuilt and updated. There is some road noise along the south side of the site. The restaurant, with a varied menu and a good value menu of the day, has a large comfortable terrace and a patio for drinks and snacks. There is an open fronted room for barbecuing and all equipment is provided. A major feature here is the huge recreational area with all manner of sports and amusements. As well as the campsite and its chalets to rent, there is a small hotel.

Facilities

One heated sanitary block is open all year, providing a quite satisfactory supply. A second, more modern block is open Apr.-Sept. only. Launderette. Supermarket (15/6-15/9, otherwise essentials kept in bar). Restaurant. Bar. Swimming pools (15/6-15/9). Tennis. Playground. Games room. Bicycle hire. Gas supplies. Torches required in some areas. Off site: Fishing and bathing in river 200 m.

Open: All year excl. 3 November - 3 December.

Directions

Site is 15 km. west of Jaca on the N240 at km. 300 (65 km. northwest of Huesca).
GPS: 42.55576, -0.75649

Charges guide

Per person	€ 4,89 - € 6,08
child (2-9 yrs)	€ 4,55 - € 5,69
pitch	€ 4,89 - € 10,80

20% discount in low season.

Zaragoza
Camping Ciudad de Zaragoza

Ctra San Juan Bautista de la Salle s/n, E-50012 Zaragoza (Zaragoza) T: **876 241 495**
E: info@campingzaragoza.com alanrogers.com/ES91040

Zaragoza is a popular en-route stop between the ports of Santander and Bilbao and the beaches of the Costa Brava. The city, however, has much more to offer as the former capital of Aragon and now Spain's fifth largest city. Primarily for short stay, transit visitors, this all year site gives impressions of concrete, metal and plastic, although it will soften in time. There are 103 touring pitches with electricity and water, which are mostly of gravel and without shade as yet. A modern bar/restaurant serves good food at reasonable prices, there are good facilities for children and the very pleasant swimming and paddling pools are welcome as it gets very hot here. The city centre is 4 km. distant and a regular bus service is available. Also on site are 70 mobile homes for rent and a 58-bed youth hostel. The site is very busy during the world famous 'Fiesta del Pilar', a nine day festival in October which culminates in a massive fireworks display over the River Ebro.

Facilities

Modern toilet blocks include good facilities for disabled visitors. Motorcaravan services. Bar and restaurant (all year). Swimming and paddling pools (30/5-30/9). Tennis. Pétanque. Multisports pitch. Play areas. Bungalows for rent. Hostel. Club and TV room. Internet access and free WiFi. Off site: Zaragoza city centre 4 km. (regular bus service 100 m. from gate). Golf 5 km. Many tours available.

Open: All year.

Directions

Follow the Autovia del Nordeste (Zaragoza ring road) southwest to leave at the junction with the N11-a. Follow signs to the city centre (Autovia de Madrid) and the site is signed to the right.
GPS: 41.63766, -0.94273

Charges guide

Per unit incl. 2 persons and electricity	€ 15,84 - € 25,16
extra person	€ 2,89 - € 4,82
child (0-14 yrs)	€ 2,57 - € 4,28
dog	€ 2,61 - € 2,68

For latest campsite news, availability and prices visit
alanrogers.com

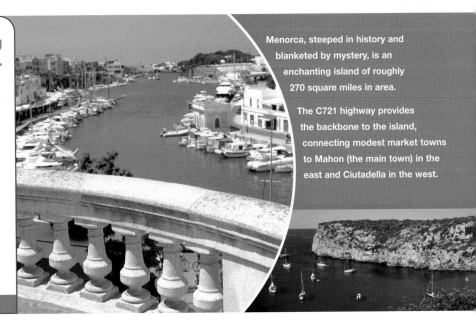

Menorca, steeped in history and blanketed by mystery, is an enchanting island of roughly 270 square miles in area.

The C721 highway provides the backbone to the island, connecting modest market towns to Mahon (the main town) in the east and Ciutadella in the west.

Mahon's classic Georgian style buildings, complete with sash windows, will endear them to the British traveller. Its impressive harbour was captured by the British in 1708 during the Spanish War of Succession. In complete contrast, Ciutadella has a more Gothic feel to it. A labyrinth of tiny streets entwine the 'little city', most of which can only be accessed on foot. Monte Toro stands proudly at the centre of the island surveying all. To the south a greener lush terrain exists with long, luxurious beaches, while to the north a giant rockery erupts riddled with caves and prehistoric finds.

Alaior
Camping Son Bou

Ctra de San Jaime km 3,5, Apdo 85, Alaior, E-07730 Menorca (Menorca) T: **971 372 727**
E: info@campingsonbou.com **alanrogers.com/ES80000**

Camping Son Bou was opened in 1996 and has been purpose built in local style providing a large irregular shaped pool with marvellous views across to Monte Toro and overlooked by a pine shaded, terraced bar and restaurant. The 313 large pitches, 143 for tourers with 10A electricity, are arranged in circles radiating out from the main facilities and clearly edged with stones. Natural pine tree shade covers most but the outer ring. Drinking water and refuse points are well placed. The ground is hard and devoid of grass except where sprinklers operate. The beautiful island of Menorca cries out to be explored. It is peaceful and tranquil, with its characteristic dry stone walls, its low white buildings with terracotta tiled roof, its beautiful coastline, ancient monuments and pretty villages with their cycle of fiestas of religious origin with the noble horse as the central element.

Facilities

Well designed toilet block of good quality, open plan in places. Some washbasins in cabins (cold water). Bathrooms and shower. Baby room. Facilities for disabled visitors. Service wash. Shop, bar, restaurant, takeaway and outdoor pool (all open all season). Tennis. Play area. Bicycle hire. Open-air cinema. Occasional barbecue with guitarist. Comprehensive activity programme. English spoken. Dogs are not accepted. Off site: Riding 4 km. Village 3 km. with sandy beach.

Open: 16 April - 16 October.

Directions

From Mahon (Mao) follow main road to Ciutadella. Go past Alaior (bypassed) and watch for restaurant on left and sign for 3.5 km. Torre Soli Nou and campsite sign. GPS: 39.92199, 4.09114

Charges 2011

Per unit incl. 2 persons and electricity	€ 29,10 - € 34,32
extra person	€ 6,56 - € 7,94
child (3-13 yrs)	€ 4,87 - € 5,34

Portugal is a relatively small country occupying the southwest corner of the Iberian peninsula, bordered by Spain in the north and east, with the Atlantic coast in the south and west. In spite of its size, the country offers a tremendous variety in both its way of life and traditions.

Tourist Office

ICEP Portuguese Trade & Tourism Office,
Second Floor, 22/25a Sackville Street,
London W1S 3LY

Tel: 09063 640 610
E-mail: iceplondt@aol.com
Fax: 020 7494 1868
Internet: www.portugalinsite.com

Most visitors looking for a beach type holiday head for the busy Algarve, with its long stretches of sheltered sandy beaches, and warm, clear Atlantic waters, great for bathing and watersports. With its monuments and fertile rolling hills, central Portugal adjoins the beautiful Tagus river that winds its way through the capital city of Lisbon, on its way to the Atlantic Ocean.

Lisbon city itself has deep-rooted, cultural traditions, coming alive at night with buzzing cafés, restaurants and discos. Moving south east of Lisbon the land becomes rather impoverished, consisting of stretches of vast undulating plains, dominated by cork plantations. Most people head for the walled town of Evora, an area steeped in two thousand years of history. The Portuguese consider the Minho area in the north to be the most beautiful part of their country, with its wooded mountain and wild coastline, a rural and conservative region with picturesque towns.

Population
10 million

Capital
Lisbon

Climate
The country enjoys a maritime climate with hot summers and mild winters with comparatively low rainfall in the south, heavy rain in the north.

Language
Portuguese, but English is widely spoken in cities, towns and larger resorts. French can be useful.

Telephone
The country code is 00 351.

Currency
The Euro (€)

Banks
Mon-Fri 08.30-11.45 and 13.00-14.45. Some large city banks offer a currency exchange 18.30-23.00.

Shops
Mon-Fri 09.00-13.00 and 15.00-19.00. Sat 09.00-13.00.

Public Holidays
New Year; Carnival (Shrove Tues); Good Fri; Liberty Day 25 Apr; Labour Day; Corpus Christi; National Day 10 June; Saints Days; Assumption 15 Aug; Republic Day 5 Oct; All Saints 1 Nov; Immaculate Conception 8 Dec; Christmas 24-26 Dec.

The Algarve, Portugal's southern-most province, is a true sunseekers paradise, offering all year round sunshine and over 150 miles of beautiful sandy beaches.

THE ALGARVE HAS ONE DISTRICT: FARO

The coast of the Algarve offers mile after mile of golden beaches and small sandy coves with interesting rock formations, interspersed with busy fishing ports. The capital, Faro, boasts excellent beaches, while the thriving fishing port and market centre of Lagos is one of the most popular destinations in the Algarve. Although the earthquake of 1755 caused great damage to Lagos, the streets and squares of the town have retained much of their charm. Within walking distance are some superb beaches, including Praia de Dona Ana, which is considered to be the most picturesque of all, and the smaller coves of Praia do Pinhão and Praia Camilo. Further inland and to the north, the hills mark the edge of a greener and more fertile region, brilliantly coloured by fig trees, orange groves and almond trees that come into blossom in the winter. Here you will also find a series of typical villages that have successfully preserved their ancestral traditions. The walled town of Silves has a Moorish fortress, 13th-century cathedral and archaeology museum. Nearby, the narrow streets of the old spa town of Monchique wind up a steep hillside, revealing magnificent views.

Places of interest

Albufeira: popular resort, daily market, good nightlife.

Cape São Vicente: south westernmost point of Europe.

Faro: monuments, churches, museums, Gothic cathedral, good shopping centre.

Sagres: 17th-century fortress.

Tavira: picturesque town, 17th- and 18th-century architecture.

Vilamoura: good sporting facilities including golf courses.

Cuisine of the region

Fresh fish and seafood are popular; the local speciality is *Ameijoas na Cataplana* (clams steamed in a copper pan). One of the most traditional dishes is *caldeiradas* (stew made with all kinds of different fish) and *sardinha assada* (grilled sardines). Given the abundance of trees in the region, figs and almonds are used a lot in desserts including *bolinhos de amêndoa* (small cakes made from marzipan and almond paste), which are moulded into the shape of fruits and vegetables in all kinds of different sizes.

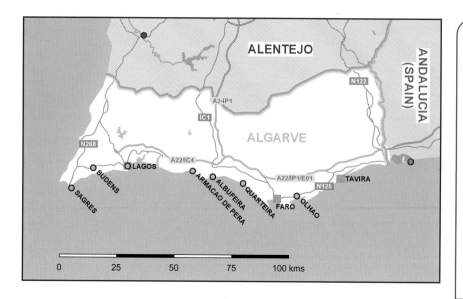

Albufeira

Parque de Campismo Albufeira

N395 Ferreiras - Albufeira, P-8200-555 Albufeira (Faro) T: 289 587 629. E: campingalbufeira@mail.telepac.pt
alanrogers.com/PO8210

The spacious entrance to this site will accommodate the largest of units (watch for severe speed bumps at the barrier). One of the better sites on the Algarve, it has pitches on fairly flat ground with some terracing, trees and shrubs giving reasonable shade in most parts. There are some marked and numbered pitches of 50-80 sq.m. Winter stays are encouraged with many facilities remaining open including a pool. An attractively designed complex of traditional Portuguese style buildings on the hill, with an unusually shaped pool and two more for children, forms the central area of the site. It has pleasant views, large terraces for sunbathing and is surrounded by a variety of flowers, shrubs and well watered lawns, complete with a fountain. The à la carte restaurant, impressive with its international cuisine, and the very pleasant self-service one; both have views across the three pools. A pizzeria, bars and a soundproofed disco are great for younger campers.

Facilities

Very clean toilet blocks include hot showers. Launderette. Very large supermarket. Tabac (English papers). Waiter and self-service restaurants. Pizzeria. Bars. Satellite TV. Soundproofed disco. Swimming pools. Tennis. Playground. Internet access. First aid post with doctor nearby. Car wash. ATM. Car hire. Off site: Site bus service from gate to Albufeira every 45 minutes (2 km). Theme parks nearby. Beaches.

Open: All year.

Directions

From N125 coast road or N264 (from Lisbon) at new junctions follow N395 to Albufeira. Site is about 2 km. on the left. GPS: 37.10639, -8.25361

Charges guide

Per unit incl. 2 persons	€ 23,50 - € 24,65
extra person	€ 5,50
child (4-10 yrs)	€ 2,70
electricity	€ 3,00

Armação de Pera

Parque de Campismo de Armação de Pera

P-8365 Armação de Pera (Faro) T: 282 312 260. E: camping_arm_pera@hotmail.com

alanrogers.com/PO8410

A pleasant site with a wide attractive entrance and a large external parking area, the 1,200 pitches at ths site are in zones on level grassy sand. They are marked by trees that provide some shade, and are easily accessed from tarmac and gravel roads. Electricity is available for most pitches. The facilities are good and the self service restaurant, bar and well stocked supermarket should cater for most needs. You can relax around the swimming pools. The disco near the entrance and café complex is soundproofed which should ensure a peaceful night for non-revellers. The site is within easy reach of Albufeira and Portimão.

Facilities

Three modern sanitary blocks provide British and Turkish style WCs and showers with hot water on payment. Facilities for disabled campers. A reader reports that maintenance can be variable. Laundry. Supermarket. Self-service restaurant. Three bars (1 all year). Swimming and paddling pools (May-Sept; charged per day; no lifeguard). Games and TV rooms. Tennis. Well maintained play area. ATM. Internet access. Off site: Bus to town from gate. Fishing, bicycle hire and watersports nearby.

Open: All year.

Directions

Site is west of Albufeira. Turn off N125/IC4 road in Alcantarilha, taking the EN269-1 towards the coast. Site is the second 'campismo' left on the roundabout just before Armação de Pera. There are further sites with similar names in the area, so be sure to find the right one. GPS: 37.10947, -8.35329

Charges guide

Per person	€ 2,50 - € 5,50
pitch	€ 3,00 - € 9,50
electricity (6A)	€ 2,50 - € 4,00

Budens

Parque de Campismo Quinta dos Carriços

Praia da Salema, Vila do Bispo, P-8650-196 Budens (Faro) T: 282 695 201. E: quintacarrico@oninet.pt

alanrogers.com/PO8440

This is an attractive and peaceful, valley site with a separate naturist area. A traditional tiled Portuguese style entrance leads you down a steep incline into this excellent and well maintained site which has a village atmosphere. With continuing improvements, the site has been developed over the years by the Dutch owner. It is spread over two valleys (which are real sun traps), with the 300 partially terraced pitches marked and divided by trees and shrubs (oleanders and roses). A small stream (dry when seen) meanders through the site. The most remote part, 250 m. from the main site, is dedicated to naturists.

Facilities

Four modern, spacious sanitary blocks, well tiled with quality fittings, are spotlessly clean. Washbasins with cold water, hot showers on payment. Washing machine. Excellent facility for disabled campers. Gas supplies. Well stocked shop. Restaurant (1/3-15/10). Bar (daily in season, once a week from 1/3-15/10). TV (cable). WiFi internet. Games room. Bicycle, scooter, moped and motorcycle hire. Off site: Fishing, golf and beach 1 km. Riding 8 km. Bus service to town (not beach) from site.

Open: All year.

Directions

Turn off RN125 (Lagos - Sagres) road at junction to Figuere and Salema (17 km. from Lagos); site is signed. GPS: 37.075427, -8.831338

Charges 2011

Per person	€ 5,65
child	€ 2,60
pitch and electricity	€ 12,15 - € 15,75
dog	€ 2,50
Discounts for long winter stays.	

Lagos

Orbitur Camping Valverde

Estrada da Praia da Luz, Valverde, P-8600-148 Lagos (Faro) T: 282 789 211. E: info@orbitur.pt

alanrogers.com/PO8200

A little over a kilometre from the village of Praia da Luz and its beach and about 7 km. from Lagos, this large, well run site is certainly worth considering for your stay in the Algarve. It has 650 numbered pitches, of varying sizes, which are enclosed by hedges. All are on flat ground or broad terraces with good shade in most parts from established trees and shrubs. The site has a swimming pool with a long curling slide and a paddling pool (under tens free, adults charged). This is an excellent site with well maintained facilities and good security.

Facilities

Six large, clean, toilet blocks have some washbasins and sinks with cold water only, and hot showers. Units for disabled visitors. Laundry. Motorcaravan services. Supermarket, shops, restaurant and bar complex with both self-service and waiter service in season (closed Nov). Takeaway. Coffee shop. Swimming pool (Apr-Sept) with slide and paddling pool (June-Sept). Playground. Tennis. Satellite TV in bar. Disco. Pub. WiFi throughout (free). Excursions. Off site: Bus service from site gate. Beach and fishing 1.5 km. Bicycle hire 3 km. Golf 10 km.

Open: All year.

Directions

From Lagos on N125 road, after 7 km. turn south to Praia da Luz. At the town follow signs for 'campismo'. The beach road is narrow and cobbled and is very challenging in a large unit. GPS: 37.09973, -8.71744

Charges guide

Per person	€ 5,80
child (5-10 yrs)	€ 3,00
pitch	€ 11,50 - € 12,50
electricity	€ 2,90 - € 3,50

For latest campsite news, availability and prices visit

alanrogers.com

Lagos

Camping Turiscampo

N125, Espiche, Luz, P-8600 Lagos (Faro) T: 282 789 265. E: info@turiscampo.com

alanrogers.com/PO8202

186

This good quality site has been thoughtfully refurbished and updated since it was purchased by the friendly Coll family, who are known to us from their previous Spanish site. The site provides 206 pitches for touring units, mainly in rows of terraces, all with electricity (6/10A) and some with shade. Twelve pitches (80 sq.m) have water and waste water. They vary in size (70-120 sq.m). The upper areas of the site are mainly used for bungalow accommodation (and are generally separate from the touring areas). A new, elevated Californian style pool plus a children's pool have been constructed. The supporting structure is a clever water cascade and surround and there is a large sun lounger area on astroturf. One side of the pool area is open to the road. The restaurant/bar has been tastefully refurbished and Roberto and his staff are delighted to use their excellent English, providing good fare at most reasonable prices.

Facilities

Four toilet blocks are well located around the site. Two have been refurbished, two are new and contain modern facilities for disabled campers. Hot water throughout. Facilities for children. Washing machines. Shop. Gas supplies. Restaurant/bar. Swimming pool (Mar-Oct). Bicycle hire. Entertainment in high season. Two cildren's playgrounds. Adult art workshops. Aqua gymnastics. Miniclub (5-12 yrs) in season. Boules. Archery. Sports field. Cable TV. Internet. WiFi (charged). Bungalows to rent. Off site: Bus to Lagos and other towns from Praia da Luz village 1.5 km. Fishing and beach 2 km. Golf 4 km. Sailing 5 km. Boat launching 5 km. Riding 10 km.

Open: All year.

Directions

Take exit 1 from the N125 Lagos - Vila do Bispo. The impressive entrance is about 3 km. on the right. GPS: 37.10111, -8.73278

Charges guide

Per unit incl. 2 persons and electricity	€ 16,20 - € 28,83
extra person	€ 3,28 - € 6,56
child (3-10 yrs)	€ 1,77 - € 3,28
dog	€ 1,01

Camping Cheques accepted.

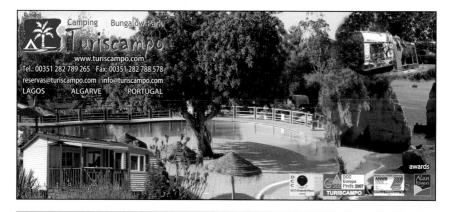

Olhão

Camping Olhão

Pinheiros de Marim, P-8700 Olhão (Faro) T: 289 700 300. E: parque.campismo@sbsi.pt

alanrogers.com/PO8230

This site, with around 800 pitches, is open all year. It has many mature trees providing good shade. The pitches are marked, numbered and in rows divided by shrubs, although levelling will be necessary and the trees make access tricky on some. There is electricity for 102 pitches (6A) and a separate area for tents. Permanent and long stay units take 20% of the pitches, the touring pitches filling up quickly in July and August, so arrive early. There is some noise nuisance from an adjacent railway. The site has a relaxed, casual atmosphere.

Facilities

Eleven sanitary blocks are adequate, clean when seen, and are specifically sited to be a maximum of 50 m. from any pitch. One block has facilities for disabled visitors. Laundry. Excellent supermarket. Kiosk. Restaurant/bar. Café and general room with cable TV. Playgrounds. Swimming pools (all year) and tennis courts (fees for both). Bicycle hire. Internet at reception. Off site: Bus service to the nearest ferry at Olhão 50 m. from site. Riding 1 km. Indoor pool 2 km. Fishing 2 km.

Open: All year.

Directions

Just over 1 km. east of Olhão, on EN125, take turn to Pinheiros de Marim. Site is back off the road on the left. Look for very large, white, triangular entry arch as the site name is different on the outside wall. GPS: 37.03528, -7.8225

Charges guide

Per person	€ 2,30 - € 4,70
child (5-12 yrs)	€ 1,30 - € 2,30
pitch with electricity	€ 5,25 - € 14,60

For latest campsite news, availability and prices visit

alanrogers.com

Quarteira

Orbitur Camping Quarteira

Estrada da Fonte Santa, avenida Sá Cameiro, P-8125-618 Quarteira (Faro) T: 289 302 826. E: info@orbitur.pt

alanrogers.com/PO8220

This is a large, busy attractive site on undulating ground with some terracing, taking 795 units. On the outskirts of the popular Algarve resort of Quarteira, it is 600 m. from a sandy beach which stretches for a kilometre to the town centre. Many of the unmarked pitches have shade from tall trees and there are a few small individual pitches of 50 sq.m. with electricity and water. There are 659 electrical connections. Like others along this coast, the site encourages long winter stays. There is a large restaurant and supermarket which have a separate entrance for local trade. The swimming pools (free for campers) are excellent, featuring pools for adults (with a large flume) and children (with fountains).

Facilities

Five toilet blocks provide British and Turkish style toilets, washbasins with cold water, hot showers plus facilities for disabled visitors. Washing machines. Motorcaravan services. Gas supplies. Supermarket. Self-service restaurant (closed Nov). Separate takeaway (from late May). Swimming pools (April-Sept). General room with bar and satellite TV. WiFi. Tennis. Open-air disco (high season). Off site: Bus from gate to Faro. Fishing 1 km. Bicycle hire (summer) 1 km. Golf 4 km.

Open: All year.

Directions

Turn off N125 for village of Almancil. In the village take road south to Quarteira. Site is on the left 1 km. after large, official town welcome sign.
GPS: 37.06666, -8.08333

Charges guide

Per person	€ 5,90
child (5-10 yrs)	€ 3,00
pitch	€ 12,70 - € 13,70
electricity	€ 2,90 - € 3,50

Off season discounts (up to 70%).

Orbitur — www.orbitur.pt · Online Reservations

Camping Orbitur Portugal

Tel:(+351) 214 857 400/9 · Mobile:(+351) 932 376 540 / 932 420 600 / 933 598 102 / 938 800 310
Fax:+351 214 857 410 / 214 872 167 · E-mail: info@orbitur.pt / bookings@orbitur.pt

Sagres

Orbitur Camping Sagres

Cerro das Moitas, P-8650-998 Sagres (Faro) T: 282 624 371. E: info@orbitur.pt

alanrogers.com/PO8430

Camping de Sagres is a pleasant site at the western tip of the Algarve, not very far from the lighthouse in the relatively unspoilt southwest corner of Portugal. With 960 pitches for tents and 120 for tourers, the sandy pitches, some terraced, are located amongst pine trees that give good shade. There are some hardstandings for motorhomes and electricity throughout. The fairly bland restaurant, bar and café/grill provide a range of reasonably priced meals. This is a reasonable site for those seeking winter sun, or as a base for exploring this 'Land's End' region of Portugal. It is away from the hustle and bustle of the more crowded resorts. The beaches and the town of Sagres (the departure point of the Portuguese navigators) with its fort, are a short drive.

Facilities

Three spacious toilet blocks are showing some signs of wear but provide hot and cold showers and washbasins with cold water. Washing machines. Motorcaravan services. Supermarket. Restaurant/bar and café/grill (all Easter and June-Oct). TV room. Satellite TV in restaurant. Bicycle hire. Barbecue area. Playground. Fishing. Medical post. Car wash. WiFi (free). Off site: Buses from village 1 km. Beach and fishing 2 km. Boat launching 8 km. Golf 12 km.

Open: All year.

Directions

From Sagres, turn off the N268 road west onto the EN268. After about 2 km. the site is signed off to the right. GPS: 37.02278, -8.94583

Charges guide

Per person	€ 4,90
child (5-10 yrs)	€ 2,50
caravan and car	€ 9,90 - € 10,90
electricity (6A)	€ 2,90 - € 3,50

Off season discounts (up to 70%).

For latest campsite news, availability and prices visit

alanrogers.com

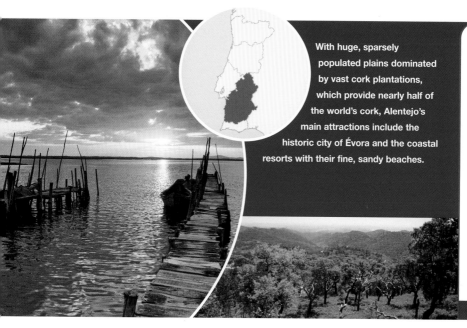

With huge, sparsely populated plains dominated by vast cork plantations, which provide nearly half of the world's cork, Alentejo's main attractions include the historic city of Évora and the coastal resorts with their fine, sandy beaches.

ALENTEJO IS MADE UP OF FOUR DISTRICTS: BEJA, ÉVORA, SETÚBAL AND PORTALEGRE

One of the most impressive cities in Portugal, Évora lies on a gently sloping hill rising out of the huge Alentejo plain. A city steeped in history, it was occupied by the Romans and Moors for centuries. With its narrow streets, of Moorish origin, and white-washed houses, it also boasts one of the best-preserved Roman temples in the country plus various palaces and monuments, the majority dating from the 14th-16th centuries. One of the more extraordinary sights can be found in the Capela dos Ossos in the church of São Francisco – adorning the walls and pillars of this chamber are the bones of more than 5,000 monks. On the Alentejo coast is the small peaceful town of Santiago do Cacém, which has two of the best beaches in Portugal. The nearby archaeological site at Miróbriga includes ruins of a hippodrome, several houses (some of which have mural paintings) and a clearly defined acropolis. Further south along the coast is Porto Côvo and the larger, popular resort of Vila Nova de Milfontes, which has a little castle and ancient port.

Places of interest

Arraiolos: ancient town, 17th-century castle, famous for its carpets.

Beja: provincial town founded by Julius Caesar, 13th-century castle.

Borba: pretty town, noted for its marble and wine.

Elvas: ancient fortress town, 15th-century aqueduct.

Estremoz: market town, medieval castle.

Odemira: quiet, characterful country town.

Reguengos de Monsaraz: charming, unspoiled village with whitewashed houses.

Vila Viçosa: attractive hillside town, 16th-century convent.

Cuisine of the region

Alentejo was traditionally an important wheat-growing region (it is frequently referred to as the 'granary of Portugal'). Local specialities include *sopa de cação* (skate soup), made from fish and bread, and *ensopado de borrego* (lamb stew). Cheeses of the region include *queijo de Serpa* and *queijos de Niza*, made from goats' milk. The *queijos de Évora*, made from ewes' milk, is smaller in size with a strong, spicy flavour. *Arroz Doce* (rice pudding topped with cinnamon) is the traditional dessert for festivals and parties and is to be found all over the country.

BEIRAS & CENTRE

FATIMA
TOMAR

SAO MARTINHO DO PORTO

0   25   50   75 kms

SANTO ANTONIO DAS AREIAS

SANTAREM

PORTALEGRE

N245

E802

LISBON & VALE DO TEJO

CORUCHE

ESTREMOZ

ELVAS

BORBA

LISBON

ARRAIOLOS   A6/E802,E90

A6,IP7

SETUBAL

EVORA

SESIMBRA

N256

IP2/E802

A2/E01

ALVITO

ALENTEJO

SANTIAGO DO CACEM

N121

BEJA

N260,IP8

PORTO COVO

N120,IC4

VILA NOVA
DE MILFONTES

N122

N263

ODEMIRA

A2/E01

ANDALUCIA
(SPAIN)

ALGARVE

For latest campsite news, availability and prices visit
alanrogers.com

Alvito

Camping Markádia

Barragem de Odivelas, Apartado 17, P-7920-999 Alvito (Beja) T: 284 763 141. E: markadia@hotmail.com
alanrogers.com/PO8350

A tranquil, lakeside site in an unspoilt setting, this will appeal most to those nature lovers who want to 'get away from it all' and to those who enjoy country pursuits such as walking, fishing and riding. There are 130 casual unmarked pitches on undulating grass and sand with ample electricity connections (16A). The site is lit but a torch is required. The friendly Dutch owner has carefully planned the site so each pitch has its own oak tree to provide shade. The open countryside and lake provide excellent views and a very pleasant environment, albeit somewhat remote. The lake is in fact a 1,000 hectare reservoir, and more than 150 species of birds can be found in the area. The stellar views in the very low ambient lighting are wonderful at night. The bar/restaurant with a terrace is open daily in season but weekends only during the winter. One can swim in the reservoir and canoes, pedaloes and windsurfers are available for hire. You may bring your own boat, although power boats, quads and motor scooters are not allowed on environmental grounds.

Facilities

Four modern, very clean and well equipped toilet blocks are built in traditional Portuguese style with hot water throughout. Washing machines. Motorcaravan services. Bar and restaurant (1/4-30/9). Shop (all year, bread to order). Lounge. Playground. Fishing. Boat hire. Tennis. Riding. Medical post. Car wash. Dogs are not accepted in July/Aug. Facilities and amenities may be reduced outside the main season. Off site: Swimming and boating in the lake.

Open: All year.

Directions

From A2 between Setubal and the Algarve take exit 10 on IP8 signed Ferreira and Beja. Take road to Torrao and 13 km. later, 1 km. north of Odivelas, turn right towards Barragem and site is 3 km. after crossing head of reservoir following small signs (one small section of poor road). GPS: 38.1812, -8.10293

Charges guide

Per person	€ 5,60
child (5-10 yrs)	€ 2,80
pitch incl. electricity	€ 14,00

Discounts of 10-20% outside June-Aug, and for longer stays. No credit cards.

Évora

Orbitur Camping Évora

Estrada de Alca Covas, Herdade Esphrragosa, P-700-703 Évora (Evora) T: 266 705 190. E: info@orbitur.pt
alanrogers.com/PO8340

Situated some 1.5 km. from the historic former provincial capital, this site is well located for an overnight stop. There is a small swimming pool and a simple small bar where snacks may be served. Most of the 285 sandy and good-sized touring pitches have 15A electricity and those in the older part of the site have well developed shade. The ground is probably not suitable for visitors using wheelchairs. The historic walled town and its castle (on the World Heritage list) and the surrounding area with its megalithic monuments are well woth visiting.

Facilities

Two toilet blocks are just acceptable. Free hot showers and British style WCs. Laundry. Motorcaravan services. Gas supplies. Bar and snacks (May-Oct). Bread to order. Swimming pool (June-Sept). Tennis. Mature play area (supervision necessary). Off site: Bicycle hire 2 km. Riding and golf 5 km. Supermarkets in the town.

Open: All year.

Directions

Site is 1.5 km. southwest of the town on the N380 road to Alcácovas. GPS: 38.557294, -7.925863

Charges guide

Per person	€ 5,10
child (5-10 yrs)	€ 2,60
pitch	€ 10,90 - € 11,90
electricity	€ 2,90 - € 3,50

Off season discounts (up to 70%).

For latest campsite news, availability and prices visit
alanrogers.com

Odemira

Parque de Campismo São Miguel

São Miguel, Odeceixe, P-7630-592 Odemira (Beja) T: 282 947 145. E: camping.sao.miguel@mail.telepac.pt
alanrogers.com/PO8170

Nestled in green hills near two pretty white villages, 4 km. from the beautiful Praia Odeceixe (beach) is the attractive camping park São Miguel. Unusually the site works on a maximum number of 700 campers, you find your own place (there are no defined pitches) under the tall trees, there are ample electrical points, and the land slopes away gently. Wooden chalet style accommodation to rent is in a separate area, but some mobile homes share the two traditional older style but clean sanitary blocks. The main building with its traditional Portuguese architecture is built around two sides of a large grassy square. It houses reception, a restaurant, bars and a supermarket. There are 'Lisbon Arcade' style verandas to sit under and enjoy a drink, coffee or meal while enjoying the view across the square to the pool, tennis courts and camping which is hidden under a canopy of trees.

Facilities

Two older style toilet blocks with British style WCs and free hot showers. Washing machines. Toilets and basins for disabled campers but no shower. Shop (June-Sept). Self-service restaurant (Mar-Oct). Bar, snacks and pizzeria (June-Sept). Satellite TV. Playground. Tennis (charged). Swimming pool (charged). Dogs are not accepted. Torches useful. Off site: Bus service from gate. Historic village of Odeceixe 2 km. Beach, fishing and sailing 4 km. Riding 20 km. Site is inside the Alentejo nature park.

Open: All year.

Directions

Between Odemira and Lagos on the N120 just before the village of Odeceixe on the main road well signed. GPS: 37.43868, -8.75568

Charges guide

Per person	€ 3,90 - € 6,10
child (5-10 yrs)	€ 2,20 - € 3,30
pitch	€ 7,80 - € 12,00
electricity	€ 3,00

Odemira

Zmar-Eco Camping Resort

Herdade ç de Mateus E.N. 393/1, San Salvador, P-7630 Odemira (Beja) T: 707 200 626
E: info@zmar.eu alanrogers.com/PO8175

Zmar is an exciting new project which should be fully open this year. The site is located near Zambujeira do Mar, on the Alentejo coast. This is a highly ambitious initiative developed along strict environmental lines. For example, renewable resources such as locally harvested timber and recycled plastic are used wherever possible and solar energy is used whenever practicable. Public indoor spaces have no air-conditioning, but there is adequate cooling through underfloor ventilation and electric fans where possible. Pitches are of 100 sq.m. and benefit from artificial shade. Caravans and wood-clad mobile homes are also available for rent. The swimming pool complex features a large outdoor pool and an indoor pool area with a wave machine and a wellness centre.

Facilities

Eight toilet blocks provide comprehensive facilities including for children and disabled visitors. Bar. Restaurant. Crêperie. Takeaway. Large supermarket. Swimming pool. Covered pool. Wellness centre. Sports field. Games room. Play area, farm and play house. Tennis. Bicycle hire. Activity and entertainment programme. Mobile homes and caravans for rent. Caravan repair and servicing. The site's own debit card system is used for payment at all facilities. Off site: Vicentina coast and the Alentejo natural park. Sines (birthplace of Vasco de Gama). Cycle and walking tracks. Sea fishing.

Open: All year.

Directions

From the N120 from Odemira to Lagos, at roundabout in the centre of Portas de Transval turn towards Milfontes. Take turn to Cabo Sardão and then Zambujeira do Mar. Site is on the left. GPS: 37.60422, -8.73142

Charges guide

Per unit incl. up to 4 persons and electricity	€ 20,00 - € 50,00
extra person	€ 5,00 - € 10,00
child (4-12 yrs)	€ 5,00

Camping Cheques accepted.

For latest campsite news, availability and prices visit
alanrogers.com

Porto Covo

Parque de Campismo Porto Covo

Estrada Municipal 554, P-7520-437 Porto Covo (Setubal) T: 269 905 136. E: camping.portocovo@gmail.com
alanrogers.com/PO8160

This is a site in a popular, small seaside resort where a fairly large proportion of the pitches are occupied by Portuguese units. However, it has a reasonable sense of space as you pass the security barrier to reception which is part of an uncluttered and attractively designed 'village square' area with some well established apartments for rent. The pitches are somewhat small but are hedged, reasonably level, all have electricity (5A) and are shaded. The beaches are a short walk and feature steep cliffs and pleasant sandy shores. If you do not want to venture out to the beach then the site has a swimming pool located behind the restaurant and with areas for sunbathing. A jolly bar and restaurant with terrace cleverly operates across the boundary of the site and it offers a varied Portuguese menu (popular with the locals) at very reasonable prices. A second smaller restaurant operates in the site in low season.

Facilities

The toilet blocks are clean with the usual amenities including hot showers. Motorcaravan services (outside gate). Restaurant (10/6-30/9). Bar with satellite TV. Shop in season. Recreation room with games and a TV. Play area. Swimming pools (10/6-30/9). Tennis. Barbecue areas. Boat trips and fishing trips organised. Off site: The village is a short walk with shops, bars and restaurants. Bus service to Lisbon 300 m. from site. Fishing 500 m. Riding 20 km. Golf 25 km.

Open: All year.

Directions

From E120-1 Cercal - Sines road (the road changes from the E120 at Tanganheira). Turn left (southwest) to Porto Covo and follow site signs. Do not be surprised to be led through a new housing estate; look for large white water tower with site logo. GPS: 37.85269, -8.78806

Charges guide

Per person	€ 2,50 - € 3,55
child (5-10 yrs)	€ 1,75
pitch	€ 5,25 - € 10,80
electricity	€ 2,65 - € 3,30
Reductions in low season.	

Santo Antonio das Areias

Camping Asseiceira

Caixa Postal 2, P-7330-204 Santo Antonio das Areias (Portalegre) T: 245 992 940
E: gary-campingasseiceira@hotmail.com alanrogers.com/PO8355

Set amongst unspoilt mountain scenery in the spectacular national park of Serra de São Mamede, Camping Asseiceira is a British owned site offering visitors a warm welcome. The Spanish border is just 8 km. away. Arranged in a small olive grove are 12 pitches with views rising up to the spectacular medieval castle and town of Marvão. This a pleasant, well looked after small site with few facilities, although the village of Santo António das Areias is only a few minutes walk with shops, restaurants and a bank. Access to the site is from a tarmac road suitable for most units. The site has a small swimming pool with a bar service from nearby and the owners are working hard to improve the facilities.

Facilities

A small clean and well equipped toilet block, built in wood, with hot water throughout. Small swimming pool with adjacent bar and terrace (June-Oct). WiFi. Off site: Village with shops, restaurants and bank 3 km. Daily train or bus to Lisbon. Golf 4 km. Riding 7 km. Fishing 8 km.

Open: All year.

Directions

From the IP1 take exit 7 onto the A6/IP7 towards Estremoz, then the IP2/E802 towards Portalegre. Continue past Portalegre to right turn for Marvão and Spain. Follow signs for Marvão and after roundabout at Portagem take first right and follow road to Santo António das Areias. At petrol station turn right down hill. Site is 400 m. on left. GPS: 39.41225, -7.35236

Charges guide

Per person	€ 3,00
pitch	€ 2,00 - € 6,00
awning	€ 3,00
electricity (16A)	€ 4,00

For latest campsite news, availability and prices visit
alanrogers.com

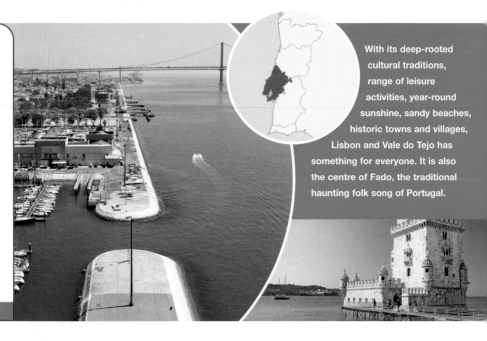

With its deep-rooted cultural traditions, range of leisure activities, year-round sunshine, sandy beaches, historic towns and villages, Lisbon and Vale do Tejo has something for everyone. It is also the centre of Fado, the traditional haunting folk song of Portugal.

THIS REGION IS DIVIDED INTO FOUR DISTRICTS: LEIRIA, LISBON, SANTARÉM AND SETÚBAL

(PART OF SETÚBAL ALSO FEATURES IN THE ALENTEJO REGION)

Standing on the banks of the river Tagus, Lisbon has been the capital of Portugal since 1255. Places of interest in the city include the medieval quarters of Alfama and Mouraria, with their cobbled streets and alleys, colourful buildings, markets and castles, and Belém, with its tower and the 16th-century Jerónimos monastery. Lisbon also boasts an assortment of museums. Not far from the capital lies the romantic town of Sintra, which has an array of cottages, manor houses and palaces. Its mountains also form part of the Sintra-Cascais Natural Park. Along the Atlantic coast, high sweeping cliffs lead down to white sandy beaches, backed by lagoons. Europe's westernmost point, Cabo da Roca, is found here as are plenty of coastal towns and villages including Peniche, Nazaré and Óbidos, a small medieval walled town with cobbled streets, tiny whitewashed houses and balconies brimming with flowers. Further inland, at Alcobaça, Tomar and Batalha, are ancient monasteries, with castles in Leiria, Tomar and Santarém. Recreational pursuits include water sports, fishing and golf. In summer there are open-air music festivals.

Places of interest

Estoril: casino, golf course and racing track.

Fátima: one of the most important centres of pilgrimage in the Catholic world.

Leiria: medieval royal castle, 16th-century cathedral, Romanesque church.

Mafra: 18th-century Palace-Convent, the largest Portuguese religious monument.

Santarém: castle, archaeology museum, Gothic convent and churches.

Sesimbra: picturesque small fishing town, medieval castle, the Lagoa de Albufeira is a favourite spot for windsurfers.

Setúbal: natural reserve, beaches, golf courses.

Tomar: 12th-century Templars' Castle, Gothic and Renaissance churches, 15th-century synagogue.

Cuisine of the region

Fish soups, stews and seafood are popular, including *sardinha assada* (grilled sardines) and *Bifes de Espardarte* (swordfish steaks). Sintra is famed for its cheesecakes, which according to ancient documents were already being made in the 12th century, and were part of the rent payments. Wine-producing regions include Azeitão, Bucelas, Carcavelos and Colares.

Caldeiradas: fish stews.

Queijadas: cheese tarts.

Pastéis de Belém: custard tarts.

Travesseiros: puff pastries stuffed with a sweet eggy mixture.

Cascais

Orbitur Camping Guincho

EN247, Lugar da Areia - Guincho, P-2750-053 Cascais (Lisbon) T: 214 870 450. E: info@orbitur.pt
alanrogers.com/PO8130

Although this is a popular site for permanent Portuguese units with 1,295 pitches, it is nevertheless quite attractively laid out among low pine trees and with the A5 autostrada connection to Lisbon (30 km), it provides a useful alternative to sites nearer the city. This is viewed as an alternative for visiting Lisbon, not a holiday site. There is a choice of pitches (small – mainly about 50 sq.m) mostly with electricity, although siting amongst the trees may be tricky, particularly when the site is full. Located behind sand dunes and a wide, sandy beach, the site offers a wide range of facilities. These include a fairly plain bar/restaurant, supermarket (all year), general lounge with pool tables, electronic games, TV room and a good laundry.

Facilities

Three sanitary blocks, one refurbished, are in the older style but are clean and tidy. Washbasins with cold water but hot showers. Facilities for disabled visitors. Washing machines and dryers. Motorcaravan services. Gas. Supermarket. Restaurant, bar and terrace. General room with TV. Tennis. Playground. Entertainment in summer. WiFi. Chalets to rent. Off site: Bus service from gate. Excursions. Riding 500 m. Beach 800 m. Fishing 1 km. Golf 3 km.

Open: All year.

Directions

Approach from either direction on the N247. Turn inland 6.5 km. west of Cascais at site sign. Travelling direct from Lisbon, the site is well signed as you leave the A5 at exit 12 and follow directions for Birre. GPS: 38.72117, -9.46667

Charges guide

Per person	€ 5,10
child (5-10 yrs)	€ 2,60
pitch	€ 10,90 - € 11,90
electricity	€ 2,90 - € 3,50
Off season discounts (up to 70%).	

For latest campsite news, availability and prices visit
alanrogers.com

Costa da Caparica

Orbitur Camping Costa da Caparica

Avenida Alfonso de Albuquerque, Quinta de Ste Antonio, P-2825-450 Costa da Caparica (Setubal)
T: 212 919 710. E: info@orbitur.pt **alanrogers.com/PO8150**

This site has relatively easy access to Lisbon (just under 20 km) via the motorway, by bus or even by bus and ferry if you wish. It is situated near a small resort, favoured by the Portuguese themselves, which has all the usual amenities plus a good sandy beach (200 m. from the site) and promenade walks. An area for touring units includes some larger pitches for motorcaravans. There are 240 pitches with electricity connections (long electricity leads may be needed). In addition, there are 140 permanent caravans. We see this very much as a site to visit Lisbon rather than for prolonged stays.

Facilities

The three toilet blocks have mostly British style toilets, washbasins with cold water and some hot showers – they come under pressure when the site is full. Facilities for disabled visitors. Washing machine. Motorcaravan services. Supermarket. Large bar/restaurant (not Nov). TV room (satellite). Playground. Off site: Bus service from site gate. Fishing 1 km. Riding 4 km. Golf 5 km.

Open: All year.

Directions

Cross the Tagus bridge (toll) on A2 motorway going south from Lisbon, immediately take the turning for Caparica and Trafaria. At 7 km. marker on IC20 turn right (no sign) - the site is at the second roundabout. GPS: 38.65595, -9.24107

Charges guide

Per person	€ 5,10
pitch incl. electricity	€ 13,80 - € 15,40

Fernao Ferro

Camping Parque Verde

Avenida do Casal Sapo, Fontainhas, P-2685-065 Fernao Ferro (Setubal) T: **212 108 999**
E: info@parqueverde.pt **alanrogers.com/PO8155**

This is very much a site for 812 permanent caravans but it has relatively easy access to Lisbon (just under 20 km) via the motorway and the impressive bridge. It is very much favoured by the Portuguese themselves. The site has all the usual amenities and a village-like central bar and restaurant complex. Most of the amenities are open all year round. There is a small area for touring units containing about 18 pitches and some larger pitches for motorcaravans. There are 20 mobile homes for rent. We see this site as useful for visiting Lisbon rather than for prolonged stays.

Facilities

The single toilet block for the touring units provides acceptable facilities. Washing machines. Supermarket. Bar, restaurants and snack bar (all year). Swimming pool and children's pool (1/5-30/9). Fitness facilities. Play area. Disco and other entertainment. Off site: Trains for Lisbon 4 km. Golf 5 km. Riding 12 km. Fishing 15 km.

Open: All year.

Directions

From the A2 toll road take exit 2 onto the N378 towards Sesimbra. Pass through Fernao Ferro and at roundabout follow for Coina into Fontainhas. Stay on tarred road meandering through Fontainhas (rua 25 de Abril) and site is on the right. GPS: 38.55056, -9.07167

Charges guide

Per unit incl. 2 persons and electricity	€ 16,00
extra person	€ 2,00 - € 3,00

Ferreira do Zêzere

Camping Quinta da Cerejeira

P-2240-333 Ferreira do Zêzere (Santarem) T: 249 361 756. E: info@cerejeira.com
alanrogers.com/PO8550

This is a delightful, small, family owned venture run by Gert and Teunie Verheij assisted by their children. It is a converted farm (quinta) and has been coaxed into a very special campsite. The pitches are on flat grass or on long terraces under fruit and olive trees. There are 30 pitches of which 18 have access to 6A electricity (long leads may be needed). There is a some shade and the site is full of rustic charm and craft works. It is very peaceful with views of the surrounding green hills from the charming vine-covered patio above a small swimming pool. You will notice the working well, no longer powered by a donkey but you can see where he used to circle to pump water.

Facilities

The single rustic sanitary building has British style WCs with hot showers. It could be busy at peak periods. Washing machine. No facilities for disabled campers. No shop but just ask and the baker calls daily. Bar with snacks and restaurant. Children's club room. Separate games and rest room with satellite TV. Artistic workshops. Internet terminals and WiFi. Swing for children. Torches useful. Off site: Bus service from town 1 km. Town has shops, bars and restaurants. Fishing 5 km. Watersports 5 km. Riding 11 km.

Open: 1 February - 30 November.

Directions

From Lisbon take A1/A23 to Torres Novas then IC3 to Tomar and N238 to Ferreira do Zêzere. Take road N348 to Vila de Rei and the site is 1 km. from Ferreira do Zêzere to the eastern side of town (do not go into the town). From Coimbra use the N238 road at an earlier exit. GPS: 39.703333, -8.278167

Charges guide

Per person	€ 3,00 - € 3,50
child (under 11 yrs)	€ 1,50 - € 2,00
pitch incl. car	€ 5,25 - € 7,75
electricity	€ 2,50

For latest campsite news, availability and prices visit
alanrogers.com

Foz do Arelho
Orbitur Camping Foz do Arelho
Rua Maldonado Freitas, P-2500-516 Foz do Arelho (Leiria) T: 262 978 683. E: info@orbitur.pt
alanrogers.com/PO8480

This is a large and roomy ex-municipal site and improvements are still taking place. It is 2 km. from the beach and has a new central complex with a most impressive swimming pool and separated children's pool with lifeguard. Pitches are generally sandy with some hardstandings. They vary in size and are unmarked on two main levels with wide tarmac roads. There is some shade and all touring pitches have electricity (5/15A). The large two storey, brick-faced building contains all the site's leisure facilities but has no ramped access. and there are no sanitary facilities anywhere on site for disabled campers. This building is somewhat sterile and the furniture is bland but there are pleasant views over the pool from the restaurant and terrace. This is a pleasant site with sound facilities for all. Some permanent Portuguese units are occupied in high season and weekends at other times.

Facilities	Directions
Four identical modern sanitary buildings (solar heating) with seatless British and Turkish style WCs and free showers. Washing machine in one. Facilities for disabled campers at the block near reception. Supermarket. Bar/snacks and restaurant (closed Nov). Bread to order (1/9-30/6). Children's club. Games room. Small new amphitheatre. Playground – supervision needed. Bus service. Doctor's room. Torches useful. Off site: Bus 500 m. Seaside town 2 km. Fishing 2 km. Three supermarkets in Foz do Arelho.	Site is north of Lisbon and west of Caldos la Rainha. From the A8 take N360 to Foz do Arelho. Site is well signed. GPS: 39.43067, -9.20083

Charges guide

Per person	€ 5,10
child (5-10 yrs)	€ 2,60
pitch	€ 10,90 - € 11,90
electricity	€ 2,90 - € 3,50

Open: All year.

Lisboa
Lisboa Camping-Parque Municipal de Monsanto
Estrada da Circunvalacao, P-1400-061 Lisboa (Lisbon) T: 217 628 200. E: info@lisboacamping.com
alanrogers.com/PO8140

This very large site is professionally operated by many uniformed staff, providing a quality service at a good price. The wide entrance with its ponds, fountains and the trees, lawns and flowering shrubs leading up to the two swimming pools, is a most attractive feature. On sloping ground, the site's many terraces are well shaded by trees and shrubs. The 400 good pitches include 170 serviced pitches on concrete hardstandings. There is a huge separate area for tents, and 70 chalet style bungalows are for hire. Central Lisbon is 8 kilometres, with two bus routes giving a regular service from the gate. A decent beach is 10 kilometres. Although a city site, it is big enough to generate a park atmosphere and when we visited we spotted many red squirrels and an abundance of birds. This is a most pleasant site for visiting Lisbon or just relaxing using the impressive facilities.

Facilities	Directions
Eight solar-powered toilet blocks contain quality facilities, including those for disabled campers. Launderette. Motorcaravan service point. Shops, bar and restaurants. Two swimming pools (with lifeguard; May-Sept). Tennis. Minigolf. Sports field. Playgrounds. Roman theatre. Entertainment in high season. General and TV (cable) rooms. Internet. Organised excursions. Off site: Excellent bus service from site gate. Lisbon city. Bicycle hire 2 km. Golf 5 km. Beaches 10 km. Riding 16 km.	From Lisbon take A5 motorway towards Estoril and site is signed from junction 4 onto the 1C17 (huge site signs at first exit to Buraca). The site is just on the right. Enter to the right of the fountain on the tiled road. GPS: 38.72477, -9.20737

Charges guide

Per unit incl. 2 persons and electricity	€ 19,00 - € 28,00
extra person	€ 5,00 - € 6,50
child (6-12 yrs)	€ 2,10 - € 3,00

Open: All year.

For latest campsite news, availability and prices visit
alanrogers.com

Nazaré
Orbitur Camping Valado

Rua dos Combatentes do Ultramar 2, Valado, P-2450-148 Nazaré (Leiria) T: 262 561 111. E: info@orbitur.pt

alanrogers.com/PO8110

This popular site is close to the old, traditional fishing port of Nazaré which has now become something of a holiday resort and popular with coach parties. The large sandy beach in the town (about 2 km. steeply downhill from the site) is sheltered by headlands and provides good swimming. The campsite is on undulating ground under tall pine trees. There are said to be 503 pitches and, although some smallish individual pitches with electricity and water can be reserved, the bulk of the site is not marked out and units are close together during July/August. About 420 electrical connections are available.

Facilities

The three toilet blocks have British and Turkish style WCs, washbasins (some cold water) and 17 hot showers, all very clean when inspected. Laundry. Motorcaravan services. Gas supplies. Supermarket. Bar, snack bar and restaurant with terrace (Easter and June-Oct). TV/general room. Playground. Tennis. WiFi. Off site: Bus service 20 m. Fishing and bicycle hire 2 km.

Open: 1 February - 30 November.

Directions

Site is on the Nazaré - Alcobaca N8-5 road, 2 km. east of Nazaré. GPS: 39.5934, -9.02783

Charges guide

Per person	€ 4,30
pitch	€ 8,60 - € 9,60
electricity	€ 2,90 - € 3,50

Off season discounts (up to 70%).

Nazaré
Camping Caravaning Vale Paraiso

186

EN242, P-2450-138 Nazaré (Leiria) T: 262 561 800. E: info@valeparaiso.com

alanrogers.com/PO8460

A pleasant, well managed site, Vale Paraiso improves every year, with the latest additions being new reception buildings and pool areas. The owners are keen to welcome British visitors and English is spoken. The site is by the main N242 road in eight hectares of undulating pine woods. There are 650 shady pitches, many on sandy ground only suitable for tents. For other units there are around 250 individual pitches of varying size on harder ground with electricity available. A large range of sporting and leisure activities includes an excellent outdoor pool and paddling pool with sunbathing areas. The adventure playground is very safe with new equipment. There is a pleasant bar, innovative takeaway selling roasts and a lower level restaurant/bar. Several long beaches of white sand are within 2-15 km. allowing windsurfing, sailing, surfing and body-boarding. Entertainment for children and evening entertainment is organised in season. Nazaré is an old fishing village with narrow streets, a harbour and marina and many outdoor bars and cafés, with a lift to Sitio. There is much of historical interest in the area although the mild Atlantic climate is also conducive to just relaxing.

Facilities

Spotless sanitary facilities have hot water throughout. Nearly all WCs are British style. Modern facilities for disabled campers. Baby baths. Washing machine and dryers. Motorcaravan services. Supermarket (1/5-30/9). Restaurant (15/5-15/9). Café/bar with satellite TV. Takeaway. Tabac. Swimming and paddling pools (Mar-Sept; free for under 11s). Pétanque. Leisure games. Amusement hall. Bicycle hire. Safety deposit. Gas supplies. E-mail and fax facilities. WiFi (free). Apartments, tents and mobile homes to rent. Off site: Bus service from gate. Fishing 2 km. Boat launching 2 km. Riding 6 km.

Open: All year except 19-27 December.

Directions

Site is 2 km. north of Nazaré on the EN242 Marinha Grande road. GPS: 39.62028, -9.05639

Charges 2011

Per unit incl. 2 persons and electricity	€ 21,20 - € 26,70
extra person	€ 3,25 - € 4,85
child (3-10 yrs)	€ 1,60 - € 2,40
dog	€ 2,90

Credit cards accepted for amounts over € 150. Camping Cheques accepted.

Outeiro do Louriçal
Campismo O Tamanco

Rua do Louriçal 11, Casas Brancas, P-3105-158 Outeiro do Louriçal (Leiria) T: **236 952 551**
E: tamanco@mac.com **alanrogers.com/PO8400**

O Tamanco is a peaceful countryside site, with a homely almost farmstead atmosphere; you will have chickens and ducks wandering around and there is a Burro here. The young Dutch owners, Irene and Hans, are sure to give you a warm welcome at this delightful little site. The 65 good sized pitches are separated by cordons of all manner of fruit trees, ornamental trees and flowering shrubs, on level grassy ground. There is electricity (6/16A) to all the pitches and 5 pitches are suitable for large motorhomes. The site is lit and there is nearly always space available. The swimming pool is very pleasant, as is the small bar and a restaurant (with vegetarian menu options). Pay a visit to the lively town of Coimbra, the roman sites in Conimbriga and the place of pilgrimage, Fatima. One can fish and swim in a nearby lake and the resort beaches are a short drive. There is some road noise on pitches at the front of the site.

Facilities

The single toilet block provides very clean and generously sized facilities including washbasins in cabins. No easy access for disabled visitors. As facilities are limited they may be busy in peak periods. Hot water throughout. Washing machine. Bar/restaurant. Roofed patio with fireplace. TV room/lounge (satellite). Internet access. Swimming pool. Off site: Bus service 1 km. Lake 2 km. Beach 11 km. Market in nearby Lourical every Sunday. Lake 12 km.

Open: All year.

Directions

From the A17 (Lisboa - Porto), take exit 5 for Carrico, turn right at the roundabout and O Tamanco is on the left. GPS: 39.99455, -8.78584

Charges guide

Per unit incl. 2 persons and electricity	€ 18,00
extra person	€ 4,00
child (up to 10 yrs)	€ 2,20
dog	€ 0,85

Winter discounts up to 40%. No credit cards.

Sâo Pedro de Moel
Orbitur Camping Sâo Pedro de Moel

Rua Volta do Sete, P-2430 Sâo Pedro de Moel (Leiria) T: **244 599 168**. E: info@orbitur.pt
alanrogers.com/PO8100

This quiet and very attractive site is situated under tall pines, on the edge of the rather select small resort of Sâo Pedro de Moel. This is a shady site which can be crowded in July and August. The 525 pitches are in blocks and unmarked (cars may be parked separately) with 404 electrical connections. A few pitches are used for permanent units. Although there are areas of soft sand, there should be no problem in finding a firm place. The large restaurant and bar are modern as is the superb swimming pool, paddling pool and flume (there is a lifeguard). The attractive, sandy beach is about 500 m. walk downhill from the site (you can take the car, although parking may be difficult in the town) and is sheltered from the wind by low cliffs.

Facilities

Four clean toilet blocks have mainly British style toilets (some with bidets), some washbasins with hot water. Hot showers are mostly in one unisex block. Laundry. Motorcaravan services. Gas supplies. Supermarket. Large restaurant and bar with terrace (closed Nov). Swimming pools (1/3-30/9). Satellite TV. Games room. Playground. Tennis. WiFi. Off site: Bus service 100 m. Beach 500 m. Fishing 1 km.

Open: All year.

Directions

Site is 9 km. west of Marinha Grande, on the right as you enter Sâo Pedro de Moel. GPS: 39.75883, -9.02229

Charges guide

Per person	€ 5,10
child (5-10 yrs)	€ 2,60
pitch	€ 10,90 - € 11,90
electricity	€ 2,90 - € 3,50

Off season discounts (up to 70%).

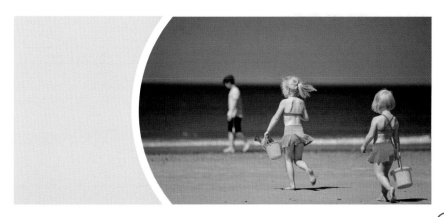

For latest campsite news, availability and prices visit
alanrogers.com

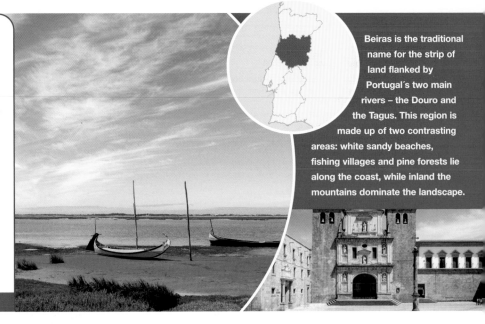

Beiras is the traditional name for the strip of land flanked by Portugal's two main rivers – the Douro and the Tagus. This region is made up of two contrasting areas: white sandy beaches, fishing villages and pine forests lie along the coast, while inland the mountains dominate the landscape.

Beiras & Centre

BEIRAS HAS FIVE DISTRICTS: AVEIRO, COIMBRA, CASTELO BRANCO, GUARDA AND VISEU

One of Europe's oldest university towns, Coimbra was Portugal's capital from 1143 to 1255. The university, founded in 1290, has kept its academic traditions, as seen in the black-capped students, in the soulful tones of the fado de Coimbra (a traditional song sung to the sound of guitars by the students) and in the Queima das Fitas (Burning of the Ribbons), a boisterous celebration of graduating students. Coimbra also boasts a Romanesque cathedral and south of the town lies Conímbriga, with the most important Roman remains in Portugal. Surrounded by the original walls, the archaeological site features an early Christian burial ground, a set of hot springs and a museum. Further north lies Aveiro. Famous for its lagoon, the town is criss-crossed by canals where colourfully painted moliceiro boats sail. To the east lies the Serra de Estrela, the highest mountain range in the country. It is home to the textile town of Covilha, attractive villages including Gouveia, Manteigas and Seia, plus the mountain resort of Guarda. Along the coast, the pretty seaside resorts of São Martinho do Porto, Nazaré and Figueira da Foz offer fine sandy beaches, good seafood restaurants and water sports facilities.

Places of interest

Belmonte: hilltop town, castle, Romanesque-Gothic church.

Bussaco: national park founded by monks in the 6th century.

Castelo Branco: 13th-century castle, medieval quarter, 16th- and 18th-century churches.

Curia and *Luso:* spa towns.

Monsanto: historic village, 12th-century castle, 18th-century manor-houses.

Viseu: remains of Gothic walls, cathedral.

Cuisine of the region

Roast pork, lamb stew, seafood and fresh fish are popular, including *truta* (trout) from the mountains of Serra da Estrela. The famous ewe's milk cheese *Queijo da Serra*, is also produced in the mountains, and can be bought at Cheese Fairs held in villages and towns throughout the region during February and March. Regional desserts include hard and sweet biscuits, pancakes and sponge cake (*ovos-moles*, *pão-de-ló*).

Chanfana: lamb stewed in red wine.

Leitão assado da Bairrada: roast pork.

Arganil

Camping Municipal Arganil

EN17 km 5 Sarzedo, Sarzedo, P-3300 Arganil (Coimbra) T: 235 205 706. E: camping@mailtelepao.pt

alanrogers.com/PO8330

This peaceful, inland site is attractively located in the hamlet of Sarzedo, some 2 km. from the town of Arganil. A spacious and well planned site, it is of a high quality for a municipal and prices are very reasonable! Delightfully situated among pine trees above the River Alva where one can swim, fish or canoe. The 150 pitches, most with electricity (15A), are of a reasonable size, mainly on flat sandy grass terraces and most shaded by tall trees. The site is kept beautifully clean and neat and access roads are tarmac. An excellent, small restaurant has an unusual attached bar with terrace.

Facilities

Sanitary facilities are clean and well maintained, with Turkish and British style WCs, controllable hot showers, washbasins in semi-private partitioned cabins and a hairdressing area. Ramped entrances make it suitable for disabled visitors. Washing machines. Bar, restaurant and snacks. Shop (July-Sept). TV room. Tennis. Off site: Bus service 50 m. River beach and fishing 100 m. Watersports 200 m. Swimming pool in nearby Arganil. Golf 25 km.

Open: All year.

Directions

From Coimbra on the IC2 take exit 8 onto the IP3 towards Viseu. Take exit 13 onto the IP6 (N17) towards Arganil and onto the N324-4 to Sarzedo (site signed). Ignore the first site sign in Avelar as there is better access 500 m. further up the road on the right, also signed. GPS: 40.23333, -8.08333

Charges guide

Per person	€ 1,60 - € 1,80
child (5-10 yrs)	€ 1,10 - € 1,30
pitch	€ 3,10 - € 7,00
electricity	€ 2,00 - € 2,40

For latest campsite news, availability and prices visit
alanrogers.com

Aveiro

Orbitur Camping São Jacinto

EN327 km 20, São Jacinto, P-3800-909 Aveiro (Aveiro) T: 234 838 284. E: info@orbitur.pt
alanrogers.com/PO8050

This small site is in the São Jacinto nature reserve, on a peninsula between the Atlantic and the Barrinha, with views to the mountains beyond. The area is a weekend resort for locals and can be crowded in high season – it may therefore be difficult to find space in July/August, particularly for larger units. This is not a large site, taking 169 units on unmarked pitches, but in most places trees provide natural limits and shade. Swimming and fishing are both possible in the adjacent Ria, or the sea, a 20-minute walk from a guarded back gate.

Facilities

Two toilet blocks, very clean when inspected, contain the usual facilities. Dishwashing and laundry sinks. Washing machine and ironing board in a separate part of the toilet block. Motorcaravan services. Shop. Restaurant, bar and snack bar (Easter, June-Oct). Attractive new playground. Five bungalows to rent. Off site: Bus service 20 m. Fishing 200 m. Bicycle hire 10 km.

Open: 1 January - 6 October.

Directions

Turn off N109 at Estarreja to N109-5 to cross bridge over Ria da Gosta Nova and on to Torreira and São Jacinto. From Porto go south N1/09, turn for Ovar on the N327 which leads to São Jacinto.
GPS: 40.67497, -8.72295

Charges guide

Per person	€ 4,30
pitch	€ 11,40
electricity	€ 2,90 - € 3,50
Off season discounts (up to 70%).	

Figueira da Foz

Orbitur Camping Gala

EN109 km 4 Gala, P-3080-458 Figueira da Foz (Coimbra) T: 233 431 492. E: info@orbitur.pt
alanrogers.com/PO8090

One of the best Orbitur sites, Gala has around 450 pitches on sandy terrain under a canopy of pine trees and is well cared for. Some pitches near the road are rather noisy. One can drive or walk the 300 m. from the back of the site to a private beach; you should swim with caution when it is windy – the warden will advise. The site fills in July/August and units may be very close together, but there should be plenty of room at other times. Besides the beach, Coimbra and the nearby Roman remains are worth visiting.

Facilities

The three toilet blocks have British and Turkish style toilets, individual basins (some with hot water) and free hot showers. Laundry. Motorcaravan services. Gas supplies. Supermarket and restaurant/bar with terrace. Lounge. Open-air pool (June-Sept). Playground. Tennis. TV. WiFi throughout. Doctor visits in season. Car wash area. Off site: Beach 300 m. Fishing 1 km. Bicycle hire and riding 3 km.

Open: All year.

Directions

Coming from the north, the site is 4 km. south of Figueira da Foz beyond the two rivers; turn off N109 1 km. from bridge on southern edge of Gala, look for Orbitur sign on roundabout it is then 600 m. to site.
GPS: 40.11850, -8.85683

Charges guide

Per person	€ 5,10
pitch	€ 10,90 - € 11,90
electricity	€ 2,90 - € 3,50
Off season discounts (up to 70%).	

Idanha-a-Nova

Orbitur Barragem de Idhana-a-Nova

Barragem Marechal Carmona, P-6060-192 Idanha-a-Nova (Castelo Branco) T: 277 202 793
E: idanha@orbitur.pt alanrogers.com/PO8360

This attractive and well laid out site is located in quiet, unspoilt countryside close to a reservoir near the small town of Idanha-a-Nova. The site has around 500 spacious unmarked pitches on wide grassy terraces and there is a little shade from young trees. Electricity (16A) is included in the price. Amenities include tennis courts with stadium-style spectator seating and a medium sized swimming pool with paddling pool, together with several playgrounds. A good supermarket, restaurant, bar and terrace complex is located centrally on site but these are only open in high season.

Facilities

Four large toilet blocks, built in the traditional Portuguese style, provide quality installations with some washbasins in private cabins, hot showers with dividers, foot baths and facilities for disabled visitors. Laundry. Supermarket (1/7-30/9). Café and bar (1/6-30/9). Restaurant (1/7-20/9). Swimming pool. Tennis. TV room. Vending machines. Medical post. Car wash. Canoe hire. Off site: Small town of Idanha-a-Nova.

Open: All year.

Directions

Using the N240, turn off at Ladoeiro onto the N354 (32 km. east of Castelo Branco) and follow signs to Idanha. After 16 km. follow signs for 'Campismo'. Do not turn towards Idanha-a-Nova or approach via this town. GPS: 39.950485, -7.187011

Charges guide

Per unit incl. 2 persons and electricity	€ 15,60 - € 26,00
extra person	€ 2,58 - € 4,30
child (5-10 yrs)	€ 1,32 - € 2,20

For latest campsite news, availability and prices visit
alanrogers.com

Ilhavo
Camping Costa Nova

Quinta dos Patos, Costa Nova do Prado, P-3830 Gafanha da Encarnação - Ilhavo (Aveiro) T: 234 393 220
E: info@campingcostanova.com alanrogers.com/PO8060

Camping Costa Nova is situated between a river (Ria de Aveiro) and the sea in a protected natural reserve. There is direct access to a large sandy beach via a wooden walkway over the dunes. The 300 grassy pitches are provided with electricity hook ups (10A). This site is ideal for those who enjoy watersports and the surroundings offer plenty of sites of interest for exploration. The site boasts a large bar/restaurant and a café with TV and internet access. English speaking visitors are welcomed and this sheltered site also attracts many for winter stays. Apartments are available for let.

Facilities

Three toilet blocks are well spaced around the site and offer adequate facilities with free hot water. Laundry room. Supermarket. Bar (all season). Restaurant (1/7-31/8). Takeaway. Snack bar. Shop. Games room. Disco. TV. Play area. Football field. Internet access. Off site: Beach 500 m. Fishing. Golf 600 m.

Open: 2 February - 31 December.

Directions

On the IP5 travelling from Aveiro east towards Barra, cross the bridge. At roundabout take third exit and site is well signed. GPS: 40.59972, -8.75139

Charges guide

Per unit incl. 2 persons	
and electricity	€ 12,70 - € 16,40
extra person	€ 2,50 - € 3,80
child (5-10 yrs)	€ 1,25 - € 1,90
dog	€ 1,50 - € 1,70

Praia de Mira
Orbitur Camping Mira

Estrada Florestal no 1 km 2, Dunas de Mira, P-3070-792 Praia de Mira (Coimbra) T: 231 471 234
E: info@orbitur.pt alanrogers.com/PO8070

A small, peaceful seaside site set in pinewoods, Orbitur Camping Mira is situated to the south of Aveiro and Vagos, in a quieter and less crowded area. It fronts onto a lake at the head of the Ria de Mira, which eventually runs into the Aveiro Ria. A back gate leads directly to the sea and a wide quiet beach 300 m. away. A road runs alongside the site boundary where the restaurant complex is situated, resulting in some road noise. The site has around 225 pitches on sand, which are not marked but have trees creating natural divisions. Electricity and water points are plentiful. The site has an inexpensive restaurant, snack bar, lounge bar and TV room. A medium sized supermarket is well stocked, with plenty of fresh produce. The Mira Ria is fascinating, with the brightly painted, decorative 'moliceiros' (traditional fishing boats).

Facilities

The modern toilet blocks are clean, with 14 free hot showers and washing machines. Facilities for disabled visitors. Motorcaravan services. Gas supplies. Shop. Restaurant, bar and snack bar (Easter, June-Oct). TV room. Play area. Bicycle hire. WiFi at the bar. Bungalows (7) to rent. Off site: Bus service 150 m. (summer only). Fishing 500 m. Indoor pool, lake swimming and riding at Mira 7 km.

Open: 1 January - 30 November.

Directions

Take the IP5 (A25) southwest to Aveiro then the A17 south to Figuera da Foz. Then take the N109 north to Mira and follow signs west to Praia (beach) de Mira. GPS: 40.4533, -8.79902

Charges guide

Per person	€ 4,90
child (5-10 yrs)	€ 2,50
pitch	€ 8,60 - € 11,90
electricity	€ 2,90 - € 3,50

Off season discounts (up to 70%).

For latest campsite news, availability and prices visit
alanrogers.com

Sátão

Camping Quinta Chave Grande

Casfreires, Ferreira d'Aves, P-3560-043 Sátão (Viseu) T: 232 665 552. E: chave-grande@sapo.pt
alanrogers.com/PO8335

Quinta Chave Grande is a good quality campsite with friendly Dutch owners. It is set in a rural valley, close to many charming old villages, yet also only 25 km. from the provincial capital of Viseu, with its museums, churches and beautiful old town centre. The site occupies a large area and there are 150 unmarked touring pitches, although some are defined by trees. Electricity (6A) is available to all but long leads may be required. Larger units can be accommodated and there is a separate terraced area for tents. Torches are essential. For those who enjoy walking there are eight marked walking tours starting from the campsite. They take between 90 minutes and four hours, and each tour provides an opportunity to see some magnificent scenery with the occasional glimpse of wildlife.

Facilities

Two modern toilet blocks, one with private en-suite cubicles for use by families and for visitors with disabilities. Service wash available. No shop but local tradesmen visit the site. Bar (all season). Swimming pool and children's pool (1/5-1/10). Fenced play area. Organised events for children and teenagers in July/Aug. Tennis. Boules. Off site: Fishing 5 km. Riding 25 km. Golf 40 km. Marked walks. Good touring area.

Open: 15 March - 31 October.

Directions

From A25 Guarda - Viseu road take exit 19, than at the IP5 take exit 17 to Sátão. Take the N229 northeast to Sátão. Site is very well signed along road and is 12 km. northeast of Sátão. GPS: 40.8227, -7.69609

Charges guide

Per person	€ 4,50
child (3-16 yrs)	€ 2,50
pitch incl. car	€ 7,00 - € 8,00
electricity	€ 3,00

Vagos

Orbitur Camping Vagueira

Gafanha da Vagueira, Gafanha da Boa Hora, P-3840-254 Vagos (Aveiro) T: 234 797 526. E: vagueira@orbitur.pt
alanrogers.com/PO8040

This is a large site set 1.5 km. from the beach and 500 m. from the Ria da Gosta Nova river. It is shaded under tall pine trees and has comprehensive facilities and reasonable prices. The 800 pitches are unmarked, on sand and pine needles with a large number of permanent Portuguese units which are here in high season and weekends at other times. Groups are taken in high season. All touring pitches have electricity (6A). In sympathy with the surroundings, the modern buildings have clean lines and include a restaurant and bar with a disco area outside where music is played at weekends. This complex extends into a large rectangle holding the extremely large supermarket and facilities listed below. The whole site is securely fenced and is kept remarkably clean. The rules of peace between 23.00-07.00 are firmly applied. This is a good family site if you do not need a pool and have transport to get you to the beach. The seaside town here is a mixture of buildings and services which seem to be unsure of which future direction to take, but the beach is excellent.

Facilities

Seven modern sanitary buildings with British and Turkish style WCs and free showers. Facilities for disabled campers (unlocked). Washing machines. Bar/snacks and separate restaurant (June-Sept). Large supermarket. Children's club. Outdoor disco. Games room. Playground. Tennis (charge). Satellite TV. Internet room and WiFi. Torches useful. Off site: Seaside town has shops bars and restaurants. Bus 500 m. River fishing 500 m. Watersports at beach 1.5 km. Golf and riding 1 km.

Open: All year.

Directions

Site is south of Aveiro. Take N109 south from Aveiro towards Mira. At Vagos take the N333 right turn towards Vagueira. Site is well signed at this turn and is just off the roundabout you arrive at on the beach road. GPS: 40.55792, -8.74517

Charges guide

Per person	€ 1,83 - € 3,65
child	€ 0,95 - € 1,85
pitch and car	€ 3,25 - € 8,50
electricity	€ 2,00

Camping Cheques accepted.

For latest campsite news, availability and prices visit
alanrogers.com

Originally inhabited by Celtics, Romans and Moors, the North is a region steeped in history. Renowned for its beautiful countryside, the River Douro winds its way past mountains, valleys, vineyards and cliffs until it reaches the sandy beaches of the Atlantic coast near the city of Porto.

THE REGION COMPRISES FIVE DISTRICTS: BRAGA, BRAGANÇA, PORTO, VIANA DO CASTELO AND VILA REAL

Situated in the north western corner of Portugal, the Costa Verde boasts lush green pine forests and unspoilt sandy beaches, dotted with picturesque seaside villages, including Caminha and Vila Nova de Cerveira. It is also renowned for its wine, being the home of Port and Vinho Verdo. Located on the banks of the River Douro, the attractive city of Porto is the centre of the Port wine trade – free tastings are offered at the wine cellars in Vila Nova de Gaia – and terraced vineyards can be found across the Douro Valley. The region is also a perfect place for walking, mountain trekking, canoeing or simply relaxing in the spa towns of Carvalhelhos, Chaves and Pedras Salgadas. Vidago has a magnificent park with swimming pools and a golf course, while the mountains of Peneda, Soajo and Gerês form the Peneda Geres National Park, an area covering 170,000 acres, with an abundance of wildlife. Vila Nova de Foz is the centre for visits to the Côa Archaeological Park, which houses one of the world's largest collections of outdoor Palaeolithic rock art, dating back 22,000 years.

Places of interest

Barcelos: medieval walled town with dungeon, ceramics museum, archaeology museum.

Bragança: medieval castle and walls, 16th-century cathedral, railway museum with 19th-century locomotives and carriages.

Chaves: Roman bridge, 14th-century castle with Archaeology and Epigraphy Museum.

Guimarães: medieval castle and walls, palace.

Lamego: medieval castle, 12th-century fortress.

Ponte de Lima: beautiful small town, Roman bridge, medieval towers, manor houses.

Viana do Castelo: town famous for its handicrafts and colourful regional costumes.

Vila do Conde: ancient medieval shipyard, famous for its manufactured lace.

Cuisine of the region

Typical dishes include *bacalhau* (dried and salted cod), *rabanadas, papos-de-anjo* and *barrigas-de-freiras* (sweetmeats). Porto has its own tripe dish *Tripas à moda do Porto.*

The Minho region is renowned for its *Vinhos Verdes*, whose vines are grown on trellises (being suspended high in the air on special frames). In the Douro region, the vines are grown on terraces, giving the impression of huge natural staircases leading down to the banks of the river. Both red and white wines are produced here including the famous *Vinho do Porto* (Port Wine).

Caldo verde: thick soup made with green cabbage, potatoes and spicy sausage.

Feijoada à transmontana: bean stew.

Porto & North

GALICIA (SPAIN)

CAMINHA ○ A3/E01

VIANA DO CASTELO
DARQUE ○

○ CAMPO DO GERES

BARCELOS ■

BRAGA ■

POVOA DE VARZIM ○ ■ GUIMARAES

VILA DO CONDE ○

■ VIDAGO

PORTO & NORTH (PORTUGAL)

A4/E82

PORTO ○ ■

A1/E01

CASTILLA Y LEON (SPAIN)

BEIRAS & CENTRE

0   25   50   75   100 kms

Caminha

Orbitur Camping Caminha

EN13 km 90, Mata do Camarido, P-4910-180 Caminha (Viana do Costelo) T: 258 921 295. E: info@orbitur.pt
alanrogers.com/PO8010

In northern Portugal close to the Spanish border, this pleasant site is just 200 metres from the beach. It has an attractive and peaceful setting in woods alongside the river estuary that marks the border with Spain and on the edge of the little town of Caminha. The site is shaded by tall pines with other small trees planted to mark large sandy pitches. The main site road is surfaced but elsewhere take care not to get trapped in soft sand. Pitching and parking can be haphazard. Static units are grouped together on one side of the site. Water points, electrical supply and lighting are good. With a pleasant, open feel about the setting, fishing is possible in the estuary and swimming, either there or from the rather open, sandy beach.

Facilities

The clean, well maintained toilet block has British style toilets, washbasins (cold water) and hot showers, plus beach showers, extra dishwashing and laundry sinks (cold water). Laundry. Motorcaravan services. Supermarket. Small restaurant/bar with snacks (all Easter and 1/6-15/9). Bicycle hire. Off site: Beach 200 m. Fishing 200 m. Bus service 800 m.

Open: All year.

Directions

From the north, turn off the main coast road (N13-E50) just after camping sign at end of embankment alongside estuary, about 1.5 km. south of ferry. From the south on N13 turn left at Hotel Faz de Minho at start of estuary and follow for 1 km. through woods to site. GPS: 41.86635, -8.85844

Charges guide

Per person	€ 2,50 - € 4,50
child (5-10 yrs)	€ 1,30 - € 2,50
cavavan and car	€ 5,60 - € 10,20
electricity	€ 2,50 - € 3,10

Off season discounts (up to 70%).

For latest campsite news, availability and prices visit
alanrogers.com

Campo do Gerês

Parque de Campismo de Cerdeira

Rua de Cerdeira 400, P-4840 Campo do Gerês (Braga) T: 253 351 005. E: info@parquecerdeira.com

alanrogers.com/PO8370

Located in the National Park of Peneda Gerês, amidst spectacular mountain scenery, this excellent site offers modern facilities in a truly natural area. The National Park is home to all manner of flora, fauna and wildlife, including the roebuck, wolf and wild boar. The well fenced, professional and peaceful site has some 600 good sized, unmarked, mostly level, grassy pitches in a shady woodland setting. Electricity is available for most pitches, though some long leads may be required. A very large timber complex, tastefully designed with the use of noble materials, granite and wood, provides a superb restaurant with a comprehensive menu. A pool with a separated section for toddlers is a welcome, cooling relief in the height of summer. There are unlimited opportunities in the immediate area for fishing, riding, canoeing, mountain biking and climbing, so take advantage of this quality mountain hospitality.

Facilities

Four very clean sanitary blocks provide mixed style WCs, controllable showers and hot water. Laundry. Gas supplies. Shop. Restaurant/bar (1/4-6/10, plus weekends and holidays). Playground. Bicycle hire. TV room (satellite). Medical post. Good tennis courts. Minigolf. Car wash. Barbecue area. Torches useful. English spoken. Attractive bungalows to rent. Dogs are not accepted June-Aug. Off site: Fishing and riding 800 m.

Open: All year.

Directions

From north, N103 (Braga - Chaves), turn left at N205 (7.5 km. north of Braga). Follow N205 to Caldelas Terras de Bouro and Covide where site is clearly marked to Campo do Geres. An eastern approach from the N103 is for the adventurous but will be rewarded by magnificent views over mountains and lakes. GPS: 41.7631, -8.1905

Charges guide

Per unit incl. 2 persons and electricity	€ 15,75 - € 24,45
extra person	€ 3,20 - € 4,60
child (5-11 yrs)	€ 2,00 - € 3,10
dog	€ 1,50 - € 3,00

Darque

Orbitur Camping Viana do Castelo

Rua Diogo Alvares, Cabadelo, P-4900-161 Darque (Viana do Costelo) T: 258 322 167. E: info@orbitur.pt

alanrogers.com/PO8020

This site in northern Portugal is worth considering as it has the advantage of direct access, through a gate in the fence (locked at night) to a large and excellent soft sand beach (400 m.) which is popular for windsurfing. There are 225 pitches on undulating sand, most with good shade from pine trees and with electricity in all areas (long leads may be needed). Some flat good sized pitches are reserved for caravans and motorcaravans. As usual with Orbitur sites, most pitches are not marked and it could be crowded in July/August. A pleasant restaurant terrace overlooks the pool. A ferry crosses the river to the town centre. The site is also convenient for visiting the medieval town of Ponte de Lima (24 km), with its white-washed houses, towers and Roman bridge, and Viana do Castelo is famous for its beautiful embroideries and festival processions.

Facilities

Toilet facilities are in two blocks, both with washbasins with cold water and hot showers. Facilities for disabled campers. Laundry. Motorcaravan services. Gas supplies. Supermarket. Small restaurant with terrace and bar (all Easter and 1/6-30/9). Open-air pool (June-Sept). Reading room with TV, video and fireplace. Playground. Tennis. Medical post. Off site: Fishing 100 m. Beach 50 m.

Open: All year.

Directions

On N13 coast road driving north to south drive through Viana do Castelo and over estuary bridge. Turn immediately right off N13 towards Cabedelo and the sea. Site is the third campsite signed, the other two are not recommended. GPS: 41.67866, -8.82637

Charges guide

Per person	€ 2,70 - € 4,80
child (5-10 yrs)	€ 1,40 - € 2,50
caravan and car	€ 6,70 - € 11,30
electricity	€ 2,50 - € 3,10
Off season discounts (up to 70%).	

For latest campsite news, availability and prices visit
alanrogers.com

Póvoa de Varzim

Orbitur Camping Rio Alto

EN13 km 13 Rio Alto-Est, Estela, P-4570-275 Póvoa de Varzim (Porto) T: **252 615 699**. E: info@orbitur.pt

alanrogers.com/PO8030

This site makes an excellent base for visiting Porto which is some 35 km. south of Estela. It has around 700 pitches on sandy terrain and is next to what is virtually a private beach. There are hardstandings for caravans and motorcaravans and electrical connections to most pitches (long leads may be required). The area for tents is furthest from the beach and windswept, stunted pines give some shade. There are arrangements for car parking away from camping areas in peak season. There is a quality restaurant, snack bar and a large swimming pool across the road from reception. An 18-hole golf course is adjacent and huge nets along one side of the site protect campers from any stray balls. The beach is accessed via a novel double tunnel in two lengths of 40 metres under the dunes (open 09.00-19.00). The beach shelves steeply at some tidal stages (lifeguard from 1-5 June to 15 September).

Facilities

Four refurbished and well equipped toilet blocks have hot water. Laundry facilities. Facilities for disabled campers. Gas supplies. Shop (1/6-31/10). Restaurant, bar, snack bar (1/5-31/10). Swimming pool (1/6-30/9). Tennis. Playground. Games room. TV. Medical post. Car wash. Evening entertainment twice weekly in season. Off site: Fishing, golf, bicycle hire and riding within 5 km.

Open: All year.

Directions

From A28 in direction of Porto, leave at exit 18 signed Fao/Apuila. At roundabout take N13 in direction of Pavoa de Varzim/Porto for 2.5 km. At Hotel Contriz, turn right onto narrow cobbled road. Site well signed in 2 km. GPS: 41.44504, -8.75767

Charges guide

Per person	€ 2,90 - € 5,40
child (5-10 yrs)	€ 1,50 - € 3,00
caravan and car	€ 6,80 - € 12,00
electricity (5/15A)	€ 2,50 - € 3,10

Off season discounts (up to 70%).

For latest campsite news, availability and prices visit

alanrogers.com

alan rogers

Insurance Service

High quality, low cost insurance you can trust

Price Beater
GUARANTEE*

Caravan
Insurance
**SAVE
UP TO
60%**

We've been entrusted with readers' campsite-based holidays since 1968, and they have asked us for good value, good quality insurance.

We have teamed up with Shield Total Insurance – one of the leading names in outdoor leisure insurances – to bring you peace of mind and huge savings. Call or visit our website for a no obligation quote – there's no reason not to – and trust us to cover your valued possessions for you.

*Price Beater GUARANTEE
Motorhomes and Static Caravans
We guarantee to beat any genuine 'like for like' insurance renewal quote by at least £25. Subject to terms & conditions.

- Caravans - **Discounts up to 60%**
- Park Homes - **Fantastic low rates**
- Cars - *COMING SOON*

Instant quote
Call **0844 824 6314**
alanrogers.com/insurance

   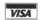

Accommodation

Over recent years many of the campsites featured in this guide have added large numbers of high quality mobile homes and chalets. Many site owners believe that some former caravanners and motorcaravanners have been enticed by the extra comfort they can now provide, and that maybe this is the ideal solution to combine the freedom of camping with all the comforts of home.

Quality is consistently high and, although the exact size and inventory may vary from site to site, if you choose any of the sites detailed here, you can be sure that you're staying in some of the best quality and best value mobile homes available.

Home comforts are provided and typically these include a fridge with freezer compartment, gas hob, proper shower – often a microwave and radio/cassette hi-fi too, but do check for details. All mobile homes and chalets come fully equipped with a good range of kitchen utensils, pots and pans, crockery, cutlery and outdoor furniture. Some even have an attractive wooden sundeck or paved terrace – a perfect spot for outdoors eating or relaxing with a book and watching the world go by.

Regardless of model, colourful soft furnishings are the norm and a generally breezy décor helps to provide a real holiday feel.

Although some sites may have a large number of different accommodation types, we have restricted our choice to one or two of the most popular accommodation units (either mobile homes or chalets) for each of the sites listed.

The mobile homes here will be of modern design, and recent innovations, for example, often include pitched roofs which substantially improve their appearance.

Design will invariably include clever use of space and fittings/furniture to provide for comfortable holidays – usually light and airy, with big windows and patio-style doors, fully equipped kitchen areas, a shower room with shower, washbasin and WC, cleverly designed bedrooms and a comfortable lounge/dining area (often incorporating a sofa bed).

In general, modern campsite chalets incorporate all the best features of mobile homes in a more traditional structure, sometimes with the advantage of an upper mezzanine floor for an additional bedroom.

Our selected campsites offer a massive range of different types of mobile home and chalet, and it would be impractical to inspect every single accommodation unit. Our selection criteria, therefore, primarily takes account of the quality standards of the campsite itself.

However, there are a couple of important ground rules:

- Featured mobile homes must be no more than 5 years old

- chalets no more than 10 years old

- All listed accommodation must, of course, fully conform with all applicable local, national and European safety legislation.

For each campsite we have given details of the type, or types, of accommodation available to rent, but these details are necessarily quite brief. Sometimes internal layouts can differ quite substantially, particularly with regard to sleeping arrangements, where these include the flexible provision for 'extra persons' on sofa beds located in the living area. These arrangements may vary from accommodation to accommodation, and if you're planning a holiday which includes more people than are catered for by the main bedrooms you should check exactly how the extra sleeping arrangements are to be provided!

Charges

An indication of the tariff for each type of accommodation featured is also included, indicating the variance between the low and high season tariffs. However, given that many campsites have a large and often complex range of pricing options, incorporating special deals and various discounts, the charges we mention should be taken to be just an indication. We strongly recommend therefore that you confirm the actual cost when making a booking.

We also strongly recommend that you check with the campsite, when booking, what (if anything) will be provided by way of bed linen, blankets, pillows etc. Again, in our experience, this can vary widely from site to site.

On every campsite a fully refundable deposit (usually between 150 and 300 euros) is payable on arrival. There may also be an optional cleaning service for which a further charge is made. Other options may include sheet hire (typically 30 euros per unit) or baby pack hire (cot and high chair).

ES84780 Camping Joan

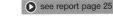
see report page 25

Passeig Maritim 88, E-43850 Cambrils

AR1 – BUNGALOW 2-4 PERSONS – Bungalow	AR2 – BUNGALOW 3-5 PERSONS – Bungalow
Sleeping: 1 bedroom, sleeps 1: 1 single, sofa bed	Sleeping: sofa bed
Living: living/kitchen area, TV, shower	Living: living/kitchen area, TV, shower
Eating: microwave, coffee maker, fridge	Eating: microwave, coffee maker, fridge
Outside: table & chairs	Outside: table & chairs, 2 sun loungers, barbecue
Pets: not accepted	Pets: not accepted

Other (AR1 and AR2): bed linen to hire

Open: 26 February - 4 November

Weekly Charge	AR1	AR2
Low Season *(from)*	€ 255	€ 353
High Season *(from)*	€ 784	€ 1064

ES84810 Camping Cambrils Park

see report page 26

Avenida Mas Clariana s/n, E-43850 Cambrils

AR1 – BONITA 5+1 – Apartment	AR2 – ALOHA – Apartment
Sleeping: 2 bedrooms, sleeps 6: 1 double, 2 singles, sofa bed, pillows and blankets provided	Sleeping: 2 bedrooms, sleeps 6: 1 double, 2 singles, sofa bed, pillows and blankets provided
Living: living/kitchen area, TV, air conditioning, shower, separate WC	Living: living/kitchen area, TV, air conditioning, shower, WC
Eating: fitted kitchen with hob, microwave, dishwasher, fridge, freezer	Eating: fitted kitchen with hob, oven, microwave, fridge
Outside: table & chairs, 2 sun loungers	Outside: table & chairs, 2 sun loungers
Pets: not accepted	Pets: not accepted

Open: 26 March - 12 October

Weekly Charge	AR1	AR2
Low Season *(from)*	€ 399	€ 350
High Season *(from)*	€ 1470	€ 1365

ES80100 Camping Castell Mar

see report page 28

Platja de la Rubina, E-17486 Castelló d'Empúries

AR1 – PAGAN – Bungalow Tent
Sleeping: 2 bedrooms, sleeps 5: 1 double, 1 single, bunk bed, pillows and blankets provided
Living: living/kitchen area, shower, WC
Eating: fitted kitchen with hob, coffee maker, fridge
Outside: table & chairs, parasol, 2 sun loungers
Pets: not accepted

Open: 21 May - 18 September

Weekly Charge	AR1
Low Season *(from)*	€ 392
High Season *(from)*	€ 820

ES80070 Camping Castell Montgri

▶ see report page 33

Ctra Toroella - l'Estartit km 4,7, E-17258 l'Estartit

AR1 – PAGAN – Bungalow Tent	AR2 – MOBILE HOME 5/6 – Mobile Home
Sleeping: 2 bedrooms, sleeps 5: 1 double, 1 single, bunk bed, pillows and blankets provided	**Sleeping:** 2 bedrooms, sleeps 6: 1 double, 1 single, bunk bed, sofa bed, pillows and blankets provided
Living: living/kitchen area, shower, WC	**Living:** living/kitchen area, heating, air conditioning, shower, separate WC
Eating: fitted kitchen with hob, coffee maker, fridge	
Outside: table & chairs, parasol, 2 sun loungers	**Eating:** fitted kitchen with hob, microwave, coffee maker, fridge
Pets: accepted (with supplement)	**Outside:** table & chairs, parasol, 2 sun loungers
	Pets: accepted (with supplement)

Open: 14 May - 25 September		
Weekly Charge	**AR1**	**AR2**
Low Season *(from)*	€ 420	€ 497
High Season *(from)*	€ 915	€ 1180

ES82330 Camping La Tordera

▶ see report page 36

Cami de la Tordera s/n, E-08380 Malgrat de Mar

AR1 – BUNGALOW 3 PERSONS – Bungalow	AR2 – BUNGALOW 5 PERSONS – Bungalow
Sleeping: 1 bedroom, 2 doubles, 1 single, bunk bed, sofa bed	**Sleeping:** 2 bedrooms, sleeps 1: 2 doubles, 1 single, bunk bed, sofa bed
Living: living/kitchen area, heating, TV, air conditioning, shower, separate WC	**Living:** living/kitchen area, heating, TV, air conditioning, shower, separate WC
Eating: fitted kitchen with microwave, grill, coffee maker, fridge, freezer	**Eating:** fitted kitchen with microwave, grill, coffee maker, fridge, freezer
Outside: table & chairs, barbecue	**Outside:** table & chairs, barbecue
Pets: not accepted	**Pets:** not accepted

Other (AR1 and AR2): bed linen, highchair to hire

Open: 3 June - 2 October		
Weekly Charge	**AR1**	**AR2**
Low Season *(from)*	€ 413	€ 553
High Season *(from)*	€ 833	€ 1113

ES85400 Kawan Village La Torre del Sol

▶ see report page 39

Ctra N340 km 1136, E-43300 Montroig

AR1 – PAGAN – Bungalow Tent
Sleeping: 2 bedrooms, sleeps 5: 3 singles, bunk bed, pillows and blankets provided
Living: living/kitchen area, shower, WC, separate WC
Eating: fitted kitchen with hob, coffee maker, fridge
Outside: table & chairs, parasol, 2 sun loungers
Pets: not accepted

Open: 1 April - 30 September	
Weekly Charge	**AR1**
Low Season *(from)*	€ 162
High Season *(from)*	€ 587

ES84800 Camping & Bungalows Sanguli

▶ see report page 46

Prolongacion Calle, Apdo 123, E-43840 Salou

AR1 – VILLA PARADISE – Chalet	AR2 – LOUISIANE – Mobile home
Sleeping: 2 bedrooms, sleeps 6: 1 double, 2 singles, sofa bed, pillows and blankets provided	Sleeping: 2 bedrooms, sleeps 6: 1 double, 2 singles, sofa bed, pillows and blankets provided
Living: living/kitchen area, TV, air conditioning, shower, separate WC	Living: living/kitchen area, air conditioning, shower, WC
Eating: fitted kitchen with hob, microwave, dishwasher, fridge, freezer	Eating: fitted kitchen with hob, oven, microwave, fridge
Outside: table & chairs, 2 sun loungers	Outside: table & chairs
Pets: not accepted	Pets: not accepted

Open: 19 March - 1 November		
Weekly Charge	AR1	AR2
Low Season (from)	€ 399	€ 308
High Season (from)	€ 1470	€ 1155

ES80600 Camping La Ballena Alegre

▶ see report page 53

Ctra Sant Marti d'Empuries s/n, E-17470 Sant Pere Pescador

AR1 – TAMARIU / FLUVIA / EMPURIES – Bungalow	AR2 – MEDITERRANEO – Mobile home
Sleeping: 2 bedrooms, sleeps 1: 1 double, 1 single, bunk bed, sofa bed, pillows and blankets provided	Sleeping: 2 bedrooms, sleeps 1: 1 single, pillows and blankets provided
Living: living/kitchen area, heating, TV, air conditioning, shower, separate WC	Living: living/kitchen area, heating, air conditioning, shower, separate WC
Eating: fitted kitchen with microwave, dishwasher, coffee maker, fridge, freezer	Eating: fitted kitchen with microwave, dishwasher, coffee maker, fridge, freezer
Outside: table & chairs, 2 sun loungers	Outside: table & chairs, 2 sun loungers
Pets: not accepted	Pets: not accepted

Other (AR1 and AR2): bed linen, highchair to hire

Open: 14 May - 26 September.		
Weekly Charge	AR1	AR2
Low Season (from)	€ 420	€ 355
High Season (from)	€ 1148	€ 994

ES80800 Camping El Delfin Verde

▶ see report page 58

Ctra de Torroella de Montgrí, E-17257 Torroella de Montgrí

AR1 – PAX 5TA – Mobile home	AR2 – PAX 6TAS – Mobile home
Sleeping: 2 bedrooms, sleeps 1: 1 double, 1 single, pillows and blankets provided	Sleeping: 3 bedrooms, sleeps 1: 2 doubles, 1 single, pillows and blankets provided
Living: living/kitchen area, heating, TV, shower, separate WC	Living: living/kitchen area, heating, TV, shower, separate WC
Eating: fitted kitchen with microwave, coffee maker, fridge, freezer	Eating: fitted kitchen with microwave, coffee maker, fridge, freezer
Outside: table & chairs	Outside: table & chairs
Pets: not accepted	Pets: not accepted

Other (AR1 and AR2): highchair to hire

Open: 16 April - 25 September		
Weekly Charge	AR1	AR2
Low Season (from)	€ 57	€ 66
High Season (from)	€ 155	€ 175

ES83900 Camping Vilanova Park

▶ see report page 60

Ctra de l'Arboc km 2.5, E-08800 Vilanova i la Geltru

AR1 – BUNGALOW SERIE 950 – Bungalow	AR2 – BUNGALOW SERIE 540 – Bungalow
Sleeping: 2 bedrooms, sleeps 6: 2 doubles, 2 singles, sofa bed, pillows and blankets provided	Sleeping: 2 bedrooms, sleeps 6: 4 singles, sofa bed, pillows and blankets provided
Living: living/kitchen area, heating, air conditioning, shower, WC	Living: living/kitchen area, shower, WC
Eating: fitted kitchen with hob, microwave, coffee maker, fridge	Eating: fitted kitchen with hob, fridge
Outside: table & chairs	Outside: table & chairs
Pets: not accepted	Pets: not accepted

Other (AR1 and AR2): bed linen to hire

Open: All year		
Weekly Charge	**AR1**	**AR2**
Low Season *(from)*	€ 714	€ 637
High Season *(from)*	€ 1155	€ 1057

PO8202 Camping Turiscampo

▶ see report page 158

N125, Espiche, Luz, P-8600 Lagos

AR1 – BUNGALOW 5 PERSONS	AR2 – MOBILE HOME 5/6 PERSONS
Sleeping: 2 bedrooms, sleeps 1: 1 double, 1 single, sofa bed, pillows and blankets provided	Sleeping: 2 bedrooms, sleeps 1: 2 doubles, sofa bed, pillows and blankets provided
Living: living/kitchen area, heating, shower, separate WC	Living: living/kitchen area, heating, air conditioning, shower, separate WC
Eating: fitted kitchen with hob, microwave, dishwasher, coffee maker, fridge, freezer	Eating: fitted kitchen with hob, oven, microwave, dishwasher, coffee maker, fridge, freezer
Outside: table & chairs, 2 sun loungers	Outside: table & chairs, 2 sun loungers
Pets: not accepted	Pets: not accepted

Other (AR1 and AR2): bed linen to hire

Open: All year

Weekly Charge	AR1	AR2
Low Season *(from)*	€ 252	€ 297
High Season *(from)*	€ 749	€ 826

PO8460 Camping Caravaning Vale Paraiso

▶ see report page 168

EN242, P-2450-138 Nazaré

AR1 – CHALET – Chalet	AR2 – APARTEMENTO – Apartment
Sleeping: 2 bedrooms, sleeps 5: 1 double, 2 singles, bunk bed, pillows and blankets provided	Sleeping: 2 bedrooms, sleeps 6: 1 double, 2 singles, bunk bed, sofa bed, pillows and blankets provided
Living: living/kitchen area, TV, shower, separate WC	Living: living/kitchen area, TV, shower, separate WC
Eating: fitted kitchen with hob, microwave, dishwasher, coffee maker, fridge, freezer	Eating: fitted kitchen with hob, microwave, dishwasher, coffee maker, fridge, freezer
Outside: table & chairs, parasol	Outside: table & chairs, parasol
Pets: not accepted	Pets: not accepted

Other (AR1 and AR2): bed linen, cot to hire

Open: All year

Weekly Charge	AR1	AR2
Low Season *(from)*	€ 315	€ 315
High Season *(from)*	€ 710	€ 712

PO8030 Orbitur Camping Rio Alto

▶ see report page 178

EN13 km 13 Rio Alto-Est, Estela, P-4570-275 Póvoa de Varzim

AR1 – BUNGALOW – Bungalow	AR2 – MOBILE HOME – Mobile home
Sleeping: 1 bedroom, pillows and blankets provided	Sleeping: 2 bedrooms, sofa bed, pillows and blankets provided
Living: living/kitchen area, TV, shower	Living: living/kitchen area, TV, shower
Eating: dishwasher, coffee maker, fridge, freezer	Eating: dishwasher, coffee maker, fridge, freezer
Outside: table & chairs, parasol, 2 sun loungers	Outside: table & chairs, parasol, 2 sun loungers
Pets: not accepted	Pets: not accepted

Other (AR1 and AR2): bed linen, highchair to hire

Open: all year

Weekly Charge	AR1	AR2
Low Season *(from)*	€ 308	€ 252
High Season *(from)*	€ 728	€ 707

VACANCES André Trigano .com

LE SPÉCIALISTE DU CAMPING

SPAIN

PORTUGAL

Travel agency Vacances André Trigano, specialised in renting luxurious chalets and mobile homes, offers you a dream holiday for all ages on campistes especially selected for their natural beauty or location near the most excting cities in Spain and Portugal. Comfort accommodations in a relaxing environment

199€* PER WEEK

INFORMATION / RESERVATIONS

0905 076 0240

Calls cost £ 0.75 per minute plus network extras. Billpayers permission needed.

vacancesandretrigano.com

* Rates from

Travelling - in Europe

When taking your car (and caravan, tent or trailer tent) or motorcaravan to the continent you do need to plan in advance and to find out as much as possible about driving in the countries you plan to visit. Whilst European harmonisation has eliminated many of the differences between one country and another, it is well worth reading the short notes we provide in the introduction to each country in this guide in addition to this more general summary.

Of course, the main difference from driving in the UK is that in mainland Europe you will need to drive on the right. Without taking extra time and care, especially at busy junctions and conversely when roads are empty, it is easy to forget to drive on the right. Remember that traffic approaching from the right usually has priority unless otherwise indicated by road markings and signs. Harmonisation also means that most (but not all) common road signs are the same in all countries.

Your vehicle

Book your vehicle in for a good service well before your intended departure date. This will lessen the chance of an expensive breakdown. Make sure your brakes are working efficiently and that your tyres have plenty of tread (3 mm. is recommended, particularly if you are undertaking a long journey).

Also make sure that your caravan or trailer is roadworthy and that its tyres are in good order and correctly inflated. Plan your packing and be careful not to overload your vehicle, caravan or trailer – this is unsafe and may well invalidate your insurance cover (it must not be more fully loaded than the kerb weight of the insured vehicle).

CHECK ALL THE FOLLOWING:

- **GB sticker.** If you do not display a sticker, you may risk an on-the-spot fine as this identifier is compulsory in all countries. Euro-plates are an acceptable alternative within the EU (but not outside). Remember to attach another sticker (or Euro-plate) to caravans and trailers. Only GB stickers (not England, Scotland, Wales or N. Ireland) stickers are valid in the EU.

- **Headlights.** As you will be driving on the right you must adjust your headlights so that the dipped beam does not dazzle oncoming drivers. Converter kits are readily available for most vehicles, although if your car is fitted with high intensity headlights, you should check with your motor dealer. Check that any planned extra loading does not affect the beam height.

- **Seatbelts.** Rules for the fitting and wearing of seatbelts throughout Europe are similar to those in the UK, but it is worth checking before you go. Rules for carrying children in the front of vehicles vary from country to country. It is best to plan not to do this if possible.

- **Door/wing mirrors.** To help with driving on the right, if your vehicle is not fitted with a mirror on the left hand side, we recommend you have one fitted.

- **Fuel.** Leaded and Lead Replacement petrol is increasingly difficult to find in Northern Europe.

Compulsory additional equipment

The driving laws of the countries of Europe still vary in what you are required to carry in your vehicle, although the consequences of not carrying a required piece of equipment are almost always an on-the-spot fine.

To meet these requirements we suggest that you carry the following:

- FIRE EXTINGUISHER
- BASIC TOOL KIT

- FIRST AID KIT
- SPARE BULBS
- TWO WARNING TRIANGLES – two are required in some countries at all times, and are compulsory in most countries when towing.
- HIGH VISIBILITY VEST – now compulsory in France, Spain, Italy and Austria (and likely to become compulsory throughout the EU) in case you need to walk on a motorway.

Insurance and Motoring Documents

Vehicle insurance

Contact your insurer well before you depart to check that your car insurance policy covers driving outside the UK. Most do, but many policies only provide minimum cover (so if you have an accident your insurance may only cover the cost of damage to the other person's property, with no cover for fire and theft).

To maintain the same level of cover abroad as you enjoy at home you need to tell your vehicle insurer. Some will automatically cover you abroad with no extra cost and no extra paperwork. Some will say you need a Green Card (which is neither green nor on card) but won't charge for it. Some will charge extra for the Green Card. Ideally you should contact your vehicle insurer 3-4 weeks before you set off, and confirm your conversation with them in writing.

Breakdown insurance

Arrange breakdown cover for your trip in good time so that if your vehicle breaks down or is involved in an accident it (and your caravan or trailer) can be repaired or returned to this country. This cover can usually be arranged as part of your travel insurance policy (see below).

Documents you must take with you

You may be asked to show your documents at any time so make sure that they are in order, up-to-date and easily accessible while you travel.

These are what you need to take:

- **Passports** (you may also need a visa in some countries if you hold either a UK passport not issued in the UK or a passport that was issued outside the EU).
- **Motor Insurance Certificate,** including Green Card (or Continental Cover clause)
- **DVLA Vehicle Registration Document** plus, if not your own vehicle, the owner's written authority to drive.
- **A full valid Driving Licence** (not provisional). The new photo style licence is now mandatory in most European countries.

Personal Holiday insurance

Even though you are just travelling within Europe you must take out travel insurance. Few EU countries pay the full cost of medical treatment even under reciprocal health service arrangements. The first part of a holiday insurance policy covers people. It will include the cost of doctor, ambulance and hospital treatment if needed. If needed the better companies will even pay for English language speaking doctors and nurses and will bring a sick or injured holidaymaker home by air ambulance.

Personal Holiday insurance (continued)

An important part of the insurance, often ignored, is cancellation (and curtailment) cover. Few things are as heartbreaking as having to cancel a holiday because a member of the family falls ill. Cancellation insurance can't take away the disappointment, but it makes sure you don't suffer financially as well. For this reason you should arrange your holiday insurance at least eight weeks before you set off.

Whichever insurance you choose we would advise reading very carefully the policies sold by the High Street travel trade. Whilst they may be good, they may not cover the specific needs of campers, caravanners and motorcaravanners.

Telephone **01580 214000** for a quote for our Camping Travel Insurance with cover arranged through leading leisure insurance providers.

Alternatively visit our website at: **alanrogers.com/insurance**

European Health Insurance Card (EHIC)

Make sure you apply for your EHIC before travelling in Europe. Eligible travellers from the UK are entitled to receive free or reduced-cost medical care in many European countries on production of an EHIC. This free card is available by completing a form in the booklet 'Health Advice for Travellers' from local Post Offices. One should be completed for each family member. Alternatively visit **www.ehic.org.uk** and apply on-line. Please allow time to send your application off and have the EHIC returned to you.

The EHIC is valid in all European Community countries plus Iceland, Liechtenstein, Switzerland and Norway. If you or any of your dependants are suddenly taken ill or have an accident during a visit to any of these countries, free or reduced-cost emergency treatment is available – in most cases on production of a valid EHIC.

Only state-provided emergency treatment is covered, and you will receive treatment on the same terms as nationals of the country you are visiting. Private treatment is generally not covered, and state-provided treatment may not cover all of the things that you would expect to receive free of charge from the NHS.

Remember an EHIC does not cover you for all the medical costs that you can incur or for repatriation - it is not an alternative to travel insurance. You will still need appropriate insurance to ensure you are fully covered for all eventualities.

Travelling with children

Most countries in Europe are enforcing strict guidelines when you are travelling with children who are not your own. A minor (under the age of 18) must be accompanied by a parent or legal guardian or must carry a letter of authorisation from a parent or guardian. The letter should name the adult responsible for the minor during his or her stay. Similarly, a minor travelling with just one of his/her parents, must have a letter of authority to leave their home country from the parent staying behind. Full information is available at **www.fco.gov.uk**

Open All Year

The following sites are understood to accept caravanners and campers all year round. It is always wise to phone the site to check as the facilities available, for example, may be reduced.

SPAIN

Cataluña-Catalunya

ES85360	Ametlla	19
ES91240	Bedurà Park	34
ES82280	Blanes	21
ES82350	Bon Repos	55
ES82400	Bona Vista Kim	22
ES85350	Cala d'Oques	32
ES81300	Calonge	23
ES80360	Esponellà	31
ES91190	Frontera	31
ES84770	La Llosa	24
ES91400	Pedraforca	45
ES84820	Pineda de Salou	35
ES85080	Poboleda	43
ES85060	Serra de Prades	59
ES91225	Vall de Camprodon	26
ES83900	Vilanova Park	60

Comunidad Valenciana

ES86200	Alqueria	68
ES85850	Altomira	72
ES86830	Benisol	66
ES85800	Bonterra	65
ES86870	Cap Blanch	65
ES86900	Costa Blanca	68
ES86850	El Raco	66
ES86120	Euro (Oliva)	72
ES87410	Florantilles	76
ES87540	Javea	71
ES86150	Kiko	73
ES86250	Kiko Rural	77
ES87400	Lo Monte	75
ES87420	Marina	70
ES86450	Mariola	67
ES87430	Marjal	69
ES85900	Monmar	71
ES87550	Moraira	71
ES85750	Oasis	74
ES86130	Olé	73
ES85600	Playa Tropicana	64
ES85610	Ribamar	64
ES85590	Spa Natura Resort	74
ES85700	Torre La Sal 2	75
ES86750	Vall de Laguar	67
ES86810	Villasol	66
ES85580	Vinaros	77

Murcia

ES87520	El Portus (Naturist)	80
ES87450	Fuente	79
ES87480	Madriles	80
ES87530	Manga	81
ES87440	Puerta	80

Andalucia

ES88730	Aldea	85
ES87830	Almanat (Naturist)	84
ES92750	Avellanos	88
ES88030	Buganvilla	92
ES87630	Cabo de Gata	86
ES88020	Cabopino	91
ES90840	Campiña	96
ES90850	Carlos III	90
ES87560	Cueva Negra	93
ES87510	Cuevas Mar	94
ES90890	Despeñaperros	96
ES92950	Don Cactus	93
ES92900	El Balcon	95
ES90800	El Brillante	87
ES87810	El Pino	98
ES88090	El Sur	95
ES87620	Escullos	93
ES87900	Fuente de Piedra	88
ES87650	Garrofa	84
ES88900	Gazules	84
ES88710	Giralda	90
ES87820	Laguna Playa	98
ES92850	Lomas	89
ES88000	Marbella Playa	91
ES92930	Orgiva	94
ES88500	Paloma	97
ES88570	Pinar San José	85
ES88650	Playa Las Dunas	88
ES92920	Puerta La Alpujarra	94
ES92760	Reina Isabel	91
ES88590	Roche	86
ES87680	Roquetas	95
ES88580	Rosaleda	86
ES87850	Rural Iznate	90
ES87490	Sopalmo	92
ES92700	Suspiro-Moro	89
ES88550	Tarifa	97
ES90780	Villares	87

Extremadura

ES90860	Cáceres	101
ES90870	Merida	102
ES90270	Monfrague	102

Castilla La-Mancha

ES90970	Batanes	106
ES90900	El Greco	106
ES90960	Mirador	105

Madrid

ES90910	Aranjuez	109
ES92000	El Escorial	108
ES92120	Monte Holiday	110
ES92100	Pico-Miel	110

Castilla y León

ES92500	Costajan	113
ES90210	Fuentes Blancas	113
ES90250	Regio	115
ES90245	Riaza	115

Galicia

ES90240	As Cancelas	120
ES89360	Bayona Playa	118
ES89380	Paxarinas	120

Asturias

ES89400	Cantiles	124
ES89650	Picos-Europa	123

Cantabria

ES89640	Molino	128
ES89730	Santillana	132

Pais Vasco-Euskadi

ES90390	Gran Zarautz	136
ES90300	Igueldo	136
ES90340	Leagi	135

La Rioja

ES92280	Berceo	138

Aragón

ES91040	Ciudad de Zaragoza	151
ES90640	Gavín	148
ES91250	Lago Barasona	148
ES90610	Ligüerre de Cinca	150
ES90600	Peña Montañesa	149

PORTUGAL

Algarve

PO8210	Albufeira	156
PO8410	Armacao-Pera	157
PO8230	Olhão	158
PO8220	Quarteira	159
PO8440	Quinta	157
PO8430	Sagres	159
PO8202	Turiscampo	158
PO8200	Valverde	157

Alentejo

PO8355	Asseiceira	163
PO8340	Évora	161
PO8350	Markádia	161
PO8160	Porto Covo	163
PO8170	São Miguel	162
PO8175	Zmar	162

Lisbon & Vale do Tejo

PO8150	Caparica	166
PO8480	Foz do Arelho	167
PO8130	Guincho	165
PO8140	Monsanto	167
PO8400	O Tamanco	169
PO8155	Parque Verde	166
PO8100	Sao Pedro-Moel	169

Beiras & Centre

PO8330	Arganil	171
PO8360	Barragem de Idhana-a-Nova	172
PO8090	Gala	172
PO8040	Vagueira	174

Porto & North

PO8010	Caminha	176
PO8370	Cerdeira	177
PO8030	Rio Alto	178
PO8020	Viana-Castelo	177

Dogs

For the benefit of those who want to take their dogs with them or for people who do not like dogs at the sites they visit, we list here the sites that have indicated to us that they do not accept dogs. If you are, however, planning to take your dog we do advise you to contact them first to check – there may be limits on numbers, breeds, etc. or times of the year when they are excluded.

Never – these sites do not accept dogs at any time

SPAIN

Cataluña-Catalunya

ES91240	Bedurà Park	34
ES84810	Cambrils	26
ES80900	Cypsela	41
ES81030	El Maset	19
ES80700	Escala	34
ES91430	Pirineus	32
ES81010	Playa Brava	43
ES85300	Playa Montroig	38
ES91230	Solsones	55
ES84200	Stel (Roda)	44
ES85370	Templo del Sol (Nat)	32
ES81400	Treumal	24

Comunidad Valenciana

ES87410	Florantilles	76
ES85600	Playa Tropicana	64
ES86810	Villasol	66

Andalucia

ES88550	Tarifa	97
ES87580	Tau de San José	96

Castilla y León

ES92540	Demanda	116
ES92510	Rio Lobos	116

Cantabria

ES89980	Playa de Isla	129

ES89930	Playa del Regaton	129
ES89990	Punta Marina	129

Aragón

ES91100	Fresneda	148

Balears

ES80000	Son Bou	152

PORTUGAL

Alentejo

PO8170	São Miguel	162

Maybe – not accepted in high season

SPAIN

Cataluña-Catalunya

ES81600	Cala Gogo	24
ES80800	Delfin Verde	58
ES80720	Medes	33
ES84820	Pineda de Salou	35
ES80090	Salatà	45

Comunidad Valenciana

ES85800	Bonterra	65
ES85590	Spa Natura Resort	74

Andalucia

ES88030	Buganvilla	92
ES92950	Don Cactus	93
ES88500	Paloma	97
ES88570	Pinar San José	85
ES88580	Rosaleda	86

PORTUGAL

Alentejo

PO8350	Markádia	161

Fishing

We are pleased to include details of sites which provide facilities for fishing on site. However, it is always best to contact sites directly to check that they provide for your individual requirements.

SPAIN

Cataluña-Catalunya

ES85360	Ametlla	19
ES80350	Amfora	50
ES80500	Aquarius	52
ES80600	Ballena Alegre	53
ES80640	Bassegoda	18
ES82320	Bella Terra	22
ES82280	Blanes	21
ES82350	Bon Repos	55
ES82380	Caballo de Mar	41
ES85350	Cala d'Oques	32
ES81600	Cala Gogo	24

ES82000	Cala Llevadó	59
ES80100	Castell Mar	28
ES82340	Del Mar	36
ES80800	Delfin Verde	58
ES80400	Dunas	51
ES82300	El Pinar	21
ES85330	Els Prat - Marius	37
ES91190	Frontera	31
ES80310	Gaviota	48
ES84780	Joan	25
ES84770	La Llosa	24
ES80150	Laguna	27
ES80300	Nautic Almata	28

ES84850	Palmeras	57
ES84100	Playa Bara	44
ES85300	Playa Montroig	38
ES80320	Riu	49
ES91420	Solana del Segre	20
ES84200	Stel (Roda)	44
ES84830	Tamarit	56
ES85370	Templo del Sol (Nat)	32
ES82330	Tordera	36
ES84860	Torre de la Mora	57
ES85400	Torre del Sol	39
ES81400	Treumal	24
ES91225	Vall de Camprodon	26

Fishing continued

Comunidad Valenciana

ES86115	Azul	72
ES86120	Euro (Oliva)	72
ES86150	Kiko	73
ES87430	Marjal	69
ES86130	Olé	73
ES86880	Playa Paraiso	76
ES85600	Playa Tropicana	64
ES85700	Torre La Sal 2	75

Murcia

ES87520	El Portus (Naturist)	80
ES87530	Manga	81
ES87440	Puerta	80

Andalucia

ES87830	Almanat (Naturist)	84
ES92950	Don Cactus	93
ES87650	Garrofa	84
ES87820	Laguna Playa	98
ES88550	Tarifa	97

Castilla La-Mancha

ES90900	El Greco	106
ES90980	Rio Mundo	105

Madrid

ES90910	Aranjuez	109

Castilla y León

ES92570	Frias	114
ES92510	Rio Lobos	116

Galicia

ES89360	Bayona Playa	118
ES89380	Paxarinas	120

Asturias

ES89440	Cascada	122
ES89500	Costa Verde	124
ES89450	Lagos-Somiedo	125
ES89600	Paz	125
ES89650	Picos-Europa	123

Cantabria

ES89700	Arenas-Pechon	130
ES89910	Barguilla	131
ES89620	Isla	131
ES89640	Molino	128
ES89980	Playa de Isla	129
ES89930	Playa del Regaton	129
ES90000	Playa Joyel	130

Pais Vasco-Euskadi

ES90450	Angosto	136
ES90350	Portuondo	135

La Rioja

ES92260	Cameros	140
ES90400	Haro	139
ES92250	Rioja	139

Navarra

ES90430	Errota el Molino	144
ES90480	Urrobi	143

Aragón

ES90580	Baliera	147
ES90610	Ligüerre de Cinca	150
ES90600	Peña Montañesa	149
ES90630	Puente	151

PORTUGAL

Alentejo

PO8350	Markádia	161

Beiras & Centre

PO8360	Barragem de Idhana-a-Nova	172
PO8060	Costa Nova	173
PO8070	Mira	173

Porto & North

PO8010	Caminha	176
PO8020	Viana-Castelo	177

Bicycle Hire

We understand that the following sites have bicycles to hire on site or can arrange for bicycles to be delivered. However, we would recommend that you contact them directly to check as the situation can change.

SPAIN

Cataluña-Catalunya

ES85360	Ametlla	19
ES80350	Amfora	50
ES80500	Aquarius	52
ES80600	Ballena Alegre	53
ES80640	Bassegoda	18
ES82320	Bella Terra	22
ES81600	Cala Gogo	24
ES80900	Cypsela	41
ES80800	Delfin Verde	58
ES84790	Don Camilo	25
ES80400	Dunas	51
ES83920	El Garrofer	55
ES85330	Els Prat - Marius	37
ES80360	Esponellà	31
ES85550	Eucaliptus	19
ES80310	Gaviota	48
ES81000	Inter-Pals	42
ES84780	Joan	25
ES84770	La Llosa	24
ES80150	Laguna	27
ES80720	Medes	33
ES85020	Montblanc Park	37

ES80300	Nautic Almata	28
ES84850	Palmeras	57
ES80330	Palmeras	49
ES91400	Pedraforca	45
ES84820	Pineda de Salou	35
ES84100	Playa Bara	44
ES81010	Playa Brava	43
ES85300	Playa Montroig	38
ES80320	Riu	49
ES83400	Rupit	45
ES85060	Serra de Prades	59
ES91230	Solsones	55
ES91440	Stel (Puigcerdá)	44
ES84200	Stel (Roda)	44
ES84830	Tamarit	56
ES85370	Templo del Sol (Nat)	32
ES85400	Torre del Sol	39
ES82100	Tucan	35
ES81700	Valldaro	42
ES83900	Vilanova Park	60

Comunidad Valenciana

ES86115	Azul	72
ES85800	Bonterra	65

ES86120	Euro (Oliva)	72
ES86150	Kiko	73
ES86250	Kiko Rural	77
ES87400	Lo Monte	75
ES87420	Marina	70
ES87430	Marjal	69
ES85750	Oasis	74
ES85600	Playa Tropicana	64
ES86220	Santa Marta	67
ES85590	Spa Natura Resort	74

Murcia

ES87440	Puerta	80

Andalucia

ES87630	Cabo de Gata	86
ES90840	Campiña	96
ES92950	Don Cactus	93
ES92900	El Balcon	95
ES87620	Escullos	93
ES87900	Fuente de Piedra	88
ES88900	Gazules	84
ES92930	Orgiva	94
ES87580	Tau de San José	96

Bicycle Hire continued

Extremadura
ES90870	Merida	102

Castilla La-Mancha
ES90970	Batanes	106
ES90980	Rio Mundo	105

Madrid
ES90910	Aranjuez	109
ES92120	Monte Holiday	110

Castilla y León
ES92540	Demanda	116
ES90230	Santiago	113

Galicia
ES90240	As Cancelas	120
ES89380	Paxarinas	120

Cantabria
ES89910	Barguilla	131
ES89620	Isla	131
ES89730	Santillana	132

Pais Vasco-Euskadi
ES90450	Angosto	136

La Rioja
ES90400	Haro	139

Navarra
ES90430	Errota el Molino	144
ES90420	Etxarri	143

Aragón
ES91100	Fresneda	148
ES90640	Gavín	148
ES91250	Lago Barasona	148
ES90610	Ligüerre de Cinca	150
ES90600	Peña Montañesa	149
ES90630	Puente	151

Balears
ES80000	Son Bou	152

PORTUGAL

Algarve
PO8210	Albufeira	155
PO8230	Olhão	157
PO8440	Quinta	156
PO8430	Sagres	158
PO8202	Turiscampo	157

Alentejo
PO8355	Asseiceira	163
PO8160	Porto Covo	163
PO8175	Zmar	162

Lisbon & Vale do Tejo
PO8480	Foz do Arelho	167
PO8550	Quinta Da Cerejeira	166
PO8460	Vale Paraiso	168

Beiras & Centre
PO8360	Barragem de Idhana-a-Nova	172
PO8070	Mira	173
PO8040	Vagueira	174

Porto & North
PO8010	Caminha	176

Horse Riding

We understand that the following sites have horse riding stables on site. Where facilities are within easy reach and we have been given details, we have included this information in the individual site reports. However, we recommend that you contact the site to check that they meet your requirements.

SPAIN

Cataluña-Catalunya
ES80150	Laguna	27
ES80300	Nautic Almata	28
ES85060	Serra de Prades	59

Andalucia
ES92900	El Balcon	95

Asturias
ES89450	Lagos-Somiedo	125

Cantabria
ES89700	Arenas-Pechon	130
ES89620	Isla	131

La Rioja
ES92250	Rioja	139

Aragón
ES90600	Peña Montañesa	149
ES90630	Puente	151

PORTUGAL

Alentejo
PO8350	Markádia	161

Spain.
Overnight.

Been to any good campsites lately?
We have

You'll find them here...

...and, new for 2011, here...

101 great campsites, ideal for your specific hobby, pastime or passion

THE
CARAVAN &
MOTORHOME
SHOWS

The best start to your next adventure...

MANCHESTER CENTRAL
CARAVAN &
MOTORHOME
SHOW 2011 MANCHESTER 20-23 JANUARY

Come and see the widest choice of caravans and a great selection of motorhomes from leading UK and overseas manufacturers. If it's a bargain you are looking for, many exhibitors are offering amazing deals that you won't find anywhere else!

INTERNATIONAL
CARAVAN &
MOTORHOME
2011 NEC BIRMINGHAM 11-16 OCTOBER

The UK's biggest selection of caravans, motorhomes, holiday homes, awnings, folding campers and of course accessories! The NEC is the first place to see all the latest products, have a great day out and find exactly what you want for your next holiday.

For more information visit:
www.caravanshows.com or emc
info@caravanshows.com

Save up to 60% on your holiday

Paying too much for your mobile home holiday?

Cantabria
page 127

Pais Vasco-Euskadi
page 133

Asturias
page 121

La Rioja
page 137

Galicia
page 117

Navarra
page 141

Porto & North
page 175

Castilla y Léon
page 111

isbon &
e do Tejo
age 164

Aragón
page 145

Catalunya
page 16

Beiras & Centre
page 170

Madrid
page 107

Balears
page 152

Extremadura
page 99

Castilla-La Mancha
page 103

Comunidad
Valenciana
page 62

Alentejo
page 159

Andalucia
page 82

Murcia
page 78

Algarve
page 154

Town & Village Index

Town & Village Index continued

Index by Campsite Number

Index by Campsite Number continued

Index by Campsite Number continued

Index by Campsite Region & Name